CROSSING
THE
BORDERS
OF
TIME

À ma Janice chérie, pour qu'elle croie toujours en moi, et pour l'aider à attendre des jours meilleurs ⸻

... ga bien
das ... ... main
Connaisse ... l'affect
j'avais ja... ... avec
mais je ...

Lorsque je t'ai revue plus tard à Dijon
pas retrouvé ce souvenir, et les principa...
que j'avais pris en une année de guerre ...
de notre rencontre une aventure banale
gagné de plus pour toi, un remords de plus p...
car j'avais peut de même conscience de ...
lâchetés. Sauf ces cependant, que jamais
t'ai complètement oublié. A villefranch...

CROSSING THE BORDERS OF TIME

A TRUE STORY OF WAR, EXILE, AND
LOVE RECLAIMED

LESLIE MAITLAND

OTHER PRESS
NEW YORK

Copyright © 2012 Leslie Maitland

Production Editor: *Yvonne E. Cárdenas*
Book design: *Simon M. Sullivan*

This book was set in 11.5 pt Janson MT by Alpha Design & Composition of
Pittsfield, NH.

Maps on pages xi and 106 by Valerie M. Sebestyen.

Lyrics from "J'attendrai" by Louis Potérat, 1938.

10 9 8 7 6 5 4 3 2 1

LIBRARY OF CONGRESS CATALOGING-IN-PUBLICATION DATA

Maitland, Leslie.
Crossing the borders of time : a true story of war, exile, and love
reclaimed / Leslie Maitland.
p. cm.
Includes bibliographical references.
ISBN 978-1-59051-496-2 (hardcover) — ISBN 978-1-59051-497-9
(ebook)
1. World War, 1939–1945—Refugees—France—Biography.
2. World War, 1939–1945—Jews—France—Biography.   3. Jewish
refugees—United States—Biography.   4. First loves—France—
Biography.   I. Title.
D809.F7M35 2011
940.53'145092341073—dc23
2011047110

Disclaimer: The events described in this book are true. The names
of a limited number of nonpublic individuals have been changed
to protect their privacy and that of their families.

For my mother, and for my father

O lost, and by the wind grieved,
ghost, come back again.

—THOMAS WOLFE, *Look Homeward, Angel*

CONTENTS

THE GÜNZBURGERS' ROUTE OF ESCAPE THROUGH OCCUPIED FRANCE, 1940–1942

ENGLAND

English Channel

BELGIUM

GERMANY

LUXEMBOURG

Lille

Amiens

Réims

Paris

Nancy

Eppingen

Nantes

Langres

Mulhouse

Ihringen

Freiburg

Dijon

Gray

SWITZERLAND

Vichy

Villefranche

Geneva

Lyon

Bordeaux

Valence

ITALY

Gurs

Toulouse

Marseille

SPAIN

Unoccupied Zone

Occupied Zone

Annexed Zone
(Alsace and Lorraine)

Reserved Zone

Prohibited Zone

– – – Family's route out of
Germany and France

↔ Sigmar's path to
incarceration

◄---► Women's flight from Gray

ONE

"WHAT'S PAST IS PROLOGUE"

DURING THE FALL that my father was dying, I went back to Europe and found myself seeking my mother's lost love. I say *I went back* almost as if the world my mother had fled and the dream she abandoned had also been mine, because I had grown to share the myth of her life. Perhaps it is common for children whose parents survived the Nazi regime to identify with them, to assume a duty to make their lives better. As my mother's handmaiden and avid disciple in an oral tradition, I felt possessed by a history never my own. Still, not as yoked as she was to life's compromises, I would prove more prepared to retrace the past and use it to forge a new future for her.

Time was running out on the present, and while my father grew weak in a lonely cave of silent bravado, it pained me to realize he would not even leave us the words that we needed. No deathbed regrets, explanations, or tears. An emotional bandit, he would soon slip away under shadow of night, wearing his boots and his mask.

When work as a journalist compelled me to leave New York for a week that October, I was anguished to lose precious time at Dad's side. Yet how fast he would fade I failed to imagine. Nor could I foresee the course of my journey: that an impetuous detour to France from reporting in Germany would send me in search of Roland Arcieri—the man my mother had loved and lost and mourned all her life. Dreading my father's imminent death and the void he would leave, I took a blind leap of faith into the past, dragging my mother behind me.

This is how one Sunday morning in 1990 I came to be visiting Mulhouse, a provincial French city just twelve miles from Germany's Rhine River border. With cousins in town, I had visited Mulhouse twice years before. But on this crisp autumn day I was drawn toward a new destination: a fourteen-story, concrete and blue brick building whose boxy design represented what passed too often for modern in Europe. Although there was nothing about this unexceptional structure on a street densely shaded by chestnut trees to attract an American tourist, I instantly sensed that this was the place I needed to find. I stood at the spot—the X on a map to a treasure buried by time—torn by contradictory feelings. I ran a very real risk of discovering something better left hidden, yet I could not understand or forgive my failure to look here before.

An ache of remorse for all the lost years mingled with nervous excitement. Just up the stairs, I would finally learn what I had always wanted to know. Who was Roland? Where was Roland? What had happened to him in the near fifty years since the cruelties of war had stolen the girl he wanted to marry? I yearned to find my mother's grand passion. Love for the dark-eyed Frenchman, whose picture she always kept tucked in her wallet, continued to pulse in her memory, the heartbeat that kept her alive. Now, at long last, I had tracked down his sister, who lived in this building, and I'd called her the previous evening.

"*Vous êtes la fille de Janine?*" You're Janine's daughter? "What Janine?" She dwelled on the name, then firmly declared she knew no Janine who had once been a friend of her brother's. All the same, moments later, she surprised me by saying she preferred not to talk on the phone, but insisted that I come to see her. Her invitation seemed a curious one, and it made me uneasy.

Inside the building that Sunday morning, the lobby was empty and silent, its only adornment some scrawny dracaenas moping in pots in the corners. On a wall near the entry, a directory of twenty-eight tenants included the family name I remembered. Had she ever married, I might not have found her. Yet Emilienne Arcieri, Roland's sister, was listed on the third floor, and a small elevator stood vacant and waiting. What would I say when I met her? How to explain my intentions in coming? Buying time to evaluate answers, I turned away from the elevator and slowly mounted the stairs.

Just a few flights above lay a glimpse of a road that my mother wished she had chosen. Blocked at the time by landslides of war, it had twisted throughout a lifetime of dreams while she went in another direction. With its pitfalls concealed, too late to turn back, it seemed cruel and ill-timed to make her confront where the path she had lost might have led her. Was that the gift I would bring her from France at this uniquely terrible moment? It was never a thing she had looked for or asked for, and I had kept my mission in Mulhouse a secret. I felt guilty about this radical shift from our faithful pattern of talking and sharing, but I knew she would try to dissuade me.

Janine had last seen Roland on Friday, March 13, 1942. On that day, pulled from his arms on the teeming docks of Marseille, she fled France with her family aboard a Portuguese passenger ship furtively heading for Casablanca to meet a freighter steaming for Cuba. Theirs was a dangerously late escape from the Nazis. Her ship from Marseille, my mother had told me, was likely the last to have carried Jews out of France before the Germans seized total control of the country. Two weeks later, the first transports of Jews to camps in the East would begin in occupied France—that part of the conquered country directly ruled by the Germans. By July, mass deportations to Auschwitz would also begin in the so-called Free or Unoccupied Zone, where the puppet French government of Marshal Philippe Pétain complied with German demands.

At eighteen, my mother prized love over survival, but the moment presented no options. Roland, then twenty-one and a Catholic from Mulhouse, would not be granted permission to leave. Janine desperately wanted to stay at his side, but she had to escape with her family. Buoyed by the optimism of youth, the lovers tried to assure one another that in less than a year the war would be over and, with peace restored, they would marry.

That long-ago hour when her family boarded the *Lipari* to flee a crazed Europe was one I so often made my mother describe that I virtually felt I had lived it. I had peered at a black-and-white photo of Roland in a small rented boat—a snapshot taken for her by a fellow passenger on the *Lipari*'s deck—and I had wondered about him. On the back, neatly written, were the words "*seul sur la mer*," alone on the sea, and in the picture, Roland's thin face and angular features looked wooden, his expression as dark as the water around him. In a white shirt and tie and long overcoat, he appeared out of place in the nautical setting. Yet he was rowing behind the *Lipari* as it made its way from the pier, bearing 448 Jews past the rosy stone forts at the mouth of the city's Vieux Port and out past the lighthouse to the glimmering Mediterranean Sea.

It was afternoon when the *Lipari* pushed away from the quai de la Joliette, the sun floating toward the horizon as the ship passed beneath the promontory where the stately nineteenth-century Palais du Pharo, built by Napoleon III, sits overlooking the water. There may have been dogs in the palace's park running free in the grass and lovers on benches enfolded in fervent embrace—just as you see there today—as boats of all sizes glided below, distant and toylike, sails furled, motors purring, in and out of that pink, twinkling harbor. Its beauty, with the vast open ocean rich with the promise of freedom, was entirely lost to Janine.

In her arms, she clutched Roland's parting present, a fragrant bouquet of mimosas—tiny, cottony, yellow flowers that he had brought to the pier. In some parts of France, wearing yellow flowers had become a sign of sympathy for Jews forced to attach yellow stars to their clothing to mark them as outcasts. But Roland's carried another, more personal meaning. "Mimosas signify remembrance," he had whispered, his face in her hair, wild in the strong sea breezes, when he clasped her to him before she embarked. The sunlit scent of the flowers surrounded the lovers in a space of their own on the fear-laden dock, as refugees swarmed all around them and elbowed each other to cross the gangway toward safety.

When they parted, the bouquet seemed a token brought back from a dream and mocked her with all she had lost. And so, turning to the railing in tears as the ship picked up speed, she dropped the stems one by one to the water, as if marking a luminous trail on the waves to find her way back to the man she adored. The flowers danced on the foam, drifted toward him, and caught on his oars, but the *Lipari* soon left Roland behind, a speck on the water. The golden dots bobbed on the swelling surface around him as he rowed back alone to the land and its war.

"Janine, I ask you here to preserve your love until the happy day when you can become my companion for life." These were the words Roland had written

that morning in her pocket-sized blue spiral notebook, filled with farewell messages inscribed by her friends. On deck, the March·wind whipped her stiff brown coat like a sail. She had the broad shoulders of a swimmer, but a waist so slim that my father would marvel that its circumference could fit in the span of his hands. She pulled her belt tighter and turned the coat's beaver collar up to her chin against the gusts that spun off the water. In spite of her grief, the ring that shone on her finger provided a flicker of pleasure and promise. It was silver with a square-cut aquamarine, the same crystalline blue as her eyes, and it served to signal their vows to each other. Roland had bought it for her a few days before in Lyon, along with a brooch of three poppies enameled in blue, white, and red—a symbol of loyalty, in spite of it all, to the humbled French flag and the Frenchman whose love would be waiting.

Alone in her bunk, Janine would open the thick, sealed envelope that Roland had slipped in her pocket at the moment they parted and would read his pledge through her tears:

> I consider you from this present day as my fiancée and future partner. You ask only to belong to me. We must wait for that reality. Our sole enemy is time! Whatever the length of our separation, our love will survive it, because it depends on us alone. I give you my vow that <u>whatever the time we must wait</u>, you will be my wife. Never forget, never doubt. . . . You see, *ma chérie*, fate has sent us a test so that our love will achieve its full greatness. You are everything for me, and I do not want to speak here of all my pain in letting you leave, going so far from me, but know that if I had to lose you, nothing good would come of my life. You are my goal. . . .

They had never seen each other again. And my mother had never forgotten.

Now, recalling the story that kept me transfixed, I froze on the second-floor landing. I had lived all my life caught up in this romance, but why had I simply assumed that Roland's sister would also remember? Could it be, as years passed, feeling trapped in a difficult marriage, my mother invented this perfect love of her youth as a balm for her suffering heart? How real was the story she'd told me? What if she'd spent a lifetime mourning a man for whom she had been a dalliance only? Then I had her pride to consider. What would it mean to deliver a message that Janine's passion for Roland had been so enduring that a half century later her daughter would cross the ocean to find him? He might be happily married with his young love forgotten—a proud patriarch now, settled and stable, with a dozen dimpled grandchildren.

I reached the third floor, groping toward an encounter entirely unscripted. A door led from the bright landing to a black vestibule where a faint orange glow guided my hand to the *minuterie*, the timed switch that would light up the hall just long enough for me to discern which apartment I wanted. There could be serious danger here in my meddling. Though my mother had long since abandoned all hope she would see him again, Roland continued to serve as her anchor. He endured for her always—laughingly lifting his drink and kissing her hand at a nameless café of the past. How could I bear to bring her sad news, only compounding her losses at the very same time that my father lay dying, and she stood so helpless beside him?

The light in the hallway switched off. In the darkness, heart racing, I thought back to the sickroom where I pictured my father clutching a dumbbell, ever in training for his unwinnable ultimate battle. Was I also betraying this resolute man I had never stopped loving, despite the conflicts between us? What would he make of what I was doing? Because one thing was clear: in the life she had lived, my mother was trained in noble acceptance, a patient trait that neither my father nor I had developed. Reared in America and schooled by him in reaching for dreams, it was *his* daughter who had traveled alone to this foreign doorstep. And while it did not occur to me then or before, but surely would later, how had my mother's eternal love for Roland changed and embittered my father?

I pressed the wall switch for more time in the light and found myself back in that cold, dreary hallway. What would I say when Roland's sister inquired, as she undoubtedly would, whether Janine was still married? That her husband, my father, was dying? Then what in hell was I doing here? I prayed I would find an acceptable answer, if only for me, as I took a deep breath, softly knocked on the door, and heard brisk footsteps approaching. In that uncertain moment, the ghost of the past and the hope of the future converged in the doorway beside me, vying to claim whatever would follow.

TWO

THE BLACK FOREST

I HAD SPENT THE NIGHT before my journey to Mulhouse in the medieval German fortress city of Freiburg, sleeping in an attic apartment of the house where my mother was born. The large red sandstone building had belonged to my grandfather in the 1920s and '30s, but on the night that I stayed there, my host was the grandson of the German hotelier who took it over when my grandparents fled. I could hardly imagine what his grandfather, who hanged himself shortly after taking over the house, or my own, who never returned there to see it or claim it, would have made of the fact that more than fifty years later, their descendants—German and Jew—would both rest there one night, after a fine dinner and good local wine, under that very same roof.

The difference was that my convivial host, Michael Stock—tall and blond with Germanic good looks—knew he belonged there, and although the house had been my grandfather's, I knew I did not. I lay awake the whole night conferring with spirits, hearing old voices echo from tales of the past. In confused half consciousness, exhausted and troubled, I lingered in darkness on the threshold of sleep. The police sirens, the buzzing motorcycles and screeching car brakes, the meandering laughter of beer-drenched students loudly returning from untamed moonlit revels seemed as much the night cries of 1940 as of 1990. In the same space where my mother, then a teenager, had fretfully worried over her father's plans for escape from the only home she had known, I felt the present slide into the past, or worse, the past come alive. By daybreak, I was gripped by a near frantic compulsion to get out of the country. Still, I had yet to realize that in crossing the Rhine, I would not only be tracing the route my mother had laid out before me, but also seeking the Frenchman who captured her heart.

• • •

It was within forty miles of Mulhouse, where I would look for Roland, that my mother's story began in Freiburg im Breisgau. On a map of Europe, Freiburg is easy to pinpoint. I am tempted to say that it sits just where Germany's profile, facing west and lustily sniffing with interest, pokes its nose over France and Switzerland's borders. But that does not do it justice, for its beauty is haunting.

Freiburg im Breisgau and its Cathedral of Our Dear Lady, nestled beside the Black Forest mountains, 1906

Founded in 1120, the town is tucked into Germany's southwest corner, an area that until 1918 was known as the Grand Duchy of Baden, in a temperate valley curtained by lush pine slopes of the Black Forest. Unusual, narrow canals line its cobblestone streets, nine miles of "very little rivers" or *Bächle* that bring an ever-flowing rush of cool, running water from the mountains to swirl like a ribbon throughout town and then empty into the Dreisam River, flowing on toward the Rhine and the border with France. The *Bächle* are only about one foot wide and have delighted generations of Freiburg's children, who jump over them, float toy boats in them, and crouch to play with their gurgling waters.

These charming canals, an elite, five-hundred-year-old university, and a majestic High Gothic cathedral soaring in filigreed, red stone splendor at the center of town have all contributed to Freiburg's well-deserved reputation as a jewel of Germany, despite its snug size.

For most of my life, however, my mother has tried to deny that this was where she was born, her hatred of the Nazis making her loathe to admit her descent from their fatherland. Asked the place of her birth, she is always evasive, relying on the tortuous back-and-forth of Alsace's control by France and Germany over the centuries to distort which nation claimed her hometown at the moment she entered the world.

As a child, I awkwardly aped her fudging and mumbling when asked to explain her background to friends. I found it perplexing that my self-proclaimed French mother lapsed into German to speak with her parents, her brother, and her sister. To this, she always maintained that her birthplace was German when her parents were born, before World War I, so that German was their native tongue, but under the treaty ending that war it reverted to France and was French at the time of her birth four years later. Her geopolitical story fooled me far longer than I should acknowledge. The truth of the matter, I eventually learned, was that the high-ceilinged bedroom at Poststrasse 6 where my mother first opened her eyes was in Freiburg (never a part of contested Alsace, although very near it), so that she, like her parents, was German.

That her rejection of everything German had actually included changing her name was another detail she always glossed over. Even her future husband discovered her original name and birthplace only after they married, when, as they crossed into Canada on their honeymoon, she was obliged to show him her passport. My father's French bride, Janine of Mulhouse, was thus disclosed at the border to be Hanna of Freiburg. Symbolically, if not otherwise, the French Canadian border was an appropriate place for the truth to come out, as her change of identity had initially occurred at a border, when she first crossed the Rhine escaping the Nazis.

On that train into France in 1938, she renamed herself Janine, choosing a name close to the one that her parents—Sigmar and Alice Günzburger—had wanted for her but were barred from selecting for political reasons. In the aftermath of crushing defeat in World War I,

German authorities deemed their first choice, Jeanette, to be overly French. Officialdom switched her name to Johanna, taking no note of the fact that the name already belonged to Alice's mother, and that it went strictly against German Jewish tradition to name a child for a living family member. As a result, my mother was simply called Hanna until the day she left Freiburg—or Hannele, with the -*le* suffix that the local *badisch* dialect attaches to nouns as a form of endearment.

Hanna was born on September 5, 1923, the very same year that the town's Nazi Party marched into being and two months before Hitler's first thwarted attempt to seize power. It was a time of such horrific inflation, with Germany staggering beneath a punishing burden of war reparations, that the midwife who brought her onto the scene left the house, pockets bulging, with five million marks for the service she rendered. Whatever the rate of exchange, my mother was certainly worth every Pfennig, but in point of fact, the money was worthless. Society reeled as the value of the mark fell from 8.9 to the dollar in 1919 to a meaningless 4.2 trillion to the dollar only four years later.

While many lost their life savings, in spite of hard times, the reconstruction required after the war helped Sigmar's steel and building supply business prosper, and the house, with its ample rooms, curving staircase, and balconies overlooking the garden in back, quietly advertised his successes. Its size and location, in the heart of a city renowned as a center of culture and learning, spoke to the strides Jews had made in social acceptance. The house sat beside a lively tourist hotel, the Minerva, just a short walk from the main post office, the railroad station, and the old picturesque hub of town. The Minerva stood at the corner where the Poststrasse and the Rosastrasse met at right angles, and across the street Sigmar and his older brother Heinrich had set up the business that carried their name. The *Gebrüder* (Brothers) Günzburger had offices and a warehouse there and a larger warehouse alongside the city's freight railroad tracks.

Each week Sigmar traveled with his chauffeur in his large black Opel sedan on sales trips through the region that bordered the Rhine. But with his office so close, on most days he returned for a warm and hearty midday meal to a home staffed by a maid, a cook, and a governess, and run with the orderliness that he demanded. The life he expected to offer his children was one of comfort, learning, duty, and discipline in a country where both he and his wife traced their lineage back for hundreds of years.

To an unlikely extent he succeeded. In spite of the Nazi assault that later made my mother an exile from a world she had thought was secure, never again would she recapture the sense of belonging that she enjoyed in Freiburg, where everyone knew everyone else and their family history through generations. Many years later, walking unrecognized on those city streets after decades of denying her birthplace, she was all the more shaken by an ambush of rage and regret that she could not have lived out the life to which she was born. She was overcome with resentment knowing that she—unlike the citizens sauntering past us or enjoying their *Würste* and their beers in the afternoon shadow of the glowing cathedral—had been uprooted and forced to run for her life from her birthplace and the country where all her ancestors lay buried.

Her mother, born Alice Heinsheimer, proudly traced her family back to 1695 in the farming community of Eppingen southeast of Heidelberg, and she treasured the artifacts confirming her background as if every inked tendril on yellowing parchment sprouted from roots dug deep in the nation. Hanna's father could similarly follow his family tree back to 1645 on either side of the Rhine. Both Ihringen, a few miles from Freiburg, where Sigmar was born in 1880, and Eppingen, where Alice was born in 1892, are quaint picture-book towns of half-timbered *Fachwerk* houses with dark exposed beams framing intricate patterns on exterior walls of cream-colored stucco. Red geraniums, bright as lipstick, gaily dress their façades in well-tended boxes beneath shuttered windows, all primly veiled in white lacy curtains.

It was only after seeing these towns that I could fully appreciate my grandfather's wry sense of humor in the ritual greeting he devised for me in my childhood, by which point—having come to terms with so much in life—his forbidding Germanic demeanor had mellowed. Snapping his heels together with the brisk pomp of a nobleman wearing a waistcoat festooned with medals, he would formally bow and intone his imaginary credentials: "Sigmar, Baron von Ihringen." He solemnly introduced himself as if lord of the manor from his small farming village. "Leslie, Countess von Eppingen," I was to reply by way of asserting more noble rank, as I extended my hand for a courtly kiss and returned his bow with a curtsy.

My grandmother's birthplace of Eppingen, far more provincial than Freiburg, was a mostly Protestant town that counted just 151 Jews among 3,622 residents in a census in 1880. Alice's father, Maier, like his father before him, was both a leader of the Jewish community and, as a member of the county council, active in civic affairs. He took over his family's thriving construction supply business and cultivated a potato field and an apple orchard just outside of town.

Too early, all this was left to his widow Johanna to manage when Maier, then just fifty-eight, died of uremia on August 27, 1913. Her youngest child, Siegfried, was only ten at the time, the belated birth of this son a surprise to everyone, eleven years after Alice was born, the last of four daughters. At Maier's death, Alice had just returned from a French finishing school for Jewish young women, and she grieved the loss of the father she worshipped. By comparison, Johanna, clad in shapeless black dresses with her steely gray hair drawn into a tight

The Heinsheimer daughters—(L to R) Alice, Lina, Jennie, and Rosie— with their brother, Siegfried, circa 1906

little bun, was cold and reserved. Alice herself never quite learned how to deal with open displays of emotion, but the death of her father with his tickling walrus mustache left a hole in her heart and seemed to influence her choice of an older man for her husband when she and Sigmar were matched with each other seven years later.

A tall, pretty, fine-featured young woman, Alice—often called Lisel—had long dark braids that she wore coiled on her head like a woven crown, very fair skin, and a profusion of freckles she viewed all her life as a personal torment. Although Sigmar would later insist that he would miss any single freckle she lacked, beginning in girlhood and ever thereafter, Alice eagerly tried any new remedy that promised to bleach them. Sadly, they kept her from seeing herself as the classic beauty she was, with a straight and delicate nose and angular cheekbones that sloped toward the point of her chin like a heart. She found reason for pride not in her mirror but rather in her family background, and she conceived of herself, first and foremost, as a faithful native daughter of Deutschland.

World War I started a year after the death of Alice's father. Her brother Siegfried was too young to be drafted, despite desperate conditions that resulted in boys of only fifteen being forced to face new horrors of weaponry—machine guns, mustard gas, and the hellfire of artillery shells. Alice, however, then twenty-two, served through the war in the Eppingen hospital, and she found satisfaction in aiding the cause of her nation by nursing the burned and the blistered, the blinded, the sick and dismembered, who had somehow survived with the rats in the cold, stinking trenches.

In rasping voices, soldiers shared their suffering with her, and when the ones still able to fight returned to the front, she scrounged candy or soap or other small luxuries to send to her favorites or those most in need of her cheering. In tiny, cramped writing they replied with thanks and bravado—"*Forward into Valhalla!*"—on the backs of war photographs they turned into postcards and sent from the field. Courtesy of the army, no stamps were required for her former patients to mail her via *Feldpost* these battlefront pictures in which they posed brandishing swords or impishly grinning amid smoking rubble, and

Alice (behind wheelchair) worked as a nurse caring for wounded German soldiers in the Eppingen hospital throughout World War I.

she received hundreds from soldiers she nursed on her ward. She preserved all their pictures and still others in which she modestly posed with her patients and colleagues. Later, wherever she moved over the next three turbulent decades, she took along also a framed, penciled sketch of herself in her nurse's cap—with her fine, perfect profile—drawn for her by one of her soldiers, as well as a letter of praise from the war-weary doctor who guided her efforts.

Alice's husband, my grandfather Sigmar, was the youngest of thirteen children born to Simon and Jeanette Günzburger, nine of whom survived to adulthood. According to Sigmar's notes inside the cover of a Hebrew prayer book now brittle with age, Simon's grandfather had been a respected eighteenth-century rabbi in Breisach, which sat on the Rhine fifteen miles from Colmar in France. But on the eve of Yom Kippur in 1793, during four days of firebombing by French revolutionary forces from the fortified town of Neuf-Breisach over the river, Reb David fled his synagogue. Escaping the shelling, Sigmar's notes say, his great-grandfather found refuge in Ihringen, and there he soon married.

Two generations later, while arranged marriages between suitable Jewish families remained the norm, the union of Simon and Jeanette was a rare love match, according to family legend. A large man with laughing eyes, full cheeks, and a thick curly beard, Simon made his living as a cattle dealer, a common trade for Jews in Germany's southwestern region. It was lonely work requiring much travel, and Simon roamed the countryside with a goal of getting home each week in time for the Sabbath. It would later be said that his amorous wife—in whose memory Hanna's parents had sought to name her Jeanette—spent his absences immersed in romantic novels and greeted him passionately on his returns, accounting for their numerous offspring. Perhaps it was the influence of fiction that inspired the exotic, non-Hebrew names Jeanette gave many of her children (among them Heinrich, Karoline, Hermann, Norbert, Marie, and Adolf), raising eyebrows of Jewish neighbors. As for my grandfather, while officially

Simon and Jeanette Günzburger with their three youngest sons, Heinrich (L), Sigmar (seated), and Hermann, circa 1882

named Samuel, he was invariably known by his Germanic middle name of Sigmar, likely because at the time of his birth in 1880, festering anti-Semitism was swelling again.

This was especially the case in agricultural regions such as Ihringen, where Jews worked as middlemen handling trade and became targets for blame when struggling peasants could not pay their debts. A religious heritage derived from Martin Luther further inflamed anti-Jewish attitudes, and the resulting lack of economic opportunity spurred several of Sigmar's brothers to immigrate to America when he himself was still a child. The fortunes they went on to earn in oil wells, diamonds, and Canadian mines would later prove crucial to Sigmar's maneuvers escaping the Nazis, while for their parents, money from America made it possible to quit Ihringen for the much larger and finer city of Freiburg.

After centuries of French and Austrian rule, Freiburg was almost 80 percent Catholic and, being so close to the western border, retained some of the egalitarian imprint of French political thought. Flourishing around an august university, it was a more liberal and cosmopolitan urban center, where the couple hoped to find greater religious tolerance, in addition to better schools for their youngest sons. As for Ihringen, Sigmar had such little regard for the town of his birth that he never again returned there or took his wife and children to see it, though it is a trip of barely ten miles. Today, the green Kaiserstuhl landscape between the two towns boasts vineyards whose grapes produce fine white wines—Sylvaner, Riesling, Traminer—and broad fields at the foot of the Tuniberg slopes, where white asparagus or *Spargel* grows thick and fleshy under dark blankets that shield it from the light of the sun.

When Sigmar, then nine, first moved with his parents to Freiburg in 1889, the city's restored Jewish community was only twenty-six years old, following more than four centuries in which Jews had been banned. In records kept in the archives, I have pondered my great-grandfather's registry there, including the fact that he and his wife were deemed "Israelites" by religion, which made them unusual. Jews had been permitted to start a synagogue in Freiburg in 1865 and a cemetery soon after. But by 1933, when Hitler took power, there were still only 1,138 Jews in the city, comprising just over 1 percent of the population, largely the same as in the rest of the country.

In high school in Freiburg, Sigmar excelled. It is a testimony to his hope in the Fatherland, his faith that reason or justice might eventually prevail, that he saved his report card and many other official papers in order someday to reclaim his valid German identity. I examine his schoolboy marks with the same maternal pleasure I have derived from the grades of my children, but it feels like spying somehow, this looking into the past to check my grandfather's progress. From country to country, Sigmar carried these records in what he dubbed his *Köfferle*, a worn brown leather valise, filled with the incontrovertible documentary proof of exactly who he had been, and it therefore became his most valued possession.

How thankful I am, in my research, for our family compulsion to preserve every document and memento. Letters and pictures, drawings and poems, programs and matchbooks, old report cards, identity cards, postcards, and wartime transit papers. Graveside speeches, telegrams sent almost one hundred years past, birth announcements, the first heartfelt scribblings of children, lined ledgers of spending, and government records that detail a culture as well as a story of persecution. The will that Sigmar wrote out by hand on the eve of his marriage, and the dog-eared booklet of Hebrew prayers and psalms that the German Army provided for Jewish soldiers marching to battle in World War I. The documents stamped by the Nazis that systematically stripped Sigmar of all he once claimed—his name and his home as well as his nation. We are all casual archivists of family history, as if preserving these fragile treasures could stop time and make the people we love at least as enduring as onionskin paper.

Prior to the war, Sigmar's wealthy American brothers provided the means for him to launch his iron, steel, and building supply business, starting in Mülhausen across the Rhine River. A bachelor, he had remained single after his mother's death in 1907 to care for his father in Freiburg, and so he commuted to work until 1914, when he was called up to four years of infantry service. In postcards he wrote home from the front, Sigmar, then thirty-three, explained that after

Sigmar as a young businessman in Freiburg

training in Konstanz with the 114th Infantry Regiment, he had been made a *Scheinwerfer*, manning battlefield searchlights. Were it not for a niece who scoured local farms to send packages of food to him daily, he would have gone hungry. Then he contracted rheumatic fever. Despite his ordeals, Sigmar stood proudly with his regiment, posing for his own wartime postcards. His demeanor suggests that this short Jewish soldier—with a thick mustache and sometimes a beard, wearing a high-buttoned uniform and a flat cap that covered the fact he had already lost most of his hair—was also a loyal German who would always revere Goethe, Nietzsche, Beethoven, and Wagner.

A telegram handwritten in purple pencil that Sigmar received at the front on January 26, 1915—the same date inscribed on my great-grandfather's tombstone—makes it clear that when Simon fell ill, his soldiering son could not have returned in time to see him alive. Bereft of his father, Sigmar decided to move to Mülhausen when he resumed civilian life after Germany's defeat in the war. His older sister Marie and her husband, Paul Cahen, already lived in that city, though its contentious history sowed perennial troubles for those who considered it home, as control of the region shifted between the French and the Germans.

In the Franco-Prussian War of 1871, France had lost Mulhouse to Otto von Bismarck, who claimed Alsace and the neighboring province of Lorraine as part of his newly unified German nation. Renamed Mülhausen, the city was forced to accept German language and culture. The Germans treated the region as occupied enemy territory, even while drafting its men into their army. Almost fifty years later, the tables were turned. With France's victory in World War I, the kaiser abdicated and went into exile. Mülhausen, along with the rest of Alsace and Lorraine, returned to French rule under the treaty signed in Versailles in 1919. Joyfully, the beleaguered city reclaimed its French name, and rancor toward Germany burned ever more fiercely.

Soon after Sigmar's return from battle, his sister Marie arranged through a friend in Eppingen for him to meet Alice. At that point, the former wartime nurse was twenty-eight years old and all too aware that with so many young men having died in the war, she could not afford to be overly choosy. When the match was suggested, Sigmar was close to forty, shorter than she, a quiet, serious, and intellectual man whose chief enjoyments came from reading and playing the piano. Qualities that might lead strangers to view him as stern and unyielding somehow also lent him a charming, childlike aura of virtue. A person of straightforward standards and firmly held morals, Sigmar never spoke ill of anyone else and would not seek advantage over his neighbor. He adhered to the laws of the country he loved because he assumed they were there for Order and Purpose. Above that, he believed in a God who ruled the universe fairly, and doing whatever he could to assist in that goal, he strove to make sure that justice prevailed.

From a young woman's perspective, there was probably little dashing about him beyond the strength and mystery that lay in his silence. Indeed, while Alice admired her reliable suitor, passion likely played no major role in inducing the playful, if bashful, former nurse to agree to the marriage, as she did after only two meetings. In the first, she served him squares of Swiss chocolate on a small silver tray and nervously poured sweet liqueur into colored-glass snifters barely larger than thimbles. In the second, she drifted to sleep and almost fell off

Alice was twenty-eight years old and Sigmar nearly forty when they were introduced after the war.

her chair while Sigmar earnestly spoke with her eagle-eyed mother, immovably stationed with them as a chaperone.

Ever after, Alice would pride herself for having shown something like wisdom and farsighted good sense in securing her future. Sigmar's brother and business partner, Heinrich, was a far better-looking, more graceful man, but comparing her own solid mate to her vain and high-strung brother-in-law over the years, Alice concluded—and tried with little success to drill into her daughters—that looks meant nothing in choosing a husband. What counted, she knew, were virtues of character on which a woman could always depend.

Alice's marriage took place in a hotel in Heidelberg, and Marie's young daughter Emilie, or "Mimi," entertained the small group of guests with Chopin piano mazurkas. A group portrait of the wedding party shows Alice, dressed in white ruffles, her eyes cast down shyly, slouching a little as if to disguise being taller than the unsmiling new husband who stands at her side. Sigmar, wearing a white bow tie and a gold watch chain looped over his tight buttoned vest, stares in dignified poise toward the future.

Sigmar with Alice and her family in July 1920, when they married in Heidelberg. Seated (L to R): Rosie, Johanna, Lina, and Jennie. Standing (L to R): Rosie's husband, Natan Marx; Alice's brother, Siegfried; Alice; Sigmar; Lina's husband, Sigmund Weil; Jennie's husband, Joseph Guggenheim; and their son, Werner.

. . .

In 1920, when my grandparents wed, the Nazi Party, founded the previous year, promulgated an overtly anti-Semitic program drafted in large part by a young Adolf Hitler. It declared that "only those of German blood, whatever their creed, may be members of the nation," and that "accordingly, no Jew may be a member of the nation." But for Sigmar, returning to French-controlled Mulhouse after the war—a German war veteran with a new German bride—proved difficult too, with anti-German sentiment in France running so high. Feeling even less welcome as Germans in France than as Jews in Germany, Sigmar and Alice crossed the Rhine once again to settle and start a family in Freiburg.

They would have to reverse this move eighteen years later, of course, when Sigmar's record as a German veteran and Alice's service nursing her country's soldiers in war could not offset the fact that they were Jews. When they married, however, Alice was especially eager to live in the bustling German university town, with its fine theater and opera. Cable cars provided easy access to cool nearby mountains for hiking and skiing, while in the summer, glacial lakes with festive beer gardens beckoned tourists from all over Europe.

By 1921, when Alice gave birth to her first child, a son she named Norbert, Nazi Party ranks grew to three thousand, and Hitler set up his unit of brown-shirted storm troopers. The party adopted the swastika, an ancient Sanskrit fertility symbol, as its insignia for banners and badges, and before long the Jew-hating exhortations of Hitler's speeches were translated into violent action. Two years later, when Hanna was born, the anti-Jewish propagandist newspaper *Der Stürmer* made its appearance; and in 1925, when the Günzburgers' second daughter, Gertrude, was born, Hitler published the first volume of his autobiography, *Mein Kampf*, denouncing Jews as "vampires" who cunningly schemed to enslave other peoples.

In 1926, the Nazis launched the Hitler Youth movement, but the three Günzburger children were too young to take note of it or of their exclusion from its popular ranks. It was not until several years later, when they tried to fit in with their peers proudly attired in Hitler Youth garb and caught up in the jubilant frenzy of pro-Nazi rallies, that the shock of their outcast status would hit them.

Alice's marriage to Sigmar changed her. The spirited young woman—known even to the Eppingen postman as the intended recipient of mail addressed simply to the impudent or "*freche Lisel*"—turned into a docile, subservient wife. Anxiously, she ministered to her husband's comforts and needs, providing a nurse's watchful attention. For as long as he lived, she buttered his bread, buttoned his shirts, drew his bathwater, and ran to lower or open the windows at his slightest hint of discomfort. If he cleared his throat, she ran for his sweater. If she sensed that Sigmar had something to say, she sternly hushed the room into silence. Pleasing him became her prime and constant concern.

Alice loved her children deeply but relegated their general care to a series of governesses whom she trusted more than she did herself to provide the training they needed for their station in life. Beyond that, unfamiliar with physical shows of affection from *her* mother, Alice in turn proved undemonstrative with her own children. A noisy smack in the air passed for her kiss, and she shied away with the quickness of instinct and a flutter of hands from any embraces, which seemed to cause her embarrassment.

Although Hanna would certainly not model her mothering style on Alice, she would later pattern her concept of the nurturing service she owed to her husband on her experience of her parents' marriage. Meanwhile, Alice's fixed aim to gratify Sigmar in every conceivable way was one that Hanna also adopted in regard to her father. Desperate to win Sigmar's loving approval and aspiring to a career as a doctor, Hanna became the obedient child between a rebellious older brother and younger sister with a mischievous penchant for upsetting their parents.

Her single instance of remembered defiance involved her balking at Sigmar's demand that she give up her treasured textbooks from a previous year to a younger child from a needy family. "I'd prefer to keep them, Father," Hanna demurred, mistakenly thinking a choice was involved. "Get them now!" Sigmar roared, lunged at his daughter, and grabbed her throat as a warning.

"Teach Father a lesson! Run away!" Norbert advised her. "Don't come back until they find you! Let Father think you're missing or dead. Oh, then he'll feel bad." He led his younger sister to a nearby park and told her to hide there all night. But as darkness descended and the park's keeper began locking its gates, Hanna realized that she herself—hungry, cold, alone, and afraid—would suffer her retribution the most. Sheepishly, she slipped through the gate and made her way home before her parents had even noticed her missing.

"*I* can't punish you, but *God* will," Alice routinely intoned with a sigh—a prophecy the children found all the more frightening for the mercilessness of this maternal submission to implacable powers. Closer at hand, Alice left the miscreant to Sigmar, and it was Norbert who generally faced the tight-lipped, eye-bulging wrath of his father, who clumsily chased him around an upholstered circular bench in the foyer, flourishing an old cat-o'-nine-tails they called a *Lavatli*. Pressed to grow up too soon by the rapid arrival of two little sisters before he turned three, Norbert landed in trouble so often that as a very young boy he felt unwanted and stewed over baseless worries that he was adopted. Craving his mother's love and attention, he tried to provoke her, repeatedly sparking her frustrated tears, and then he felt guilty.

"*Even if I'm your stepchild and am always treated like an afterthought, I don't care, I'm already used to it,*" he wrote at age eight in a childish hand on broadly lined paper. "*Greetings and kisses from Norbert who loves you even if you don't love him back. I want to be good again. . . . I put this note next to your bed. Please take it.*"

Yet when Sigmar hired a rigid new governess to assume the challenge of molding his children, she proved far more effective than even the strictest of fathers could have desired. The arrival of Fräulein Elfriede, who took a sadist's delight in secretly abusing her charges, soon became the overriding event of their childhood. Blindly, Alice and Sigmar ceded her total control. To the children, however, the governess's cruelty, which they were too afraid to reveal to their parents, made her seem the very embodiment within their own home of the Nazi terror seizing the nation.

Only thirtyish herself at the time, Elfriede was a hard-bodied athlete with womanly curves, a shock of blond hair, and a prizefighter's coarse, flattened features. Her unrelenting and disciplined training, she assured Sigmar and Alice, would boost their children's inner resilience. If it did that, it also helped inculcate in Hanna a lifelong fear of all authority figures, as well as a hunger for approval that later prevented her from straying from what was expected of her. She learned to accept whatever life dealt her. And at times when she might have pursued her own path, both before and during her marriage, she felt constrained by duty—first to her parents and then to her husband and children—to put her own interests aside in deference to others.

Fomenting a rivalry that would dog their relationship always, Fräulein Elfriede fanned competition among the three siblings, especially between the two sisters, which diminished the closeness that might have made up for what they missed from their parents. The governess insinuated that she would spare the child she preferred the brunt of her tortures, a tactic that encouraged the three to vie for her favor in spite of the fact that they all despised her.

"I claim Fräulein Elfriede's right arm!" Norbert would shout as they left on a walk. "And I get her left!" Trudi would hastily add. So

Trudi (L), Hanna, and Norbert in Freiburg, in a photograph taken for Sigmar's fiftieth birthday in 1930

they left Hanna to straggle behind, her siblings triumphantly gloating over their shoulders. The whole family called Hanna the nebbish, the timid one—a rare Yiddish word allowed in the household—and her fearfulness drew cold ridicule from Fräulein Elfriede.

"*Ich strafe dich mit Verachtung,*" I punish you with my utter contempt, the governess sneered, averting her eyes as if the mere sight of the girl were too repulsive for any person of substance to bear.

Whether it was part of her nature or a reflection of her support for Hitler's insistence on cultivating a "brutal, domineering, fearless, cruel" generation, Fräulein Elfriede cracked down on the children much as the Hitler Youth movement cracked down on their non-Jewish peers. Night after night, she ordered them to take icy showers in front of each other, timed which child could endure the cold and shame longest, and urged the winner to claim a toy from each of the others. She forced them into boxing matches and made them leap, seated atop each other's shoulders, from the high diving board at the Eppingen town pool before they had even learned how to swim. She locked Norbert outside on the terrace in thunderstorms and often imprisoned Trudi in a small, dark cupboard under the eaves where dirty linen was stored. Whenever Fräulein Elfriede caught the girl falsely denying some naughty behavior, she marched her through town with a humiliating sign on her back that proclaimed her to all as "the Lying Gertrude."

For Hanna, however, most dreaded of all were games of hide-and-seek in the mountains near the crumbling ruins of an old castle tower, games that Fräulein Elfriede expressly designed to prey on her fears of being abandoned. On her first visit, Hanna was moved by the grandeur of the location. From the misty crest of the Schlossberg, her view stretched over Alsace, well into France and the smoky blue ridge of the Vosges, while at the foot of the mountain, Freiburg sat a perfect toy town with its orange tile roofs and several high, pointed steeples. At the stroke of the hour, the bells of its churches all rang out in jumbled succession, their various peals dancing like goats on the flowering hillsides. But Hanna's rapture surveying the scene was abruptly cut short when Fräulein Elfriede demanded that she cover her eyes and then disappeared with Norbert and Trudi. Sobbing as she searched in vain through the pine-scented woods and the clouds that were drawn to the top of the mountain, Hanna was mortified to imagine them laughing at her from the place they were hiding. With comfortable glee, they would witness her terror and later describe it, she knew, to all their classmates.

Sigmar and Alice, unengaged in the inner lives of their children, saw none of this, but they appreciated the fine *Kinderstube*, or upbringing, the Fräulein provided. She taught the girls to sew and crochet, to knit and embroider, and she schooled all three in athletics and manners. The girls took separate lessons in posture and walking, being trained to place toe before heel and move as if gliding. Their achievements were put on display in the evenings, when Fräulein summoned them into the parlor to recite a poem for their parents or to play a small piece of music on the accordion before being dismissed to their rooms. Over time, their fear of Fräulein Elfriede grew so overpowering—while their relationship with their parents grew ever more formal—that the children felt incapable of revealing to Alice and Sigmar what they had learned of their governess's pro-Hitler leanings.

"I sing the song of the one who does me most good," had long been her motto. And now, one afternoon, as Fräulein Elfriede put on her coat, the children caught sight of a Nazi Party swastika hidden beneath her lapel. Frightened by the discovery, but more fearful still of her retaliation if they disclosed it to their parents, they were cowed into silence and pledged for their own sakes to mask her ugly political secret.

With the promulgation of the Nuremburg Laws in 1935 and their strict delineation of contacts permitted between Germans and Jews—including a ban on Jews hiring Aryan domestic employees under the age of forty-five—Fräulein Elfriede quit the household. It was a wonderfully unexpected result of the new Nazi rules. On the day that she left, the three children sat on the staircase as the hated young woman descended, each beating a metal pot with a big wooden spoon—a primitive drumroll to herald their freedom. Down the steps that wound to the street like a conch shell, the governess brushed past their knees with the sangfroid of a ramrod: her lips were clamped shut and she said not a word.

Much later, however, after the war, they heard from Fräulein Elfriede again when she wrote Alice in New York imploring her Jewish former employer to send her clothing and food. But in an uncharacteristic act of defiance, Hanna (Janine, by then) insisted that Alice ignore these entreaties. In her memories of girlhood, Fräulein Elfriede would ever loom large, wielding absolute power, like an advance guard of the Gestapo and the insidious emblem of the Reich's creeping evil. "I'll never come see you again," Janine vowed to her mother, shocking them both with her threat, "if you send that cruel Nazi witch as much as a toothpick."

Janine destroyed Elfriede's letter, but Alice's trove of long-preserved papers contains several from another former domestic employee, Agathe Mutterer, who used to come to the Poststrasse house to iron the laundry. She was seventy-four years old in 1961 when she obtained the Günzburgers' New York address and, after an absence of twenty-three years, wrote from Freiburg:

Many difficult years have passed since our life together on the Poststrasse. How I used to love to come to you in celebration of ironing, when your three darling children made a ring around my ironing board, played the accordion for me, and brought me little chocolates to eat! I felt so at home in your dear family.

Since then, there has been much suffering, we have grown old, and almost all the relatives are gone. But I would be so happy if I could hear from you and know that you still are alive. Be happy that someone in the old homeland is still thinking of you with gratitude. May God always protect you.

In 1936, the same Agathe Mutterer had inscribed in Hanna's childhood autograph book a message that would later prove amazingly prescient: "*My very good, dear Hannele,*" she wrote. "*Learn to carry your suffering patiently. Learn to be understanding and learn to forgive. Learn to love, and it will help you.*"

THREE

DIE NAZI-ZEIT

IT WAS EARLY SPRINGTIME 1933 in the Black Forest Valley, and a mantle of snow still collared the mountains. In Freiburg, fragrant March violets crept on schedule out of the earth, and cone-shaped blossoms of pink and cream dressed the chestnut trees. But even in this university town in the balmiest corner of Germany, the simple joys of awakening spring would soon be eclipsed by a thunderous new political storm. This was the start of the *Nazi-Zeit*, the Nazi Time, as Germans now refer to the period, as if it arose like any other natural season.

On March 31, Sigmar was stunned to discover himself immediately and directly affected by a headline that blasted across the top of Baden's Nazi Party newspaper, *Der Alemanne*, trumpeting a war against Germany's Jews as well as a boycott of all Jewish-owned firms. ACHTUNG! BOYKOTT! it read, naming scores of Freiburg businesses that Germans were exhorted to shun, beginning the following morning, by order of Joseph Goebbels, Hitler's *Reichsminister* and head of Popular Enlightenment and Propaganda, himself a former Freiburg student. The list included the Gebrüder Günzburger. "Jews want to destroy Germany!" the newspaper warned, announcing the nationwide boycott with a barrage of exclamation points. "In the future, no German should buy from the Jews!"

Printed in Fraktur, the gothic font widely used by the Nazis until they abruptly banned it in 1941 when Hitler deemed it outmoded, the paper urged the citizenry to rally that evening at eight fifteen at the Münsterplatz, the splendid square of the city's cathedral. Here, at the market set up around the cathedral each morning, generations of burghers had gathered to haggle with weatherworn peasants over baskets and pushcarts filled with products and produce,

*On March 31, 1933, the front page of the Nazi Party newspaper in
Baden,* Der Alemanne, *declared war against Germany's Jews and
announced a boycott of all Jewish-owned firms.*

richly arrayed under bright striped umbrellas. That night, however, in
place of fruits and flowers, sausages and cheeses, olives and noodles,
black-and-red Nazi banners emblazoned with swastikas dominated
the cobblestoned square, as citizens amassed to shout new battle cries
at their old Jewish neighbors.

"Hitler has taken the rudder," Hanna recalled hearing Sigmar be-
moan to his brother Heinrich just eight weeks before, on January 30,
when the Nazi leader maneuvered to seize power as chancellor. She

Freiburg's market on the Münsterplatz: the late-Gothic building on the left, with arches, is the red-colored Historische Kaufhaus (Historical Merchants' Hall).

had puzzled over her father's metaphor then, but shortly after ten in the morning on April 1, Sigmar's reasons for worry grew clear, as brown-shirted Nazi storm troopers formed a sidewalk phalanx outside his office. A curious crowd gathered to watch as they daubed the windows with crude yellow Stars of David to brand the business as Jewish and therefore off-limits.

It was Hitler's stated objective to protect the purity of German blood through the elimination of Jewish "pollution," and economic restrictions marked his first step. Though Sigmar, Alice, and their assimilated peers took care to present themselves always as true *Germans* of Jewish faith—any difference of identity a matter of religion, not race—Nazi dogma expressly outlawed that view. As a result, German Jews now anxiously redoubled efforts to distance themselves from the alien presence of *Ostjuden* rushing over their borders from Poland's poor ghettos, those Orthodox Jews who attracted embarrassing public attention with their raven black clothes, beards, mangled German, and fringes.

By contrast, Freiburg's main synagogue, an imposing stone structure near the university, was a liberal one where, even in prayer, most men eschewed traditional skullcaps or yarmulkes and instead covered their heads with the same dark fedoras they wore on the street. Religion had a place in their lives, but within the greater community they were secularized. Hence Sigmar, like his non-Jewish counterparts, spent Saturday mornings at work in his office, and though he did not permit his wife and children to write, sew, or play on the Sabbath, he magnanimously awarded himself dispensation to continue smoking his favored cigars. "God forgives *Sigmärle*," he would say with a shrug and a grin, by way of explaining his happy personal compromise with the Almighty.

He hewed more carefully to what the community expected of him just days after Freiburg's first Nazi rally, when, despite the ire aimed at Jews, he persisted in having Hanna deliver paper-wrapped packets of Passover matzo to each of his best Gentile customers as a neighborly gesture. Hanna loved the eight-day holiday and its special breakfasts of *Matzekaffee*—matzo soaked in large cups of coffee, sugar, and milk—yet she dreaded her annual springtime chore.

"*Guten Tag*," she would say as instructed, bobbing a curtsy with practiced politeness as she reluctantly made her visits through town. "I am the daughter of Sigmar Günzburger, and he would like you to have with his compliments a sample of our Passover matzo."

Popular German folk wisdom had held that matzo worked to help ward off lightning, so it became traditional for Jews in some parts of the country to have their children bring the unleavened bread to non-Jewish neighbors at Passover time. New Nazi efforts to fan public outrage over the medieval "blood libel" charge failed to grant Hanna reprieve from her rounds. Indeed, she was obliged to make her deliveries again the following year, even as the lurid anti-Semitic propaganda vehicle, *Der Stürmer*, published a fourteen-page issue devoted to the Jews' alleged ritual murder of Christian children in order to use their blood to make matzo.

Coinciding with Easter, however, Passover gave Hanna and Trudi the pleasure of a new dress, coat, hat, and shoes for public display. After each shopping trip with Alice for this purpose, the girls looked forward to showing their father their new finery, knowing ahead of time exactly how he would tease them. "Oh, but I already know all about it," Sigmar would say with an air of great wisdom acquired from the rumor mill on the town's busy square. "Everyone's been talking about it on the Rotteckplatz!" And when the day itself finally came to parade their new things and they appeared dressed for synagogue, Sigmar would thump the heavy mahogany table that sat in the foyer and then clasp his hand to his chest as if overcome by the sheer delight and surprise of their beauty.

"*Was werden da die Leute sagen?*" What will the people say when they see you? he would ask in wonder, a rhetorical query that always elicited blushes and laughter. The joy of this moment was tempered, however, by having to stand next to their mother as she turned aside all compliments about their appearance.

"*Ach*, they're nothing so special," Alice would say with a dismissive wave of her hand that was meant to be self-effacing, when acquaintances stopped her to comment on the charm of her daughters in their matching ensembles—always light blue to enhance Hanna's eyes, always red for her copper-haired sister.

Hanna, Trudi, and Norbert studied Hebrew in after-school classes, and on Friday nights they sang in the synagogue choir. At services, where women and girls were relegated to the balcony, Hanna's thoughts wandered in spite of her will toward pure-minded devotion.

The Freiburg Synagogue was consecrated in 1885 and destroyed by the Nazis in 1938.

A child who was acutely aware of the sudden potential for danger and loss and who groped in lonely spaces for the comfort of love, she believed in prayer as a kind of insurance. In the austere sanctuary, she struggled to find the smiling embrace of a benevolent God who might forgive a child's secret doubts. Instead, she encountered a God who terrified her with thoughts of how she would pay for the sin of ignoring His Law, with its intricate rules and stern retribution. The reign of God in her world mirrored the authoritarian rule she knew in her home, and the probability of displeasing God or Sigmar engendered not only fear but also a smoldering sense of guilt that was already a driving part of her nature.

At the Rosh Hashanah holiday marking the Jewish New Year, for instance, the Günzburger children were expected to write to their parents

Hanna's 1934 New Year's letter to her parents, written in the hard-to-decipher script called Sütterlin, *taught in German schools from 1915 to 1941*

and critique their own past behavior. With their best handwriting in flowery letters that they placed like offerings on their parents' pillows, they
annually extended their thanks and pledged to mend their performance
at home and in school. The tone of their letters hardly varied at all:

"*I promise to work harder to please you in the New Year,*" Hanna wrote,
for example, at age eleven in 1934. "*I won't give any fresh answers. I will
try hard to excel in school.*" And at Rosh Hashanah when she was twelve:
"*In the last year, I was sometimes bad. For that I ask you from the bottom of my
heart to forgive me. May God make me do only good things and give you all the
love and good luck you deserve. So wishes your faithful daughter.*"

In an effort to gain her father's respect, Hanna worked to find biblical questions she might raise with him during the family's outings
each Sunday, when Buhler, the chauffeur, often drove them to the
so-called *Alter Friedhof* or seventeenth-century Old Cemetery, where
the ancestors of the town's Catholic elite lay buried. There—his
preferred weekend pastime—Sigmar led them on tours through the
elaborate graves, expounding upon the generational histories of the
entrenched Freiburg families whose mossy tombstones he found so
intriguing.

But whenever Hanna asked him about God or death or the reason
for evil, Sigmar's answer was curt and unyielding. "We don't question these things," he sternly rebuked her. Ever after, she cringed to
recall how shocked he had been when she tried to show off her biblical insight by sharing the news she had heard from a friend—that
Adam and Eve were really chased out of Eden *not* for chastely eating
a forbidden apple, but for angering God by engaging in sex with each
other. "Who told you such a thing?" Sigmar demanded, and he directed her never to speak with her theological expert again.

Ever aiming to please, in school Hanna was a hardworking and excellent student. Her prize-winning entry in a penmanship contest
requiring the use of a highly formal, complicated Germanic script
called *Sütterlin* was hung on display in a local museum, and she set
her sights on winning the top academic prize in her class, for which
Sigmar had held out the reward of a new bicycle. When her marks
won top ranking, however, school officials refused to grant her the

prize because she was Jewish, and Sigmar made no allowance for that injustice.

As a result, she never got the new bike she craved until she bought *me* a shiny white Schwinn when I was eleven, outfitting it with near-giddy delight with baskets and bell and red handlebar streamers. Then thirty-six, she occasionally rode it around town while I was in school. Yet those solitary excursions up and down the empty hills of suburban New Jersey could not have brought the same joy she had tasted in daydreams, pedaling in all gleaming splendor through the bustling streets of the center of Freiburg, until she arrived at her school, greeted by the admiring glances of all her classmates.

With new laws on education in 1933, the Reich decreed that the proportion of non-Aryan students in German schools should be reduced to a maximum of 5 percent, ousting thousands of Jewish children from their classrooms and forcing them into ad hoc Jewish schools. The Central Committee of German Jews set rules for these schools that called for teaching the children about both sides of their lives, the Jewish and German, about the contributions each had made to the other, and about the tensions dividing them now. Under grave existing circumstances, "the entire education must be directed toward the creation of determined and secure Jewish personalities," the committee said, because "the Jewish child must be enabled to take up and master the exceptionally difficult struggle for survival which awaits him." In light of her top academic performance, Hanna was allowed to remain, a token Jew, in the German *Höhere Mädchenschule* (the Higher Girls' School).

"Now here is the perfect example of a young lady with distinctively Aryan features," a Nazi Party official observed to her class, his hand on Hanna's shoulder, during a visit to lecture the students on how to recognize non-Aryan facial characteristics. No one dared contradict him, but the incident inspired Hanna's teacher to get even with her for "passing" as German. When Christmastime came and the class was preparing its annual play, he assigned her the role of the *Christkind*, the Christ child, whose part called for bearing a sack with a gift for the class. Hanna entered the room with the bag slung over her shoulder, and her classmates rushed from their seats to circle around her, eager to see what Baby Jesus had brought them. But when they tore open the wrapping, she was ashamed to discover the present the teacher selected was a large framed picture of Adolf Hitler. The only Jew in the class, Hanna flushed in humiliation to have been forced to deliver, as if a sacred gift, the Führer's picture to hang in the schoolroom, and she wept as her classmates hooted with laughter.

Generally speaking, her fellow students nevertheless treated her kindly, even as fear of Nazi reprisals against their parents compelled some of them to ask her to sneak around to their back doors whenever she came to play at their homes. In school, each time a teacher entered a classroom, Hanna had no choice but to join with her classmates, jumping to their feet and shouting *"Heil Hitler!"* with a Nazi salute, until it became such a habit for her that she accidentally greeted the rabbi that way when she encountered him walking alone on the street.

At Monday morning flag-raising ceremonies in front of her school, Hanna's classmates all wore the Bund Deutscher Mädel (League of

Freiburg's Adolf-Hitler-Strasse, lined with Nazi banners and flags, between 1935 and 1940. To create a street grand enough to honor the Führer, the city's main thoroughfare, the Kaiserstrasse, was linked to other streets to the north and south.

German Girls) uniforms that Hitler Youth leaders prescribed for girls: navy skirts with white blouses, white kneesocks with tassels, and wide leather belts and bandoliers. In an effort to blend in, Hanna persuaded Alice to buy a white blouse and socks for her and to have the dressmaker produce a similar kick-pleated skirt. The bandolier, the most desirable part of the outfit, was, of course, not accessible to her. But walking home to the Poststrasse one day after school, she was drawn to a crowd of cheering young people who stood gathered near the train station in front of the Zähringer Hof, one of the city's finest hotels. Garlands of flowers draped the doorway, and bloodred Nazi banners flew from the windows. The children were shouting and waving to a room several floors high above, calling for "dear Göring," Hitler's chief aide, "to be so kind as to come to the window."

Lieber Göring, sei so nett,
Komm doch mal ans Fensterbrett!

Over and over they chanted their couplet, their clear children's voices insistent and charged with excitement, until the uniformed figure of Hermann Göring appeared at the window and acknowledged their adulation with an exemplary Nazi salute. Below him stood a generation determined to rise, phoenixlike, from the devastating defeats their parents had suffered in war and under its onerous treaty. But in the cheering crowd on the street, there was at least one young Jewish girl, confused and uncertain, whose voice mingled with those of her German peers.

Many years later, when I was a teenager, my father would bring my mother to tears of frustration and anger at the dinner table when he rebuked her for the passive compliance of Jews who had, out of fear, complied with Fascist commands instead of rebelling.

"What would you have had me do? I was a child. What could any of us do?" she would stammer, her eyes brimming, on the many occasions this issue arose. She never cried out of sadness, but only to drain unvented anger, accumulated over a lifetime and squelched into silence. It was one of the common disputes that sparked my increasingly protective feelings for her, as my father persisted in maintaining that Jews themselves handed power to Hitler through docile acceptance of their own annihilation. He would raise his fist, slide his jaw forward, narrow his eyes, and snarl through clenched teeth, "I might have gone down, but *I* would have taken a bunch of Krauts with me."

That summer, as usual, the children left to spend their vacation with their grandmother Johanna in Eppingen, a trip always made special by Alice's having friends and relations greet their train at numerous stops on the way, bringing them treats. *"I can't believe how many people we have met, and everybody gives us something,"* Hanna enthused in a letter home, describing their journey. *"We couldn't close the suitcase anymore, we had so many chocolates and goodies!"* A day or so later, they reported their shock to discover a new sign on the gate of the Eppingen pool, which led Alice to threaten to summon them back: JUDEN UND HUNDE VERBOTEN, Jews and Dogs Not Permitted. Undeterred, Hanna wrote Alice, begging to stay:

> Even though we can't go swimming anymore, there is still more to do here on vacation than in Freiburg. We tease the geese and play with the horses and chickens. Today we spent in the garden watering the plants. We wore nothing but our undershirts, panties, and aprons. We were barefoot. That's how we hopped around the whole day. We plucked all the plums from the tree and stuffed them into our underpants. Don't worry, Trudi has no freckles yet, but you

Hanna (L) and Trudi picking daisies on summer holidays in Eppingen

have to send us a new tube of bleaching cream because she will soon run out. . . .

Listen to this, Mother. Yesterday, a man was here who told us that you, Mother, were a terrible flirt! Don't you say anything more to us! (Excuse the grease spot on this letter. It came from a pickle sandwich I am eating just now.) You, dear Mother, are a world-known lady here. Everybody one meets knows the Lisel.

When the children returned to Freiburg in September, Sigmar and Alice had not forgotten the notice posted at the Eppingen pool. Channeling their need to belong—if not in the larger community of the town, then with their peers—Sigmar enrolled all three in the Bund Deutschjüdischer Jugend (League of German Jewish Youth), one of two Jewish recreational clubs. The other youth group had a Zionist outlook and a more daring agenda, but still adamant in his sense of himself as a true German, Sigmar ruled out his children's joining a movement whose stated goal involved emigration.

Meanwhile, Hitler Youth membership soared to nearly six million. Widening economic restrictions seriously threatened the livelihood of Jews now forced out of civil service positions and jobs in education, law, culture, and science. Hitler had won dictatorial powers, the ranks of storm troopers had swelled to over two million, and beginning with Dachau near Munich, four concentration camps ostensibly for political prisoners had already been opened. Even though 90 percent of German voters approved Hitler's powers, Sigmar still harbored hope that the situation would change and that leaving their homeland would prove unnecessary.

Increasingly grim circumstances led to changes at home as well. Alice spent much of her time closeted with her friend Meta Ellenbogen, who for many years had rented a top-floor room in the house, supporting herself by selling coffee. A timid and lonely woman with hair dyed jet-black and the fine bones and nervous demeanor of a small, flitting bird, she sat talking in Alice's bedroom late into the night, flying upstairs only when Sigmar entered and methodically began to loosen his leather suspenders. Downstairs, the retired, impoverished army officer whom Sigmar had met in the war and had allowed to live rent-free in the basement with his wife and two children abruptly moved out, fearful now of being known to live with Jews. But before long, a different tenant moved into the house.

Therese Loewy was a fifty-four-year-old widow whose husband, Alfred, had been a mathematics professor and academic colleague of the eminent existential philosopher Martin Heidegger. On May 27, 1933—with the pomp of a national holiday, the singing of the Nazi anthem, the roaring "*Sieg Heil!*" and Nazi salutes—Heidegger, having joined the Nazi Party, was installed in the prestigious post of rector of the Albert-Ludwigs-University in Freiburg. Admirers flocked to the city from all over Germany to hear his rector's address, but Alfred Loewy, being Jewish, was not invited. Although only sixty, he was blind by then and relied on Therese to lead him to a seat in the last row of the jammed auditorium to hear his former student extol the truth and greatness of Hitler's National Socialist movement and the fresh beginning it offered the country. The role of science and philosophy, the new rector declared, was to lend power to the Nazi political program as the means of realizing "the historical mission of the German people."

Pledging to revive the primordial, indigenous power of German *Blut und Boden*, blood and earth, in the academic life of the Reich, Heidegger announced that he would stem within the university the encroaching foreign threat of the Jews. And so, when the dean of the Mathematics Faculty soon sought his help to allow Loewy to retain his position despite the general purging of Jewish professors, Heidegger refused. When Herr Professor Loewy then requested emeritus status as a last-ditch attempt to maintain ties with his students and continue his thirty-six years of research at Freiburg, Heidegger wrote his former mentor that "any further pursuit of your plea is hopeless." Two years later, Alfred Loewy died brokenhearted, and Therese, whose only child had died in infancy, was ordered to vacate her home.

Touched by her plight, Sigmar invited the widow to move in with his family, who all shifted rooms to make space for her. But the arrangement made everyone testy. Frau Loewy, an Orthodox Jew and a pianist who gave lessons to adults, including Sigmar, repeatedly grumbled to Alice that the children disrupted her teaching, and the children resented the changes her presence imposed. Swathed in the black clothes of mourning, stooped by grief, and understandably bitter, she seemed to cast a pall on the house as she sat at the Bechstein grand piano that had been Alice's fiftieth birthday gift to Sigmar, softly singing and playing Gustav Mahler's "Songs on the Death of Children." On Saturdays, when her own maid was off and Sabbath piety barred Frau Loewy from working, Alice took over making her bed and bringing her water to bathe. Never before having seen Alice in that kind of role, her children objected that their unfriendly boarder was turning their mother into her servant. Alice's own help in the house had been greatly diminished by the prohibitions of the Nuremberg Laws, but not a complainer—not then and not ever—she kept silent about helping Frau Loewy and firmly instructed the children to say nothing to Sigmar.

With Alice distracted and Fräulein Elfriede no longer in charge, Norbert recklessly seized greater freedoms. Like Hitler and Einstein before him and almost every other boy in the country, he had been a fan of Karl May, the enormously popular turn-of-the-century German writer of adventure stories featuring a noble Apache Indian chief named Winnetou and his German blood brother, Old Shatterhand. May's tales fed on a romanticized, Germanic longing for the mythologized realm of innocent nature and depicted glorified battles between forces of good and evil. Drawing on their popularity, the Hitler Youth movement devised competitive hide-and-seek exploits called Trapper and Indian, as well as violent war games that encouraged boys to engage in bloody fights with each other—all designed to hone them as soldiers. But even had he not been barred as a Jew from these rough adventures, Norbert's interests veered in another direction.

The irrepressible uncle I later adored was a handsomer version of the film noir actor Robert Mitchum and shared the screen star's bad boy pursuits. "Booze, broads, it's all true. Make up more if you want," the actor was famously quoted as saying, and my uncle, too, would indulge in such robust enjoyment of life that I always picture him with his head thrown back laughing in total abandon. He smoked and drank to fatal excess, while his pursuit of women was so blithely unchecked by his own or his paramours' marital status that his love life persistently got him in trouble. In the face of persecution and war, Norbert began to practice romantic skills early.

A strikingly good-looking teenager in 1936, he courted danger in defying Nazi laws against *Rassenschande*, defiling the race, by flirting with German girls, who were now definitively forbidden to him. Besides that, Alice never knew where to find him, he gave no accounting, and his rash rebelliousness threatened them all.

One evening when Alice stood at the window in tears, ineffectually pleading with him to come in to dinner or else face Sigmar's punishment later, Norbert shouted back from the street with a threat of his own. "I'm going to tell everyone that you and Papa plan to throw Papa's guns in the river tonight!" he called out, having overheard his parents discuss the need to dispose discreetly of Sigmar's World War I pistols in response to new laws against Jews owning weapons. Her son's words rang in her ears, reverberating over the streets, bouncing off mountains. She felt certain they would ricochet back to the Gestapo. The next day, Sigmar and Alice decided to send Norbert away to Alice's sister in Zurich until Hitler lost power or until the whole family could emigrate.

In August 1936, Berlin hosted the Summer Olympics, and Hanna, full of national pride, insisted on wearing a celebratory Olympics pin on her collar. Around the world, despite the systematic exclusion of German Jewish athletes and the racial insults hurled at black contestants, the Olympics proved a stunning triumph for the Nazi propaganda machine. It managed to create a false façade of social harmony and prosperity that duped the international press and foreign dignitaries attending the games into believing that reports of German oppression and militarism had been unfairly and grossly exaggerated.

After the theatrical pageant came to an end and the world's eyes turned away, the warning notice the children had found at the Eppingen pool began to appear everywhere—on shops, on theaters, and on the Poststrasse also. Until then, a week had rarely gone by without Sigmar's handing Hanna a *Krügle*, a small earthenware pitcher, to take next door to the bar at the Hotel Minerva to have filled with special wine for his dinner. But one evening as she approached the hotel with her pitcher in hand and the cherished Olympics insignia pinned to her blouse, she was faced by that same large new sign on the familiar door: JUDEN UND HUNDE VERBOTEN.

Stopping bewildered and shocked on the steps, she hardly knew which frightened her more—violating the sign by proceeding inside the Minerva, or returning to Sigmar with an empty *Krügle*. Before very long, Rosemarie, the hotel keeper's daughter, would reluctantly tell Hanna that they could no longer be seen playing together. At her parents' insistence, their games of collecting horse chestnuts and trapping chocolaty maybugs in jars would come to an end.

Shortly thereafter, not a political movement but a physical one stemming from a medical problem would prevent Hanna from playing with anyone. Whenever she bent at the waist, she experienced a very sharp pain in her spine, and she began to question all her friends, hoping to learn the ailment was common. Throughout the day she would hunch and curl over, arching her back like a cat, testing to see if the pain might be gone. Loathe to worry her parents, she told them nothing about it, which led them to view her repetitive movements as a new nervous tic, and they told her to stop. Then her Eppingen grandmother observed to Alice that Hannele looked a little bit "tilted" and required constant reminders not to stand crooked. Soon Alice made it a point to enter the bathroom while her daughter, then thirteen, was taking a shower and was alarmed to notice a long purplish bruise that snaked down Hanna's back.

"You wait and see, she'll have tuberculosis of the bones," Hanna overheard Alice fretfully whisper to her sister-in-law Toni, who accompanied them a few days later to the university hospital for X-rays. "Today's the twenty-seventh and my father died on the twenty-seventh. *Gott im Himmel*, of all days, we should *never* have come here today."

With the eventual diagnosis of Scheuermann's disease, a decalcification of the spine that generally occurs in adolescence, the family received a dire prognosis: if Hanna grew any taller, she would very likely develop a hunchback. The edges of five vertebrae showed decomposition, worsened by the rigorous daily athletics program imposed by the Nazis in school and Fräulein Elfriede at home. Alice took her to Zurich to be seen by her sister's son-in-law, a pediatrician, and called for her brother, by then a doctor in London, to join them in Switzerland to consult on her treatment.

Today doctors know that the condition resolves spontaneously without deforming the spine, but in late 1936, they ordered Hanna to bed for almost a year in the hope that with rest and without weight-bearing stress, her back might grow straight. Added to the awful regimen were vitamins, calcium, and cod liver oil. Hanna spent four months confined to bed at home, during which time her classmates—*none* of them Jewish, she would always remember—visited daily, bringing her schoolwork so she would not fall behind. But when her back failed to show the expected improvement, it was resolved that she spend the next six months in a children's rest home in Arosa, a secluded aerie in the Swiss Alps.

Hanna passed her days there alone on a frosty mountaintop terrace, surrounded by towering pine trees laden with snow. Lying flat on her back, unable even to read, encased in a fur sack on a hard wooden cot, she reposed in fear and in silence while the other young patients went skating and skiing. In deference to her cousin in Zurich, who referred so many patients, the sanatorium insisted on giving Hanna a room of her own instead of housing her in the dormitory with the other girls.

Dr. Pedolin's Kinderheim, *a sanatorium for ailing children, in Arosa in the Swiss Alps*

Due to the increasing difficulty of crossing the border, moreover, her family was unable to visit her there. And so, stunned one morning to find blood on her sheets, and never informed about her maturing body's natural cycles, Hanna concluded that she was dying.

Like Heidi, she finally came down the mountain from her lonely retreat, but she brought with her a horror of the number 27, a unique superstition that was as overpowering as it was irrational, enduring, and unusual for her.

"Can't you hold on until midnight?" my mother urged, for example, as I rushed off to the hospital in labor on the afternoon of July 27, 1987 to give birth to my own daughter. Be it her father's rigid Germanic discipline or the influence of living in fear under a Fascist regime, my mother normally avoids confrontation at any cost. Yet about the number 27 she is unyielding. On a crowded airplane, for instance, she once flatly refused to take her seat in row 27 and insisted my father travel the aisle to find fellow passengers willing to trade seats before take-off. And this time, at least, her vehemence left him no choice.

"You see those people seated in the twenty-seventh row?" my father pointed out drily once they had switched seats and were airborne. "I should warn you—if *they* go down, *we* go down also."

The concept of collective doom was one she was used to, but the goal of escape, the personal struggle toward life and renewal, was like hope through a storm, the thing that prevailed.

FOUR

THE SIDEWALK OF CUCKOLDS

By THE TIME Hanna returned from Arosa in late 1937, the growing number of legal, economic, and social restrictions on German Jews had forced Sigmar to accept the urgent need to get out of the country. Their immediate world was shrinking around them, and escape had become his critical goal, never mind the loss of their home or his business. But he had waited so long that it was no longer easy to gain entry anywhere else. For months, he struggled to secure visas to immigrate to the United States, but with Jews by the many thousands seeking admission, his written pleas went unanswered, and his subsequent trips to the visa office in Stuttgart proved equally fruitless.

The following March, declaring a need for Lebensraum or living space in the east, Germany annexed Austria, where jubilant crowds welcomed Hitler's troops into Vienna. Almost immediately, Jews were violently attacked on the streets, the women forced to their knees to scrub sidewalks and gutters. Mass arrests of Jews in Germany began in June, and soon synagogues in Munich and Nuremberg were burned to the ground.

At an international conference on the refugee question held that summer in France, at Evian on Lake Geneva, the scope of the problem loomed large. Many of the thirty-two participating countries offered sympathy. Very few offered asylum. Although a quarter of Germany's six hundred thousand Jews had fled its borders since 1933, France had accepted only 10 percent of them. With Austrian Jews now swelling the tides of refugees, the British not only tightened restrictions for England but also refused to accept Jews into Palestine. American quotas were kept tightly in place, as polls showed that the majority of Americans viewed Jews negatively and believed them to be a threat to the nation. Those who sought to curb immigration argued to President Franklin Roosevelt that the Depression still demanded putting domestic needs first. As a result, between 1933 and America's entry into World War II eight years later, only about one hundred thousand Jews were admitted.

"It will no doubt be appreciated," an Australian delegate announced at the Evian conference, "that as we have no racial problem, we are not desirous of importing one." And Canada said that in terms of welcoming refugees, "none was too many." Afterward, it was bitterly noted among Germany's desperate Jews that *Evian* spelled backward yielded *naïve*, which was what they saw their hopes to have been, when they expected the conference to offer them someplace to go.

Sigmar now aimed his efforts at France, believing that what remained of the small building supply business he had launched in Mulhouse before he was married, along with the fact that his sister lived there, might help win admission. Then perhaps they'd have greater success winning American visas as "stateless" refugees stranded in France, he reasoned, than they'd experienced applying from Freiburg. And so, week after week, Sigmar traveled to the French consulate in Karlsruhe in pursuit of French visas, and he hired agents both there and in Mulhouse to lead him through thickets of requirements and charges. While his sister Marie's son, Edmond Cahen, a lawyer in Mulhouse, helped him with legal papers, in the end Sigmar was obliged to pay what he termed "a present to a certain gentleman" in Mulhouse, a lifesaving bribe, to obtain the French visas he guiltily realized others might not have afforded.

By the time the family managed to leave, Sigmar was impoverished: he and his brother Heinrich were coerced into paying more for the privilege of fleeing than they received from the forced sale, at only a fraction of its true worth, of the prosperous firm they had founded in 1919. On April 7, based on an official ruling by the Freiburg Chamber of Commerce, two other brothers—Albin and Alfons Glatt, who had worked for competitors of the Günzburger brothers—took over what the chamber described as the "non-Aryan" firm, along with its buildings and vehicles, its warehouses full of supplies, and its ample customer lists.

Alice with Sigmar (L) and Heinrich, his brother and business partner, in Freiburg, mid-1930s

As to the house at Poststrasse 6, Sigmar sold it to his next-door neighbor, August Schöpperle. The hotel owner was confident that the political turmoil and migrations of war would bring even more travelers with money to Freiburg and was planning to use it to expand the Minerva. In haste to depart by the time their papers came through,

The Poststrasse, with the Hotel Minerva at the corner. Beside it to the right is the Günzburger home at Poststrasse 6.

Sigmar had been in no position to bargain and had sold Herr Schöpperle the house at a price that was also far below its actual value. But it hardly mattered, he grimly acknowledged, given the fact that he was barred from taking money out of the country.

Technically, it was arranged that "all things happened legally," Dr. Hans Schadek, then Freiburg's chief archivist, explained when he showed me the relevant records on one of my visits. He described how, seeking funds for armaments, the Nazis pillaged Jewish wealth by means of imposing taxes that conveniently managed to total the sum of every emigrant's assets. Revenue from the sales of the family's home and business was deposited into blocked accounts at the Oberrheinische Bank that were nominally in the Günzburgers' names, but from which they could make no withdrawals without state approval. No such approvals were granted. Official taxes on "Jewish wealth," flight taxes, bank fees on the taxpaying transactions, and punishing fines would eventually claim all that they owned through pretexts the Nazis wrote into law.

"*Ich bin Jude*" (I am a Jew), read the form Sigmar was obliged to fill out on June 30, 1938, before emigrating, declaring his remaining worth at that point. And for this purpose, it also described him as a member of the German state, no longer a citizen, yet still subject to the rules of the Reich. Having already signed away everything, however, there was nothing much left for him to declare. Almost every category of assets on the four-page form thus earned the same answer: *Nichts* (nothing). Money? *Nichts.* Real estate? *Nichts.* Other expected capital? *Nichts.* The only items of any value still in his possession besides their furnishings were three now-dubious life insurance policies, a gold watch, and the simple gold rings he and Alice had exchanged at their wedding.

All this brought them to the warm mid-August morning in 1938 when they were to leave. Hanna, now almost fifteen, awoke to the familiar cooing of doves on the rooftops and the buzz of the electric cart ferrying mail to the post office at the end of the street. From the Hotel Minerva next door came the familiar clatter of dishes and pans, the smells and the banter of the kitchen staff preparing guests' breakfasts. It had always been a private pleasure for her to sit at the window and spy on the sophisticated foreign tourists who lingered on the hotel

Vor Ausfüllung des Vermögensverzeichnisses ist die beigefügte Anleitung genau durchzulesen!

Zur Beachtung!

1. Wer hat das Vermögensverzeichnis einzureichen?
Jeder Anmeldepflichtige, also auch jeder Ehegatte und jedes Kind für sich. Für jedes minderjährige Kind ist das Vermögensverzeichnis vom Inhaber der elterlichen Gewalt oder von dem Vormund einzureichen.

2. Bis wann ist das Vermögensverzeichnis einzureichen?
Bis zum 30. Juni 1938. Wer anmelde- und bewertungspflichtig ist, aber die Anmelde- und Bewertungspflicht nicht oder nicht rechtzeitig oder nicht vollständig erfüllt, setzt sich schwerer Strafe (Geldstrafe, Gefängnis, Zuchthaus, Einziehung des Vermögens) aus.

3. Wie ist das Vermögensverzeichnis auszufüllen?
Es müssen sämtliche Fragen beantwortet werden. Nichtzutreffendes ist zu durchstreichen. Reicht der in dem Vermögensverzeichnis für die Ausfüllung vorgesehene Raum nicht aus, so sind die geforderten Angaben auf einer Anlage zu machen.

4. Wenn Zweifel bestehen, ob diese oder jene Werte in dem Vermögensverzeichnis aufgeführt werden müssen, sind die Werte aufzuführen.

Verzeichnis über das Vermögen von Juden
nach dem Stand vom 27. April 1938

des Samuel Günzburger , Kaufmann, Eisenhändler
der (Zu- und Vorname) (Beruf oder Gewerbe)

in Freiburg i. Br. , Post — Straße, Platz Nr. 6
(Wohnsitz oder gewöhnlicher Aufenthalt)

Angaben zur Person

Ich bin geboren am 29.12.1880

Ich bin Jude (§ 5 der Ersten Verordnung zum Reichsbürgergesetz vom 14. November 1935, Reichsgesetzbl. I S. 1333)
und — deutscher — Staatsangehörigkeit — staatenlos —.

Da ich — Jude deutscher Staatsangehörigkeit — staatenloser Jude — bin, habe ich in dem nachstehenden Vermögensverzeichnis mein gesamtes inländisches und ausländisches Vermögen angegeben und bewertet.

Da ich Jude fremder Staatsangehörigkeit bin, habe ich in dem nachstehenden Vermögensverzeichnis mein inländisches Vermögen angegeben und bewertet.

Ich bin verheiratet mit Lisl Günzburger geb. Heinsheimer
(Mädchenname der Ehefrau)

Mein Ehegatte ist der Rasse nach — jüdisch — nichtjüdisch — und gehört der israel. Religionsgemeinschaft an.

Angaben über das Vermögen

I. Land- und forstwirtschaftliches Vermögen (vgl. Anleitung Ziff. 9):

Wenn Sie am 27. April 1938 land- und forstwirtschaftliches Vermögen besaßen (gepachtete Ländereien u. dgl. sind nur aufzuführen, wenn das der Bewirtschaftung dienende Inventar Ihnen gehört).

Lage des eigenen oder gepachteten Betriebs und seine Größe in Hektar? (Gemeinde — Gutsbezirk — und Gutsnamen, auch grundbuch- und katastermäßige Bezeichnung)	Art des eigenen oder gepachteten Betriebs? (z. B. landwirtschaftlicher, forstwirtschaftlicher, gärtnerischer Betrieb, Weinbaubetrieb, Fischzuchtbetrieb)	Handelte es sich um einen eigenen Betrieb oder um eine Pachtung	Wert des Betriebs RM	Bei eigenen Betrieben: Wenn der Betrieb noch Anderen gehörte: Wie hoch war Ihr Anteil (z. B. 1/3)
1	2	3	4	5
/	/	/	/	nichts

II. Grundvermögen (Grund und Boden, Gebäude) (vgl. Anleitung Ziff. 10):

Wenn Sie am 27. April 1938 Grundvermögen besaßen (Grundstücke, die nicht zu dem vorstehend unter I und nachstehend unter III bezeichneten Vermögen gehörten):

Lage des Grundstücks? (Gemeinde, Straße und Hausnummer, bei Bauland auch grundbuch- und katastermäßige Bezeichnung)	Art des Grundstücks? (z. B. Einfamilienhaus, Mietwohngrundstück, Bauland)	Wert des Grundstücks RM	Wenn das Grundstück noch Anderen gehörte: Wie hoch war Ihr Anteil? (z. B. 1/3)
1	2	3	4
/	/	/	nichts

¹) Nichtzutreffendes ist zu durchstreichen.

Vermögensverzeichnis (VO v. 26. 4. 38)

The official form—the Inventory of Jewish Wealth, in accordance with the Reich law of April 27, 1938—on which Sigmar reported no longer having any assets: "nichts" terrace, enjoying their food and their papers and quietly conversing. Now she, too, would be traveling, but the mysterious thrill she had always imagined as she studied those tourists was replaced by dread in leaving her birthplace for the unknown.

"*Wir wandern aus. Wir wandern aus*," her father had warned them so many times without her ever believing he meant it. The verb he had used means *to emigrate*, but also—too aptly, she feared—to wander, to roam, to travel like nomads.

Across the room, her beloved Käthe Kruse doll drooped on a shelf, its painted blue eyes accusingly staring. Her only doll had been the patient in so many of her first medical efforts that, with its soft stuffed body scarred by long lines of stitches and stained in the cause of science by myriad greasy ointments, Hanna had already decided to leave her behind. They were traveling by train, but a van would carry their pared-down household possessions, including Sigmar's cherished grand piano. To accommodate the smaller space they would have in their Mulhouse apartment, they were taking furniture only from the living room, dining room, and master bedroom. For the children, their beds. Art, silverware, crystal, and china found space in the truck. Clothes and books were carefully chosen. Still, they were uncommonly lucky to be able to leave with that much.

Once the truck pulled away, Sigmar approached the wide oak doorway with a little screwdriver. There were tears in the eyes of this man so ill accustomed to showing emotion as he reached up to unfasten the five-inch long carved wooden mezuzah that he had hung on the entryway of the house, creating space that was sacred, on the day that he and Alice moved in as newlyweds. Never adept with his hands, Sigmar took off his glasses and angrily wiped at his eyes as he tried to fit the slim head of the screwdriver into the slots of the two stubborn screws that held the mezuzah to the doorframe, welcoming those who entered the house. Once it came down, he saw the tight, yellowed scroll of parchment rolled up inside it with the familiar prayer inked by hand in minute Hebrew letters, admonishing faithful adherence to God's commandments—among them the holy duty to teach His words to new generations.

Sigmar took that mezuzah wherever they moved in the years that followed, an artifact of a world destroyed, but he would never rehang it, as he never regained a home of his own. No, he never regarded his small New York City apartment as worthy of consecration by such an imposing ritual object; instead he nailed to his American doorway a small, unobtrusive version made of indeterminate metal. But twenty years after the day he ruefully carried it wrapped in his handkerchief over Germany's border, Sigmar presented the Freiburg mezuzah to my mother and father, who attached it to the first house that they bought, the house my mother resolved never to leave, despite my father's persistent entreaties and his efforts to lure her to bigger and better.

That sorrowful day she left Freiburg was always in mind. Norbert had been called home from Switzerland in order to move to Mulhouse with the rest of the family. Carrying valises, they walked in silence to the corner and turned left at the Minerva onto the Rosastrasse where a sign announced that the Gebrüder Glatt—New Aryan Ownership!— had taken over the firm from the Günzburger brothers. Sigmar vowed that someday they would come home to Freiburg to win it back. Still, as he passed the company's gates on the way to the station nearby, his mouth was set in a fixed, bitter line, and averting his eyes, he denied himself a last look at all that he had worked to accomplish.

Good wishes and comforting words filled their tense parting moments, as a small group assembled to see the family off. There was Fräulein Ellenbogen, who still occupied her small attic room in the house, not yet having found someplace to move, with so many Jewish homeowners already gone. Frau Loewy had rented rooms in the home of a Catholic butcher a few blocks away, a difficult choice for an Orthodox Jew who kept strictly kosher. She was not at the station, having said her good-byes a few days before, but there was Buhler the chauffeur. He had named his son Norbert in honor of the Günzburgers' son and had continued working for Sigmar long past the time that having a Jewish employer made sense for a German. Now he clasped hands with his passenger of so many trips, neither one daring as their roads separated to voice his deep feelings. Before the coming war's end, Buhler's son Norbert, still a teenager, would sacrifice an arm for the Führer fighting in Russia—the field of Germany's greatest casualties in World War II—while Sigmar's Norbert would later be posted to Germany, a vengeful soldier in the victorious army of his new American homeland.

Sigmar's longtime secretary, Elisabeth Hipp, brought chocolates to sweeten the travelers' journey. For the rest of his life, Sigmar would find occasions to send Fräulein Hipp money, and she, in turn, regularly sent back little German books of Christian devotional verse or evangelical tracts, as well as calendars with brightly colored botanical pictures labeled in both German and Latin. These my grandfather presented to me. I still have most of those books (never read) and calendars (never used) on my shelves even now, unable, of course, to find the right day after so many years to start throwing them out. When it comes to discarding these things of the past, I can never think of an answer that pleases my heart—the reason to get rid of them *now* instead of last week or eight months or twelve years ago—which is probably why everyone always gives them to *me*. A family Dumpster for memories' traces. I hold on to them all—Sigmar's cigar butt from the day that he died, Alice's veil of black lace—as if I could use them to conjure their owners, to bring them back once again.

Beyond that is my link in the chain of possession that has guarded not just these simple tokens of everyday life, but also the family pictures and papers and letters that have survived generations of turmoil to land at my door. I have become a trustee, a conduit, and to honor the past, I must pass them along, "keeping faith with those who sleep in the dust," as the prayer book tells me. It is, I see clearly, much like the way I increasingly think of the Jewish tradition. In the face of the odds, the forces that time and again have sought to destroy it, the suffering of those who died to preserve it, who am I—who am *I* in these easy times for us here—to toss it aside, to abandon it now? From the beginning, the Jewish narrative has always been a story of journey, recalled and retold in each generation. Among those who have lived an exodus within their own times and have stubbornly carried their faith to new lands, it is left to their children to save and transmit it to those who come later, forging behind.

The train that carried my mother's family out of their ancestral home, a perilous five years after Hitler seized power, stopped at the border, where Reich officials examined their exit visas and verified they were each taking no more than 10 Reichsmarks (under $2.50) out of the country. The heart-stopping terror my mother remembers as the scrutiny continued for much longer than seemed necessary was so indelibly etched in her soul that I have watched her relive it time and again, whenever a situation requires producing identification. Going through customs, returning from any trip outside this country, is an encounter she fears—in part because it involves showing a passport that lists her real birthplace, and because it empowers an official to search and ask questions before granting her entry. "If a doorman looks at me hard," she has confided, "I still get that feeling, my knees begin shaking."

She arrived in Mulhouse with her new French name. As a result, her old autograph book, in which friends inscribed little poems, aphorisms, and colorful drawings full of whimsy and talent, includes entries from 1938 addressed either "Liebe Hanna" or "Chère Janine," based on whether the entry was dated before August or later. At the border, Hanna-now-Janine buried the German girl living inside her. Then she allowed France to change her, a transformation she quickly embraced to create a new life.

"After four weeks in France or six weeks in America, we pretended to be Frenchmen or Americans," Hannah Arendt wrote firsthand of the German Jews' efforts to reshape themselves and their lives, an assimilationist struggle typified again and again by my mother in every new country. "In the first place, we don't like to be called *refugees*," Arendt also declared, explaining how degraded German Jews felt after fleeing their homes, stateless, unwanted, and empty-handed.

It was unnerving, when I read Arendt's words, to remember how deeply my mother had hated my father's derisive nickname for her, which he tended to use as a verbal stiletto whenever she voiced her own contrary views on political issues. The "Ref," he would say, knowing each time how the term would wound her. "Listen to the Ref." But in my mind, the Ref was the woman who slipped into my high school pep rallies and, to her own surprise, cried—tears that sprang from some unexplored zone that had a great deal to do with all she had been through. Unnoticed, she stood in the back of the rowdy auditorium and quietly cried when she saw me alone on the stage, performing routines that required two batons at a time, the captain of the baton twirling squad—a role so totally out of character for me—a serious girl, insufficiently "bouncy" in my father's opinion.

It was also the Ref, I see now, who would not permit me to step down from the squad when the war in Vietnam somehow made my white tasseled boots, thigh-high satin skirt, and towering majorette's hat of black bunny fur unappealing to me. The flags, the salutes, the marching and music—in that era it all seemed uncomfortably militaristic. I had a moral responsibility, my mother insisted, not to abandon the squad. Privately, though, I had my suspicions: the girl forbidden to wear the bold bandolier and tasseled kneesocks of the Nazi girls' troop in Freiburg, the girl who needed to master French, Spanish, and English and in each of them fretted over her accent, was the very same person who wanted her daughter to strut in the happy parades that took over the streets when our football team won and when crowds waving American flags stood waiting on Main Street to cheer us on Memorial Day. And so when my closest friend resigned from the squad, this refugee's daughter had no choice but to stay, *to belong*, and to point her silver baton toward the flag while a wobbly school band bleated its way through her mother's adopted national anthem.

In what would prove to be just the first stop on a six-year journey from Freiburg to safety, the family settled into a two-bedroom second-floor apartment at 18 avenue Roger Salengro in Mulhouse, overlooking the chestnut and pine trees of the parc Salvator in the back and just up the street from the ivy-wrapped Lycée de Jeunes Filles that Janine and Trudi would be attending. When the girls' school began taking boys in 1971, its name was changed to the Lycée Michel de Montaigne, its fifth name change in a century, all four earlier ones reflecting the switches of language required by the back-and-forth status of French and German control of Alsace. So, too, the region's mixed background spawned a distinctive double-tongued dialect that its own citizens mocked by mingling French and German in rhyming ditties that my grandmother Alice often recited to me when I was a child:

> *Voulez-vous Kartoffel soupe?*
> *Non, madame, je danke vous.*
> *Je n'ai pas appetite dazu.*

All the same, in Mulhouse, despite her prior academic success, Janine's French was deemed insufficient for her to continue at her own class level, and she was required, chagrined, to drop back two grades. And excluded as she had been as a Jew from joining her Freiburg friends at joyously nationalistic Hitler Youth rallies, now she felt branded as a German and thus different again from most of her classmates. So in her young teenage years, a point when girls yearn more than anything to fit in with their peers, Janine became an outsider, a careful observer of the people and culture around her. She tried to blend in, but, afraid to make overtures, at the same time developed a reticent stance she would never abandon and that others often mistook, believing her proud and coolly standoffish.

To the extent she could look forward to starting school in a new country in a new language, Janine was pleased to think that at least she'd be stylishly dressed in the new wardrobe Alice had ordered before leaving Freiburg. Since they could not take their money with them, Alice spent what remained after multiple taxes on indulging her two girls in ways she had not done before and could never do later. On the momentous day she landed in France, for example, Janine tottered off the train in unforgettable pain on her first pair of high heels, chosen in navy blue leather to match the outfits she envied on her classmates in Freiburg. There were also fresh summer dresses in floral prints—dresses I found in my mother's closet and wore myself in high school and college—and blue silk pajamas with tops so beautifully made that the sisters would wear them as blouses. But on their second day in Mulhouse, Aunt Marie took them to buy the drab buff-colored smocks that the lycée required from the moment the girls entered school in the morning until the end of the day. With long sleeves and buttons up to the neck, the smocks completely covered Janine and Trudi's custom-made clothes, introducing a French sense of *égalité*, if not *liberté*, to the new German students.

It was here, too, that for the first time the Günzburgers joined a community with a significant number of other Jews, a result of the fact that after its revolution, France became the first European nation to grant Jews full citizenship, gradually leading their numbers to double. In search of freedom, many Jews had long since crossed over the Rhine to find themselves in a place where entire populations of farming towns had started turning their backs on the fields—on seasonal labor and nature's careless tricks and privations—in exchange for long and hard, but regular hours in textile factory jobs. Chemists and colorists, artists, engravers, machinists, and workers with specialized skills were employed by the thousands in flourishing printworks that already by the eighteenth century had transformed Mulhouse into a major manufacturing center, producing fabrics for a growing international market.

Widely forbidden in Europe from owning land, Jews thrived in this industrial setting, working as merchants wholesaling textiles and later on producing apparel. Over time, the Jewish community grew, winning sufficient acceptance that by the point Janine arrived in Alsace, her class at the lycée was divided into three different groups— Protestant, Catholic, and Jewish—to study religion. A Hebrew teacher came to the school expressly to teach Jewish students about their own faith, and the Günzburger children were surprised to find a welcoming circle of Jewish friends who eased their adjustment to the French way of life.

For Janine, this meant taking part in a social ritual that continues today in a great many cities and small towns of Europe, as locals derive their prime entertainment in the late afternoon from the sheer pleasure of strolling and greeting each other. In Mulhouse, the street where they walked was the rue du Sauvage, where at number 25 in 1859, the French Army captain Alfred Dreyfus was born. Himself the son of a wealthy Jewish textile manufacturer, Dreyfus would ignite a hugely divisive political crisis throughout France when his persecution on trumped-up charges of treason exposed anti-Semitism in the French military.

The well-stocked shelves of a gourmet grocery store filled the Dreyfus house the last time I saw it, and the rue du Sauvage was reserved solely for walking. But even in the days when trolley cars ran down the street and war threatened, it was here that young people gathered, and there was one side of the street that they favored. The other side, ever avoided, was informally known as the *trottoir des cocus*, the Sidewalk of Cuckolds. Regrettably, how it came to be nicknamed for husbands whose wives are unfaithful is a tale long buried in folklore.

As it happened, it was on the rue du Sauvage where Janine first saw Roland and, though he was on the side of the street across from the Sidewalk of Cuckolds, their story right from the outset involved a triangle. A classmate of Janine's—Roland's sometime girlfriend Yvette—pointed him out during a break from his studies in college, and in the instant that Janine saw him talking with friends, she knew his was a face she would always remember. He was tall and lean, with an ocean of wavy brown hair and a laugh that stopped time, but eyes that carried her dreaming into the future. In that moment, lured by desire, she left girlhood behind, like her Käthe Kruse doll, once loved but outgrown, slumped on a shelf in a vacated house.

FIVE

THE TATTLER'S STONE

BETWEEN THE RHINE RIVER and the granite Vosges Mountains, in the heart of Mulhouse, the old city hall or *mairie* is an improbable Renaissance building of bubble gum pink and bright painted gold that presides over the pretty place de la Réunion like an elaborate wedding cake on a dessert buffet of cookies and pies. A work of gleeful imagination, the structure is covered entirely with mischievous trompe l'oeil decorations that appear to be ornate architectural details and statues, but are all just part of a painted façade.

How curious, then, to discover slowly that this confection's only real, three-dimensional detail, save for a notable double staircase in front, is a stern directive toward peaceful civic behavior. This is delivered by way of a grotesque bald female head carved from a twenty-five-pound stone, which hangs from a wall on a thick metal chain and is known as the *Klapperstein* or Tattler's Stone. Staring down on the street with bulging eyes, flushed cheeks, an anguished brow, and a swollen tongue that lewdly protrudes from its mouth, the head bears a warning to passersby in old rhyming German: "I am called the *Klapperstein*, well known to those with a nasty mouth," it says in translation. "Whoever takes pleasure in quarrels and disputes must carry me through the streets of the city."

According to historical accounts of life in Mulhouse, the town punished gossips, quite often women, by parading them on market days, either on foot or seated backward on a donkey, with the heavy *Klapperstein* hung from a rope around their necks and sometimes also a sign on their backs confessing their slander. A placard dating to 1576, preserved in the building, announces that being condemned to carry the *Klapperstein* for indulging in speech deemed "vulgar, insulting,

The Klapperstein *or Tattler's Stone, hanging from
the pink and gold* mairie *or city hall in Mulhouse,
France*

slanderous, or hurtful" would punish the culprit and serve as a useful example to others. Early on, this was hailed as a valuable goal in a town as provincial as Mulhouse, with little to offer, then or now, in the way of distractions. In a place so inbred, discretion was crucial. Still, in the story of love and loss that my mother shared with Roland Emil Léon Arcieri, wagging tongues in the town of his birth would eventually play a significant role.

Roland's family background was partly Italian. His mother, Léonie Christophe, came from a French village west of the Vosges. His father, Emil, was the son of a shoemaker from a village near Genoa who had migrated to Lutzelhouse, an Alsatian village in the Valley of the Bruche, sixteen miles southwest of Strasbourg. As a result of

Léonie and Emil Arcieri with their
daughter Emilienne and son, Roland

the 1870 war that put French Alsace in Prussian hands, Emil was born German. He was drafted to serve as an Imperial Guard for the kaiser and then to fight in the German Army in World War I, even as his French father-in-law was seized by the Germans and died in a detention camp. Such were the not uncommon family tragedies in that contested border region, where generations of Alsatians found their nationality reassigned by history and the vicissitudes of war.

Emil and his brother Joseph had moved south to Mulhouse to work in the sales office of a Lutzelhouse-based textile firm before World War I. Joseph sold cloth of plain white or ecru, and Emil traded in the printed cotton fabrics that brought the region world renown. Both brothers would spend their lives working for the same company, sheltered beneath the patriarchal umbrella typical of the Alsatian textile business of that era and linked always to their native village.

The Arcieris—the name means "archer" in Italian—were a close-knit family, Catholics in predominantly Calvinist Mulhouse. And although Roland's Italian surname would eventually help him hide his Alsatian roots when confronted by Nazis in occupied France, his parents' decision to have him circumcised when he was five years old would eventually lead to unforeseen dangers. Seared in his mind was the terrifying ordeal of being held tightly on his mother's lap while the pediatrician in Mulhouse, hoping to cure an infection, snipped off his foreskin in the procedure that is traditionally performed on Jewish infants for religious reasons. But the horror of that memory would later pale beside his ongoing dread as a young man in the war years that a forced inspection inside his pants—called a *Hosenprobe*—by Jew-seeking Nazis would, in consequence of that critical snip, prompt sufficient suspicion for them to arrest him.

Born on May 23, 1920, Roland was the Arcieris' only son, the middle child between two doting sisters, and he grew up first in an apartment near the center of town and later in a fine house on the rue du Ventron, on the fashionable green hills of the Rebberg section overlooking the city. Owing to his father's wartime absence, he was seven years younger than Emilienne, the couple's first daughter, and in every way possible, unaccountably different. While she was a shy, ungainly girl with dark, mournful eyes slanting beneath heavy brows, Roland was a beautiful child with thick curls and fine features.

In contrast, as well, while his sister was devout and conscientious, as a teenager Roland could not be called a hard worker, indulging instead in sports and pastimes with friends who admired his looks and charisma, his humor and pure dedication to creating for all, and not least himself, a very good time. "*Le plus qu'on est fou, le plus qu'on rigole*," the more one is crazy, the more fun one has, was his only half-joking perspective on life. No grand ambition inspired him to study. Indeed, he willingly considered himself the black sheep of the family and confessed, not without self-satisfaction, "If everyone walks in one direction, I go in the other—that way there's less traffic."

This guiding principle involved no grave complications until the spring of 1937, when he set his normally lenient father's pointed goatee aquiver by failing to pass his examinations at the lycée. For "reasons of vanity," Roland announced to his parents, he simply could not repeat the same year, and certainly not in ignominy at the same local school. He spent weeks in his father's office that summer writing to boarding schools, seeking admission to one that would let him move up, even provisionally, to the next grade. When he finally found an all-boys school in Nancy run by Jesuit priests who agreed to his terms, he persuaded his parents to permit him to leave. "I'll never pass if I stay here," the young man insisted. "I have too many friends. You must fence me in."

Except for brief visits home from Nancy at Christmas and Easter, he was thereafter confined to school grounds and would pass his first baccalaureate the following spring near the top of his class. On his return home in the summer of 1938, however, after his uncharacteristically arduous studies, he was eighteen years old and starved for female companionship when he met Yvette, one of the Jewish girls who befriended Janine when she arrived in Mulhouse.

That fall, back in Nancy, Roland wrote to Yvette every week, sneaking his letters into the mail in violation of school rules, undeterred by the fact she never wrote back. It therefore came as a shock, a blow to his manhood, when he came home for Christmas to discover the girl of his frustrated boarding-school dreams ice-skating arm in arm with somebody else. Worse, amid whispers and giggles, he learned that Yvette had been regularly reading his love letters aloud to her friends. Mortified that his expressions of ardor had been so callously mocked, he returned to school feeling profoundly betrayed. No longer in use, the *Klapperstein* offered him no retribution. Nor could he know that he *had* won a heart he would hold for all time with the stream of letters he lovingly penned. Janine had heard them and never recovered.

How it secretly thwarted my sense of romance as a child when my mother added an unwanted prologue to my favorite story, that Roland's first passions had been inspired by . . . Yvette! Only years later did I realize the psychological truth that her struggle to win Roland's attention and trust actually caused her to treasure him more. Because Roland was wounded in love before they met, Janine had to woo him, and the challenge to win him became an obsession.

But I wanted to hear that their love had been perfect, created in heaven right from the start. Roland and Janine were Romeo and Juliet as far as I was concerned, the future of their innocent love subverted by forces and hatreds beyond their control. It therefore came as singularly satisfying to learn in sixth grade that even Shakespeare had conceived of his Romeo as first infatuated by another girl, *Rosalind*, who would "not be hit by cupid's arrow." Only then is the young romantic allowed to meet the one true love he would break all rules to wed and for whom, in despair, he would give up his life.

. . .

Within a few months of moving to Mulhouse, Janine was enjoying herself as never before. She had new friends, kind teachers, and unusual freedom, especially after her parents decided, now with only two bedrooms, to rent a small maid's room on the building's top floor to house their two daughters. As a precaution, Alice and Sigmar kept Norbert with them in the downstairs apartment in order to track his comings and goings and make sure that their girl-crazy son didn't get into trouble in the hours he wasn't working with Sigmar. Together they were trying to revive both the faltering pipe-fitting business that had been left to Sigmar's sister Marie on the death of her husband and the virtually dormant building supply business that Sigmar had launched in Mulhouse before he was married. Now fifty-eight, minus the luxury of his car and driver, Sigmar trudged through the countryside on foot and by train looking for customers and finding it hard to make any money.

Alice, meanwhile, was coping alone for the first time in her marriage with laundry, cooking, and housework, with few friends except for Marie, who thankfully lived around the corner. In frustration, she watched Norbert abandon the business studies he had pursued in Switzerland so as to help his father, while her girls shook off the reins of their strict German upbringing. She worried especially to see Janine fall under the sway of Lisette, Marie's eccentric, irreverent daughter-in-law.

A vivacious young woman of determined opinion, Lisette displayed a fierce intelligence that brought fire to her beauty. She was nineteen when she married Edy, Marie's only son, and sparks flew between the two women as Lisette, whose own mother had died at her birth, delighted in shocking her mother-in-law and defying conventions.

Lisette's overtly sexual language, spirited wordplay, and philosophical wit left her listeners gaping, and the more stodgily proper they were, the more she felt it her duty to disturb and provoke them. Speaking in rhyme, she tossed bawdy double entendres over their heads. She also provided Janine, twelve years younger, with a startling new role model of a woman who claimed independence—a right she asserted throughout her life—regardless of how her sudden departures affected her children. There would be six children in all, ranging from thirteen to thirty-three by the time she and Edy divorced. Of the eldest, twin daughters, one was born severely disabled due to the fact that the obstetrician, initially failing to realize the need for a second delivery, waited too long.

Elisabeth "Lisette" Hauser Cahen in 1932 with her twin daughters

Even as Alice fretted over Lisette's freethinking influence upon Janine, and regretted Norbert's stunted schooling, and worried about their lack of income, and hated Sigmar's weary travels, and missed her home and extended family, there was no bemoaning leaving Freiburg. Grisly reports from across the border proved they had fled not a moment too soon. Already, thousands of German Jews had been deported to camps—their locations and nature largely unknown—and Hitler's reach was expanding.

When, at the end of October 1938, the Nazis expelled eighteen thousand Polish-born Jews from Germany, sending them off by train with neither possessions nor money, the enraged son of one such uprooted Jew fatally shot a minor official at the German embassy in Paris. Violent reprisals on November 9 and 10 unleashed unprecedented terror and destruction throughout Germany, including Freiburg. Storm troopers torched more than one thousand synagogues, feeding bonfires with holy texts, scrolls of the Torah, and ritual objects. Joined by unrestrained mobs, they smashed windows of tens of thousands of Jewish shops and homes; they attacked and murdered Jews on the streets and filled concentration camps with about thirty-five thousand others, roughly 10 percent of the Jews still left in the country. In what was dubbed *Kristallnacht*, crystal night—a lyrical name for a pogrom—the Nazis shattered not only glass, but also any illusion that the Reich would uphold moral justice. In Freiburg, historically esteemed as a bastion of scholarship and culture, the grand nineteenth-century synagogue was burned to the ground.

Seized in the roundup was Sigmar's brother Heinrich. According to a certificate of incarceration later issued to him by the International Red Cross, Heinrich Günzburger, prisoner number 21973, then sixty years old, had been arrested on grounds of being a Jew. As with most of the ten thousand Jewish men imprisoned at Dachau in the wake of *Kristallnacht*, his release a month later came with a warning to get out of the country. The goal of purging Jews from German-held lands thus began with forced emigration, and Heinrich wasted no time in fleeing to Mulhouse. He hoped from there to reunite in Geneva with his wife, Toni, and prayed that having sent their two sons to Buffalo, New York, a few years earlier, they, too, would soon qualify for American visas.

On the day that Heinrich arrived in Mulhouse, Sigmar met him at the train station and encountered a broken man, horribly burned, trembling, and near catatonic. His red eyes stared blankly back into themselves, and tears rolled down his gaunt gray cheeks. One arm was a long, garish wound from elbow to wrist, the skin charred and oozing, split raw and open down to the bone. In the jammed barracks at Dachau, Heinrich had been wedged against a fiery wood-burning

stove when a Nazi officer commanded the inmates to stand at attention for hours. The first man to speak or move a muscle, the officer
barked, would be shot on the spot. So Heinrich stood rigid, his nausea
at the stench and pain of his own burning flesh only checked by his
harrowing fear.

It fell to Alice to clean the burned arm and change his bandages
several times daily, a gruesome reminder of her bloodstained World
War I service, when she'd nursed that same generation of Germany's
soldiers. Within days, when a telephone call came from the wife of
her cousin in Frankfurt, Alice collapsed. On the night of the madness, the woman reported, storm troopers had crashed through their
door and ransacked their home. When her husband, the director of a
Frankfurt opera company, demanded an explanation from them, the
intruders answered by beating him up and then dragged him away.
Two days later, one of the men returned to shove a small cardboard
box into her hands. It held ashes—all that remained of her husband,
who was shot in the back attempting escape. Or so she was told. "See,
he's home again," the unidentified messenger spat out the words.
"Didn't I promise we'd bring him back to you soon?"

From Zurich came better news that Alice's mother Johanna and
the rest of the family—Alice's sister Rosie, her brother-in-law Natan
Marx, and her niece Hannchen—had managed to get out of Eppingen before *Kristallnacht*, albeit penniless. Weeks earlier, two members
of the brutal Nazi paramilitary force called the *Schutzstaffel*, or SS,
had barged into the Heinsheimer store; they took Natan's volunteer
fireman's helmet, confiscated the family's passports, and examined the
business's records. Then the SS demanded the sale of the store, their
house, and their land and required them to turn over the proceeds as
taxes in exchange for their passports. After eight generations in the
same modest village, the family was ordered to clear out, but was left
with so little they needed a loan from a cousin in Holland to secure
transportation. Johanna took refuge with another daughter in Zurich,
while the Marxes—having applied for visas years before Sigmar acknowledged the need—escaped from Europe on a ship to New York.

Two days after *Kristallnacht*, German Jewry was collectively fined
one billion Reichsmarks for the destruction leveled against it, a

The Heinsheimer family store on the Brettener Strasse in
Eppingen with Maier and Siegfried in the doorway and
Alice on the left in the window above them

punishment to be paid through the confiscation of 20 percent of the
property of every Jew, including many who already had left. In Sigmar's case, notice of the new fines arrived in Mulhouse, a chain of
documents informing him of sums withdrawn by the Nazi government from the bank accounts he had been forced to abandon. The
same Germanic compulsion for order that led the Nazis to keep meticulous records, thorough accounts of money and corpses, dutifully
prompted Sigmar to register as required with city officials wherever
he landed. As a result, the Freiburg authorities knew just where to

find him. Every few months they notified him of thousands of additional Reichsmarks in taxes they had deducted from his blocked bank accounts, on top of the many thousands he'd paid before leaving Freiburg. In a form letter he received in Mulhouse that January, the Nazi authorities threatened that if they had any difficulty in collecting the extra taxes, he would first be charged interest; after that, they would send agents to find him, and he would be forced to reimburse the Reich for their efforts, as well.

In addition to claims paid to Freiburg's finance department, Sigmar received notice of heavy taxes withdrawn from his seized accounts to pay Eppingen: Alice's birthplace had targeted her for inclusion in the fines imposed on its Jewish community for the *Kristallnacht* destruction of the synagogue there. He was also informed that the Reich would be confiscating the equivalent of 20,000 French francs in exchange for its generously "permitting" him to do business in Mulhouse. According to the Nazi regime, although it operated under a different name (*Mesanita*) in a foreign country, any business he ran in France should properly be considered an offshoot of the former Günzburger Brothers' firm, now in the hands of Aryan owners.

That April, Sigmar wrote to the Freiburg finance authorities outlining arguments seeking reductions. Could the flight tax be deducted from the Jewish wealth tax? Sigmar inquired into the truth of that rumor. A curt reply arrived two days later. "*Ein Abzug der Reichsfluchtsteuer an der Judensvermögensabgabe ist nicht zulässig.*" A deduction of the flight tax from the Jewish wealth tax is not permitted. Conversely, the city added with contorted logic, the Jewish wealth tax *might* have been deducted from the flight tax had Sigmar *not* fled, if he had remained a resident of Germany until after *Kristallnacht*. But because he had emigrated before January 1, 1939, all taxes would remain unabated. In closing, the letter directed that in case he had further questions, he needed to send return postage if he expected an answer.

There was nothing for Sigmar to do but file all these papers in the worn leather briefcase where I found them so many years later. Brown by now and frayed at the edges, many of the documents bear the stamp of the *Finanzamt* with the Nazi insignia of an eagle spreading its wings astride a globe whose center is filled with the swastika's twisted black cross. They reveal how the finance department changed his name in accord with new regulations—to *Samuel Israel* Günzburger—to show he was Jewish, while withdrawing so many extra "tax" payments from his accounts even after he fled to Mulhouse that the funds on deposit were entirely depleted.

In my grandfather's many replies, I would see signs of the person whose unwavering faith in the difference between right and wrong guided his every transaction. Even in New York at age eighty, he would walk several blocks back to a supermarket on Broadway to return an extra nickel of change, lest the cashier have to pay for the error out of her pocket. In his polished black wingtips, herringbone topcoat, and soft gray fedora, he would slowly make his way back to the store with the deliberateness of a business mogul concluding a matter worth millions. A man who would later rouse himself on his deathbed to remind his grief-stricken wife to pay the rent and the rest of her bills on the first of each month, he never altered the standards he set for himself. Until *Kristallnacht*, Sigmar had fully believed in the ultimate restoration of justice in the land of his birth, but now optimism gave way to despair.

Still, Sigmar kept his fears to himself so as not to alarm his traumatized brother about their additional losses in Freiburg or, much worse, about what he now understood to be Hitler's goal to eliminate German Jewry entirely. Heinrich spent all his days in a chair, staring out a large picture window, totally silent, his eyes fixed on the clock in the parc Salvator behind the apartment. The clock's face, a circle of color embedded in grass, was made entirely of flowers that were changed with the season. Its hands kissed the fading petals of time as the hours and days passed, the weeks and the months, bringing the world ever closer to war, just twenty years after the last one had ended.

But Janine did not seem to notice. Much as the plants in the clock lived by their own biological time, unperturbed by the mechanized sweep of the arms that measured their days, so did she—unaffected as yet by the ticking time bomb just over the border—continue to bloom in her own youthful rhythm. Her attention as a teenager was focused on her circle of friends and on a single, special new interest. Having heard Yvette read Roland's letters aloud all that fall and having seen him in person at Christmas, she was, above all, eager to meet him. Love, like "the light of the heart," as Balzac described its effect on a provincial young girl, kindled a fresh sense of wonder. The memories are hers.

· · ·

One spring afternoon in 1939, as Janine and Yvette strolled after school on the rue du Sauvage, they spotted a group of young men on the corner. *"Regarde! C'est lui! Roland! Il est rentré,"* Yvette whispered to Janine, indicating the tallest among them. Roland had returned. As the two girls approached, he noticed and stiffened, shifting uneasily from foot to foot as he rested lightly on a long, furled umbrella, in the style that British prime minister Neville Chamberlain had made chic for the moment. Unaware that Roland had bitterly learned of her sharing and mocking his letters with friends, Yvette chattered gaily, coquettish, oblivious of his tepid response. But as the two talked, Janine indulged in studying him, as if some glorious mythological being had suddenly alighted to earth in her path. His slim face had high cheekbones and a sensitive mouth, and his velvet brown eyes shone with gentleness. She blushed when he turned and caught her staring at him, like the maiden Psyche stealing forbidden glimpses of the sleeping Cupid, her lover, by candlelight.

Roland Arcieri, photographed in Mulhouse, 1945

This time, Yvette introduced them, and Roland quickly endeared himself further by praising the very thing that always embarrassed Janine most, so often casting her as an outsider in her own estimation that she tended toward silence. "What a delightful accent you have!" he observed with a beckoning smile. To Janine, it suddenly seemed as if her family's migration from Freiburg had been uniquely designed to deposit her on that corner in France at that precise moment. It was predestined, she told herself, and she vowed with urgent resolve she had not felt before to do whatever it took to make a permanent place for herself in the life of this man whose poetic expressions of love, although addressed to somebody else, had already managed to win her heart.

That summer, more than a month before Hitler stunned Europe by announcing a nonaggression pact with the Soviets, storks folded their spindly legs to nest in the bell towers of Mulhouse, red geraniums danced in window boxes, and printers laid patterns of ink on new bolts of cotton fabric, as they had done for centuries. Trudi left on a vacation visit to cousins from Düsseldorf who resettled in Belgium, and Yvette was setting off on holiday too. But she had grown intrigued by Roland once again, her interest whetted by his strange indifference when they met at Easter time, and calculating that he would soon come back from school in Nancy, Yvette bemoaned to her friends that she could not be home to welcome him there.

"Do me a favor," Yvette asked Janine, who ever after remembered this conversation that made her feel as sneaky as a thief in the night. "Keep an eye on him for me. Make sure he doesn't find someone else before I get back to town."

When, soon after Yvette's departure, Roland found Janine, it eased her conscience to think that fate was to blame, as her good fortune in catching his eye began with a game of spin the bottle. Janine and Norbert had just discovered the game at a party earlier that summer and were quick to appreciate the face-saving factors that have long ensured its popularity as a facilitator of first sexual contact: how the random selection of partners for kissing so easily reduces fears of rejection, commitment, baring one's feelings, or going too far. Still, the challenge remains to hide any reaction as the bottle is spinning and starts to slow down, to prevent lips from moving in silent entreaties for it to point to the person one would choose on one's own, if given the chance and adequate nerve.

For Janine the air hummed, and the walls themselves started turning when Roland Arcieri sauntered into the room, and with a smile and a half wave to them all, pulled up a chair. At nineteen, he was a few years older than the others, and he took in the scene with bemused detachment that left them to wonder whether he'd deign to join in the fun. It was then, however, that he spotted Janine and recalled having met her before on the street with Yvette. "*Ah, midi moins dix,*" he said under his breath, remembering the way that she stood a little bit tilted, at an angle that faintly suggested a clock's minute hand at ten minutes to noon. Had he noticed then how pretty she was?

She was tall and slender with auburn hair that curled to her shoulders, no longer restrained by Fräulein Elfriede's insistence on neat chin-length bobs. Her light blue eyes were large and wide set, and the near-level curve of her brows lent her an innocent air of serious purpose. Her nose was straight, not small or large; her skin clear and lovely. To the extent she would have changed any feature, she would have preferred a more generous mouth, and so she lightly enhanced it with lipstick, which carried the risk of her father's displeasure. Now she realized Roland was looking her over and forced herself to return his regard, bravely meeting and holding his eyes.

"Come on, Roland! It's your turn," someone shouted to general approval until Roland started laughing, stood up, stubbed out his cigarette, and then, with a playful wink at Janine, agreed to take his chance with the bottle. Her heart was pounding. How could she stand to watch him kiss someone else! What to do if the bottle landed on her? Oh, if only she could have escaped on a pretext, but leaving now might well be construed as insulting to him.

Roland bent down on one knee to spin the empty wine bottle, a roulette wheel of kisses that held everyone rapt. Living inside each fragile rotation of the flashing green glass, Janine became as one with the bottle, round and round until she felt dizzy, turning and wobbling, directing its outcome through prayer and will. The bottle skittered sideways, clattering on the uneven planks of the floor, hit a chair leg, then slowed down and stopped moving, pointing closely enough in Janine's direction for Roland to select her. The archer's aim had been perfect; Cupid himself could not have done better.

Janine looked up and studied his face for signs of dismay or derision she hoped not to find. Surely, she worried, he would have preferred the bottle to land on one of the girls he had known so much longer! Nervously clutching the edge of her seat as he approached, she tried to ignore the rest of them staring. The warmth in her cheeks told her they had gone pink, and to hide them she reached down to yank up her white ankle socks and then kept pulling at them, her chin grazing her lap, as if she might draw the short socks straight over her head. At the very same time, she regretted not having worn something more alluring than her old floral-print dress with its childish puffed sleeves and high ruffled collar. At least she had added a blue ribbon belt to gather the waist, which helped to show off her figure a little.

Then he was waiting, grinning, in front of her chair, and he reached for her hands. She stood just before him, and his eyes smiled deeply into her own. And when he kissed her right there in front of them all, it was no schoolboy's peck on the cheek or anything like her mother's too-noisy and brusquely self-conscious smack in the air. His wide mouth was firm as his lips met her own, and like an explorer planting a stake in new soil, he claimed her right then for the rest of her days, and she responded with all the need and desire, the yearning for closeness that she had stifled as long as she could remember. There was only Roland and this kiss that transformed her.

The room had grown silent, all of them gaping, then suddenly the others started to cheer. "So that's what you learned in college!" one of the boys snickered, breaking the general tension with laughter. "Well, now it's your turn, Pierrot," another proposed. But for Roland and Janine, still standing together, the game was over. Janine felt her heart racing and her face glowing red as she sank back into her chair, mostly determined not to glance in Norbert's direction. She could feel him studying her and sensed disapproval, the rules he set for his sisters not the same ones he imposed on himself. With a stab of guilt—her chief aim in the past having been pleasing Alice and Sigmar—she realized she would have to find some way of bribing her brother never to tell her parents what happened.

. . .

Was it that kiss that later made my mother so wary that I might too soon discover how souls can meld when lips touch lips? Was it the pain of loving but losing Roland that seemed to make her so intensely protective that the significance she placed on a kiss exploded past reason or my understanding? When I reached the age of going to parties or later on dates, she would always sit waiting until I returned, and there was no disguising the time when the antique French chinoiserie clock on the wall outside her room ceased its regular tick for a moment, pregnantly hiccupped, and then chimed the hour.

The first question Mom asked was always the same. "Did he try to kiss you good night?" she would probe in a tone of concern. I'd find her reading in bed or on the steps, smoking or filing her long, Revlon-red nails, depending on whether my father had gone to sleep yet. My mother looked straight in my eyes and studied my face every time to determine whether a kiss—either empty and careless or pulsing with feeling beyond all forgetting—had affected me in some permanent fashion.

"You can't let someone kiss you too soon," she would lecture, her own youthful romance tucked away in the past at those moments. "He won't respect you. You'll get a bad reputation because he'll tell all his friends. . . ."

What did I know at that point of my mother's time with Roland in Mulhouse? I had heard of their regular meetings on the rue du Sauvage, sharing pastries and talking, playing volleyball and swimming in the Ill River where the young people's sports club gathered that summer, with Hitler growling just over the border, preparing shortly to pounce upon Poland. An infrequent daytime movie, she said, some hiking, a bike ride, hours in the bookshops, poetry, talking. Much later, however, standing with her on an unseasonably chilly May day on a bridge overlooking the same Alsatian river, swollen with silt and heavy spring rain, other memories revealed why he was the one she had never forgotten. With Roland, her introduction to the opposite sex had been exceedingly tender and loving. What she found in his arms was a goal in itself—shelter from all the ugly turmoil swirling around them. As the threat of war grew closer each day, they seemed to exist, wearing blinders, in a world of their own.

Friday, September 1, 1939, four days before Janine's sixteenth birthday, she and Roland lay hidden in a cradle of moist brown earth on the banks of the Ill, with the tall silver grasses that served as their curtain tickling their legs. A light wind rustled the leaves of the willows, and ducks flew over their heads to land on the water and float downstream in pairs. Roland and Janine were wet from a swim, and Roland, slim and bronzed by the sun, rested his weight on one elbow as he smoothed back her hair from her brow and bent down to kiss her. His hand gently stroked her neck and her shoulders and his fingers traced the damp edge of the yellow wool bathing suit her mother had bought her, just a girl-child, the previous summer before leaving Freiburg. Then he lowered his head to place a single warm kiss in the hollow of her throat, a place so soft and private it startled them both. "*Quelle beauté*," he murmured, his voice a caress, his cheek against hers, as both of them struggled for breath—shyly, discreetly—still clasping each other.

An hour later, after biking back home and dashing upstairs to the apartment where she knew her parents would be beginning to worry—ready to light Sabbath candles and sit down to their ritual dinner of barley soup and beef flanken—she was instantly struck by the heavy silence. Alice and Sigmar sat there not speaking, and the table had not yet been set. They barely looked up as she came through the door, and she was shocked that her mother was crying, a crumpled linen handkerchief from her trousseau, *A.G.* finely embroidered on one of its corners, balled up in her hand.

So they knew, she thought, oddly calm in that instant. Someone must have spied her with Roland at the river, she imagined, and rushed to offer her parents a detailed report. She wondered whether her parents would read even more on her face—a new fire in her eyes or a blush on her cheek. Yet steeled this once by unpracticed defiance, she was unwilling to diminish or dirty her memory of that afternoon with some awkward attempt to explain it away or to accept any censure for having done wrong. In her mind's eye, she summoned the people they had seen at the river and tied the odious *Klapperstein* around all their necks in a phantom parade of staggering figures, and she tried to guess who might have betrayed her.

It was then that she noticed the suitcases lining the hallway, a map spread out in front of her father, and the headlines of the evening paper that still lay on the table screaming the news. Hitler's army had overrun Poland, while his warplanes and tanks attacked Polish troops, cities, bridges, and railroads. In a world-changing Blitzkrieg of fire and terror, the Germans rained death and destruction on Poland, even as she and Roland had lain in the long summer grasses. In response to the invasion of Poland, she read, France and England had warned that unless Hitler withdrew, treaty obligations would impel them to war.

Janine stared at the web of roads on the map spread out on the table and at the suitcases lined up like some ragtag army, ready to march, crookedly running the length of the hall. Her father was talking, looking at her. *War. Too close to the border here in Alsace. Hitler invading.* She heard only fragments of what he was saying, but sensed everything starting to topple around her. Her mind rushed back to Roland, to the green, lazy river, as if, starting over, she could take a different route home in order to enter a happier scene when she came through the door. She remembered the distant day she had outraged her father by sharing the bold theological news that it wasn't really for eating an apple that Adam and Eve were exiled from Eden, but rather for their sexual exploits. Having only just left the arms of Roland, was she, too, now to be punished for trading kisses and indulging in love? *Wir wandern aus.* Again. But where could they go?

SIX

GRAY DAYS, PHONY WAR

PANIC DESCENDED ON ALSACE during those uncertain days of early September 1939, as a nationwide mobilization called army reservists back to their units, workers hauled sandbags to bolster air raid shelters and windows, curfews abruptly clamped down on nightlife, and civilians made contingency plans for fleeing their homes—easy targets for shelling from over the Rhine. The banks shut their doors. The government declared martial law, advised hospitals to truck their patients out of the cities to safer, more rural locales, and banned international telephone and telegraph services, which added to the mounting fear and confusion. Strict new regulations called for carrying gas masks and pocket flashlights at all times and rushing to shelters when sirens were sounded.

In Mulhouse, city officials distributed personalized emergency cards informing residents in both French and German what region would welcome them in case evacuation from Alsace proved necessary. Janine's evacuation card, No. 9150, preserves the official instructions, among them the warning that the cards themselves were to be "preciously guarded": Be sure to take along family papers and valuables, provisions for four days (bread, biscuits, canned goods, concentrated milk for the children), as well as individual cutlery, glasses, and blankets, and a good pair of shoes. The total baggage weight per person should not exceed 30 kilos [about 66 pounds] for those without personal means of transportation. Close shutters and windows, turn off the sources of water and gas, remove electrical fuses, and lock up securely. "For the rest," it advised, "rigorously follow all instructions given by the military or civil authorities, particularly those that will be displayed when the moment arrives."

The evacuation card issued to Janine by the city of Mulhouse in 1939 in anticipation of a German invasion over the nearby border

Despite such precautions, the situation remained tentative, a war of nerves with the Germans. No one seemed ready to say whether actual war was at hand or whether hope still existed that Hitler would relinquish his claim on the Polish city of Danzig, halt his eastern attack, and back down. The papers were filled with ironies that made it hard to assess the state of affairs. It was reported that the actress Norma Shearer, vacationing on the Riviera with the suave French star Charles Boyer and his wife, had been summoned by Hollywood to rush "home to filmland." At the very same time, however, large advertisements proudly declared, FROM SEPTEMBER 1ST TO 20TH THE WHOLE WORLD WILL MEET IN CANNES FOR THE FIRST INTERNATIONAL FILM FESTIVAL. They promised "three weeks of splendor and enchantment" along the resort's lively Croisette, lined by princely hotels and colorful Mediterranean beaches.

Bizarrely, a menacing letter from Hitler to French premier Edouard Daladier, warning that a "new bloody war of annihilation" would unfold unless his demands for land were accepted, appeared in the newspaper beside an upbeat ad from the German spa city of Baden-Baden. It guaranteed "a peaceful and hearty welcome and unequaled possibilities for rest and recreation" for clientele from abroad and assured potential guests that "despite certain reports about scarcity and quality of food," meals and service remained as fine as they had been in the past.

Still, denouncing the terms of the 1919 Treaty of Versailles as "intolerable" and bellowing fresh demands for Lebensraum, Hitler refused to withdraw from Poland. Consequently, on September 3, first England, then France reluctantly declared that Hitler left them no choice but war.

Interrupting their packing, the Günzburgers anxiously gathered around the radio that night to hear Premier Daladier's emotional five-minute broadcast to the nation: "The cause of France merges with that of justice," he said. "Frenchwomen and Frenchmen, we are making war because it has been imposed on us. Each of us is at his post on the soil of France in this land of liberty where the respect for human dignity finds one of its last refuges." He closed with a rousing "*Vive la France!*"

Within hours, Hitler's first unprovoked assault on the Allies—the sinking of the British ocean liner the *Athenia*—resulted in the deaths of 112 passengers, the majority of them women and children. With that, German Jewish refugees in Alsace confronted with new urgency the terrifying possibility of Hitler's troops pursuing them from over the Rhine. Quick escape from the border region became their priority, even as war with their native country made their status in France an open question.

A German Army veteran, Sigmar faced a dilemma much like the one he encountered after the previous war, when he first attempted to settle in Mulhouse. To the French, he was German—mistrusted as an enemy, with no way to hide his name or his accent. To the Germans, he was a Jew—a stateless pariah and fair game in any territory he might be found. While prudence left him no other choice, moving from Alsace meant leaving the one part of France where he felt somewhat at home, where a Germanic name and dual national heritage were well understood and Jews well established. Thus, with a heavy heart, Sigmar studied maps, consulted friends, and made frantic arrangements to get Trudi home from her cousins in Brussels that weekend.

How sorely he missed the roomy Opel sedan he had been forced to give up to the Glatts! Transportation loomed as a serious problem, not just for the immediate family now, but also for his sister Marie and her longtime Jewish housekeeper, Isabelle (Bella) Picard, from whom she was inseparable. Both now in their sixties—one a widow, the other unmarried—they looked to Sigmar for their escape. Marie's son Edy had already been called up to the French Army as a captain, while Lisette and their children were evacuating to a town in Burgundy known to Lisette from summer vacations. Marie's only daughter, Mimi, married to a prosperous French Jewish silk merchant in Lyon, was staying put in her spacious apartment steps away from the grand place Bellecour. But Marie and Bella were afraid to go there, believing with Sigmar that hiding in the provinces would make them less attractive as targets, both of Germans and shelling, which they expected to start near the border at any second.

That Monday, with the first of what would become a full ledger of loans from relatives, Sigmar sent Norbert to buy a car to carry them south for fear that traveling by train, passport checks could invite

The Rosengart was reputed to be the cheapest and smallest car produced in France in the late 1930s.

trouble. But it was immediately apparent that the bright red Rosengart with the tall front grille in which Norbert returned could not possibly carry them all, let alone fit everyone's barest essentials for an absence of unknown duration. It was the cheapest and smallest car produced in France at the time, mocked as resembling a soapbox on wheels.

Sigmar stood mute in front of their building when Norbert called him downstairs to admire it, and he studied the small two-door coupe with glum disappointment. Then, still not a driver, he awkwardly climbed out of habit into the cramped backseat, where even sitting alone, he realized this one little car would not suffice. Never before a man to seek favors, now, looking toward a menacing future, Sigmar saw that the price of pride vastly exceeded his ravaged budget. Mentally, he leafed through his address book for someone who owned a car and might be willing to help them. He came up with one man, Joseph Fimbel, a teacher and Marist lay brother with whom he had slowly developed a friendship based on the hours they spent discussing religion. So many hours, in fact, that Alice suspected Monsieur Fimbel nourished a private hope of converting her husband.

But if his Catholic friend harbored such aspirations, it was a thought that Sigmar may have unintentionally fostered through his genuine interest in exploring the church's mysterious spiritual beauty. Already in Freiburg, besides his regular visits to the old Catholic graveyard, he had loved wandering through the majestic cathedral, its air fragrant with incense, hundreds of white candles flickering prayers in the half-darkened vaults. He would listen, entranced, as the organist bobbed over his keys, the deep chords of immense pipes throbbing in the ancient stones under his feet. Sigmar stood with respect as his neighbors sank to their knees to speak with a God who had suffered their pains, and his hand gripped the burnished wood of the pews almost as if he truly belonged there.

And yet, expedient as conversion might have been at that hour—a test Jews had repeatedly faced through the centuries—Sigmar could not have imagined renouncing the faith of his fathers. His appreciation for the kingdom of God he saw expressed in the church was romantic, aesthetic, something apart from the Jew that he was, much as he loved Wagner's *Ring* without reservation, ignoring the uncomfortable fact that the music's creator had seen little value to the existence of Jews. Indeed, while it sometimes occurred to him that his own Creator no longer cared much for Jews either, Sigmar had been wont to slip out of the Freiburg Cathedral with the furtiveness of a wayward husband leaving his lover, ever chary of being spotted by *Herr Rabbiner* Julius Zimels, the immaculate rabbi who strolled through the town wearing dove-colored spats and a fine homburg hat. That the rabbi would sanction his ecumenical tourism struck Sigmar as doubtful, while he believed Monsieur Fimbel not only welcomed his interest, but also honored its limits. Their friendship was based on such firm and mutual regard for each other that, as Sigmar expected, the teacher readily agreed to assist him, all the more as he was planning to get out of Mulhouse with similar haste.

For Sigmar, the next pressing question of where to go involved such a gamble that he made a decision based on little more than a letter and Monsieur Fimbel's convenience. Sigmar had received the letter a few months earlier from a former Freiburg acquaintance. The man was a cattle dealer who wrote of being comfortably settled on a farm he had bought on the outskirts of the small town of Gray in the dairy region of Franche-Comté, southwest of Alsace along the Swiss border. A Jewish mayor, Moïse Lévy—who was also a senator representing the Haute-Saône department of Franche-Comté in the National Assembly—governed the town of some six thousand people, he wrote, which contributed to a friendly atmosphere for refugees escaping the Germans. Beyond this information and the knowledge that Gray was less than four hours away, not far from Dijon and sited on the Saône River, Sigmar knew virtually nothing about it. Certainly it had the advantage of being much closer to all that they knew than their official evacuation assignment to the country's extreme southwest corner near Spain, which Sigmar chose to ignore for the moment.

Monsieur Fimbel, meanwhile, had his own reasons for going to Gray. Not quite forty-two—though already bald and starkly attired in a white shirt and black suit he seemed older—he had been born in Mulhouse under the reign of the Germans. Marked all his life by his Alsatian background and memories of German oppression, when drafted to fight for the kaiser in 1914, he had fled to Belgium and spent four years in hiding rather than having to side against France. In an unsuccessful attempt to pressure his parents to disclose his whereabouts and then oblige him to fight, the Germans had gone so far as to imprison the couple.

After the war, he joined the Catholic order of Marist teaching brothers and, pledging himself to their vows of poverty, chastity, and obedience, advanced as director of one of their schools. But now, in view of the fact that the French Army requisitioned his school building for use as a military hospital, Monsieur Fimbel aimed to transfer his program to Gray. The pious educator encouraged Sigmar to come along, and his help in moving the family would be the first of many instances in which his aid proved crucial to refugees hiding in France.

Only two hectic days after war was declared, they were ready to leave. This put their departure on September 5, Janine's sixteenth birthday—a memory that, no matter how fleeting, would shadow every birthday thereafter. She chafed at being swept up in a drama that seemed to have so little to do with things that truly mattered to her, as if she were forced to fight in a battle launched long before she was born. Running again seemed more awful than having been chased from her birthplace the previous year, because while the first move was wrenching, she had been especially happy in Mulhouse and trusted that it would remain a safe haven. Her chief sorrow, losing Roland, was as vast as the all-encompassing joy he had brought. Seeing herself through his eyes had transformed her. Who would she be when she no longer found herself in the love that he mirrored? Time and circumstance, both so limited, had lent them restraint, but unfulfilled passion only heightened her longing. She would have risked any danger to stay in his arms.

Aside from Roland, she had done well in school both socially and academically, earning the top prize in chemistry even while handicapped by tackling new subjects in a largely strange language. The school principal's evaluation at the end of her first trimester—"She has made progress in French, but not enough yet to follow a class properly"—had swiftly turned into praise for her application in becoming "*une très bonne élève*," a very good student.

As the family prepared to flee again, she had no grounds to hope they would be firmly established anytime quickly, which made her indifferent to where they were going, except that she wanted an address to give to Roland so he could write her. Assuming, of course, that he wouldn't forget her. Better *not* to announce where they were going, Alice finally snapped in annoyance when Janine persisted in asking, not daring to tell her mother the reason. As for themselves, they would find out soon enough.

At present, not knowing where they would live or how much space they would have, Sigmar told them to pack very little. With no time to waste, they would have to abandon almost all their belongings and hope for the chance to return for them later. In a halfhearted attempt to appear optimistic, he even suggested they might move back to Mulhouse before long. He was, after all, duly impressed by France's defensive barrier of concrete fortifications known as the Maginot Line, which ran almost the length of the French–German border, more than four hundred miles from Basel to Belgium, with hundreds of subterranean bunkers, hidden trolleys, and highways. Then, too, having experienced Germany bested before, he consoled himself by counting on Britain and France to crush Hitler soon.

Still it was wiser, he thought, not to dwell on that view. His focus was on packing essentials and rushing away before the Germans stormed over the border. The sole valuable he agreed to take in the car, Alice's sterling silver flatware, he loaded with his documents and family pictures into his old leather *Köfferle* and entrusted to Bella. When Sigmar discovered that instead of packing her clothes, Janine had filled her suitcase with books, favorites of hers and Roland's, he dumped them all out on the floor in vexation.

"*Bisch du verrückt?*" Are you crazy? her father demanded, reverting to the *badisch* dialect that would always remain most comfortable for him. But his edict on packing only the basics did not extend to his piano music, its pages all marked with Frau Loewy's instructions; this he slipped into his bag in spite of the fact he could not take his Bechstein, whose gleaming wood surface he lovingly covered with blankets.

The small caravan left Mulhouse that Tuesday with Norbert at the wheel of the Rosengart and Trudi beside him, and with Janine morosely crammed into the narrow backseat beside Sigmar's *Köfferle* and the mountainous Bella. The housekeeper in her light cotton dress was rolled into a big, fluffy ball with her knees drawn up to her chest and her arms folded on top of the ample shelf of her breasts. Sigmar, Alice, and Marie rode with Monsieur Fimbel, who led the way out of the fear-gripped city, past the school and the synagogue, the candy-colored town hall and the languid river. Janine's eyes searched the streets, hungry for an unlikely last glimpse of Roland. Not permitted to leave the apartment once war was declared and never allowed to use the telephone, she was distraught at being unable to say good-bye and find out whether the Arcieris planned to stay in Mulhouse or also retreat from the border. As an Alsatian-born veteran of the kaiser's army, she knew, Roland's father was unlikely to be more eager than Sigmar to greet the Germans and risk their finding a new use for him on behalf of the Reich.

In tandem, the two cars headed southwest, on roads punctuated by khaki-clad soldiers and jammed with vehicles laden with luggage and piled high with mattresses and pyramids of household possessions. On this second day of the war, however, travel seemed easier than expected, with little happening to make them believe the conflict had started. For months to come, moreover, as a quiet fall tumbled into a bitterly cold but equally quiescent winter, Janine would often reflect with remorse that she might have spent that time with Roland, had her family not fled from Mulhouse so precipitously.

Until late spring, France and Germany would sit passively, if nervously, frozen on opposite sides of the Rhine without either launching a full-scale assault. Indeed, while military training and the building of warplanes rushed forward on both sides of the Channel, Hitler publicly disavowed any interest in land to the west, and no armed German soldier crossed over the border to France. As the waiting game lingered, some came to believe that actual fighting might never erupt. It was a period the French came to call the *drôle de guerre*, the phony war, in which except for some action at sea, both sides largely hung back in defensive positions behind the security of their Maginot and Siegfried lines, at the same time urgently plotting and arming for battle. In England, Prime Minister Chamberlain called it the Twilight

War; other British officials declared it the Bore War; and in Germany too, they came up with a darkly humorous name for this strange interlude of passive aggression. There it was dubbed the *Sitzkrieg* or the sitting war.

On the day they left Mulhouse, though, the Günzburgers could not have foreseen more than eight months of stillness lying ahead, or Janine would have been even more disconsolate than she was, as the tiny four-cylinder Rosengart puttered along on bumpy back roads and past well-tended vineyards and wide rolling fields edged by Queen Anne's lace and mustard. They pulled into Gray in the late afternoon. With an abrupt shifting of gears and screeching of brakes that startled the passengers napping around him, Norbert stopped short as the car carrying their parents pulled to the curb and suddenly parked in front of a building whose Renaissance façade of richly carved stone, like many in Gray, was marred by old peeling shutters and unpainted grillwork.

Why was Alice getting out of the car? She darted into a small notions shop and, emerging with a package, headed to the Rosengart and tapped on the little half window in back where Janine was sitting, miserably staring off into space. Moist curls framed Janine's forehead and her cheeks were flushed red, by both the hot sun of early September and the pressure of Bella, slumped against her like a thick sack of flour, sleeping again, and now lightly snoring.

"*Herzlichen Glückwunsch zum Geburtstag, Hannele,*" her mother said. Heartfelt good wishes on your birthday. "I'm sorry it's not a good birthday for you. Hopefully next year things will be better." Alice smiled as she passed the packet through the window. Inside was a blue plastic rain hat printed with tiny white flowers and with strings for tying under the chin. It was almost identical to one that Janine had noticed and admired aloud, walking with Alice in Mulhouse the previous week, before everything had horribly changed. Janine was touched and broke into tears that had waited all day for an excuse to erupt, like an afternoon storm after hours of heat lightning. "A birthday gift for a rainy day," Alice said, patting her shoulder through the car window.

As darkness fell over the Saône River, they drove soberly up the Grande Rue, the town's main thoroughfare, past an eighteenth-century apothecary shop where the sculpted heads of four women

above the arch of each shuttered window unblinkingly met their arrival with stony suspicion. The street mounted a hill from the banks of
the river toward the top of the town, where the church and an unexpectedly beautiful town hall presided—its Flemish tile roof fantasti-
cally patterned in large diamond shapes of olive green, black, orange,
and yellow.

That first evening in Gray they checked into the Hôtel de l'Europe,
where Marie and Bella would spend the next months, even after the
rest of the family moved into a few shabby, unfurnished rooms in
what they were told was the town's oldest building—a ramshackle
fifteenth-century structure on a small winding street, the rue de la
Malcouverte or "the street of the badly covered." Lacking the most
rudimentary comforts, these accommodations offered no running
water, no plumbing, no electricity, and no heat. The family slept on
wooden crates; a pail on the terrace served as their "outhouse," while
in order to bathe, they gratefully filed once a week into the common
bathroom of Aunt Marie's hotel. Fleas infested their rooms, and they
were soon pocked with nasty bites. For drinking water, there was a
pump out back, a source they shared with the prostitutes who lived
in the building directly behind them and who, short of business with
so many men drafted in expectation of war, lounged in the courtyard.

Alice dealt with life in Gray without complaint, impressed by the
general spirit of brave acceptance she witnessed as Frenchwomen
sent their children alone into safety or fled their homes carrying virtually nothing, their valuables sewn into the clothing they wore. For
the good of the nation, the government urged "calm and sangfroid,"
advising residents to observe the strictest discretion in speech because
"the ears of the enemy" were everywhere, listening.

In the face of these things, Alice felt fortunate to have her family
together, and she consoled her two daughters with uplifting tales of
the wealth and comfort that would await them after the war, when Sigmar could finally claim the inheritance left by his two older brothers
who had died in New York. They had left many millions, with Sigmar,
Heinrich, and Marie all named in their wills. "After the war, we'll be
very rich," Alice promised, "and we'll live in a beautiful house again
and eat lots of good food and wear fine clothes." For now, however,

they would have to rely on what funds Maurice, Aunt Marie's son-in-law, could send from Lyon as a loan against those expected bequests. "In case I die before then, just don't bury me in this horrible dump of a town," Janine griped to her mother.

Once viewed as a snob by her children, Alice faced every fresh hardship with stoicism and even good cheer. "We must count our blessings!" was the lifelong philosophical lesson that she would take from a second ordeal of living through war. Stories kept filtering over the border about hundreds of German Jews killing themselves to avoid deportation to what were being described as "modern ghettos" in Poland, and the Nazis predicted that within a few months, *all* of Germany's Jews would be gone. It was reported that German officials had discussed this bold project with their allies in Moscow and that Kremlin leaders had raised no objection. Jewish men were sent first, put to work in occupied Poland to build living quarters, Alice read in the paper, and their wives and children would be sent on to join them. There was talk of Jews everywhere soon being deported and resettled in camps to the east, but how they would live there was never made clear.

The same week the Günzburgers arrived in Gray, the French Ministry of Education announced that school would begin as expected on October 2 and that students should attend classes in the towns where they were, rather than return home to their regular schools. With Monsieur Fimbel's assistance, Janine and Trudi were enrolled in a mostly-boys school, and while more refugees turned up within its gates every day, the new German girls attracted attention.

"You *can't* be Jewish," a native of Gray named Claudia insisted to Janine once they had gotten to know one another. As a student in Freiburg, Janine had experienced little outright anti-Semitism from her classmates, and she steeled herself as she waited to learn where this conversation was heading. "Why's that? What do you mean?" Janine asked, uneasily eyeing the students gathered around them under the trees in front of the school. "Everyone knows that Jews all have horns," Claudia told her, bringing her hands to both sides of her head.

Some fifty years later, however, it was Janine who could not recognize her former classmate when they encountered each other by chance on the street. We were together on her first trip back to Gray since the war, a bright autumn morning in 1989, when a tall, gray-haired woman, bent over a cane and wearing a long black dress and sensible shoes, stopped us at the top of the town to speak with my mother. She was slightly winded from having climbed up the steep flight of stone steps that led from the Malcouvert to where we were standing outside the town's Renaissance church.

"I feel that I know you," the Frenchwoman said to my mother, as she adjusted her weight on her cane on the uneven ground and set down a net shopping bag of groceries. She peered intently at Janine, at her cropped blond hair and her loafers, her turtleneck sweater and pants and black leather jacket, as if trying to see into the past to find someone with whom she once had something in common.

"*Je m'excuse.*" My mother smiled at the woman. I'm sorry, that's impossible. Her voice was gentle as she answered in French.

"*Mais vraiment, j'en suis sûre,*" the stranger replied. I'm certain I know you.

"No. That's not possible. I live in America. I'm an American," my mother insisted. The other woman paused several seconds, looked into her eyes, shook her head and moved on.

"*Eh bien, au revoir.*" Until the next time, she called resignedly over her shoulder. There was something wistful in the way she waved without turning around. As if she knew better.

"I wonder why that old woman thought that she knew me?" my mother mused aloud as we watched her gingerly make her way across the cobblestoned plaza. I turned in surprise. "Isn't it possible that you *did* know her when you lived here?" I ventured. "After all, that was a long time ago."

Her face went blank as she considered my words, and her memory reached back through the years, deducting the changes that age would have wrought. "Claudia," the name suddenly fell out of her mouth. "How stupid of me! Of course, you're right. That was Claudia, my friend, I'm sure of it now." She spun around to call after the woman, but the plaza was empty, and the tall, stooped, dark figure was gone. Mom's face was stricken as her eyes searched the square. "Oh, what a shame! Claudia! I wish I'd spoken with her!"

But I could see what had happened. For my mother, the past existed at such a remove that returning to scenes she had known in her youth seemed impossible to her without literally turning back time. Perhaps that was why she had failed to go back to search for Roland all those years, I suddenly realized. The past was such a closed book to her now that she did not imagine she could ever find her way back, or that, if she did, there would be anyone left to welcome her there.

• • •

When Janine first arrived in Gray at the age of sixteen, her sense of place in the world had become elastic. In the previous academic year, as a newcomer to France starting school in Mulhouse, not knowing the language, she was ashamed of being demoted. Now when asked where

The Lycée Augustin Cournot, which Janine and Trudi attended in Gray

she belonged, she seized the chance to jump herself recklessly a grade ahead. In the humanities she felt confident that she could manage, but in math and science this proved a more daring adventure, especially as she harbored the goal of becoming a doctor. That October, in addition to her regular classes, she embarked on a difficult course of nursing studies aimed at preparing for medical school. Over the span of a year, she filled many books with copious notes, all in French and exquisite handwriting, detailing the causes, symptoms, and cures of innumerable maladies from appendicitis to tuberculosis, along with explanations of the body's intricate systems and functions. She studied nutrition and hygiene and sexually transmitted diseases, as well as emergency treatments for all sorts of problems: asphyxiation, coma, shock, poison, fractures, heatstroke, even gangrene. Eagerly, she threw herself into these medical classes, but when it came to her regular schoolwork, she was far less engaged.

"She is behind in her work," her mathematics teacher groused on her report card, and the principal, while praising her ready spirit to learn, suggested that she could do better and called upon her to "redouble" her efforts. So much of her sense of self, of her worth in the family, had always included winning her parents' approval by succeeding in school that this new situation felt confusing and frightening. She could not disappoint them, but neither could she admit having lied on her registration about the level of education she had completed. And so she was forced to depend on the boys, who were only too happy to help one of the very few girls in their class. During exams, her Gallic gallants would go to the bathroom and leave her their answers, and citing a need of her own for leaving the classroom, she would retrieve them a few minutes later. Where the boys were concerned, she confided to Trudi, for the sake of her studies, she couldn't afford to discourage their interest.

Still she thought of Roland with each waking moment, imbuing him with all the perfection that first love, and a love so abruptly stymied by external forces, could ever embody. Each daisy she picked in the fields provided the means for testing love's strength. "*Er liebt mich,*" she recited, plucking a petal for each of the options. "*Mit Herzen, mit Schmerzen, über alle Maßen, ganz rasend, ein klein wenig, gar nicht!*" He loves me, with heart, with pain, beyond all measure, wildly, a little bit, not at all. Based on the number of petals on the flower in hand, she tried engineering the outcome she wanted through the right choice of ditty, as they varied in length according to language. "*Il m'aime, un peu, beaucoup, à la folie, pas du tout!*" He loves me, a little, a lot, madly, not at all. Least risky, of course, but least lyrical was the binary English, which she had just started learning and reserved for those days when she most needed a boost: "He loves me, he loves me not; loves me, loves me not; loves, not." Having lost control over her future, it brought some satisfaction to tinker with fate, and Janine felt compelled to do whatever she could to get the right answer.

In school, she sat at her desk with her mind on Roland, combining her own name with his as she idly doodled on notebook pages, symbolically reuniting with him through a blending of letters to create a single identity out of the two. *Roljan*, she wrote in elaborate letters. *Rolanine*. She drew a lopsided heart around that odd appellation, teasing herself with the now-impossible notion of joining with him, and added a border of flowers, specimens unknown to science blooming over the page.

She got away with these things without attracting her teachers' attention, but when the school distributed gas masks to all the students, fearing attacks such as those France remembered with horror from two decades back, she ran into trouble. Day after day, as the uneventful *drôle de guerre* gradually lulled everyone into complacency, she decided to make better use of the cylindrical, gray metal gas mask container that students were expected to carry to and from school on long shoulder straps. The hideous masks made them all look like space aliens with huge glassy eyes and crinkly snouts, and the imminent threat of attack that seemed frightening at first when war was declared by now seemed somewhat silly.

One day after school, a new friend with unusual skill as an artist, Marie Louise Gieselbrecht, decided to decorate the plain surfaces of their gas mask containers, which were shaped like tall, narrow cans of a size suited to carry a bottle of wine. The Gray postmaster's daughter, known to all as Malou, covered her own with a modernistic, abstract design, and on Janine's she painted a whimsical scene of Snow White and the Seven Dwarves frolicking in a colorful circle, the first Disney animated film having delighted the world just two years before. Enchanted with the result, Janine removed the gas mask, hid it at home, and decided to use the container instead as a purse.

Only days after, as sirens blared through the school for their first air raid drill, the students were told to put on their gas masks and rush to the basement. Unmasked—her container found to be housing only her lipstick, her comb, her key, and some money—Janine was punished with a week of detention. The former nebbish of Freiburg ever after felt proud of her insouciance while facing the perils of wartime. When war with the Germans broke out for real the following spring and four-minute sirens signaled not practice drills, but possible bombing attacks from the skies over France—blue skies that cracked open like robins' eggs—Janine would flat out refuse to hide underground.

By then, thanks to a loan from Maurice, the family had moved with Marie and Bella to a grand apartment on the avenue Victor Hugo near town hall. Their second-floor rooms were rented from native Graylois by the name of Fournier, both husband and wife making it clear they cared less about helping Jews displaced by the Nazis than about earning money, as food grew scarcer and the future more doubtful. The Fourniers continued to live in the ground-floor apartment and could be seen, dressed in their finest, their arms clasped behind them, taking circular walks every day after lunch, around and around the same flowerbed in their very own garden. There, directly in back of the building, a wooden trapdoor in the ground opened to steep steps that descended to a dark and dank basement, where the residents— landlords and tenants—were expected to wait out air raid drills that were ever more frequent. It was black down below (no candles permitted) with bare stone walls as cold and as clammy as death and with a sharp smell of mildew infecting the air. Each movement in the tight, confined space, the kiss of fabric on skin, caused someone to jump or cry out for fear of having been grazed by a foraging rat.

When sirens wailed over Gray for the third time within days, and Sigmar called everyone to head for the shelter, Janine decided that dying above would be preferable to going back down. The instructive drawings she saw in the papers of little stick figures looking like ants in happy survival and comfortable shelter under mountains of rubble failed to inspire her. "If they bomb the house and it crumbles on top of the shelter, we won't survive, we'll only be trapped down below," she maintained, defying her father by refusing to move.

Alice stamped her feet in frustration, looking to Sigmar to order Janine to the door, but Marie spoke up first. "She's right," Sigmar's sister said simply, sitting back down. And as she would not go, the constant Bella decided not to go either, and then wordlessly Trudi also sat down. "*Do* something!" Alice uncharacteristically glared at her husband. Sigmar shrugged; his eyebrows appealed to the heavens— either to God's higher wisdom or to the grace of the pilots who might look down from their bombers and pity a father, thereby agreeing in mercy to spare them all.

Earlier, though, as the phony war dragged on through the winter, the greatest threat to survival in Gray came not from bullets or bombs but from the terrible cold. In their large, empty, unheated apartment, the family huddled together for warmth in one little room off the kitchen. But the chamber pots under their beds froze over at night-time, and their fingers, red and raw, swelled to the point they broke open like knockwursts. Inside or out, they wore coats and hats all the time, even in school, and to guard against slipping and falling down steeply sloped streets, they resorted to wrapping their shoes with coarse rags. Longingly, they remembered the potbellied stove left be-hind in Sigmar's old office in Mulhouse, and since there was still no sign of impending German invasion, the temptation arose to retrieve their things. They decided that Sigmar would go, taking Janine along chiefly because her French was more fluent.

Having already obtained their wartime identity cards as foreign-ers residing in France, they now had to apply at town hall for safe-conduct passes, setting out their travel plans in detail and their reason for going back to a zone of evacuation so close to the Rhine. The towns of Alsace were largely deserted, and an eerie silence prevailed even in Strasbourg, its largest city, whose three hundred thousand residents had been moved. And yet, almost one hundred days after the declaration of war, fighting had not erupted on French soil, and after strengthening the Maginot Line, the French confidently believed the Germans knew better than to try to attack. As a result, Sigmar felt no particular fear about traveling back toward the border, and even Alice raised no objection.

Years later, Janine would recall that while the Rosengart remained parked in front of their building in Gray, they went by train because neither she nor her father knew how to drive it, and besides, gasoline was stringently rationed. Once in Mulhouse, they arranged to ship their belongings to Gray, but by now Sigmar seemed even more keen to lay his hands on his office stove than on his piano, however treasured. And to his overwhelming delight, the stove turned out to provide not just the prospect of warmth, but also a welcome source of tobacco, which—deprived of cigars—he craved so intensely that he sometimes stooped to salvage butts from the ground when no one was watching.

Inside the small stove, he found piles of cigar and cigarette butts that he had discarded while emptying ashtrays in the spring and summer before their departure. Since then, the French government had raised the price of tobacco, and so, unwilling to risk leaving the butts to be scavenged by movers transporting the stove, he scooped them all out. In the cold weeks that followed his return to Gray, despite stiff, frozen fingers, Sigmar sat and contentedly rescued such shreds of tobacco as the butts still contained in order to roll himself new cigarettes—scrawny and stale, yet better than nothing.

For Janine, however, the highlight of her brief return to Mulhouse came when she spotted a close friend of Roland's on the street. She called out to him and ran to catch up in order to learn what news he could share.

"Is Roland still here or have they left town too?" she breathlessly asked. Her heart stopped as she waited to find out whether he had been called up to the army, an image so terrible that she had not even been able to put it to words as part of her question because hearing it said would have made it too real.

His friend filled her in on what happened in the months she was gone. "Roland left with his family in early October. I think he said they were going to stay in Villefranche."

In spite of her mother's stern warning that respectable girls should never take the initiative in their dealings with men, Janine was thrilled by the thought of making contact with Roland again. She needed to find his address and Villefranche on a map, and she knew Malou's father, the postmaster, would be the person best able to locate it for her. But when she got back to Gray and reached Malou's apartment beneath the domed, windowed rotunda of the town's incongruously grandiose post office building, she discovered the issue to be far more complicated than she had imagined.

"Which Villefranche did you have in mind?" Monsieur Gieselbrecht asked when she got up the courage to bring him her question. The name meant the same as *Freiburg* in German, *free city*, a center of trade; hence, there were many scattered through France. Like a doctor impressing a patient who is already worried over the state of her health with more information than wanted or needed, the postmaster, checking a book, rattled off at least nine towns with that name in varied directions. It would take more than a year for Janine to discover that Roland's Villefranche was only down the river from Gray, on the banks of the Saône outside of Lyon. For now, however, she had no idea where to find him and feared she might never see him again.

Before very long, Norbert was out of reach also. That December, just before Christmas, then only eighteen, he had taken a bus to nearby Vesoul to inquire about joining the French Foreign Legion. A military unit made up of multinational volunteers assigned to operations abroad, the Legion was seeking recruits to fight, in case need arose, in North Africa. Although most other young men in town had already been drafted, as a German refugee, Norbert would not be accepted into the French Army. He had nothing to keep him busy in Gray. He hated the Nazis and was eager to prove it. Besides, his status as a native German in France would be even more difficult if the *drôle de guerre* turned real and fighting began. Since the declaration of war, the French had already started interning "undesirable strangers." The announcement on December 21 that male refugees of military age would be welcome to volunteer for the Legion offered what seemed a better solution.

The Legion was known for not asking questions, for caring little about its volunteers' backgrounds, not even demanding men's actual names or their motives for joining its ranks. While some volunteers historically signed up for family or personal reasons, political turmoil had often provided a potent incentive. In Mulhouse, Norbert had heard about mass enlistments of French Alsatians who went into the Legion in 1871 out of despair when the conquering Germans grabbed that disputed part of the country. Its motto—*Legio Patria Nostra*, The

Legion, Our Country—spoke to its role as a homeland for swash-buckling men divorced from their roots, men who were loners or with nothing to lose.

Norbert disappeared for a day to enlist in nearby Vesoul without telling his parents his plans. He had never been one to speak of the dreams that dwelled in his heart, and with his carefree, convivial nature, he did not seem the type to risk danger for glory, so Sigmar and Alice could not have imagined such a decision. Upon his return from enlisting, he poked fun at his new burst of courage, borrowing a determined and dignified greeting from the old Karl May hero he had loved as a boy: Winnetou, the great Indian warrior.

"How!" Norbert said, his voice primeval and deep as the forest. His face was fierce, his shoulders thrown back, and he raised his right hand in a classic Indian greeting, but nobody laughed. He winked, and they stared, uncomprehending.

Many years later, when my libertarian father was cheering at Barry Goldwater rallies and urging whole-hog incursions into Vietnam, along with anything else it might take to crush the Communists there, my mother would vow to break my draft-age brother's kneecaps herself before she would let him go off to war. In 1940, by contrast, with the enemy's evil so clear, its potential so great, its threat lurking in shadow just over their doorstep, Sigmar and Alice heard Norbert out and, despite their fear for his safety, could not justify their desire to restrain him.

Norbert himself seemed at ease with his choice, except for the indignity of having to submit the long shiny hair of which he was proud to the indiscriminate shears of the Legion. It vexed him to picture himself sharply turned out in a new uniform only to have his person topped off so unfashionably. Before he left, the family went to a photographer's studio for a group portrait, stirred by the stark realization they could not guarantee ever all being together again.

The parents, as the three siblings always referred to Alice and Sigmar, posed sitting in hardback wooden chairs with Norbert standing behind them, flanked by his sisters. He is dressed in a self-styled uniform consisting of a coat with a wide leather belt that sits smart at his waist and a muffler dashingly wrapped around his neck; somehow, though, he already looks older, as his eyes dart away toward some future action. His sisters are wearing identical navy blue coats, custom-made in Freiburg, with gray Persian lamb trim at the collar and pockets, and Alice is somberly clad all in black, save for a ruffle of white at her throat. Her hands are tightly clasped in her lap, the knuckles pale and protruding, as she stares opaquely into the distance. Janine gazes down at the ground, inscrutable, her thoughts clearly elsewhere, while Trudi alone, her face like her mother's shaped like a heart, permits the faintest of smiles to flirt with the camera. But Sigmar, as ever, focuses bluntly ahead, his double-breasted coat all buttoned up, his gray hat perched flat on top of his head, and his hands on his thighs. A defiant furrow creases his forehead, and the corners of his mouth slope to a frown beneath the brush of his squared-off mustache.

It was a scene the photographer was coming to know and shooting more often than the bashfully formal wedding pictures that once had provided the bulk of his business. There was a similar theme to these pictures made on the eve of departure: while pictures of weddings glistened with hope, these new ones showed fear that crouched in dark spaces and sat heavy on shoulders as all of France braced once again for the fighting to start.

Alice and Sigmar seated, with Trudi (L), Norbert,
and Janine, shortly before Norbert left Gray for
Morocco with the French Foreign Legion

SEVEN

TRAVELING SHOES

JANINE WAS OUT BUYING a new pair of shoes when two policemen knocked at the door and arrested her parents. She was just walking up the avenue Victor Hugo in time to see the police car pull away from the building, and when it sped by she had to look twice to take in the fact that the man and woman in the backseat were Sigmar and Alice.

"Wait! Where are you going?" Janine called out, clutching her purchase as she bolted behind the black Citroën. Except for the car and herself, the street was deserted, and the rising edge of alarm in her voice sounded incongruous to her on this sunlit May morning. She chased the car as far as she could, until winded and panting, she had to give up. Alice twisted around in her seat, and her hand flew to the window in a tentative wave, but distance and speed erased her expression, while Sigmar stubbornly gazed in another direction. Confused, Janine helplessly watched the car disappear. Then, like a courier snaking through enemy lines, the disturbing suspicion slipped into her mind that her father may have ignored her on purpose to keep the police from nabbing her too.

But where were they taking Alice and Sigmar? Never the sort to fool with the rules, her parents could not have done anything wrong. Their respect for bureaucracies' even most cantankerous mandates duly reflected their birthplace and training. So she calmed herself with the observable truth that the police were not German but French, and the French as far as she knew had not shown themselves hostile to Jews, at least not in this town where Moïse Lévy governed as mayor. Assessing the scene, Janine realized her father was dressed, as was his habit, in a gray pin-striped suit, white shirt, and tie, which he usually fixed with a small, pearl-topped gold stickpin. In short, he did not appear at quick glance like a man who had left in a hurry or skimped on his careful morning toilette, so she couldn't imagine what the trouble might be. Some formality, surely, involving their papers, no reason to worry, but she had looked forward to sharing her purchase with them—to modeling her shoes around the apartment and to hearing her father's good-humored response whenever he saw her wear something new.

"A-a-h," Sigmar would say, his voice exploring three distinct tones. "What will all the people say when they see you?" He would examine her feet and then nod his head appreciatively. "Madame Schlumberger!" he'd add with a grin, likening her to the elegant wife of a prominent textile magnate in Mulhouse.

Climbing the hill coming home from the store, Janine had rehearsed a speech defending her purchase: loafers, the color of pecans, with white insets on top and pairs of white tassels. It was a great luxury to get something new, Alice had cautioned, and with everything so stingily rationed now that the fighting had started (soldiers' boots require leather!), these shoes would have to last her the year. With those thoughts still in mind, it took a few moments—replaying the scene of her parents' departure—before the understanding took hold that something conceivably awful had happened. That the person now holding the stylish brown loafers was not the same girl who just minutes before, paying for them, had counted out francs and proudly presented the necessary ration ticket to be snipped out of her booklet. Not the same girl who had sat in the store debating brown versus blue, heels versus flats, and had eagerly studied her very own feet, still ready to dream that so beautifully shod, they would take her away from the war to a magical place. She had imagined herself like a female Mercury with wings on her feet, flying off in these shoes to Roland's waiting arms, because despite these months of political chaos, the war still seemed less a dangerous threat than an unfair intrusion into their romance. Not yet seventeen, she had been floating above the perils around her, made brave by the fact that her hunger to find Roland inspired the only campaign that mattered to her.

Later and always, however, pricked by guilt, Janine would remember having been blithely trying on shoes at the very same time that the police were leading her parents away. So it is that the mind seems to stitch the unthinkable moment into the simple everyday fabric of the banal. We remember precisely what we were doing when tragedy struck almost as if we could posit some logic, some cause and effect, or some justice involved. Or at least, when rationale fails, there is time and place, the reliable signposts of chronology and geography, to provide some context for what has occurred. Ah yes, I remember exactly, I was doing *that* when it happened, *that* when I heard. Those pecan-brown loafers—who could forget them?

Early that evening, Alice returned home alone and exhausted. Dark circles shadowed her eyes above her sharp cheekbones, and she had removed the pins that generally held her hair in a ladylike coil, so that now her braids dangled over her shoulders, lending her the look of a girl. The police had taken her and Sigmar straight to the *gendarmerie*, she said, and held them in separate rooms for frightening hours of interrogation. Over and over, they had probed the same issues, as if they would jolt her or trick her into changing her answers, yet she could not figure out what they wanted to hear.

"*Vous êtes allemande? Deutsche, oui?*" You are German? one asked her. The description implicitly carried a tired accusation. "So, you tell us you worked in a German Army hospital in the last war. What brought you to Gray? Why are you here?"

But Sigmar's record as a German Army war veteran troubled them more. With Hitler's troops marching now in their direction—not through, but *around* the Maginot Line to the north—all foreigners were suspect. The French authorities thought it possible that Sigmar, then not quite sixty years old, had been planted in Gray, a spy for the Germans, a fifth columnist, and they could not take the chance of letting him go. Fear of sabotage raged as the *Wehrmacht* moved closer.

"Why did you come here?" the police demanded. "How long are you staying? Who are your contacts? How are you spending your time? If you're not working here, where are you getting the money to live on? What was your business in Germany? Why did you leave there?"

Sigmar's answers seemed irrelevant to them. "Very sorry," they told him, "higher orders, of course, but we have to detain you." How long they would hold him remained undetermined. Yes, they understood that he had escaped *to* France to get *away* from the Germans, that his only son was serving in North Africa with the *French* Foreign Legion, but they could not take the risk of allowing a possible enemy spy to remain at large with war erupting. They would hold him that night and move him in the morning to a fortress in Langres, a town about thirty miles northwest of Gray.

The charge? He was branded an enemy alien, a category in which he was far from alone. Under national law, they told him, they were rounding up all German men and many women between seventeen and sixty-six years of age among refugees in the region in case spies or sympathizers were hiding among them. The police captain confided to Sigmar that the group actually included another Günzburger, a man who also maintained that he had sought refuge in Gray after fleeing the Nazis in *his* hometown of Freiburg. Beneath the friendly façade of sharing a tidbit of information, the policeman's tone was insinuating.

"You already know one another?" the officer said. "Interesting . . . And both of you Günzburgers just happened to move into Gray by coincidence only?"

In any event, urgent times required extra precautions. The officer shrugged. An exception in the regulations permitted him to let Alice go because Trudi was under sixteen; by virtue of youth, both girls were technically exempt from suspicion, while Marie and Bella enjoyed the protection of French citizenship. The officer in charge told Sigmar that during his absence—hopefully brief, as France would certainly gain victory soon—his female relations were welcome to stay on in Gray, and there was no reason to fear that they would be harmed. But had Sigmar heard, by the way, that spies for the Germans were so godless and crafty that some were thought to be hiding as nuns in the midst of the pious French population?

· · ·

The German invasion of France that sparked Sigmar's arrest began with Hitler's assault on May 10, 1940, on the three neutral states of Luxembourg, Belgium, and The Netherlands, as Nazi troops slammed over the 175-mile front extending from the North Sea to the quickly irrelevant Maginot Line with a muscular phalanx of

GERMAN INVASION OF FRANCE, MAY–JUNE 1940

motorized infantry and fire-spitting, fast-moving tanks as had never been seen in warfare before. Hitler's carefully plotted three-pronged attack aimed to divide his enemies' forces. To the south, one German division played to French expectations by moving against the Maginot Line. To the north, the Germans drove into The Netherlands and Belgium, luring the strongest Allied divisions to mount a defense. And between those assaults, the Germans launched the most crucial incursion. Later dubbed the *Sichelschnitt*, or cut of the sickle, it sliced through the dense Ardennes forest of Luxembourg and south Belgium and from there into France near Sedan, above the northernmost point of the Maginot Line.

For all of the money and effort that had gone into constructing an impregnable barrier against Nazi attack, the Maginot Line simply did not extend far enough, leaving France's 250-mile border with Belgium unfortified. Yet it had penned the French leaders into passive and outmoded thinking. Theirs was no match for the Germans' fiercely aggressive approach to the war, any more than the creaky French air force could rival Göring's fearsome *Luftwaffe*. Stunned by an onslaught from which they had felt secure and protected and disheartened by the prospect of battle, French leaders succumbed to defeat right away.

"We are beaten!" French premier Paul Reynaud despaired, wakening Britain's prime minister Winston Churchill with a frantic telephone call on just the fifth morning into the war to sound the alarm that the fall of France was already at hand. Undeterred by the military might the Allies assembled—the bombers and fighters, tanks and heavy artillery, as well as ground force divisions amassed by the French, British, Belgians, and Dutch in a belatedly united campaign—the Germans had proved themselves more agile and mobile. They were practiced at smashing by land or diving by air over the borders of Europe, a wake of flames and of death trailing behind them. Once the Germans invaded around the stunted French fortification, any retreat meant inviting Hitler to penetrate farther. Among the French, there was little stomach for the scale of losses they had endured by the end of 1918, when they counted 1.3 million dead—one out of every five men between twenty and forty-five—as well as one million crippled among the eight million men called up to fight.

The German attack, moreover, came as France was already struggling to cope with a massive refugee problem. Defeat in the Spanish Civil War the previous year chased more than four hundred thousand Spaniards and disheartened volunteers from other countries over the border. The French interned many under inhumane conditions in camps like Gurs constructed along the Spanish frontier. Now, from the east, millions of new refugees surged through the country ahead of the German advance. In panic, German Jews, Poles, Belgians, Dutch, and Luxembourgers jammed the roads, overwhelming the French ability to deal with them while simultaneously fighting to hold back Hitler's armies. The refugees—many of them stateless, impoverished, unable to speak French—helped fan the xenophobia already in place. And as half the 350,000 Jews living in France when the Germans invaded were recent arrivals, their numbers were viewed with mounting dismay.

By June 10, as the Nazi war machine continued its overwhelming drive across France, and as Italy, lusting for plunder, joined the struggle on Hitler's side, the French government fled to Bordeaux from Paris, leaving the capital an "open city" for the victorious Germans to enter without firing a shot. On June 14, the swastika flew on the Eiffel Tower's exquisite iron lattice. German soldiers goose-stepped under the Arc de Triomphe and toasted their victory on the Champs-Elysées. Less than a third of the three million residents of central Paris were still there, the rest having joined the terrified masses—comprising almost a quarter of the native French population of forty million—swelling the roads as they fled from their homes.

For the demoralized French Army, confronting civilian panic on so large a scale further disrupted their efforts to impede the merciless German assault. Many soldiers threw down their guns and simply deserted. Other divisions barely could move, wedged in place by the aimless masses searching for safety. By the thousands, the fleeing French poured into Gray from the north, crossed its Stone Bridge over the Saône, and headed toward Dole. With German troops ready to storm the town, Alice and Marie, desperate with fear, realized the time had come to join the exodus scrambling to run—farther west, farther south. They could not risk waiting for Sigmar's return.

Nine months after the family's arrival in Gray, in the face of dwindling public transportation, the Rosengart still sat parked on the street with no one to drive it. Aunt Marie had repeatedly urged Janine and Trudi to learn to drive, but after only two lessons they gave up, both preferring to spend their time with the *Eclaireuses* or French Girl Scouts, rolling bandages for the army. The sisters jumped at the chance of being included when Mayor Lévy's granddaughter asked them to join, and they felt proud to help fight the Nazis. Besides, the small car regularly stalled, and they were embarrassed to have to climb out and crank it; and as neither Sigmar nor Alice knew how to drive, the girls saw no reason why they should, either.

Now, having no other recourse, trying to imagine what Sigmar would do to escape from Gray, Alice sought out Monsieur Fimbel. The plan devised by Marie—counting on her daughter-in-law's resourcefulness to save them—involved meeting up with Lisette and her children in Arnay-le-Duc in Burgundy and then for them all to flee south together. Monsieur Fimbel agreed to take them that far, but said he would have to rush right back to Gray to be at the helm of his school when the Germans invaded. There was no time to tarry! He would drive Alice, Marie, and Bella in his own car and recruit one of his teachers to drive the Rosengart with Janine and Trudi. Assuming there was gasoline to be had, he counseled, they would undoubtedly find some other refugee in Arnay-le-Duc more than willing to serve as their driver. At worst, down the road, the car being valuable, they could use it to barter for other assistance.

The five women packed a small suitcase each and closed their door on everything else. Before leaving, Alice paused to write Sigmar a note in the event he escaped from Langres and got back to Gray before she did:

> *Lieber* Sigmar, We are going with Marie and Bella to join Lisette in Arnay-le-Duc and hopefully will move south from there. God willing, we will try to come back here as soon as we can. I beg of you,

please take care of yourself! *Gruß und Kuß.* Greetings and Kisses,
Your Lisel

The next few days' travels made the trip from Mulhouse to Gray
when war was declared the previous fall seem like a casual family outing. Their first stop, Arnay-le-Duc, northwest of Beaune, was a trip
of just a few hours, which they made on back roads to avoid running
into German divisions. They arrived to bedlam in the historic main
square, filled with soldiers and refugees all in confusion and terror
over what to do next. But in the midst of the crowd they found Lisette,
who had shrewdly sized up the situation and instantly grasped that
under the circumstances, it was *chacun pour soi*, each for oneself, and
they had to be sharp to seize the advantage.

A fleet of empty ambulances was just preparing to pull out of the
city under the escort of the retreating French Army. The best possible
plan now, Lisette advised quietly, was for Marie, Bella, Alice, Janine,
and Trudi to wangle a ride to safety with the ambulance corps. Meanwhile, she and her four children would seek cover at a farm owned
by the parents of their governess in Brive-la-Gaillarde, if only she
could think of a way to get there. When her eye fell on the Rosengart,
Lisette asked Alice to lend her the car and began searching the square
for a fresh volunteer to take the wheel. In her arms she struggled to
carry Françoise, her disabled eight-year-old daughter, while her other
twin daughter and two sons, then four and two years old, clung to the
skirt of the governess who trailed behind her. Running to the French
general in command, Lisette permitted herself to break into tears.
She summoned every bit of helpless allure as she begged for compassion, pointing first to the group of women from Gray who stood
self-effacingly off to the side; then at the children hiding behind her;
and finally at the shiny, red Rosengart, still barely driven. The others
watched in wide-eyed amazement as the general gave her his total attention, even sympathetically nodding at points.

Then he smiled, patted her cheek, shouted the name of a soldier,
and instructed Lisette to load her children into the car. With the
governess in front and the four children crowded in back, the soldier
leaped into the driver's seat and started the engine. Before Lisette

understood what he was doing, the soldier saluted and roared off down the road without saying a word. Lisette, Marie, and the others stood staring in shock.

"Is this some kind of joke?" Marie asked, as her daughter-in-law peered into the distance as if she expected the car to turn around and come back. But the general was suddenly there at her side. "I have children of my own, you know," he said. "Now take the rest of your family and get into that ambulance there." He jerked his head toward one of the vans—a big red cross painted on its roof—then turned to muster his men for departure. "We're getting ready to pull out. Hurry up now."

Lisette stood gaping into the distance, unable to move. Then she jumped to life and turned to Marie. "Get in, go with them," she ordered her mother-in-law and her entourage, herding them toward the ambulance. "I'm going to get my bicycle and go after the children, and if I have to pedal all the way to the Mediterranean, I'm going to find them. I'll get word to you later." And with that, Lisette disappeared.

Over the next two days, the women jolted on wooden benches that ran along the sides of the ambulance in a convoy that crawled down a road clogged by everything that could move or be moved. With all of France now on the run from the German offensive, the roads to the

Sigmar's sister, Marie Günzburger Cahen, mother of Edy and Mimi

south were choked. Everyone thought they'd be safer the farther they went and that the countryside would be safer than cities. It was almost as if with the Boches advancing, the entire French population would claw its way over rocky frontiers or hurl itself howling into the ocean.

The pace was numbing, progress measured in feet as the long convoy of new ambulances wound through the terrified throng of people on foot and packed into cars that were piled high with belongings; people on horses and wagons, pushing carts and carriages, leading cows, goats, sheep, and chickens, or stumbling under the weight of bulging valises. Some of the aged or ill were ferried in wheelbarrows or wheelchairs. Frenzied couples darted everywhere, trying to keep their children together. Hysterical parents stood at the roadside in tears, shouting for children adrift in the mayhem. For months thereafter, newspapers would run long daily columns of classified ads alerting family members where to find one another, many thousands having been separated at the stations while they fought to board trains or having lost track of each other along tumultuous roads.

Despite Europe already in tatters, millions behaved as though they believed that there was still somewhere to go beyond Hitler's reaches. Mattresses were stacked atop cars as if they could offer protection from dive-bombing Stukas that plunged, sirens screaming, with swastikas riding their tail fins at ninety-degree angles straight to the earth. Waves of these bombers strafed the fields and the roads, defiling the air with smoke and fire and the shrieks of the fearful and the cries of the wounded.

With a deafening wail, warplanes streaked toward the ambulance carrying the Günzburger women. The driver slammed on his brakes and ran to the back to throw open the doors. He half pulled his five passengers out of the van, shoved them beneath it, and scrambled beside them for shelter, mumbling prayers. Marie cried out in pain, not hit but bruised, as she fell forward on top of a stone. German machine guns nipped the length of the road, before the planes rose and veered off toward more valuable sites to deposit their deadly four thousand-pound payloads.

Moving on, the ambulance fleet wove through small towns, greeted in one by jubilant news that the United States had entered the war. The townspeople were laughing and crying, singing and dancing and throwing flowers at the convoy, but all too soon the rumor turned out to be false. While newspapers were not to be found, improbable stories were passed down the line, and the women had no way of knowing what to believe. That Hitler was dead or that the Reich had already seized Britain? That the pope had taken his life, or that the Russians had entered the war and were bombing Berlin? A peace treaty, some insisted, was about to be signed! For those on the road, as for those in the towns whose radios offered only music, no news, an accurate state of the moment could not be discerned. Terror reigned where knowledge was wanting.

After sunset, the ambulance fleet and the soldiers pulled into a schoolyard to wait out the night. Spotting Janine, the general sent her to fetch water so he could shave. As the hours ticked by, punctuated by the staccato thud of bombs in the distance, the women tried to ignore their hunger and find rest on the ambulance benches. Through its windows, they watched the black bowl of the night lit by explosions along the horizon. In darkness, the van was filled with the sounds of Marie groaning in pain. There was no way to help her, but Alice understood that Sigmar's sister must have broken some ribs as she dove under the ambulance during the air raids.

The next afternoon, when the convoy rolled into Vichy, a fashionable spa town on the Allier River near the center of France, Marie was clutching her side and flatly refused to continue. She took in the sight of countless exhausted travelers sleeping all over the parks and under the city's covered arcades amid their belongings and declared that, if need be, she was ready to join them in making her bed on the street. Hotel rooms were doubtless scarce, the stores and banks all were closed, the trains had stopped running, and the ambulance convoy was planning to leave, but Marie would not budge, which left Alice no choice.

"*Vous êtes folles, les Boches arrivent!*" You're all crazy, the Krauts are coming! the young driver exclaimed, waving his arms back toward the road as if he could already spot them advancing. He shook his head in disbelief as he handed down the valises to Janine and Trudi, who did not disagree. While the three older women collapsed in a park, the sisters searched for someplace to stay and were grateful to find two rooms in a run-down hotel. Alice put Marie into bed and then announced her intention, in keeping with strict regulations pertaining to their refugee status in France, to register their arrival in Vichy, along with the address where they were staying. The girls could hardly believe they had heard her correctly. Register *here*, register *now* in the French city hall? As *Germans* in France with the *Wehrmacht* invading? As *Jews* on the run from the Nazis with the Germans advancing? The idea was preposterous and, surprising herself by confronting her mother, Janine openly argued against it. Registering now was more dangerous than breaking the law, she maintained, but even at this moment of crisis, Alice could not be dissuaded from fulfilling what was expected of her.

"We don't even know how long we'll be staying. Let's wait a few days," Janine persisted.

"*Sei nicht so frech!*" Alice burst back with a warning glare, unaccustomed to Janine's being so cheeky. Janine fell silent. But as Alice marched off to find city hall, Janine caught up and linked her arm through her mother's. She distrusted the wisdom of where they were going, but could not help looking around her with interest. Under normal circumstances, visiting Vichy would have been an adventure. Indeed, even now, after months of seclusion in the stillness of Gray, she marveled at this bustling resort with its elaborate architecture—the Grand Casino, the Opéra, and the lavish hotels near the triangular parc des Sources, where, since the times of the Caesars, well-heeled, health-conscious tourists had flocked to the restorative waters of twelve thermal springs. But any semblance of Vichy's glamour was lost that night when—drawn to the windows of their hotel rooms by the overbright lights and thundering roar of invasion—the women watched German panzers roll down the street and over manicured gardens, mowing down flowers and trees and anything else that lay in their path.

By morning, all was changed: German troops filled the streets and red-and-black Nazi banners flew from city hall where Alice and Janine had registered the previous day. When Janine left the hotel, unthinkingly heading to mail a letter to a friend back in Gray, she stopped short at the sight of German soldiers grabbing refugees off the sidewalks and loading them onto a large open truck. She heard people crying and watched in horror as a soldier beat an old, bearded man until he toppled, bleeding, into the gutter. The man's arms pitifully flailed as he tried to ward off the soldier's kicks, but again and again, the booted foot slammed into him until he stopped moving.

"*Stehen Sie auf, Sie jüdisches Schwein!*" the soldier shouted, yanking the man's limp body up toward the truck. Janine could not associate this terrible scene to any human behavior she had witnessed before. She remembered Uncle Heinrich's condition on returning from Dachau after *Kristallnacht*, and she was stunned by a new apprehension of the dangers they faced. What would happen to Sigmar when German soldiers broke down the gates of the prison in Langres and discovered him there?

Janine's heartbeat was drumming so fast and loud in her ears she thought the soldiers might hear it as she remembered her mother's candid responses to the registry's questions about where they had come from and where they were staying. Under her breath, she cursed Alice's slavish adherence to law, as she rushed back to warn her mother and aunt that they had to move out right away for fear that the Germans, tracking down registered Jews, would search their hotel. With that, the relationship between mother and daughter shifted irrevocably. From then on, Janine realized, her mother would always require her children's protection and guidance. A month away from her forty-eighth birthday, ripped from her country and language and now also her husband, Alice was lost.

That night the women slept in a hat shop next to the railroad. Marie remembered the owner as a man who had worked for her husband in Mulhouse before moving to Vichy. The milliner was Jewish, and he agreed to lend them money and provide them shelter for a few days while they tried to find other housing that would not require them to present passports. It proved a curious but welcome respite as Janine tried to blot out the scene of the vicious beating she had watched in the street. Willfully, she forced it out of her mind, and with practice, she would make it a habit to steer her thinking away from things that upset her. She would hide the bad thoughts away behind doors in her mind with so much success she could later forget they ever were there.

She was aided that night by a happy distraction. While Alice and Marie stretched out to sleep on top of the counters and Bella dozed in a chair, the two sisters amused themselves by trying on hats in front of the mirrors. Bypassing feathers and ribbons and velvets with veils, they preened for each other in mannish dark felt fedoras, trying to emulate Marlene Dietrich. Janine's favorite hat, unpurchased but never forgotten, was a deep navy blue. She tilted it this way and that and bent down the brim over one eye for a look that spelled sultry sophistication, all as she pictured Roland and imagined how she would model it for him. How much more mature, more womanly, she seemed to herself since they had parted the previous autumn. Where was *he* now? When she lay down on the floor on top of her coat for a few hours of rest, she dreamed she had passed Roland in the teeming human parade on the road—people trudging in hope and despair toward some destination promising safety, when all it actually offered was a place to be frightened other than home.

EIGHT

OCCUPIED

NEAR SIX IN THE EVENING on Friday, June 14, Italian warplanes dropped bombshells on Gray, the biggest one being the bone-chilling news that German forces were about to attack. Most residents, like the Günzburger women, had already fled. But a small band of four hundred steadfast Graylois who remained in town braced themselves for the dubious honor of being invaded on the very same day that Hitler achieved his most glorious triumph: his Eighteenth Army had just taken Paris.

The Italians had jumped into the war only four days before, with France's defeat already in sight. They descended on Gray at the *Luftwaffe*'s orders—like heralds for their more powerful allies—bombing the normally busy quai Mavia on the left bank of the Saône, the gas company, and the perimeter of Gray's railroad station, where trains evacuating equipment and troops from the Maginot Line monopolized tracks and prevented departures. Frantic refugees and bands of disorganized soldiers jammed the station as they clamored for trains, and a Red Cross canteen strained to feed them with meager resources.

The next morning, with German troops moving on Gray from across the river, leaving a trail of fire and dead civilians and soldiers behind them, French Army engineers set dynamite to blow out three bridges over the Saône, hoping to thwart the German offensive. In the early afternoon, three great explosions rocked the small city as its bridges went flying, cutting off traffic over the Saône and temporarily halting the flow of electricity, water, and gas.

The battle that followed that day began with two uneven forces fixing their sights on each other over the river. A ragtag assortment of defending French soldiers—outmanned, outgunned, and sadly outfoxed— was forced to retreat only hours after the fighting had started. Crossing the Saône on their own inflatable dinghies, in boats they found moored along the right bank, or by land over one small bridge that had not been destroyed, the Germans advanced in relentless assault. Their powerful tanks and artillery bombarded Gray's empty streets, and their bombers, streaking in waves overhead, torched the crest of the town as well as the level sections close to the river. Buildings burst into flame, and by late afternoon the hellfire devouring their beloved church's bell tower seared the soul of the small Catholic city. A French captain would later describe the dirge of the church bells—partially melting as they dropped from the tower in a burning hail of stones and debris—tolling their last, a death knell that mourned the town's forced surrender.

Within the hour, Nazi storm troopers seized control of the town. Later that evening a German officer strode into Monsieur Giesel-brecht's post office to demand that the mayor be summoned to the foot of the damaged Stone Bridge to receive orders. While the citizenry fled, the mayor had stayed on in Gray to assist its defenses. But the imperious German commander was not disposed to negotiate terms with the French official who arrived at the bridge—tall and patrician, wearing a suit and a bow tie.

"*Sénateur-Maire Moïse Lévy.*" The mayor introduced himself with the slightest of nods.

"*Sie . . . Jude?*" You . . . a Jew? the German lieutenant colonel reportedly sputtered at hearing the name, amazement leaving him virtually speechless, which turned out not to matter, as he and the mayor could barely understand one another. The officer fished for a monocle that he fixed in his eye, then studied the elderly Frenchman as if searching for something beside the Old Testament name that might betray his unsuitable lineage. Unflinching, Mayor Lévy stood erect for inspection with a full head of close-cropped snowy-white hair and a curling mustache with a smile of its own. "*Juif? Oui!*" he replied, no sign of fear on his dignified features, as witnesses later described that encounter.

Instead, Gray's Jewish mayor, then seventy-seven, was the first man in town to show open resistance to German orders of occupation, orders that began by imposing a curfew and quickly moved on to restricting resources. The Germans wanted all the French wounded removed from

Gray's longtime Jewish mayor, Moïse Lévy, was also a senator in the National Assembly.

the hospital to make way for their own injured soldiers. Then they commanded the firefighters to stop using water to extinguish the flames still claiming buildings all over the city. Water was strictly reserved for the Germans, for their men in the hospital or installed in town barracks. They refused to yield to entreaties or accept proof that the local water supply could amply fulfill everyone's needs while also putting out fires now rapidly spreading. As a result, personal consequences be damned, Mayor Lévy assumed authority for saving the town by overturning directives given his firemen. Elected as mayor first in 1912, after twenty years as town councillor, Lévy had won city hall many times over and counted on having his instructions obeyed.

According to André Fick—a Mulhouse-born teacher who resettled in Gray to serve as Monsieur Fimbel's assistant, became a good friend to Janine, and later wrote about life there under the Germans—the mayor inscribed his own edict on the back of a business card he gave to the firemen: "*Senator-Mayor Moïse Lévy gives the order, under his personal responsibility, to continue fighting the fires.*" Thus for the next ten days and nights, as his word somehow prevailed, the town battled the blazes that threatened buildings and homes, especially as French-British bombing missions continued to target the German invaders after Gray was defeated.

· · ·

On city halls all over the region, the black swastika was hoisted in place of the tricolor as the Germans swept south and west from Sedan and fanned out across France, their troops swarming like locusts from Switzerland's border toward the Atlantic. On June 15, after little more than one day of fighting, the Germans succeeded in seizing Verdun with losses of fewer than two hundred men, a goal they had failed to achieve in ten months of fighting in 1916, despite a death toll eighty times higher. President Roosevelt rejected an urgent plea for assistance, and the British failed to provide sufficient support to persuade the French of their wholehearted commitment as allies. Less than three months before, Great Britain and France had agreed that neither side would make a separate peace with the Germans, but now the situation had changed. Overwhelmed, France capitulated.

On June 17, in a radio broadcast from the French government's Bordeaux encampment, Marshal Pétain, the beloved eighty-four-year-old hero of Verdun in the previous war, announced that he was replacing Prime Minister Reynaud, who had resigned. Pétain, who blamed the British for France's collapse, announced he would seek an end to the fighting through an armistice to be negotiated in "a spirit of honor." The next day, however, Brigadier General Charles de Gaulle, having escaped to London, broadcast his own appeal to the French to take heart and pursue the fight against Hitler. He said he was ready to start assembling an army.

"France has lost a battle, but France has not lost the war!" De Gaulle exhorted the French to stand firm with the forces of freedom. "Has the last word been said? Must hope disappear? Is defeat final? No!" This call to arms prompted Pétain to denounce as cowards those who had fled avoiding surrender. He arranged to have a military court try the rebellious de Gaulle in absentia and that August, with de Gaulle still safely in London, condemn him to death. As for Reynaud, Pétain had him arrested, and he was held prisoner in Germany until after the war.

While the governments of The Netherlands, Belgium, and Luxembourg opted for political exile after their armies surrendered rather than do business with Hitler, Pétain welcomed the idea of peace talks as a means of ending the war and resuming a national life that was more or less normal. The losses of battle incurred in only six weeks already weighed heavy: a toll of ninety thousand French dead, two hundred thousand injured, and nearly two million prisoners of war.

But the terms of armistice signed on June 22 were not up for discussion as Pétain had suggested. Rather, they were handed down as a diktat from Hitler himself at a meeting elaborately staged in the same railcar in the forest of Compiègne where the Treaty of Versailles sealed Germany's ignominious defeat in World War I. Worse, the armistice purposely mirrored in significant ways the punishments that the earlier treaty imposed on the Germans. Now it was the Germans' turn to demand the French Army be cut to a maximum force of one hundred thousand, and they strangled the French economy in a tightening noose of reparations that amounted to 60 percent of its income. But harshest of all were the conditions set forth for occupation, which provided for Germany to rule the rich northern two-thirds of the French mainland and Pétain's government to retain limited control of the southern third only. The occupied north gave the Germans Paris, the coastlines along the Atlantic as well as the Channel, access to Spain, and the vast majority of France's population, industry, food, and resources.

The border between the Occupied and the so-called Free Zone (later changed to the more ominous Unoccupied Zone) would be controlled like one between two different countries, requiring special German permission for the French to cross over the line from one to the other. The Reich recaptured Alsace and Lorraine, and Hitler outlined a so-called Reserved Zone (including Gray) that he slated for annexation sometime in the future, with an extra presence of Germans in charge from the start. In an effort to strip the people of Alsace and Lorraine of their French self-identification, even wearing berets was forbidden. The French language there was banned in churches, in schools, and in commerce, and French names of people and places were forced into German.

In Mulhouse, the fanciful pink *mairie* now became the *Bürgermeis-teramt*, as did city halls all over the region, while the conquering Germans also changed the names of main thoroughfares to honor the Führer. This they would do all over the country. But where else could the name change have proved so mordantly witty by virtue of being so unwittingly apt, when new signs for the Adolf-Hitler-Strasse were posted along the rue du Sauvage, the Street of the Savage?

During the next few years, young men and women of Alsace and Lorraine would be required to join the Reich Labor Service, their boys pressed into the Hitler Youth corps, and their men drafted to fight for the Germans. French prisoners of war would be held until permanent peace was established, which ultimately led to three-quarters of the nearly two million French prisoners being kept by the Reich through five years of war. The armistice further required the French to hand over all anti-Nazi German refugees living in France, which obviously had dire implications for the Jews who had fled there, escaping from Hitler.

New attacks linked Jews with Communists and Freemasons as the combined historical cause of most of the miseries inflicted on France. Before long, newspapers and propaganda depicting Jews as thieves and rats began calling for the French government to suppress the "vermin" who, for their own greedy reasons, had pushed the nation into the war.

It was hardly a jailbreak, but Sigmar escaped from the Fort de la Bonnelle in Langres as the German Army closed in and his French guards—morally queasy about leaving inmates locked up while they themselves ran away—opened the gates of the dungeon and advised all their captives to do what they could to save their own necks. Together with the other Günzburger from Gray, with whom he'd grown friendly, Sigmar fled over a footbridge of logs that spanned the moat encircling the fortress, took to the woods, and wound through the fighting in an effort to travel back to his family. Not having witnessed the hysterical panic that drove most of the French to flee as far as they could from the Germans as they advanced, he assumed he would find the women where he had left them. Now, as the fighting raged around the two German Jews with the same name, and they struggled to stay out of sight while sneaking southeast toward Gray, their fears

The guardhouse of the nineteenth-century Fort de la Bonnelle in Langres, where Sigmar was held under suspicion of being a spy for the Germans

grew with every step. To be caught by the French might mean being mistaken for German spies and, under pressure of battle, could result in their being shot on the spot. To be captured by Germans certainly augured no better result.

Without any money and no place to sleep, they were tired, dirty, and terribly hungry, as they traced the German invaders' scarred and smoking path to the Saône. But relief at reaching the water turned to despair when they discovered the bridges to Gray destroyed. From one severed span to the next, the two men followed the river and scrambled down the slippery banks. They were weighing the risks of swimming across when they found a battered old rowboat tied to the trunk of a willow, half hidden in the tall river grass, minus its oars. Together—more or less in cahoots, after all, as the police had suggested long weeks before—they dragged the old vessel into the water and, ignoring the soft black stew of leaves coating the bottom, they got on their knees to try to paddle the boat with their hands.

Without oars, of course, it was challenging to keep it moving ahead. Their knees, shoulders, and back muscles ached as they desperately stretched to pull through the currents. Aiming to land at the green slope of a picnic spot on the opposite shore known as "the beach" to the locals of Gray, they labored for hours. Drawing closer, they could not fail to notice the absence of Notre-Dame's bell tower, with its three-tiered crown and watchful French cock. Horrified by the hole in the skyline, both men stopped paddling. Their puckered fingers rested on the rough, splintered gunwales, while the wind gently rocked them. Though the day was warm, they shivered at the sight of smoke that curled like an Indian signal from the rubble of buildings that lay flattened and smoldering. Sigmar's apartment on the avenue Victor Hugo was frighteningly close to the ruins of the church. He felt old and exhausted, not ready to deal with what he might learn. How he wished he could sit there, peacefully drifting as the sun set on the darkening river and fires licked the night orange.

In the time that Sigmar spent locked up in Langres, his friend Joseph Fimbel had become Gray's man of the hour. He had risked his life atop ladders, joining the firemen in battling blazes. He stood beside Mayor Lévy at the cemetery where the local priest led combined funeral rites for a score of men, women, and children killed in the battle and bombing. And with his perfect knowledge of German, he was named by Mayor Lévy commissioner in charge of relations with the

Joseph Fimbel (center) assisted the firefighters after bombing raids set Gray aflame.

German *Kommandantur* as part of a special city committee to establish order under the Occupation. Among their first problems was feeding the people. The Germans issued a punishing ruling that barred millers from delivering flour to bakers, ordering them to use only the flour previously stored by the French military. That flour, however, now reeked of petrol that the French Army had poured over its own stocks before the invasion to ruin it in case the enemy seized it. The resulting baked goods were rancid and seemed to the French—tied to the land through their bread—to epitomize all the privations of war.

"Until these supplies are used up, no other bread will be delivered to the population," the German authorities warned. They also directed that bakers wait twenty-four hours after baking bread before selling it, which meant the baguettes turned stale and dry before reaching the table. For the Graylois, this bread would linger forever on memory's palate with the foul aftertaste of humiliation.

Life was increasingly governed by new sets of rules, some imposed by the Germans directly, others sent down from the French prefect of the Haute-Saône to regional mayors. Cafés were to be open to civilians only between eleven and one and between five and nine in the evening; driving was forbidden between ten in the evening and five in the morning; traveling by car *or* bicycle required authorization from the nearest military headquarters or *Kommandantur*; all firearms were to be surrendered at town hall; and all publications, including posters, were to be submitted to the German authorities for review and approval before being printed.

The front page of a censored edition of *La Presse Grayloise* sent the people a message to bear up under a grim situation that they had, in large measure, brought on themselves. The same theme was drummed into France as a whole through the censored newspapers that spread the will of the Germans, thinly camouflaged as objective reporting.

"Beloved people: one word, a single directive. Work. The French people want to work to repair past errors committed under the guidance of its bad shepherds," *Paris Soir* said on June 24, as in following days it advocated faith in Pétain, obedience to German commands, and strict economy in every household. News photographs showed clean-cut German soldiers socializing with bevies of lovely French girls, obviously enjoying themselves. "Not as evil as alleged," applauded the caption, urging a positive view of the occupiers.

Resources, meanwhile, grew even scarcer as the ceaseless influx of weary refugees shambling through Gray, traveling back to the homes they had fled just a few weeks before, swelled the numbers of homeless and hungry. To assist them, Monsieur Fimbel established a welcome committee and opened a shelter in a girls' school just up the street from the Günzburgers' vacant apartment. In the Ermitage Sainte-Marie, they served six thousand three hundred free hot meals between June 21 and August 6, while also providing new German-approved visas, coupons for gas, and a wall on which distraught travelers could publicly post pleas for news of lost family members and information on how to reach one another.

It was here, somewhat dazed, locked out of his apartment, and gripped by fear over the fate of his family, that Sigmar spotted Joseph Fimbel. Though shamed by his filth, Sigmar fell into the tall Marist's arms and, abandoning his usual reserve, allowed himself to take comfort—the first he had known since his arrest—in the enveloping warmth of the other man's friendship. Dry sobs choked his words, then, reverting to German, he started to stammer out questions.

"*Meine Familie?*" he asked. "They are not home! Where is Lisel? Janine and Trudi? My sister and Bella?" He did not pause for an answer before he had listed them all.

Monsieur Fimbel described his trip with the women to Arnay-le-Duc just two weeks before and tried to assure him that, almost certainly, they had run farther south from the path of the German incursion and would make their way back as soon as they could. His eyes smiled through thick glasses. "Have trust in the Lord," Monsieur Fimbel said, invoking the God that both of them shared. "Patience. I know He will bring them back safely."

Sigmar was hardly alone, however, in his distress. The prefecture of Vesoul estimated that 18,500 residents of the Haute-Saône who had joined the desperate flight south had yet to return to their homes in the region. *La Presse Grayloise* spoke to the awful doubts plaguing countless others not only in Gray but in towns and cities all over the country: "Many Graylois have come home this week; each day we see the return

of friends for whom we were worried; in friendship we embrace one another with tears in our eyes. But there are still so many missing. Where
have they gone? ... The current impossibility of any communication
by mail only makes our painful uncertainty all the harder to bear."

. . .

At the end of the month, Sigmar's women were transported back to
Gray in a hearse. Considering the fact that they had traveled to Vichy
by ambulance, their mode of return might have seemed tragic, but the
choice had more to do with the state of the times than of their health.
Their driver was a former acquaintance of Marie's, who borrowed the
hearse from a friend in the funeral business because he had no other
means to ferry them all. It was an open hearse that attached to a car,
and while Marie and Alice sat inside with the driver, Janine, Trudi,
and Bella perched in the trough reserved for the coffin. In case of rain,
they were armed with an umbrella.

In spite of its heavy occupation by Germans, Alice had insisted
on returning to Gray in hopes of reconnecting with Sigmar. She was
sick with worry, not knowing what might have happened to him,
locked in prison when France was defeated. In Vichy, after leaving
the hat shop, Alice and the others had moved into a rented room
where each night, out of the depths of sleep, her unconscious wails
gave voice to the tension she stifled all day. Her fear for her husband
and uncertainty over how best to protect her daughters played out
in nightmares, as she tossed and thrashed under the covers of the
bed that they shared. By the end of a week, she announced her intention to leave, asserting that she would feel safer in occupied Gray
with Sigmar—God willing they'd find him!—than here in unoccupied Vichy without him.

It was a long and uncomfortable ride during which they crossed
paths with what looked like the entire German Army, pressing ahead
in triumphant good cheer from the opposing direction. From the
backs of their trucks, young *Wehrmacht* soldiers waved their caps in
the air as they passed and even dared smile and shout greetings to
Janine and Trudi. But leery of attracting attention that could result in
their being stopped and forced to show identification papers revealing

them to be stateless and Jewish, Alice ordered them to keep their heads down, avoid all eye contact, and pretend to be sleeping. After riding for hours on bumpy backcountry roads, Janine awoke from a nap to find that a call of nature that had begun as a whisper outside of Vichy had now, inconveniently, turned into a roar.

"Just squat inside the open umbrella," Trudi advised her. But with an unending convoy of German trucks passing, Janine rejected her sister's idea and knocked on the driver's rear window to ask him to pull off the road for a moment. Then she ran by herself into the woods, hurriedly pulled off her panties, and dropped to the ground.

"*Halt! Was machen Sie hier?*" a loud voice demanded behind her. She whipped around to see four German soldiers aiming their weapons straight at her back, and she froze in terror, heart thumping, like a rabbit caught nibbling garden petunias. One of the soldiers pointed his gun barrel toward the panties that Janine still clutched in her hand, and they all burst out laughing.

"*Allez!*" the soldier in charge ordered in French as she cowered before him, trembling, uncertain whether they intended to grab her or shoot her if she attempted to run. Still aiming his weapon, he jerked his head past the woods toward the roadside where the hearse was parked waiting, and the soldiers' laughter continued to ring in her ears, not only until they reached Gray but for decades that followed.

The first person they met when they finally drove into town turned out to be the wife of the fellow German prisoner with whom Sigmar fled Langres. The hearse was mounting the rue du Marché when they saw the woman from Freiburg, by now a more familiar acquaintance, emerge from a shop.

"They're back, your father is back!" she called out to the girls, who sat numbly surveying the rubble around them. At the car window, she told Alice their husbands had made their way home a few days before, and she advised looking for Sigmar in the shelter set up at the school on the avenue Victor Hugo, luckily spared the worst of the bombing.

"Who knows?" The other Frau Günzburger shrugged, shaking her head, when Alice expressed alarm as to why Sigmar had chosen a shelter instead of going back to their own apartment on the very same street. "Maybe he couldn't get in. Perhaps he just couldn't face the idea of being alone there without you." Then, too, she added, gesturing to the crush of shoppers lining the pavement behind her, he probably didn't have money or food. "It's *schrecklich*, there's nothing to eat here but *Dreck*," she grumbled in German, heedless of who overheard her. "The Nazi dogs are keeping it all for themselves. We're practically starving, but *Gott sei Dank*, we're still alive and together."

"Yes, yes," Alice politely agreed, impatient to drive on, to rush to the shelter. "We must all count our blessings."

When they reached the top of the hill, and the driver pulled up in front of their building, Alice handed the keys to Marie and told them all to go in without her: she would go search for Sigmar. It was characteristic of her relationship with her husband that she kept all intimate moments and all expressions of feeling between them totally private. Indeed, though she saved many boxes of letters and postcards from friends and admirers, leaving them for me to discover, when she reached her nineties she contrarily destroyed all the love letters and notes that Sigmar had sent her during their short engagement and very long marriage. "Those letters are personal," my grandmother said, unapologetic, and she could not be dissuaded from feeding them to the random gluttony of her building's incinerator. Like doves shot out of the sky, they fell fluttering down the cold metal chute in the hallway, straight to the fiery maw in the basement.

What happened when Alice ventured into the Ecole Supérieure de Jeunes Filles to seek out her husband among the displaced and new homeless of Gray is therefore a secret. Neither Alice nor Sigmar ever discussed it, but the girls and Marie leaned out the window to peer into the street and saw the couple pass through the gates of the schoolyard and slowly walk toward them.

Sigmar's suit jacket was folded over his left arm, his shirt and trousers were grimy and wrinkled, his shoes were stiff with mud from the river, his hat was battered, and he needed a shave. All the same, his right arm was bent at the elbow, and Alice's forearm rested on his, as if they were strolling down the Kaiserstrasse on a Sunday in Freiburg. Except now this street too, like the rue du Sauvage in Mulhouse and countless others in Europe, was called the Adolf-Hitler-Strasse; they themselves were in occupied France, along with the Germans; and before very long they would have to make plans for fleeing again. At the moment, however, they both seemed content just to walk side by side, not even talking, until they reached the door of their building, where Sigmar glanced up to the second-floor window at his daughters and sister—their faces like angels above him—watching and smiling.

"Sigmar, Baron von Ihringen," he announced himself to his female audience with click of his heels, a sweep of his hat, and the hint of a bow. Then he indulged in a grin and the wave of a hero home from the war, and he opened the door for his giggling wife and entered the building, as Janine and Trudi flew downstairs to greet him.

NINE

A TELLING TIME

"Give me your watch, and I'll tell you the time." That was the joke on the street that wryly summed up for the occupied French how the victorious Germans viewed coexistence. But the time the French got from the Germans was not even theirs. The Germans advanced French clocks by an hour to match the time in Berlin, their bells all tolling together the time of the Führer. It was the *Nazi-Zeit* on an hourly basis.

For Senator-Mayor Moïse Lévy, who had held one city office after another for almost a half century, time was quite simply up. On July 20, 1940, the day that Gray marked the completion of temporary repairs to the mutilated bell tower of the church by crowning its flattened roof with a bouquet of fresh flowers, the German military authority removed him as mayor and named Joseph Fimbel as his successor.

The Jewish official was out of town when the announcement was made. As senator of the Haute-Saône, he had left in early July to participate in the National Assembly meeting in Vichy that would grant full authority to Marshal Pétain. The elderly general had chosen Vichy—far from the borders and blessed with hotel rooms—as the seat of his government in exile from Paris. Before long, his collaborationist regime would become synonymous with the name of the spa, and the Unoccupied Zone would be dubbed the *Zone Nono*, once the French understood that "Free Zone" was just a misnomer for an illusion.

Convening that summer, however, the legislators still hoped to preserve what they could of French self-rule. They arrived in Vichy in a furious temper, not only shamed by the debacle of total defeat by the Germans in battle, but also enraged by what they condemned as new treachery at the hands of the British, their own former allies. In the first week of July, alarmed by the French armistice with Hitler and fearful that, as a result, the Germans would seize control of French warships, Churchill decided he had no choice but to destroy the French fleet—a defensive move he would later acknowledge was "unnatural and painful." With Operation Catapult, the British attacked French ships anchored off the coast of Algeria at Mers-el-Kébir and at other ports, killing more than one thousand two hundred French sailors and wounding hundreds of others. The fact that the British wreaked so much destruction helped to drive the horrified French farther into the arms of the Germans.

"France has never had and never will have a more inveterate enemy than Great Britain," Pierre Laval, Pétain's deputy, told the senators meeting at Vichy on July 4. "We have been nothing but toys in the hand of England, which has exploited us to ensure her own safety." The only way to restore France to its entitled position, he urged, was "to ally ourselves resolutely with Germany and to confront England together." The following day, stung by betrayal, France broke off diplomatic relations with Britain.

On July 10, gathering in the all-too-appropriate venue of the spa's Grand Casino, the Assembly gambled away French citizens' freedoms. The great-grandson of the Marquis de Lafayette stood among 80 parliamentarians opposing the motion, but 569 others fell into line with Laval and Pétain and voted to change the constitution. Now France turned on itself, blaming its downfall on disease from within. Its weakness resulted from moral pollution encouraged by the suspect, secular, and foreign influences of the Jews, the Freemasons, and the Bolsheviks; this was exemplified by the Socialist Popular Front of Léon Blum, who had served in 1936–1937 as France's first Jewish prime minister. Or so it was charged. Albert Lebrun, the ineffectual president of the Third Republic, ceded power to Pétain without resigning. And in a sharp right-hand turn, the Assembly empowered the marshal to impose a new constitution by personal order. That evening, this man who had started his life as the son of a farmer and rose to glory in old age issued three sweeping decrees that anointed him chief of state, granted him total control, and adjourned the National Assembly indefinitely.

Like a strict but well-meaning grandfather, Pétain would impose discipline on a nation of unruly children led astray by questionable

Pétain's Révolution Nationale lumped together Jews, Communists, Freemasons, and the influences of laziness, drink, and egoism as responsible for the fall of France.

friends and now brought to heel with a new set of goals. Liberty, equality, fraternity—the old trinity of democratic France's soaring ideals—gave way to a new triumvirate—work, family, homeland—that Gaullists would mock as already a failure. Its status, they said, amounted to this: "work: unobtainable; family: dispersed; homeland: humiliated." It fell to the Germans, with Pétain as their front man and doddering puppet, to secure the foundations of a demoralized, bitter, and teetering France. The answer they found was totalitarianism.

· · ·

In the third week of August, almost a month after Moïse Lévy attended the meeting in Vichy, black-booted German soldiers barged into the fine yellow mansion of Gray's former mayor across the street from the promenade des Tilleuls. He needed no explanation when the *Wehrmacht* officers brushed him aside and without invitation rudely proceeded to tour all the rooms, jotting down notes on their tasteful appointments. Then he received an order in writing: he had twenty-four hours to give up his home, fully furnished and outfitted

*Mayor Möise Lévy's familial home at n° 1 de la Grand Rue
was confiscated by the Germans and turned into a residence for
Wehrmacht officers.*

with all its linens, dishes, and silver. The next day, as men in the park
met to play boules, city firemen pulled a red truck in front of the
house to help Monsieur Lévy remove those personal items he was
permitted. But only when the Germans arrived, prepared to add pressure, did he come out the door, ashen and feeble, leaning on the arm
of an aide, while tearful townspeople gathered to watch him depart.

Throughout September, remaining in town in stopgap lodgings
though relieved of his duties, he would frequently visit town hall to keep
up with events. In early October he would move to Paris, occasionally
sending contributions to Gray for his pet social projects. But he would
never again return to his birthplace except to be buried in Gray's Jewish
cemetery—a locked enclave on the outskirts of town, where visitors only
rarely seek entry to add a small stone to the now ill-tended grave sites as
custom prescribes, as a tangible token of eternal remembrance.

Near a wall sprouting patches of lichen and moss, the Lévys' imposing family tomb records in marble Moïse's many achievements:
*Sénateur-Maire de Gray, Vice-Président du Conseil Général de la Haute-
Saône, Chevalier de la Légion d'Honneur,* and *Commandant de Mérite Social.*
It also includes a memorial to his son, René Baruch Lévy, a chemist
who was thirty-six in 1943, when he was deported to a Nazi death
camp, seven months prior to the death of the mayor.

"*Assassiné par les Allemands au camp de Birkenau,*" is engraved on the shiny gray stone to remember René Lévy's murder at the hands of the Nazis. "*Mort pour la France!*" Dead for France! The same words are also inscribed on a monument that lists him among twenty-three other Jewish Graylois deported to death camps, all lacking graves. An Yvonne and a Lucie, a Marcel and a Louis, a Paulette, a Clarisse—all dead at Auschwitz, all of them honored as dying for France, not victims but martyrs ennobled through sacrifice, as if willingly made in the name of their country.

As for the mayor, there could never be recompense for the loss of a son. Yet there was something a lifelong politician might well have enjoyed: a permanent place in the minds of some of Gray's people—the last who remember or the few who may ask—through a street named in his honor after the war.

• • •

In the first months of occupation, the Günzburgers fared better than had Mayor Lévy, because even with one thousand Germans ensconced now in Gray, no one attempted to oust them from their apartment. What made this doubly surprising was that their interim home at 12 rue Victor Hugo was just a few steps away from the headquarters the Nazis established at number 8, where a swastika menaced the street on a *Wehrmacht* flag above the front door. And more astonishing still was that they not only managed to live undisturbed by their *Wehrmacht* neighbors, but that a German lieutenant was actually billeted in their apartment! Far from becoming a threatening presence, however, the officer who moved in with them, taking the smallest bedroom close to the kitchen, behaved in a manner polite and considerate. On that point, they all granted him sincere credit. He arrived late in the evening, left in the morning, asked no questions, created no trouble and, to the contrary, often brought them small gifts of food from the Germans' canteen, richly stocked with all the provisions the victors withheld from the average French table: a little meat, sugar, or butter and the treat of fresh bread untainted by petrol. He even told Janine, when he caught her admiring his bicycle at the foot of the stairs, that he would keep his eye out to find her one too.

At such close quarters, the family could readily see there was no way of hiding the facts they were Germans *and* Jewish. Yet the dilemma of how to deal with a German officer under their roof was awkward at best and inherently frightening. Was their courteous boarder a fellow German who might at one time have been a friendly acquaintance, a schoolmate, a neighbor, or a customer's son? Or a Nazi who held their lives in his hands, because with only a word he could have them deported?

For Bella there was nothing confusing about how to regard the *Wehrmacht* troops who marched past their windows each morning that summer en route to swim in the chilly Saône River. Bare chested, wearing only trunks and shoes, the soldiers paraded their hard-muscled bodies before the townspeople. They invaded the streets in confident ranks, singing "Erika" or "Heidi-Heido" robustly in German—warriors embodying Hitler's Aryan ideal. In response, Aunt Marie's housekeeper daily rushed to the windows and yanked closed the tall shutters facing the street, deploring the sight of these vainglorious men as an inappropriate spectacle from which Janine and Trudi and all decent women ought to be shielded.

At the river themselves, the girls tried to ignore the young German soldiers who showed up in their off-duty hours to relax in the sun. Afraid to seem rude, they found it hard not to reply when directly addressed, yet they refrained from any friendly response that could suggest they were willing to carry things further. Fraternizing with the enemy would not be viewed kindly and represented even more risk for girls who were Jewish.

One afternoon, as Janine and her friend Malou sat on a bench in the grass, reading and talking, Malou jumped to her feet to confront a German soldier who was taking their picture. Not for her to wind up on exhibit in some German scrapbook, the butt of jokes in the barracks or the barbs of the Fräuleins he might later attempt to make jealous back home, or to let it appear she had willingly posed, a too-friendly local, scantily clad, welcoming the soldier's advances! She demanded his film, and he acceded. Then, not yet invited to sit, but granted an audience by virtue of his gracious surrender, he stood chatting with them, and it was shortly disclosed that this soldier working so hard to

*Marie-Louise "Malou" Gieselbrecht, Janine's
closest friend, in a boat on the Saône River*

pursue conversation was, by coincidence, a native of Freiburg. Heinz
Rosenstihl, just twenty-two, gaped in mirrored surprise at the news
that Janine had come from the very same town, each of them hence a
Freiburger *Bobbele*. Delight filled his face, and he suggested that Janine
might know of his family through their stable and riding school in the
bucolic eastern part of the city called Littenweiler. And before very
long, as invariably occurs when travelers run into someone who hails
from their town, Janine began to probe for details, the temptation to
hear about friends left behind and inquire about home chipping away
at her wall of reserve.

Adrift in the war, this boy and this girl, soldier and refugee, German and Jew, spent a few happy minutes exploring their common
Black Forest childhoods. Memories hung in the warm summer air:
the fair at the Meßplatz, the view from the Schauinsland, the bubbling *Bächle*, steamed noodle cakes drenched in caramel sauce, *Spätzle*
and pretzels. By the next time they met by chance at the river, Heinz
Rosenstihl had decided to save her. He felt especially drawn to this
pretty young woman, whom he could almost believe he had known
as a child. Somebody's classmate, the friend of a friend, a blue-eyed
young girl he had passed in a park or a bakery or maybe on skis in the

mountains long before she had captured his fancy on the banks of the Saône.

"Hitler will take over the whole world, including Palestine, but I can save you," he solemnly told her. He sounded pleased by his noble intention and looked to Malou, like him a Catholic, to help Janine accept the inevitable. "That's the only way you'll survive. All the Jews are going to be killed, but I'll marry you and take you home to my family in Freiburg. We'll tell everybody that you lost all your papers, and then we'll make up whatever we have to. Your family will be happy to know that at least one of you will be left alive. And, who knows, there's a chance that from Germany you might be able to help them somehow."

Janine sat stunned into silence, but Malou chewed on a long stalk of grass as she sized up the soldier's husband potential. "Don't be too quick to say no," Malou whispered to Janine. "He's not bad, you know, and he may have a point. Let's give it some thought." But Janine was already standing, collecting her things.

"Thank you," she told him. "Really, *wirklich*, it's kind and brave of you to make such an offer, but we should not even be seen here with you, talking together in public this long." Flustered, she pulled on her skirt and blouse, slipped on her shoes, stuffed her towel and book in a bag, and granted him a smile of good-bye in place of openly shaking his hand.

"*Ist er verrückt?*" Sigmar exploded when Janine got home and told him what happened. He instructed her never to speak with the soldier again (the young man's sanity being called into question), even though he conceded knowing Freiburg's Rosenstihl family and remembered them as respectable people. For Janine, of course, it mattered little what her father thought of the soldier's background, as her own marital interests stopped short in Mulhouse. The German's proposal had drawn her thoughts to Roland, and she realized that if *he* had suggested leaving her family and escaping the Nazis through Christian marriage, the ring might have already been on her finger, with safety just a side benefit of everything else she desperately wanted. She prayed for God's help in finding the man she adored, while never exactly confessing his name for fear that Abraham's God of judgment and vengeance might fatally frown on her choosing a Catholic. Why trouble the Lord with details, she figured, at a time when He was already so busy with world-shaking matters? After the war, she would hopefully find a way to persuade Him—or at least her own parents—that Roland's different faith should not be cause to keep them apart.

For now divine intervention seemed necessary. With Alsace and Lorraine swallowed into the Reich, even contact with Mulhouse was out of the question. On July 16, a German order expelled all Jews from Alsace, with thousands given just one hour's warning before being forced to assemble in the Mulhouse synagogue courtyard to be loaded on trucks and carted out of the Occupied Zone. The reports that traveled to Gray began to fill in the shadows that shaped Private Rosenstihl's warning. But a week or so after his sudden and daring marriage proposal, Janine found herself summoned to her school principal's office. An unsmiling, ferretlike man with dark thinning hair and a little mustache, the principal had worked himself into a rage.

"What do you think you're you doing, fraternizing with a German soldier?" he demanded, indignant. "Certainly, as a Jew, mademoiselle, you should understand the perils of this! Have you really no shame in front of your people?"

"Monsieur, I don't know what you mean," Janine replied in confusion, but with a brusque wave of his arm, he cut her off.

"Then I'm sure you can tell me why Private Rosenstihl came here to see me! He claimed he wanted to marry you in order to rescue you. He suggested that *I* talk to your father to win his consent. But I refuse to get involved in this matter! And I'd advise you in the strongest possible terms not to get involved with him, either, although it appears I'm already too late."

The next time the soldier from Freiburg approached her as she and Malou lay in the grass at the river, Janine did not shrink from voicing annoyance. Now his desire to protect her without her permission struck her as crazy and oddly pretentious.

"*Maintenant, ça suffit!*" That's enough! she snapped in French at the crestfallen soldier, calling the thing to a halt and punishing him by refusing to speak the *badisch* dialect that had been like a verbal vacation for them. "I'd rather die with my parents than escape with you. How could you think I'd go off and leave them? I can't marry you, and now I can't even speak to you either."

       . . .

In my younger years, I wanted to trust that the French had all been resisters, if not actively flouting personal danger, then at least in the way that they viewed their invaders and the suffering the Nazis inflicted on Jews throughout Europe. This was before the French publicly searched their own historical record through films and books and trials that explored their actions during the war, and it clearly reflected my mother's perception and all she had told me. Her love for Roland, her friendships with Malou and others, her embrace of their country instead of her own disgraced homeland, and *oui*, her careful decision to paint herself as having been French from the day she was born—all of these went into the mix that turned me into a Francophile.

My identification with the mother I worshipped translated cleanly into a love of the country where she happily lived during four otherwise terrible years of Europe's worst turmoil. With the razorlike moral distinctions acceptable only in childhood, I therefore grew up dividing the villains and heroes in all of her stories with a line far more fixed than their changeable borders. As the Nazis were evil, I blocked out the language my grandparents spoke, which I heard every day all around me, while my studies of French leaped ably ahead, thanks to a private instructor—the French widow of an American soldier—retained by my mother for weekly lessons.

Indeed, Mom never said anything to suggest that the French had ever collaborated with Hitler, while she claimed to have encountered more blatant anti-Semitism in the United States than she had *personally* experienced in France, or even in Germany, for that matter. To me, this stark, unfamiliar assertion raised the threat that Jews were at risk in America also, and I could not help but cringe every time she made it. I had no grounds to refute the way that she sidestepped accounts of French persecution, maintaining instead that the French, victims themselves, had been forced in the 1940s to yield to the will of the conquering Nazis. She could no more blame France than bury her love for Roland.

In recent decades, scholars have offered more damning accounts, showing that although many French harbored no particular hatred of Jews, the French government under Pétain zealously leveled sanctions against them. What Pétain described as collaboration, a viable means of coexistence with Germans within France's borders, quickly gave rise to endorsement—emulation, in fact—of policies aimed at destroying the Jews. In some cases, the Vichy administration readily jumped forward, enacting sanctions even before the Germans required them, while some of the measures the French imposed early on were even harsher than parallel statutes the Nazis devised.

Between the Germans and Vichy, the situation for Jews in both parts of the country began changing quickly. Neither zone represented a reliable haven for a population of Jews that had swelled from 150,000 in 1919 to 350,000 by World War II, among a total French population of 40 million. Another 400,000 Jews would pass through France in those years as stateless refugees hoping to find safety elsewhere, only to find themselves caught in the grip of the Vichy regime, which willingly handed off many thousands to the Germans. On a psychological level, how could the French despair for Jews deported to camps as long as 1.5 million of their own men were being held by the Reich as prisoners of war, most not free to come home until Hitler's defeat?

A representative anti-Semitic cartoon of the Vichy era depicts the hooked-nosed "Patriotic Jew," apparently a financier, congratulating himself with these words: "500,000 francs for the nation, 1 million for the Jewish Marxists. I have served the Jewish people well again today."

That August 1940, Vichy unleashed one of its first assaults upon Jews by repealing the Marchandeau Law, which had outlawed racist attacks in the press. This enabled Hitler's propaganda machine to begin feeding the public the same sort of anti-Semitic vitriol it had spewed years before to incite the Germans. The date of this action, August 27, sent chills through my mother, as did the date two months before when French prisoners were marched out of Gray on June 27 to be sent into captivity over the Rhine. "It figures—you know today's date," Janine remarked as she and Trudi stood on the street sadly watching them leave.

Yes, in the course of my research into her story, I, too, have been struck by how often that number she dreads reappears. On September 27, 1940, as Germany signed a Tripartite Pact with Italy and Japan aimed at keeping America out of the war, the Nazis called for a census of Jews and imposed the first anti-Jewish ordinance on the Occupied Zone. It would not go unnoticed that the date of the measure came exactly 149 years from September 27, 1791, the day that a vote of the National Assembly made France the first country in Europe to offer Jews full citizenship.

It was March 27, 1942, when the first German transport sent more than a thousand Jews from detention in France to death at Auschwitz. On May 27, 1943, the National Council of the Resistance first met in Paris and, led by Jean Moulin, voted to place its confidence in de Gaulle to restore the Republic. But the daring Moulin—soon captured and brutally tortured by the Gestapo in Lyon—died in custody on a train bound for Germany. On July 27, 1944, the Germans moved to crush the Resistance, gunning down five French patriots in front of a Lyon café on the place Bellecour, where their bodies were left sprawled on display as a warning to others. A memorial marking the spot where their blood stained the sidewalk lists the names of all the Nazi camps that befouled the countries of Europe. Among them, the death camp of Auschwitz, where two million captives were murdered, was liberated by Soviet troops six months after the Lyon slayings. The date, January 27, 1945, is now annually observed as International Holocaust Remembrance Day.

Is there some benefit, then, to fixing one number, as my mother has done, fearing one day a month as being portentous? The answer could only be yes if it left twenty-nine others for breath to come easy, but that was not the case here. Vichy imposed two broad-ranging *Statuts des juifs* on the so-called Free Zone on October 3 and 4, 1940, banning Jews from many public and private professions and placing them in a lower position under French law. Foreign-born Jews could be arrested and interned in "special camps" or assigned to distant compounds under surveillance, a ruling that carried grave implications.

French Jewish leaders reacted with respectful but vigorous protests, noting that Jewish citizens remained, as ever, faithful to France. In a statement decrying the measures, Chief Rabbi Isaiah Schwartz called for equality and affirmed that "no values could be dearer to us" than those of "work, family, and homeland" that Vichy had chosen to define its regime. "We will respond to a law of exclusion by unswerving devotion to the homeland," the rabbi wrote to Marshal Pétain, who did not respond. Like Alfred Dreyfus decades before, French Jews now refused to allow their victimization to shake their sense of themselves as true citizens, loyal to country. In 1940, moreover, on the defensive again, French Jewry insisted that citizenship guaranteed them rights of protection that the stateless refugees who had swarmed over their borders could not hope to claim. And so, much like my mother acting on instinct, keeping faith with that country and pretending to be what she wanted to be, the Jews of France proudly asserted their right to be French. They needed to trust in France as their savior, or else they had nothing.

TEN

CROSSING THE LINE

SIXTY-ONE YEARS from that summer in Gray when my mother peeked through the shutters on the avenue Victor Hugo to watch German soldiers in swimsuits march to the river, I arrived in August 2001 to find a muscular swirl of triathlon runners and cyclists jolting its drowsy Renaissance streets. In the Saône's choppy waters, what appeared to be seals were swimmers in wet suits, shiny and black, racing downstream. And as crowds cheered contestants from all over France, a message of life and renewal rang through this town, always linked in my childhood to stories of war.

My appointment that day was with André Fick, a former top aide to Gray's Mayor Fimbel. He was then eighty-four, and as racing cyclists swarmed through the town, I was surprised to meet him astride a bike, too, cruising his street and gallantly watching for me in case I had trouble finding his house. I'd remembered his name from wartime documents my mother had shown me, letters on which his official signature had worked like a lifeline during the years the Germans were there. Without André Fick, my own existence would have been doubtful. Yet in the instant we met, I disappeared, for he leaped over years and mistook me for Janine.

"Ah, it's wonderful to see you," he said, his tone unusually formal for an avowal that proved disarmingly candid: "*Vous savez, j'ai toujours eu le béguin pour vous.*" You know, I've always had a crush on you. He clasped my hand, reclaimed Janine in my eyes and my voice and, lured by memories, slipped through a chink in time to a faraway moment when living in danger brought depth to relations. Behind heavy glasses, tears brimmed in his light blue eyes, and for one selfish instant

I wanted to be her, my mother, the source of a dream he had never forgotten.

The son of a Mulhouse grocer, André Fick had been a devoted young Marist who studied and taught in Fimbel-run schools. Drafted into the French Army on the eve of the war, like so many other Alsatians he avoided going back home after defeat in June 1940 for fear that the Germans would force him to fight for the Reich. Instead, he eagerly followed Monsieur Fimbel to Gray, where, at just twenty-three, he took on the job of city liaison to the German command during more than four years of harsh occupation.

In his own written account of that difficult period, *Gray à l'Heure Allemande* (Gray in the time of the Germans), André Fick tells how the forces that occupied Gray gave shape to defeat for its downhearted people. For each, he says, the ordeal inevitably became something different. Some lost all that they had in the bombings and fires and dwelled on the shaky edge of existence. Some suffered the absence of a husband, a brother, a son, or a father imprisoned by Germans in mysterious camps. Many, especially women, were crushed by the burden of scrounging for daily subsistence, while others cunningly worked the black market, growing wealthy by milking the hunger of neighbors. Some were resigned, accepting the long Occupation with stoicism. Others believed resolutely in Marshal Pétain and that he would do the best for the country. The thirst for liberty and a gut-deep revulsion provoked by the Fascists prompted some, but not many, to risk their lives and join the Resistance. Others crept into the underground fight less for the aim of subverting the Nazis than as a means to evade the roundup of Frenchmen condemned to labor over the Rhine. With no way to guess how long the domination would last, fear and powerlessness weighed on the town like a low-lying fog.

The rules under which they endured, Fick recalled, multiplied daily in inverse ratio to the dwindling food in their larders. *Verboten*, forbidden: the right to assemble in public in groups of more than three people. *Verboten*: displaying the humbled French flag or French decorations. *Verboten*: photographing the exterior of any buildings or listening to foreign radio stations, especially London's. *Verboten*: singing the "Marseillaise" and engaging in any political action. *Verboten*: to travel without official approval.

The problem in Gray was the same one confounding local authorities throughout the Occupied Zone, required under the armistice "to conform to the regulations of the German authorities and collaborate with them in a correct manner." But what did that mean? Among the Graylois, citizens viewed collaboration with an added measure of dubiousness based on the fact that Mayor Fimbel and his assistant were native neither to Gray nor even to the Haute-Saône department. As Alsatians, moreover, both spoke fluent German and seemed quickly to win the trust of their masters.

To the dismay of the people, propaganda posters papered the walls of the town and encouraged its men to enlist for German factory jobs, and by the *Kommandant's* orders, each issue of the local newspaper ran similar ads. "An end to the hard times!" the text declared. "Papa is earning money in Germany now!" And yet the Germans undermined their recruitment campaign with other posters openly hinting that their own men in Gray would usurp both the love and the hearths the French left behind: "Abandoned people, place your faith in the German soldier!" A handsome, uniformed *Wehrmacht* officer smiled from these posters with contented French children embraced by his arms. Small wonder that the volunteer rate proved so unsatisfying that by 1943 the Nazis would resort to forcing the French to work in German factory jobs, to stand in for their laborers sent into battle and thereby step up production of war supplies.

Still, recognizing the potential for German soldiers to compromise Gray's lonely women, the town's celibate mayor reluctantly acceded to the *Kommandant's* order to set up a brothel. Monsieur Fimbel saw to it that prostitutes were imported from Dijon and Paris and that the bordello was furnished and kept sanitary. Costs were charged to the maintenance of the German occupied forces, with the bills to be paid by the people of France. But after the war, there would still be a handful of women, native to Gray, publicly shamed for fraternization. Among more than ten thousand other Frenchwomen later accused of "horizontal collaboration" with German soldiers, they were dragged to the city hall plaza and forced to submit to having their scalps entirely shaved.

Attempting to help Gray's population survive beneath the yoke of oppression, André Fick and the mayor needed to run a few stealthy steps ahead of the Germans. With a golden rule of "discretion and silence," Fick told me, they shielded the town from cruel Nazi excesses, using deceptions and lies to ward off reprisals and rescue many who would have been victims. They intervened to help the Graylois and, even as they manipulated to gain the trust of the Germans, the two Alsatian Marists subtly schemed right under their noses.

"We waged war against them," André recalled on the day that I met him. "Not with guns and bayonets, but a war all the same, a war that we waged in writing and meetings." And yet there were those, he sadly confided, who, regarding him as well as the mayor as tools of the Germans, maligned them in whispers as collaborators who helped to enforce the victors' demands. "The people of Gray saw me go to the *Kommandantur* every day, and they viewed that as shady. They saw me go with my documents, and they said, 'He's a collaborator.' That's the normal reaction. My actions, like those of Monsieur Fimbel, were not always well understood by the population. They saw us go every day, but it was *not* to lick the boots of the Germans, but to press for favors for the people of Gray."

. . .

All through the summer and fall of 1940, Joseph Fimbel continued to visit with Sigmar, his old Jewish friend. For warmth, as autumn set in, they sat at the kitchen table near the potbellied stove retrieved from Mulhouse, Alice doing her best with limited rations to offer the mayor simple refreshment. Even before the outbreak of fighting the previous winter, coupons dispensed at the *mairie* had fixed the amount of bread, meat, sugar, wine, flour, fats, soap, and charcoal allotted townspeople, based on their age and the work they performed. Once the Germans took over, claiming most of the food for themselves or for export to feed their country and troops, they held the Graylois to a diet of approximately one thousand six hundred calories a day, a limit they later cut almost in half. There were also restrictions on purchasing bicycle tires, textiles, and shoes, which led to new styles with soles made of wood. An informal bartering system quickly arose, with cigarettes readily serving as money.

In that first autumn of occupation, Gray's agricultural setting provided residents with more copious food than those who lived in cities could find. There were fruits and vegetables in the marketplace on the broad cobblestoned plaza before town hall, and butter and eggs often available at nearby farms. And so, on the evenings the mayor came by, Alice was pleased to see him cheer up her husband and unstintingly served him her kitchen's best, along with a cup of hot bouillon, a small glass of wine, or weak so-called coffee brewed out of chicory.

The two friends still occasionally sparred in religious debate, but increasingly, current events led to political worries, and one evening the mayor arrived to find Sigmar engulfed by hurt feelings that focused their talk on the tactical problems involved in escape. That afternoon's mail had brought a postcard from Marie's son Edy, writing from relative safety in Switzerland, where, as a military man seeking asylum, he'd been interned since France fell. What appeared on the surface as a genial family message from him actually bore oblique instructions that caught Sigmar's eye and on closer inspection stirred his resentment.

"*This would be a nice time to pay a visit to Mimi. Bring Bella,*" Edy had guardedly written his mother. Postcards were the only mail the Germans allowed the Graylois to receive from outside the Occupied

Sigmar's nephew Edmond "Edy" Cahen, a captain in the French Army, was held in Switzerland under terms of asylum after the Germans conquered France.

Zone, and unless their subject was tightly focused on family matters, censors destroyed them. But between Edy's lines, Sigmar read a clear warning, one he found troubling not for its message, but rather for what it left out. Take Bella and maneuver *now* to get out of Gray and the Occupied Zone and into the so-called Free Zone by going "to visit" Mimi in Lyon, Edy advised. Of Sigmar and Alice, of Janine and Trudi, Edy wrote not a word. No, the nephew Sigmar loved like a son had no word for them, nothing, despite all Sigmar had done to shield Edy's mother and Bella since fleeing Mulhouse the previous year.

"*Amène Bella. Amène Bella,*" Sigmar muttered under his breath, indignant that Edy would instruct Marie to bring the housekeeper while blithely ignoring the rest of the family. Shame at reading his sister's mail without her permission, albeit a postcard, prevented Sigmar from raising the issue with her. The unexpectedness of his nephew's counsel also caught him off guard. Prohibited as a Jew from owning a radio and relying for news on the local newspaper—with *La Presse Grayloise* now heavily censored by the German *Kommandantur*—it was hard to know how the war was progressing. Carefully molding public opinion, the paper prominently featured reports of German triumphs in battle and warned that French "terrorists" faced execution.

So, Sigmar wondered, was it better to sit tight in Gray, where his friendship with Fimbel offered protection? Or would they be safer, as Edy suggested, in the unoccupied sector controlled by Pétain, a man who could not be expected to stick out his neck to save foreign-born Jews who ran there to hide? Even assuming they might be safer in Lyon, could they obtain transit papers to allow them to leave? Where would they live? And what about Norbert? They had heard nothing from him since he left with the Legion. Now that France was out of the war, what if his son made his way back to Gray only to find the family gone?

He decided to broach these questions to Fimbel when the mayor came to see him that evening, but his friend began by relaying terrible news. As part of a broad-scale roundup of Jews in Baden and other German border regions, the Nazis had deported to the French camp of Gurs every last Jew they could still find in Freiburg. Sigmar sat stunned. Fräulein Ellenbogen, Frau Loewy, all their friends still in

the city when he'd fled with his family from Freiburg to Mulhouse—
had they escaped, or had they been seized? His own complacency,
remaining this long in occupied Gray, now seemed insane. Survival
meant evading the Germans, not living as literal neighbors with the
Kommandantur headquartered in the town's former Chamber of Commerce just two doors away from the family's apartment. With new
urgency, Sigmar laid out his dilemma to Fimbel, who described in
sobering detail the hurdles involved in crossing the border to the so-
called Free Zone.

The border was virtually sealed, Fimbel said, unless one acquired a
safe-conduct pass, which required approval from the German *Komman-*
dantur. With demand rising daily, desperate applicants swamped town
hall with requests for permission to cross the Demarcation Line between the two zones. Once processed by the French, all paperwork went
to the German command. But the Germans systematically rejected any
requests from Jews, and even non-Jews had to prove compelling reasons
in order to gain the passes they needed: sick or dying relatives, children or parents in need of help, or faltering businesses that demanded
attention. The postmaster, Malou's father Monsieur Gieselbrecht, was
secretly signing false papers that testified to telephone calls received at
the *Poste* from outside the Occupied Zone, urgently summoning people
home. As to fellow Alsatians who now risked being forced to fight in the
German Army, Monsieur Fimbel was providing false identity papers to
help them slip out of sight before they were drafted.

According to André Fick, among Frenchmen from Alsace-Lorraine
whom the Germans would eventually draft to fight for the Reich in
bloody Eastern Front battles, many deserters fled to Gray, having
heard that the Alsatian-born mayor could arrange their "rebirth." He
gave them new names and work as laborers assigned to restore the
war-torn farmland around the city. Trusted *passeurs* smuggled some
to safety in Switzerland or over the line to the Unoccupied Zone, and
later helped others escape to North Africa to join what was left of the
Free French Army. Mayor Fimbel hid some escapees in trucks that
carried supplies to larger towns like Dijon, where he reluctantly left
them to plot their next moves, and he personally drove others up to

the border, where a well-placed bribe of cognac, champagne, tobacco, or coffee could help raise the barriers. When the Nazis started hunting down Jews, the Marist mayor would help them flee, too, saving scores by furnishing them with transit papers, by warning targets of impending arrest, and by hiding others in the secluded countryside homes of his former students.

For his clandestine efforts, Joseph Fimbel depended upon a close, loyal team, and he soon suggested to Sigmar that Janine might come to work for him at the *mairie*. Her fluency in German and French, he said, would be valuable in helping his office cope with the flood of requests for safe-conduct passes. She could not be officially paid, but the job would offer unspoken potential. From a desk in town hall, Janine would deal with the many who frantically begged for papers to cross out of the zone and would help them fill out their forms in ways that bolstered their reasons to leave. Every few days, prepared to face questions, she would be sent with a stack of requests to the *Kommandant*, who examined these papers and signed the ones he chose to approve.

In retrospect, it is hard to believe that neither the mayor nor Sigmar addressed the risk of such regular contact with the German command, and that Janine herself, at just seventeen, would brave the perils of serving as an emissary between the *mairie* and the *Kommandantur*. Yet she leaped at the chance with enthusiasm and an unfamiliar sense of importance. She would later observe that the job in which she was so out of place that it put her in danger—a German Jewish refugee working in daily contact with a *Wehrmacht* commander who assumed she was French—made her feel, for the first time since leaving Roland, that her days had meaning and that she belonged. Applicants arrived at her desk with fear of rejection etched on their faces, and she tried to assist them. In front of the Germans, she did not let on that she was Jewish *or* German, and granted license to pretend to be French, she clung to that guise from that moment forward.

A new identity card, signed and stamped with the seal of the city and made out for her by André Fick, her supervisor, gives touching proof of his zeal to protect her. All the requisite information is duly recorded: her real name, along with the blue whorl of a fingerprint and a picture in which she appears completely untroubled, full cheeked,

Janine's new identity card, prepared by André Fick, attempted to conceal her German nationality.

wide-eyed, fresh, and smiling, in a ribbed turtleneck sweater with a pin at her throat:

SIZE: *1 meter 68*
HAIR: *chestnut*
MUSTACHE: *none*
EYES: *blue*
NOSE: *straight*

FACE SHAPE: *oblong*
SKIN COLOR: *light*
DISTINGUISHING MARKS: *none visible*

Domicile? The answer, *Gray*, is one André Fick wrote in script at least four times the size of any other word on the card. But as to nationality, he scrawled a response in letters so tiny, obscured beneath the stamp of the city, that even with a powerful magnifying glass, the answer remains intentionally indecipherable.

Decades later, when I sat with him in front of the fireplace of his tidy home, André remembered that Trudi and Malou had found his fondness for Janine amusing. Trailing behind him, openly giggling, they made him self-conscious when he walked the streets, already feeling confused and troubled by such tender yearnings for Janine as bred guilt in the face of his spiritual goals. His longtime intent of following in his role model's footsteps—he still recalled confessing to her—would require affirming the same Marist vows that Mayor Fimbel had taken and bar him from marriage. Yet he had despaired that his affection for Janine pointed to weakness that might preclude a celibate life.

"I envisioned our having a future together," he said of Janine. Nostalgia for the long-lost girl who awakened desire overwhelmed the fact that his wife, Marguerite, was seated beside him. "But in any event, Janine said no to my vision. As she was a Jew, and I was Catholic, it just couldn't work, especially given the state of the world."

What went unsaid in 1940 and again in 2001 was that Janine had already given her love to another French Catholic who came from Mulhouse. And while Roland seemed as remote to her during her time in Gray as a matinee idol, his claim on her heart precluded all other suitors. Indeed, Janine's love for Roland had grown stronger. It burned bright and pure, untarnished by any sort of careless word or fickle deed that may dim love's ardor when, being together, a couple take each other for granted.

. . .

The *Kreiskommandant* in charge of the town was fiftyish, a *Wehrmacht* reservist called back to duty to sit at a desk, not a young, rabid Nazi flexing his muscles or a man like the captain in breeches and boots who daily rode his powerful horse through Gray's humble streets, making a splendid show of himself. That is how André Fick recalled the top officer who figured in my mother's account like a cipher, a symbol, a uniform only, a hollow man in whom I might see all of Nazism's evils or view as the rote overseer of an occupied town.

Every few days after beginning her job with the mayor, Janine entered this *Kommandant*'s office and proffered the laissez-passer, or *Ausweis*, papers to sign while she stood at his desk and considered the way he handled this work. Subordinate officers streamed in and out, the telephone rang, and weightier matters demanded attention, distracting his thoughts. The Führer's black eyes glared at her from a framed photograph affixed to the wall, but the *Kommandant* was polite in his dealings and rarely demanded more information than the papers provided. As weeks wore on, she wanted to think he was growing bored by the process, that he rushed through it faster, with less concentration, whenever the sheaf she presented was thick. On pressure-filled days, he barely bothered to read the applicants' names and their destinations, and while there were other instances when he eyed them sharply, she gradually started feeling emboldened. She moved closer in to his left, leaning over the desk, and ventured flipping the pages for him—a considerate girl— so the tops of the sheets, including applicants' names, were partially hidden. She also dared some brief conversation, assuming her French was better than his and that he would not detect a German accent that would betray her refugee status and reveal her as Jewish.

A scheme had started to form in her mind: if she slipped an extra application into the pile she presented for signing, leaving blank the names of the would-be travelers, the *Kommandant* might unwittingly sign it, enabling her family to use the pass themselves. If the German officer noticed the error, she would pretend it was simply an honest mistake. "*Oh, je m'excuse!*" She practiced shock and dismay in front of the mirror, eyes round in horror, hands clasped to her chest. She would snatch the faulty application away, berating herself with abject disgust. "But how can this be? What a stupid mistake! I don't understand how this could happen, *Herr Kommandant!*" What would he do? Would he instantly guess she had done it on purpose or chalk it up to her youth and sloppy work habits?

In mid-November, Janine decided to act, but resolved not to discuss it beforehand with anyone. She did not need to hear the dangers sketched out, as she had already done so in ample detail to frighten herself. Nor did she want to invite attempts to dissuade her, which she feared might be easy. Two weeks earlier, the Germans had suddenly evicted them from their apartment on the avenue Victor Hugo, its convenience as an officers' lodging, just steps away from the *Kommandantur*, having attracted official attention. While Sigmar suspected that the landlord no longer felt comfortable renting to Jews and had offered it up to the occupiers, the Germans in any event requisitioned whatever homes and buildings they wanted. Mayor Fimbel had helped the family relocate, yet merely venturing out on the street grew ever more perilous, and Sigmar was gripped by the urgent need to escape.

And so, as Janine steeled herself to proceed with her plan, she yearned above all to impress her father, who was bound to be grateful and think her resourceful; yes, among all her motives that one stood out—the ever-present, aching compulsion to gain Sigmar's respect. To rescue the family—what could be better? It excited her, too, to imagine telling Roland how she had managed all on her own to bring the family over the line, because if ever they managed to wiggle out of this dull little town, perhaps she would even be able to find him!

She resolved to act on a Monday, when the pile of applications had grown over the weekend, and she slipped in her own close to the bottom, by which point in his labors she hoped the *Kommandant*'s attention would flag. She shrank from the thought of arousing his anger—a thunderous storm she had already witnessed—so the ruse had to work the first time she tried it. If it failed, and he caught her "mistake," she would never dare seem so careless again. At the very least, if he noticed the application lacking a name, the German would loudly complain to the mayor, and that, she knew, would embarrass her father by reflecting unfavorably upon Monsieur Fimbel. Clearly, it might also result in her being discharged.

Over and over Janine played the scene out in her mind. Still, she had not anticipated having to lean on the *Kommandant*'s desk to steady legs that threatened to buckle or that her pounding pulse would thrum so loudly she thought he could hear it. The *Kommandant* was signing the papers, and, as she turned the pages for him, her heightened state of nervous alert exaggerated every detail: the metal scratch of his fountain pen as it changed people's lives, the tick of his watch, each dark hair or meandering vein on his bureaucrat's hands, the late-day stubble that shadowed his jaw, the roll of skin that bulged like a *Wurst* over the back of his uniform's collar. She tried to ignore authority's trappings in favor of things that made him more human: generously, she attempted to picture a sweet-faced wife, children who missed him and longed to hear the clack of his bootstep nearing their door.

Janine's nervousness grew with each paper he signed, approaching the one on which she depended. He paused, pulled out a box of cigarettes, absently tamped one down on his blotter, lit it, sighed, and leaned back in his chair. For one crazy second, she considered asking for a cigarette to bring home to Sigmar, like a big, shiny bow on top of the gift of a signed *Ausweis*. But she forced herself to encourage the *Kommandant* to get back to task: "*Nous en avons beaucoup aujourd'hui,*" so many today, she observed in a tone meant to apologize for the added burdens she brought his office. "*Oui, zu viel,*" too many, he said, awkwardly mixing both tongues, but he glanced up and gave her a resigned smile before bending back to the tedious job. She averted her eyes, afraid her delight would give her away when he signed hers.

"*Gut. Fertig,*" he said, finally done. He screwed the top on his pen, stood the sheaf on end on the desk, straightened the edges, and placed them back in the folder he handed to her. He had clipped together the ones he denied and made no mention of any on which the applicants' names had been missing. "*Merci, mademoiselle.*"

"*Vielen Dank, Herr Kommandant.*" Gratitude bloomed in her heart so sincerely that she forgot where she was and answered in German. Then she turned and hurried out of the room, eager for privacy to rifle the file for the paper she wanted.

"*Auf Wiedersehen!*" the amiable soldier who always sat guard outside the *Kommandant*'s office, eager to flirt, called down the stairs. But before his words could pierce the bubble of joy in which she was floating, the red door to the street banged shut behind her, and she was gone.

• • •

On November 20, 1940, André Fick came to see Janine off at the station, and they exchanged farewell gifts. She had painted a little landscape for him, a tranquil house in a sunny setting, and he had saved his limited pay to buy her a gold-plated bracelet. Who could say when, if ever, they might meet again? It worried André to see Janine head into the unknown, all the more when he discovered that the family's arrangements called for her to travel by train through the Occupied Zone without so much as her father's protection. Monsieur Fimbel was driving Sigmar, Alice, Marie, and Trudi straight to the border, where the mayor would add his official support to get them across. But his car couldn't hold more than five people or their many valises, so Janine was leaving by train one day ahead of her parents, accompanied by Malou, who was moving to Lyon to attend dental school.

Besides being encumbered with a dozen pieces of family luggage, the girls were charged with added responsibility for Bella and her sister, Pauline, who had unexpectedly turned up in Gray two weeks before, begging to add her name to their papers. To make matters worse, the two aging sisters all too closely resembled the ugly propagandist depictions of Jews widely being displayed by the Nazis. And the fact that ulcerous sores on Pauline's swollen legs made walking slow and painful for her did not augur well for quickly escaping from tight situations. Beyond such immediate doubts as to the wisdom of Janine's traveling unguarded, André also realized that life in the Unoccupied Zone would not necessarily guarantee German Jewish refugees the level of safety they seemed to expect. This impelled him to prepare another, more important farewell present: two letters, carefully worded on official Gray City Hall stationery, both misspelling the family name (using an *s* instead of a *z*) to make it more French.

In the first, written in both French and German but aimed at appeasing the Germans in case the refugees were stopped en route, he falsely attested that "*Monsieur and Madame Gunsburger and their children will leave our city to return to their domicile in Lyon.*" As their address he cited the Lyon apartment that actually belonged to Marie's daughter. In the second, meant for the French under Pétain, he provided a character reference: "*I, the undersigned Mayor of the City of Gray, certify that during the entirety of their stay in our city, the family S. Gunsburger has conducted itself in the most satisfying manner and has always demonstrated the best Francophile feelings.*"

RÉPUBLIQUE FRANÇAISE

Mairie de Gray

(Haute-Saône)

TÉLÉPHONE 91

Objet :

Gray, le   19.Oktober   19340.

Certificat.   Bescheinigung

Nous soussigné,Maire de la   Der Unterzeichnete Bürgermeister
Ville de Gray,certifions que Monsieur   bestätigt dass Herr und Frau Gunz-
Madame GUNSBURGER et leurs enfants,   burger ihren die Stadt GRAY verlas-
vont quitter notre ville pour rejoin-   sen, um ihren neuen Wohnsitz LYON,
dre leur domicile à Lyon,rue de l'ho-   99 rue de l'Hôtel de Ville, zu er-
tel de Ville .   reichen. (adresse von M.Goldschmidt
      En foi de quoi nous avons   Lyon)
délivré le présent pour servir ce que
da droit.   Der Bürgermeister
                                          I. V.

To help the Günzburgers escape the Occupied Zone, André Fick falsely attested under the seal of the city that the family's regular domicile was in Lyon, in the Unoccupied Zone.

As he had done several times before on official letters aimed at helping Janine's family—even when, twisting facts, he placed himself in jeopardy—he signed these for the mayor, *A. Fick*, and to each signature boldly added the stamp of the *mairie*.

"Just in case . . . these may one day prove useful," he said. He shrugged as if to discount their value, reluctant to put new fears in her mind.

"*Chagrin.*" Sorrow. That was the word he used more than six decades later, when he tried to describe the scene at the station, when "Janine went into exile" and for the first time he had shyly opened his arms to embrace her. Both had wept, full of regret for the sweet and clumsy dance of their friendship, never defined and now ending. Then he stood on the platform and waved until the train and the girl disappeared from his life, chugging down the tracks into the hazy vanishing point of an uncertain future.

The first leg of the trip took the four women southwest to Dole, where they planned to change onto a northwest train bound for Dijon. Leaving from there the following morning, a third train would carry them to the border crossing where they'd arranged to rendezvous with the rest of the family. As an added precaution, Malou's father, an Alsatian by birth and a German Army veteran of the previous war, had made contact with an old army buddy, now a general in charge of that border location. Monsieur Gieselbrecht explained to his former comrade-in-arms that his daughter was crossing with dear Jewish friends, and the German general replied with assurance that he would personally meet them and warrant they made it safely over the line. But just before the women reached their first destination, German soldiers strode through the train, ordering everyone to get off in Dole. "Last stop! *Alle müssen aussteigen!*" they shouted. All passenger trains in the region were canceled until further notice.

In despair, the women sat in tears on their trunks in front of the station, when a German lieutenant, strolling by, stopped and courteously offered to help them. He and another soldier were heading for Dijon that same afternoon, he said, driving two large *Wehrmacht* trucks with space to spare for two lovely girls. If the girls could wait, he and his friend would shortly return in the trucks to collect them, and, if the girls would promise to dine with them when they reached Dijon, he was sure to find room for their considerable luggage. If Pauline and Bella were willing to ride in the back of a truck, they were welcome to hitch a ride too. That the soldier suggestively winked at this point while describing the bargain was not reassuring, but with no other way to advance toward the border or alert the family of their predicament, the girls saw no option but to accept.

As soon as he left to go for the trucks, however, Malou attacked the valises and furiously started yanking off tags. "How could your father have let us go off with Jewish names plastered all over this stuff!" she demanded. "Günzburger! Cahen! Picard! Doesn't he realize what's going on? We must be crazy! Who knows whether that guy already noticed the names on your tags and just left to get help to arrest us? They'll probably drive us to Dijon, try to have some fun on the way, and then turn us over to the Gestapo."

Within the hour, two open-backed trucks drew up in front of the station. As the lieutenant had promised, he and his fellow soldier loaded the luggage into one of the trucks and then boosted Bella and her lumbering sister into the back of the other. The only item that Bella took with her was Sigmar's little brown suitcase packed with his papers and Alice's silver. The lieutenant invited Malou into the cab of his truck, Janine climbed into the cab of the other, and they set off. As the day quickly darkened and they drove through the woods near Besançon, Janine and her driver chatted pleasantly. She allowed herself to trust that the soldiers, both in their twenties, were simply out for some innocent female companionship and had no intention of causing them harm. Suddenly, the other truck, leading the way, swerved to the shoulder and slammed to a stop. Both doors burst opened, Malou leaped out the passenger side, waving her arms and berating the German, while he jumped from the driver's side, shouting back at her, red faced and louder.

"*Vous êtes des salauds!*" You bastards! Malou was screaming. Her hot words smoked in the cold night air. "I hate you! You think Jews and Communists are problems for France? You Boches are the ones destroying our country! I only wish you'd all drop dead and leave us in peace! I want nothing to do with any of you! Go to hell!" The soldier was glaring at her, and Janine rushed to his side in an effort to calm him.

"Please, please, you must understand," she begged, grabbing the lieutenant by both arms and babbling excuses. "Her only brother—she loved him so much—he was killed last June in the fighting," she found herself lying. "She's still mourning for him. But her father is Alsatian, and just like you, he was an officer in the German Army in the last war. Malou doesn't mean what she's saying. I swear, that's just grief you hear talking! This has nothing to do with you. You have to believe me!"

The officer's arms were folded in front of his chest, and he sullenly stared into the woods. A drizzle had started, the raindrops audibly tapping the dry, brittle leaves that lay on the ground, and Janine was shivering. She remembered Bella and Pauline huddled together in the back of the open truck and couldn't imagine what they would do if the Germans abandoned them with all their bags at the side of this black, forsaken road, with the rest of her family waiting for them.

"Please understand," she repeated, ashamed of the desperation she heard in her voice. The soldier turned on his heel.

"*Ja, ich verstehe*," he finally said, his voice clipped. "These are not simple times." He beckoned to Malou. "Come on now," he said, his voice softening, "get back in the truck. We have to move on."

Outside Dijon, the lieutenant pulled off the road again, waved the second truck over, and came to its window to consult with his comrade, prompting Malou to rush over behind him. The lieutenant pressed for arranging hotel rooms before going to dinner, but Malou, reminding him of Bella and Pauline—cold, wet, hungry, and tired—sketched out another plan of her own.

"Why don't you drop us at the station, so we can leave our maids with the luggage to wait for us there?" she brightly suggested. "While you gentlemen find us rooms, we'll change into something pretty. Then we'll gladly join you for dinner and anything else you have in mind. Bella and Pauline won't mind spending the night on a bench at the station."

When they reached the city, and the soldiers drove off, promising to return for them within the hour, Malou proposed that she and Janine hide for the night in the stalls of the ladies' restroom. Pauline and Bella would remain in the waiting room, prepared to provide a convincing account when the Germans showed up: the girls, they were instructed to claim, had already left for the evening to meet up with them. They had said not to worry, they would probably not be back until morning, since they were planning to spend the night with the soldiers in a hotel. Sorry, no, they left no other message.

After rehearsing the story, the girls went into the restroom, locked themselves into two stalls, and tried to rest. The air in the station was clammy and cold, but they drifted into a light, fitful sleep until a few hours later, when an attendant barged into the bathroom, banging on doors and calling their names. "Janine! Malou! Janine! Malou!" she sang out their names in a volume that easily carried out to the hallway where the soldiers were waiting and hollowly echoed through the cavernous station.

"There are two German soldiers outside looking for a Malou and Janine. *C'est vous deux?*" the wide-eyed attendant clutching a broom asked in a hush when the girls slid open the bolts and peeked out of the stalls. They would later debate whether the woman had believed their denials. "*D'accord,*" okay, she said, nodding, and she left to report to the soldiers that the girls were not there. Come morning, Janine and Malou emerged and rejoined Bella and Pauline, and with great relief they managed to catch a train to the border.

Janine never recalled the name of the town. What she distinctly remembered was feeling deserted and panicked when she went with Malou to find Monsieur Gieselbrecht's friend, the German general who had promised to help them. Pauline and Bella remained at the station with the baggage, while the two girls set off on foot for the German's home, having been told to meet him there and not at the local *Kommandantur*, where their visit might prompt unwanted attention.

At a fine country house surrounded by a low stone wall, Malou told Janine to wait outside while she went in to meet the general and explain their needs, which included retrieving the baggage and Bella and Pauline from the train station and taking them all to the border crossing. But long minutes passed, and then so did hours. Malou did not reappear, and Janine grew increasingly frantic, pacing the street and watching the door. She was afraid for her friend, but just as afraid of ringing the bell and blundering into Malou's maneuvers. At long last, when the door opened, Malou bounced down the steps, tossing her head of shiny curls and smiling back at the general over her shoulder. Janine sprang to her feet and searched her friend's face, alarmed to think what might have kept her so long.

"Oh, what a time we have had!" Malou gaily announced. "The general gave me a splendid lunch and he's been telling me about all the daring exploits he shared with my father during the war."

By the time the general sent a truck to the station and personally drove Malou and Janine to the crossing point, the family was already there, apprehensively waiting. Introductions were made, Mayor Fimbel shook hands with the German, and Sigmar doffed his hat, inclined his head in a respectful bow, and offered the general effusive thanks. With perfunctory scrutiny, the general glanced at their papers, then he ordered a soldier to lift the barriers and, snapping his fingers, he summoned others to carry the luggage across. The women sailed through the border onto the terra firma of the Unoccupied Zone with the grace and refinement of dancing a waltz.

In three separate runs, Mayor Fimbel and Sigmar then shuttled the women and baggage to the nearest train station where they would leave for Lyon. It was the last the two men would see of each other. As the gangly Alsatian and his short German friend clasped one another in a farewell embrace, they called on the God they shared to protect them both through the perils lying ahead.

And yet, who could have predicted the future course of events? Before the end, the Jew would escape the fate the Nazis intended. But the mayor of Gray, a man suspected by his townspeople of being a little too cozy with the occupiers, and even disdained by some as a collaborator, would be arrested by the Gestapo and then deported to Buchenwald.

．　．　．

On the holiday morning of May 1, 1944, when the *mairie* was closed and the streets were festive, agents of the Nazi secret police sent from Dijon, acting on orders from the Gestapo in Paris, burst into the school Saint-Pierre-Fourier in Gray, where Monsieur Fimbel had continued to live and to work while serving as mayor. Armed with pistols and submachine guns, a commando raid of about sixty men— German SS and military as well as members of the traitorous French

Milice all dressed in black—followed them in and tore though the school hunting for Alsatian deserters and members of the Resistance they had come to suspect the mayor of hiding. The Nazis left with five people, including the mayor, and threw them in prison in Dijon for interrogation and torture.

Having believed for years that their hand-picked mayor was doing their bidding, the Germans now understood the mask he was wearing. Fimbel was actually running his own covert intelligence network, eventually even printing counterfeit cards of laissez-passer in the newspaper office, so that people marked for arrest, resisters and Jews, seemed to disappear into the air only hours before they were to be seized.

"We could fool the Germans for quite a long time because they were rather naïve," André Fick told me, "but there arrived a moment when it didn't work anymore."

Three months later, Fimbel scrawled a message on a piece of wrapping paper that found its way out to his friends in Gray through a sympathetic German monk (Alfred Stanke, later renowned as the Franciscan of Bourges) who worked in the prison: "I am on a list of those leaving," Fimbel wrote. "Do not worry about me. I will return soon. God will guard me. . . . My heart is with you."

According to André Brissinger, a fellow Marist who wrote a detailed account of Fimbel's year-long ordeal in the grip of the Nazis, Gray's mayor was sent by train with eighty others to the woods of Compiègne, not far from the spot where the Germans accepted defeat in 1918 and where Hitler laid down the terms of French surrender in 1940. There, on August 17, 1944, the SS forced Fimbel and hundreds of French deportees into sweltering cattle cars without food or water for a journey that lasted four days and ended in death for many of them. Among the dead were those shot in reprisal for thirty prisoners who managed to gouge a hole in their car and jump from the train into uncharted darkness that looked better to them than what they could see, or what they foresaw of their destination. Using dogs and searchlights, the guards gunned down or captured and viciously beat about twenty of them, and the following morning they exacted random revenge as a warning.

"*Wer kann Deutsch sprechen?*" Who speaks German? the SS officer in charge of the convoy strode down the tracks shouting, as the cars were thrown open and the cowering prisoners blinked in the sunlight. Joseph Fimbel made the mistake of proving too useful. Once again, Brissinger says, he engendered distrust when actions inspired by a longing to help tragically backfired.

"What are you going to do?" Fimbel brashly inquired of the German, after translating an order for ten of the prisoners to climb down from the train and strip off their clothes.

"Shoot them," the Nazi retorted.

"No! I beg you, don't do that!" Fimbel cried out, trying to marshal reason to save them. "Look, these are very old men. What is left of their lives will already be short. Why shoot such old men?"

"Yes, of course, you're right," the SS guard said, his voice the essence of reasonableness. He ordered the original ten back on the train and pointed to ten of the youngest on board to climb down in their places to face execution.

"Take me instead! Take me!" Fimbel insisted, already seeing the blood of young lives staining his conscience. But the ten were dragged off, followed by SS men carrying pickaxes and shovels. Gunshots exploded the peace of the forest.

Those prisoners still conscious were pleading for water when the train reached Buchenwald, the notorious Nazi labor camp on the outskirts of Weimar where fifty-six thousand suffered and died. Among its eighty thousand survivors at liberation was Léon Blum, prewar France's Jewish premier, who was blamed for defeat, condemned to life in prison by Marshal Pétain, and then, in 1943, turned over to Hitler.

Upon arrival, Fimbel's seemingly lifeless body was stripped and his Marist ring yanked from his finger before he was piled on top of a cart of cadavers headed to the crematorium. When a fellow inmate noticed him moving, he was revived, only to be sent with five hundred others to a grueling satellite camp to work in a salt mine where life meant beatings and torture, starvation and illness, topped off with a month-long death march in 1945, as the Nazis realized the Allies were coming.

On September 11, 1944, when the American Army liberated Gray, clocks were restored to their proper French time. Three months later, the local committee of the liberation elected a Jew to serve as mayor.

Joseph Fimbel, freed by Soviet soldiers, returned to Gray on May 23, 1945, weighing eighty-six pounds: the hollows of hunger were caves in his cheeks, and his shriveled skin was waxy and yellow. Like most of the clothes he had worn through his life, his striped camp uniform failed to cover his long, bony limbs. But Joseph Fimbel insisted on wearing those same wretched rags of the camp on his first night back in Gray, which he spent on his knees through long hours of prayer at Notre-Dame's altar. He later arranged for a plaque to be placed at the entrance to the chapel in grateful dedication to Mary, the Holy Mother whose compassionate smile and promise of grace had sustained him throughout his descent into hell.

This plaque would prove his only memorial in Gray, besides the portrait that hangs in the town hall gallery of mayors. On May 1, 1954, however, a decade after his arrest by the Nazis, the French government honored his actions by naming him a Chevalier of the Legion of Honor. Fellow deportees from the Buchenwald subcamp appeared at the ceremony, expressing appreciation and lending witness to the courage and selflessness of Joseph Fimbel's service to them in the face of tremendous personal peril. The grand rabbi of Lyon sent a message thanking him for individually saving at least sixty Jews, and the Germans, too, would later honor him for his postwar endeavors promoting forgiveness and friendship between the two countries.

The Catholic mayor of Gray, Joseph Fimbel, was deported as a political prisoner to the concentration camp of Buchenwald near Weimar, Germany.

"When Fimbel returned from Buchenwald, that's when people recognized the work he had done, because during the Occupation, there was always a certain suspicion," André Fick said, describing the day the Alsatian mayor finally won the respect he deserved.

André also gained recognition, in 1958, when he was awarded the Military Cross of the Resistance in a ceremony on the town hall plaza. Yet, despite the passing of decades and Fimbel's death in 1978, it remained his keenest desire for Gray to pay homage to the former mayor by dedicating a street in his name. When I volunteered my support to such a campaign, his wife shot him a look of definitive warning. This was clearly a road they had traveled before, and Marguerite did not intend to go back where it led or to revive the uncomfortable feelings the issue provoked for their neighbors, many of

André Fick was decorated with the Croix de la Résistance in 1958.

whom apparently still nurtured conflicted views on Mayor Fimbel's performance in Gray under the Nazis.

"Moïse Lévy has a street named for him, and he did far less!" André complained to his wife. A childlike tone of indignation made his voice quaver. "Moïse Lévy was the administrator of Gray for a much longer time, but in an *époque* that was *bien banale*, humdrum and peaceful. To do what Fimbel did for four years under German occupation, to save so many people—that deserves more!"

Marguerite stared at him and did not reply. The petite white-haired lady was a serious force. After waiting in silence, André turned to me and threw up his hands. "My wife does not want me to pursue it, and I cannot go against her," he said. "I would have liked to do it out of fidelity to him—my patron, my director, my teacher—out of gratitude to him."

Near sunset on that day of Gray's races in 2001, after the last contestant had crossed the line, André Fick took me to the top of the town to the Basilique Notre-Dame. In retirement, he had become the church organist, and he was pleased when I asked to hear him play. Through the organ, he had continued serving the town while finding his personal form of devotion to Mary—not the one he imagined at twenty-three, in the thrall of his mentor, but one that he could fully express with a wife at his side. We arrived just as the priest was locking the doors, but with dispensation graciously granted, Marguerite and I followed her husband up the spiral stone steps of the fifteenth-century church into the organ's high vaulted home. With little ado but evident pride in his church, André started to play, drawing the stops and pressing the keys. Music swelled through the nave, and the humming chords of his hymn rose through the restored bell tower to drift in the twilight, surprising the town that was spread out below us, preparing for dinner. His impromptu recital was a peaceful close to a day that had wakened to the tumult of athletes speeding through narrow Renaissance streets, crowds cheering at corners, and loudspeakers blaring. That evening, I would leave feeling grateful for the quiet bravery of all the Ficks and the Fimbels—people who risk their lives to wrestle with power in places whose names are not even footnotes in history's pages.

ELEVEN

THE SUN KING

On Christmas Day of 1940, Roland Arcieri happily found himself alone in Lyon with a room of his own, the princely sum of 30,000 francs in his pocket, and the world at his feet. He was twenty years old when he maneuvered off the bus from Villefranche, and despite the burden of all his possessions, he felt buoyed by a new and electric feeling of freedom. The rest of his family had left Villefranche to move back to Mulhouse just the previous day. But he felt no self-pity as he crossed the bare ground of the place Bellecour at a time when even the Sun King looked lonely and cold atop his bronze horse in the square, and everyone else was celebrating with family members, making do with such feasts as rations allowed. Rather, as Roland prowled the city, now quiet and empty, he viewed its streets as his for the claiming. He discovered it all with the fresh eye of youth and a conqueror's glee, undoubtedly equal to any sense of triumphant arrival that even King Louis XIV had known.

Roland surveyed his domain in leisurely fashion. "No point in rushing," he was known to joke with a shrug of the shoulders. "We'll all arrive at the end of the month at the very same time." He paused on the sidewalk beyond the barren sweep of the square and its simple border of skeletal trees that left it begging for more decoration, put down his bags in front of a bookshop, and peered in the window. The shop was gated and closed. But as Roland stared into the gloom, it was almost as if he might already catch a glimpse of himself perusing book titles—works of biography, history, and literature, and even the odd, naughty bit of *grivoiserie*—browsing, unhurried, through stacks of books laid out on the tables, no longer bound to run for the bus to Villefranche at the end of the day.

Ah, the pleasure of knowing his time was his own, finally freed from his father's ten p.m. curfew and being called to account for every coin that fell out of his pocket. He was more than ready to dive into life, *la bonne soupe, la grande liberté*! Never mind his tight student budget or his father's well-meaning yet tedious warning that the money he gave him was intended to last for two or three years. He took note of intriguing bars and cafés that he had never before had time to explore and permitted himself to thrill in the knowledge that everything strange would soon be familiar. Then there would be a new kind of pleasure—feeling at home in this elegant, cosmopolitan city, a man in the world, making his way. At last his life was truly beginning.

He had come to Lyon for the ostensible purpose of studying law. This is what his father believed, and he therefore tried, at least for a while, to believe it himself. For the previous year, while commuting to classes, he had also fulfilled his military service by attending twice-weekly officer training sessions and made the one-hour trip to Lyon by bus every day. His family had decamped from Mulhouse to Villefranche six weeks after war was declared, when the textile firm that employed his father and uncle acted well in advance of any invasion to shift some operations out of Alsace. The firm had mills in Villefranche, a small commercial, industrial town northwest of Lyon, chiefly distinguished as capital of the Beaujolais winemaking region.

Here, as part of the company's managerial class, the Arcieri brothers resettled in style in a spacious villa just a bike ride away from a stretch of the Saône that was verdant and tranquil. The house was not far either from the lively main street, the rue Nationale, which rolled over a hill through town like a great wave, bereft of trees or even the simple appeal of a planned public square. Except for the local church and a few houses of historical merit, the street's unbroken façade of four-story buildings with shops on both sides included little of any real interest or beauty. Still it drew out the crowds for the ritual promenade in the evenings, which served here, also, as prime entertainment with the promise of people meeting each other.

In this provincial milieu, a young man like Roland did not go unnoticed. Tall and exceedingly handsome, he exuded an air of brooding reserve and poetic detachment that only added to his allure.

Conversely, he could transform the slightest occasion into a party by way of his own wholehearted, delighted engagement, and as the only son between two loving sisters, he responded to women with natural charm. His silken attentions were validating without being demanding, and by always displaying impeccable manners, he put women at ease. Innately, he knew how to make them feel lovely and wanted, reflecting their most attractive view of themselves.

Before long, the young man who had shyly shared first kisses with Janine as they lay in the river reeds of Mulhouse fell under the spell of a woman a decade older than he. The moral distinctions that strictly confined the sexual rites of his generation would not have allowed him to take advantage of a respectable, inexperienced girl. But when the beautiful wife of a high-ranking French reserve officer called up to war invited Roland to sample a full range of intimate pleasures, he could find no reason not to accept. Set aside was the fact that her absent husband happened to be one of his father's important business associates.

She was a former haute-couture model from Paris. Roland suspected she'd met and married her textile magnate through a thread in the weave of fabric and fashion, expecting a life of luxurious privilege. With her husband at war, however, she was bored and cut off in her place of safekeeping in crusty Villefranche, sufficiently bored, it would shortly be clear, to risk introducing a special young man to the petaled secrets that bloomed in her bed. Within a few months of the Arcieris' arrival, she had picked Roland out on the rue Nationale. But it was his father, Emil, who inadvertently brought them together by hosting a company dinner that first Christmas in town where they wound up sitting across from each other. Before the main course at the city's best restaurant, her wriggling toes were creeping under the cuffs of the young man's trousers and brashly teasing their way up his calves. She smiled and daintily sipped at her wine and exchanged pleasantries with all of the guests, company people with their spouses and children, even as she pursued her adventure.

After the New Year, she approached Emil at the office to ask a favor. She was planning an extended visit to Lyon, she said, and wondered if she might borrow Roland to help with her luggage on the train to the city. There was too much for a woman like her to manage alone. But when Roland showed up at her door as requested, he was nonplussed to discover she had already sent her baggage ahead and so was encumbered only by a small alligator train case and a high-strung fox terrier named Pepi. She insisted nonetheless that Roland come along, and when they descended in Lyon and reached her hotel, she was pleased to invite him up to her room. In the period that followed, instead of pondering inheritance law, Roland attended his own private classes in a subject of far more immediate interest. This understandably helped to chase Janine from his thoughts and succeeded in making the *drôle de guerre* all the more *drôle* as long as it lasted.

. . .

The Arcieris assumed they were safe in Villefranche until the fighting broke out the following spring of 1940, and when the Germans arrived within twenty miles of town, they reacted in terror with everyone else. Loaded in two cars and a truck filled with bolts of company fabrics, the Arcieris joined the mass exodus, traveling over the volcanic peaks of the Massif Central, southwest toward Toulouse and the border of Spain. When they ran out of gas, they readily measured and traded yard goods for distance, the fabric that always paid them their wages serving them now directly as money. Indeed, its value was even more reliably stable than the teetering franc, given the fact that the country itself stood naked and shuddering while the Germans pursued their relentless assault.

By June 19, 1940, five days after the Germans took Paris, Lyon declared itself an open city, avoiding attack by permitting the *Wehrmacht* to enter without opposition. The same day, a swastika flew over the entrance of its ornate city hall; German military bands exultantly marched on the place Bellecour with tubas, trumpets, drums, and trombones; and the beloved place des Terreaux with its opulent Bartholdi fountain and outdoor cafés was transformed into an assembly point for enemy troops and the spot the *Wehrmacht* selected for parking its trucks. Before the Germans' withdrawal from this first occupation of Lyon the following month, ten thousand French prisoners of war would be locked into its Part-Dieu barracks and most then deported to face nearly five years in prison over the border.

The Wehrmacht *parked its trucks on the beautiful place des Terreaux behind Lyon's seventeenth-century hôtel de ville (city hall).*

With the unexpected fall of the country, the Arcieris returned to Villefranche, where they remained until almost the end of the year, when their company summoned them home to Mulhouse. The armistice, by shifting the border once more and labeling Alsatians as Germans again, placed the Arcieri sons, Roland and his younger cousin André, at new risk. Although born in the period Alsace was French, they could now be forced to take up arms for the Führer. But Roland's parents would not play along: they decided instead to leave him behind in the Unoccupied Zone, where the hazards of being twenty years old, fit, and Alsatian were far less likely to result in his being sent into battle. André, then sixteen, would return to school in Mulhouse, his parents convinced that before *he* reached the age of conscription, the British would also cave in to Hitler and the war would be over. It was thoroughly inconceivable to them that four years later, England would still be toughing it out with the help of its allies, and André would be caught in the carnage of Hitler's attempt to overtake Russia. Among 130,000 young Alsatians forced to fight for the Reich, André made it back, but there were 36,000 others who would never return.

As 1940 drew to a close, before going back home, Emil arranged the details of life for his son in Lyon. He rented a room in a war widow's apartment in a sedate part of town, secured him a part-time job in a notary's office, and urged him on with his study of law. None of which Roland would have chosen: the widow's apartment remote and confining, the job ill paying and dreary, and the law a subject of dubious value in a world where authority devolved from force of arms. Who, Roland wondered, decided these matters, all the harsh new rules and restrictions that popped up every day in official pronouncements from Vichy? Where was the law endorsed by the people that gave Germans the right to dictate from Paris? That empowered Pétain—a man Roland viewed as a senile, self-righteous, sanctimonious toady— the right to act on behalf of the nation? Just days before, Pétain had banished from Lyon its beloved mayor, Edouard Hérriot, who had served in that post for thirty-five years, but had opposed the armistice with Hitler and abstained from the parliamentary vote that granted the marshal unlimited power. No, from Roland's perspective, the law didn't make much sense anymore. "*Le droit mène à tout,*" his father had told him. The law leads to everything. To which Roland had retorted, "*Oui, le droit mène à tout—à condition d'en sortir!*" Yes, it leads to everything, on the condition that you can escape it.

Ambition was still not the thing that sparked Roland to action. Not the glitter of wealth, the rescue of country, the lust for battle, or the cause that captured his talents and time. The confusion of his national background—Italian, French, German, Alsatian—only fed his cynicism. He saw himself as less inclined to fight for ideals than to dwell in ideas, as an observer or critical thinker rather than as a reformer or soldier. Little use did he find for nationalism, militarism, or even patriotism that set populations to destroy one another, laying claim to individual freedom. Although reared as a Catholic, he distrusted the hold of religion that tended to choke the joy out of life through rigid, judgmental codes of behavior and the sting of guilt whipping the conscience. His convivial spirit favored inclusion, and—while Vichy fell in step with the Nazis and anti-Semitism crept into the open—he would notice only in retrospect that his own closest friends all had been Jews.

Politically, Roland was decidedly liberal, and he reacted with disdain and revulsion to the rightist "rehabilitation" of France fustily championed by Marshal Pétain. That past November, when the marshal paraded through Lyon to rally morale and garner support, Roland had remained at home rather than witness the crowd's adulation, but the city's newspapers described it all. Four months after the German Army withdrew from Lyon, banner headlines attested to the public acclaim that served to create the aura and pretense, at least for a day, of a populace thrilled by the outcome of war that imposed defeat but avoided destruction.

WITH ALL ITS SOUL LYON ACCLAIMS PÉTAIN, the front page of *Le Nouveau Journal* declared on that Tuesday, November 19. Pictures showed the old Verdun hero standing in uniform in the back of an open car with motorcycle escorts guarding his flanks, as he rode through the streets saluting the thousands who packed the sidewalks and fervently cheered all along the route of procession. People still smarting from France's ignominious fall yearned to find the resolve of a leader— someone to blaze a trail to the future by restoring a version of France that was lost in the past—in a man over eighty who slept during meetings and was ready to do the enemy's bidding.

Roland tried to blot it all out. He rushed headlong and laughing toward what he enjoyed, rejecting Vichy's dour nose-to-the-grindstone perspective in favor of his own manifesto. With everything in a state of upheaval, what sense did it make to worry or work or save for the future? With the country grappling with transition and loss, he would content himself with owning the present. *On verra ça après la guerre*— we'll see about it after the war—was the motto Roland adopted. He quit his stifling notary job, started cutting law school lectures, and spent his days with like-minded students who directed their competitive zeal to winning at cards—belote and bridge the games they favored. After the armistice the previous June, when his paramour of six lively months returned to the arms of her husband home from the front, Roland plunged into bridge as a daily obsession. In that he excelled, his observant nature and analytical skills adding to his luck as a player. Freely he spent the money he had, particularly once his parents left him to live in Lyon alone.

On n'est jamais aussi bien servi que par soi-même. His father's old maxim provided a measure of justification: one is never as generously served as by oneself. But in his case, in serving himself, he also genially treated his friends. His own munificence tugged at his pockets and stretched them wider than they were deep, a condition that worried him not at all.

As in Villefranche or Mulhouse before, but now on a far more glamorous scale, Roland found his way in the evenings to the route of Lyon's informal parade. It progressed up and down the broad rue de la République, one of the main boulevards of the Presqu'île, the vital center strip of the city, whose name describes its formation as "almost an island." It is a long, narrow, bustling peninsula between two rivers: the Saône to the west, the Rhône to the east, with twenty-eight bridges then spanning their waters. (The Germans would later bomb twenty-seven.) Streetcars ran on the rue de la République in both directions, their overhead cables tracing spidery webs against the sky. And just as Roland had determined in Mulhouse, with streetcars obscuring the view of the opposite sidewalk, it was essential to walk on the "right" side. After all, why waste one's time on the *trottoir des cocus* and miss spotting the friends one most hoped to encounter? Here he instantly sensed that the west was the side where the young people walked, and among the throngs, Roland bumped into a fellow university student, Roger Dreyfus, whom he had known slightly in Mulhouse and latched on to now as the closest of friends.

A thin young man of twenty-two with straight dark hair, jug ears, and angular features, Roger was not only Alsatian, but also, given his name, unmistakably Jewish. This was a fact that Roland never stopped to consider when they decided to live together and rented a room

Roger Dreyfus, Roland's closest friend and roommate

that suited their most dramatic sense of themselves. It was a small, bohemian bachelor pad at 27 rue Puits Gaillot, across from city hall and the Opéra, at the foot of the rue de la République. It meant four flights of stairs, sharing a bed, forgoing a kitchen, and making do with a bath in the hall, but from their garret window with a view of the Rhône, they were face-to-face with the eight white marble female figures in classical robes posed along the roof of the Opéra. In the morning when he opened his shutters and when evening came and he closed them again, Roland greeted the one on the corner, an encouraging muse with a lyre in her arm.

In the winter of 1941, a month or so after his move to the city, Roland was strolling on the rue de la République when, from a block away, he spotted Janine. He could tell who it was by the way she was standing: *midi moins dix* as she tilted a tiny bit to the left. Her sister, Trudi, was with her, and they had stopped to examine a window display, so despite his self-imposed interdiction on rushing and his reluctance to appear overeager, he quickened his pace to catch up with them.

He was halfway there when Janine noticed him coming, a fantasy materializing out of her dreams—hatless, his overcoat billowing behind his long legs, a furled umbrella like a sword at his side. Everything and everyone else on the street turned blurry around him. There was only Roland, smiling now, raising his hand to catch her attention, a gesture confirming the reality of him. Silence descended—everything muffled but the crazy, dancing beat of her heart. In how many ways had she imagined this moment in the year and a half since they had parted, never knowing when, if ever, she might see him again? The force of her love for this beautiful man left her breathless. Even in the cold winter air, with nightfall approaching, her face felt hot, and she knew she was blushing. Her legs, rooted to the sidewalk, prevented her from running to him. How should she greet him? There was no way to guess what, if anything, she might mean to him now.

She grabbed Trudi's arm and spun her sister away from the window to look down the street. "Quick, quick!" she gasped. "Look who's headed in our direction—it's Roland! What should I say?" Before her sister could reply, he was standing before her, and Janine could not contain a radiant smile. "Roland!" she cried. It was the only word that came to her and the only thought that mattered now.

"*Eh, voilà!* Can it be true? The famous Günzburger sisters!" he greeted them jovially. "This is incredible! I never expected to run into you here! How long have you charming ladies been in Lyon? Have you really been here all of this time since leaving me behind in Mulhouse to fend off the Boches by myself?"

Uncertainly, Janine extended her hand, but Roland ignored it. He took hold of her arms and floated a gentle kiss past each cheek, more brotherly than she would have preferred. He brought a light, mocking air of ceremony to this unplanned reunion, lifting the weight of significance from it. Then he turned to Trudi and gave her the same, the grin and the kisses that promised nothing and yet had the power to evoke the unspeakable picture of his being involved with some other girl.

Janine felt unprepared and scrutinized. She regretted not having had time at least to fix her hair and lipstick before he saw her looking so rumpled. She could barely remember what she was wearing and felt herself shrinking, having imagined so many more private, perfect, romantic encounters than this accidental public meeting. So blandly polite and casually pleasant, equally pleasant to her and to Trudi. She struggled to find her voice, simultaneously self-conscious and ready to launch herself into his arms.

"What, have we been *here* all this time?" She repeated his question as if in a trance. "No, no, until mid-November we were in Gray, a little town on the Saône. But there's nothing there, no reason you'd know it." She fell silent, afraid to seem nosy, yet she needed to know where he had been for more than a year, while her most desperate desire had only been for a letter from him. "But what about you? I'd heard your family had gone to Villefranche, but there are so many, I couldn't imagine which one you'd gone to. I only hoped you weren't called up to the army. . . ."

Roland threw back his head and laughed. "Which Villefranche? Are there really that many? I spent almost all the time not far from here in Villefranche-sur-Saône. If only you'd dropped a note in a bottle, it could have floated straight downstream to me! Or you yourself might have taken a swim and come for a visit! Now, *that* would have been a friendly gesture in these miserable times."

"Oh, if only I'd known—I would have liked to." The words tumbled out, sounding plaintive and needy to her, but he just laughed again.

"*Oui*, I do seem to recall that in Mulhouse you enjoyed an occasional dip in the river," he teased.

She was mortified, sorry to have made it so clear how much she had missed him. She thought she might cry and looked at the ground, but seeing her redden, Roland rescued her feelings with a straightforward question.

"So where are you living? Are your parents and brother here with you also?" he asked, and then cut her off, interrupting her answer. "No, wait—we can't stand here like this on the street. This really calls for some celebration." He stepped between the two sisters, linking arms with a girl on each side, nodded his head toward a little café, and drew them along. "I insist," he said. "You must have time for a coffee with an old friend, or something that passes for ersatz coffee these days."

In the event, they had to settle for cups of Bovril, the beef paste tea that was becoming a staple, with everything else so meagerly rationed. It had the limited virtue of being warm. And with Roland's legs bent under the table next to her own, Janine felt certain that champagne at Versailles could not have been more golden or festive. Prolonging the moment, she sipped it slowly while studying him: the slim wrist and fingers holding his cup; the square jaw, an imperturbable stiff upper lip, yet a sensual mouth; his inquisitive brows framing dark, gentle eyes; the thick chestnut hair of his Italian grandfather. When he pulled off his muffler and carelessly dropped it onto his lap, she noticed that he had gotten so thin she could see his Adam's apple rise and fall above his shirt collar each time he swallowed. It made him look young and vulnerable, and Janine wondered if he was eating enough. She felt drugged by the overpowering, delicious nearness of him.

"Now, I want to hear everything," he said, tipping back in his chair. He blinked his eyes tightly shut for a second—a habit, she'd noticed— as if he could bring the world into more sensible focus when he decided to look around again. With his eyes closed, she freely admired the face she had missed. "How did you happen to come here?" he asked, his eyes without warning again meeting hers. "Why Lyon? Where are you living? You still haven't told me."

Together, Janine and Trudi told him about their sojourn in Gray, about their father's awful detention in a dungeon in Langres, and about their frenzied flight to Vichy with Alice and their Aunt Marie courtesy of the French Army when the Germans attacked. Though they luckily found Father back in Gray after the armistice, it was too dangerous to stay there with the Nazis in charge, and so with Marie's daughter living in Lyon, this was a natural move. Not easy, though, to obtain transit papers! Of course they felt very much safer in the Unoccupied Zone, and the parents appreciated that their cousin Mimi's husband had proved exceedingly helpful in getting them settled.

As she chronicled all that had happened since their last parting, Janine realized that nervousness was making her babble. But still she went on—the most amazing news not yet recounted. Norbert had enlisted in the Foreign Legion the previous winter and shipped out to Morocco. For a year they had been worried sick about him—no news at all. Then, hard to believe, not one week after arriving in Lyon, Alice ran into him on the rue de la République, where he was sitting and shining shoes. "*Un vrai miracle!*" Janine exclaimed delightedly. With France out of the war, the Legion had released him into the Unoccupied Zone. Better to come to the cousins in Lyon, Norbert had figured, rather than make his way back to Gray and meet up with the Germans. Mimi was bound to be in touch with Marie and could tell him where and how the family was.

"Mother threw her arms around him and wept for joy," Janine continued. "But you can guess how she felt to find her darling son in such a condition. Norbert told us that right on the spot, Mother started to scold him: 'Norbert! What on earth are you doing? Now you live like a beggar and shine shoes in the streets? Why didn't you go straight to Mimi when you arrived here? She could have helped you.'"

At this point in her story, Janine regretted providing so much detail. It would feel shameful and disloyal to the family to tell Roland what her parents had been aggrieved to learn: that Norbert had, in fact, gone directly to Mimi when he arrived in Lyon, but she had done no more than lend him a few francs and point him to the shelter for refugees where he was living when Alice discovered him homeless and hustling for money. Quickly, Janine changed the subject.

Mimi's husband, Maurice, had rented them a wonderful apartment on the place Gabriel Rambaud, just a block off the Saône. "Number 14," she pointedly dropped the address, hoping Roland might remember it. It was on the fifth floor of a corner building with a wraparound terrace and very much nicer than they had expected. The flat was spacious and had glass doors looking onto the terrace, offering a clear view of the turrets of Fourvière, the basilica perched across the Saône on a hilltop above the city. She decided not to mention that given the shortage of fuel, glass walls meant their rooms were dreadfully cold. Nor did she let on that lacking a bath or shower, they had to pay to bathe at the Hôtel Claridge, where she and Trudi economized by sharing a weekly tub.

"But what about you?" Janine asked him, finally embarrassed by the uninterrupted sound of her own voice. "Where are *you* living? Is your family here with you, too, or are they still in Villefranche?"

"No, I'm all alone and, like Norbert, sadly in need of a little mothering myself," he offered with an exaggerated frown, prompting her to blush again. In a feeble effort to appear more chic, she had pushed up the sleeves of her woolen sweater, and her bare forearm felt tantalizingly close to Roland's hand on the table. How she yearned for his touch or to clasp his hand in her own. "My family went back to Mulhouse at Christmas," he said, "and by now I'll bet they're all forced to speak German. By the way, Hannele," he recalled her Germanic nickname with a mischievous grin, "I really must commend how much your French has improved. You've learned a lot since the last time I saw you." He tipped his head in admiration, but then another wicked smile crept to his lips. "Those boys in Gray must be good teachers." He turned and patted her hand in approval—paternalistic and condescending, not the touch she'd longed for throughout the months she had dreamed only of him.

"Speaking of family, I think it's time we headed home," Trudi interjected with a meaningful glance. "The parents will be anxious and waiting for dinner."

Roland checked his watch. "Ah, I had no idea it had gotten this late! How selfish of me to have kept you so long!" He turned around, raising a finger to summon the waiter, and then stood to help them on with their coats. Janine averted her head to hide the tears that sprang to her eyes and wondered how to control her expression, as once again the man she loved disappeared. Her cup of Bovril was already empty, yet pretending to find one more sip still at the bottom, she hid her face behind the rim in order to gain a moment to compose herself. Retrieving his umbrella from behind his chair, Roland moved aside, allowing the sisters to exit before him. As they filed out the door, Janine furtively dabbed at her eyes and tried to put on a mask of acceptance.

"It's been wonderful to see you," she said on the sidewalk, forcing a smile and extending her hand.

He arched his brows in a look of surprise. "*Si vite que ça?*" So you're that eager to get rid of me now? "I was about to suggest a pleasant café on the rue des Cordeliers where we could all meet again tomorrow afternoon." He tucked his muffler into his coat and paused to look up the street toward city hall. "By the way," he added, "did either of you happen to know Roger Dreyfus in Mulhouse?" He didn't bother to wait for an answer. "Roger and I are rooming together, and if he's free, I'll bring him along. I'm sure you'll both like him. *A demain.* I hope you can make it. Say five o'clock." He gave them the address, lightly kissed them again on both cheeks, turned, and was gone.

Without Trudi as witness, by the time they got home, Janine would have suspected herself of inventing it all, even as for the rest of the night she critically picked over every single word she had said. Why, if really compelled to prattle along in a breathless barrage, had she failed to mention the things that might have helped her win his respect? That might even have made him a little bit jealous? How she tricked the *Kommandant* into signing their papers! How the soldier from Freiburg, stationed in Gray, courted disaster in wanting to save her and make her his wife! How André Fick, in love with her also, endangered his own life to help her family cross over the line! *Those* were the stories she should have related, that might have actually piqued his interest in her, casting her in a more glamorous light. She should have, she could have, and surely she would have, given more time; and still she berated herself for nattering at him.

Full of rekindled desire and anguished self-doubt, she relived each jewellike second of their reunion and vowed to be different—more contained and much more elusive—the next time they met. Joy and despair wrestled all night for control of her mood, and she kicked herself for having neglected to learn his address, which made the next meeting all the more crucial. Having no phones, the only way to guarantee contact was to manage to keep each planned rendezvous. There was no way to reach him to alter arrangements or make excuses if her parents clamped down. She knew that she was facing a challenge. Despite the twenty-eight bridges of Lyon, she would have to start building one of her own in order to span the distance between them.

TWELVE

J'ATTENDRAI

"*SHH! JE T'EN PRIE! ARRÊTE DE PARLER ALLEMAND!*" Mimi hissed a warning to Alice as she guided her down the rue de l'Hôtel de Ville toward her Lyon apartment. I beg you! Stop speaking German! She glanced apprehensively over her shoulder, flashed her aunt a look of annoyance, and buried her face in her upturned fox collar. "It won't help any of us if you go on announcing yourself as a refugee to every stranger who happens to hear you!"

Chastened, Alice fell silent. The memory of Poststrasse 6 shimmered through angry tears that welled in her eyes, and she allowed herself to recall a time when it was right and natural for her to speak German, when being Frau Günzburger meant being somebody, and when she could have opened the door of her own fine home to Sigmar's niece, with her elegant wardrobe and bleached blond hair, and taught her about hospitable welcomes.

As it was, the sudden sting of rebuke from Marie's daughter overwhelmed the message her warning contained. Unemployment, war, defeat, and scarcity had helped Vichy malign the hundreds of thousands of Central European refugees who had fled into France in that decade. And as Mimi and other French Jews well understood the need to conform to a homogeneous national image, they feared that an alien hodgepodge of desperate Jews, not speaking the language, chased from their homelands but claiming a kinship, would undermine their social acceptance.

Alice heard only the personal slight. She recoiled on the sidewalk while Mimi stopped to unlock an exceptionally fine wooden door the color of amber, with cascading fruits and flowers in sculpted relief on long center panels. Pairs of decorative white marble columns flanked

*The doorway of the Lyon apartment building
at 99 rue de l'Hôtel de Ville (now rue du
Président Edouard Herriot), where Emilie
Cahen Goldschmidt and her husband,
Maurice, lived with their three children*

the entrance to number 99, where a classical sculpture adorned the graceful arch of the doorway. It showed a horned devil lurking beneath a marble bench where two dimpled cherubs innocently sat and played with a bird. He seemed to attest to the hidden presence of evil, like a symbol of inescapable doom.

Upstairs in Mimi's salon, her husband, Maurice Goldschmidt, sat with Marie, Sigmar, Janine, and the eldest of his own three children—a son, Elie-Jean, at the age of fifteen a prodigy in music and mathematics. Every eye was focused on Sigmar, reading aloud a letter from his nephew Herbert in New York. He stopped midsentence as Mimi entered the room, Alice morosely trailing behind her. His niece sniffed the air and wheeled toward her husband.

"You're serving *real* coffee, Maurice?" Mimi demanded before greeting the others, with a scowl that borrowed resentment from previous grudges and condemned the squandering of precious supplies. Maurice stared at the ivory fringe of the carpet. Where his wife was concerned, he had learned to adopt the virtue of silence.

Indeed—squat, balding, and considerably older than she—Maurice appeared perpetually puzzled that the beautiful Mimi had ever accepted his marriage proposal. He had long closed his ears to the gossip about it, that two successive disappointments in love had impelled her to marry not for romance, but in order to put an end to pity, as well as to win an affluent lifestyle. Still, the unfortunate truth that the first of Mimi's heartbreaks involved her own cousin Herbert meant that her pain was revived every time someone mentioned his name.

Herbert was the handsome and debonair son of Marie's and Sigmar's older sister Karoline. Though he and Mimi had fallen in love, full of ambition in his early twenties, he had sailed for New York, pledging to marry his cousin as soon as he earned the means to support her. With loans from Sigmar, he had launched himself in the American steel business, and his letters relayed a tale of success until he crashed with the stock market in 1929. By the time he climbed back, Herbert reported home with remorse that honor impelled him to marry an American woman, his former secretary, who had stood faithfully with him through penurious years when it was largely her salary that kept him afloat. He wrote with the hope that the passage of years had dimmed his cousin's feelings for him and said he was certain that a lovely young woman of Mimi's talent and charm would

Sigmar's nieces and nephews in the early 1920s (L to R): Herbert Winter,
Emilie "Mimi" Cahen, Jacob Winter, Gretl Winter, Edmond "Edy" Cahen

never lack for admirers. But the death of her second fiancé, slain in a violent robbery, completed her heartbreak. Rumor had it that inconsolable sorrow prompted Mimi to marry Maurice, a prosperous silk merchant, and that she opted to seek in wealth and status the elusive satisfaction she yearned for in love but never had found.

Since then, her esteemed position in Lyon social circles had come to define her, and she professed full confidence that her immediate family would remain safe under the protection of the French state. In fact, despite the menace of new anti-Jewish regulation, she refused to acknowledge that Vichy was initiating its own course of persecution beyond what she saw as the collaboration that Hitler imposed.

"Qu'est ce qui se passe?" What's going on here? she said now, scanning the solemn faces around her. "What's that you're reading, *Oncle?*"

Sigmar explained that he had heard from his cousin Max Wolf, who had fled from Belgium to Brive-la-Gaillarde near the center of France and who, having applied for Cuban visas to get out of Europe, was urging them all to try the same route. Cuba was a clever backdoor for entry into the United States, Sigmar went on, and it offered the prospect of quicker escape than dealing with quotas for stingily granted American visas. Truly, one had to face reality now. Toward that end—Sigmar's tone shifted with evident pleasure—Herbert had volunteered to act as their sponsor and even to cover their travel, if needed. He was proposing to pay for their tickets through deposits with the Hebrew Immigrant Aid Society in New York, which was working with the American Jewish Joint Distribution Committee to secure space for Jews on refugee ships chartered to sail from Marseille or Lisbon. One extra bit of very good luck was that Herbert's wife had a brother, a businessman with American government contacts in Cuba, who might help procure their U.S. visas from Havana, after they landed.

Sigmar said he was ready to begin the cumbersome process of applying for visas, which he supposed would also involve a trip to Marseille to see about passage across the Atlantic. The shortage of oceangoing ships from neutral countries required booking travel with confirmed reservations in order to get their visas approved, while visas also demanded a perplexing raft of other official documentation.

Nonetheless, here was a plan, and he was enthused. He put down his letters and beamed at the circle. But he had failed to consider how the subject of Herbert would upset his niece or even to think how the abrupt prospect of abandoning home and country would explode at the feet of his French relations.

"Absolutely out of the question! I will eat at my table! I will sleep in my bed!" Mimi jumped from her chair, and a black and towering wave of rage, years in the building, spilled over the room. She glared at Maurice as if she had caught him plotting a crime.

"For you Germans, this may be just the right answer," she snapped at Sigmar. "Cuba! *Allez-y!* Go ahead! But we are pureblooded French. *Pur sang.* Do you understand?" The term was a cold echo of the racialist themes espoused by the Nazis. "We have no intention of leaving our country. This whole discussion is absurd and alarmist." She cut off the subject with a short, angry laugh. "Herbert!" she scoffed. "*Sans blague!* No kidding! So Herbert's the hero planning to save us? I'd sooner place my faith in the marshal."

While shocked to hear her father addressed in that way, Janine was secretly thrilled by her cousin's pronouncement. The idea of moving again was intolerable now that Roland had reentered her world. And Cuba! Where was that? She couldn't remember. Besides, the French were not Nazis, and time would prove, as it generally did, that Father had schemed and worried for nothing. Why, they had stewed in Gray for nearly a year before any actual fighting started, a year that cost her incalculably in terms of the time she had lost with Roland.

Sigmar stood, kissed his sister, turned to Maurice, and extended his hand. He was grateful to this openhearted nephew by marriage who had unstintingly lent him money to tide them over since their leaving Mulhouse. "Perhaps it's best if we discuss this later," he murmured, "after you've had time to think and talk it over with Mimi." Alice and Janine dutifully followed him to the door, as Mimi moved to collect their coats. She did not try to conceal her impatience to be rid of her uncle and his pessimism, yet when she came to Janine, Mimi paused, still holding her cousin's coat in her arms.

"I don't know how you can wear those woolly black stockings," Mimi observed, as her eyes came to rest on Janine's dark legs and wooden-soled shoes. Her own, luxuriously encased in silk, were shining pink and ended in high-heeled, open-toe pumps of brown alligator. "I wouldn't be caught dead wearing those things!"

Janine did not answer. Given the means, she would certainly have opted for silk, but such finery was beyond imagining now. Nevertheless, for the gift of Mimi's rejecting the notion of running from France in fear for their lives, Janine would gladly forgive her cousin's insensitive insult. She would even bestow a kiss on each powdered cheek and flash what passed for a genuine smile.

In ensuing weeks, Norbert found work managing the bookstore for a correspondence school across the Rhône, and he persuaded its Jewish owner to hire Janine to handle the business accounts, a job for which her training amounted to zero. (Her government-issued identity card

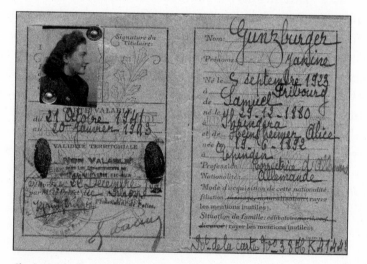

Janine's identity card in Lyon describes her profession as a corrector of German.

as a foreign worker vaguely and inaccurately described her as a "German corrector.") The school shipped books, assignments, and tests throughout the country to students pursuing their studies by mail because time or funds or location made attending high school classes unfeasible. But a perk of the job was the plausible pretext it offered

Janine to seek out Roland on the rue de la République in the late afternoons, once she hatched the idea of having the school hire him to
grade student papers in history and literature.

Unable to recapture what she'd shared with Roland in her final weeks
in Mulhouse, she became a satellite in his entourage. She was thankful
for any time in his orbit yet endured in a state of besotted frustration.
After work, she joined groups of young people who sat in cafés on the
place des Terreaux behind city hall, where Bartholdi's fountain—a
chariot drawn through the waves by four straining horses—appealed
to their zest to forget the war and get on with life. But Roland was so
taken with his card games and the companionship of fellow students,
regardless how little he actually studied, that he barely seemed to notice her there, hungering for any sign of affection that would validate
her devotion to him. To have found Roland, only to have him still out of
reach, was a shattering disappointment. The fantasy that had nourished
her spirit, soothing the nightmares of persecution, had fed rapturous
dreams of impassioned reunion. Now she berated herself for her fool-
ishness in having magnified her importance to him.

While her days were shaped by longing to see him, their meetings—
mostly by way of her persistently searching, knowing he would be
strolling the rue de la République or cavorting with friends in habitual haunts—generally proved deflating and painful. Desperate to win
his attention and then his heart, she combed through her days for interesting nuggets to share. Roland had only to bring up a book he had
read to send her dashing off to a bookstore, where, lacking the means
to buy it, she would devour as much as she could without provoking
a salesclerk's displeasure, just to learn enough to discuss it with him.

• • •

That March 1941, news of the death of Alice's mother, Johanna, arrived from Zurich, where she had lived in despair with her daughter Lina since fleeing Eppingen. (Alice rushed to Zurich for the
funeral, but by the following year, neutral Switzerland would close
its borders to Jews and even turn refugees back to the hands of the
Nazis.) In the same month, German officials informed Berlin that the
French government had interned forty-five thousand foreign Jews

in camps in the Unoccupied Zone, as permitted under the law enacted by Vichy the previous October. "The French Jews are to follow later," their report asserted of the Vichy internments, which by then outnumbered those that the Germans enforced in the Occupied Zone. By June, sweeping new legislation expanded the Vichy government's right to intern *any* Jew, foreign *or* native, for *any* reason, including suspicion of being a Jew. A revised *Statut des juifs* further excluded Jews from jobs and professions and mandated a scrupulous new census, requiring them to register in person with details of their residence, family background, and financial assets. Two weeks later, the General Consistory, the chief administrative body representing French Jews, voted in favor of cooperation befitting a loyal citizenry.

In July, further legislation empowered Vichy to seize Jewish property through an aggressive program of Aryanization already in place in the Occupied Zone. Citing the goal of erasing "all Jewish influence from the national economy,"· it provided for the confiscation of any Jewish-owned property. Authorities arrested the poorest Jews first under the pretense that internment, however miserable, reflected humanitarian motives. The betrayal long dreaded by France's native-born Jews—that they would be lumped with disenfranchised Jews who, being new to the country, could not expect its equal protection—sharply became reality now.

In the face of these alarming new rulings, Sigmar embarked on the first of many trips to Jewish aid agencies in Marseille seeking papers and passage out of the country. Week after week, Trudi accompanying him to help with translation, he traveled by train and then trudged to the office of HICEM (an international subsidiary of the Hebrew Immigrant Aid Society) on the rue de Paradis on a peak overlooking the city, and then downhill to the Joint Distribution Committee. Widely known as the Joint and based in New York, the agency had been founded in 1914 by wealthy American Jews to aid needy coreligionists overseas. Now its critical mission became one of rescue. It maintained an office in Marseille on the broad avenue of la Canebière, steps away from the feverish port where refugees flocked in fearful pursuit of any conceivable means of escape from Europe. Among them, time after time, came Sigmar and Trudi. Yet each time, confronting the chaos and competition, the endless waiting for visas and papers, and the bureaucratic delays caused by Vichy's morass of new regulations, father and daughter returned to Lyon with nothing but the certain assurance they would have to journey to Marseille again.

They needed French exit visas, transit visas, and entry visas for admission to Cuba. Exit visas required application to the prefecture (the governmental agency responsible for administering national law on the local level) in the department or region where they resided, which for Lyon was the Préfecture du Rhône. At the discretion of the prefecture, they might well be required to apply to their local police for certificates attesting to their good behavior. They needed travel passes just to go to Marseille to pursue further papers, and once they got there had to apply to the Préfecture des Bouches-du-Rhône. This office, covering the department of southern France that included Marseille, had been delegated responsibility by the Ministry of the Interior to assign rare space on one of the very few ships available to refugees who managed to get their papers in order. If Herbert succeeded in purchasing their tickets, they might bypass the difficult step of obtaining in France the American dollars required to pay for the voyage. All the same, permits were valid for only a limited period, and if any expired before the rest were secured, rules required obtaining renewals or starting the process over again.

"They can just kiss my ass!" A shocked Trudi reported the first vulgarity she had ever heard from the lips of her father, who erupted after a rescue worker explained why the dossier of papers Sigmar believed was finally complete would still not suffice to permit them to leave.

Meanwhile, aid agencies suffered the same frustration and anger. HICEM valiantly struggled to coordinate the demands of consular offices, shipping firms, and the Vichy administration. But the agency's efforts were hampered by a lack of funds, ships, and countries willing to grant admission to Jews, as well as by governmental inertia, indifference, and endless red tape. American consulates in occupied Europe ceased operations by the middle of June, and laws passed that month in the United States sharply limited the granting of visas. Under the pretext of security concerns that spies and subversives could sneak into the States as refugees, Jewish immigration was virtually forced to a halt.

Anti-Semitism in federal government offices even tarred the Jewish aid agencies themselves with suspicion of serving as secret tools for the Germans to maneuver Nazi agents onto American soil. But as the American Foreign Service Association later confirmed, "The official U.S. policy was that Jews were not to be granted American entry visas, as it would not be wise to upset any government that might become legitimate and important in Europe, and therefore a possibly valuable ally." Consequently, between the attack on Pearl Harbor in December 1941 and war's end in 1945, ninety percent of the visa quotas set aside for would-be immigrants to enter the United States from countries in Europe controlled by the Nazis went unfilled.

. . .

In the days that she wasn't traveling with Sigmar, Trudi was put to work helping Alice in the tedious task of *ravitaillement* or provisioning, which entailed standing on lines in the continual hunt for food.

Janine (R) wears the Mulhouse insignia on her sweater as she poses with Trudi, Norbert, and the cat Munnele on the balcony of their Lyon apartment at 14, place Rambaud.

In the apartment, the absence of crumbs emboldened the mice to the point that they showed up at the table for regular meals with the entitlement of family members. When Sigmar brought home a cat to keep them at bay, the cat learned to filch as well as the mice, brazenly snatching food from Alice's hands before she could get the plates to the table. When the cat made off with the delectable treat of a slice of liverwurst that Alice had waited all day in the cold to obtain, it sparked not only tears of vexation, but also a permanent longing for that kind of sausage that none in the family would ever outgrow. When Trudi managed to snare the prize of a single egg, all five of them selflessly argued so much about who should eat it that over the days they genteelly procrastinated about its consumption, the egg went bad, and they had to throw it away. They tried to brew coffee from roasted peas, learned to live on a diet of yellowish turnips called rutabagas, and relied for lunch on a carrot or an apple, saving for breakfast their single slice per person that was their daily ration of a dry mix of grains masquerading as bread.

But even here in the Unoccupied Zone, they were far from alone in their terrible hunger, with the Germans requisitioning the bulk of French food to ship over the border. Hunger became a paramount political issue. Across France housewives marched in food demonstrations, undermining the popularity of Marshal Pétain, the grandfather who purported to stand for traditional values yet failed to provide for the family's supper. When stores lacked even what rations prescribed, starvation forced people to buy at inflated black market prices—as much as ten times higher than usual. Although this practice was technically outlawed, officials often had no choice but to close their eyes to it. Eventually, however, black marketeering offered the pretext for arresting those perceived as politically suspect, which proved useful in meeting Nazi quotas for both slave laborers and Jews to be deported east to feed the voracious fires of the camps.

The slang term *le système D*, from the verb *se débrouiller*—to manage resourcefully to straighten things out—summed up the finagling required for survival. When the opportunity came to buy something scarce, people snapped at commodities they themselves did not need just to resell or trade them for other things that they wanted. When, for instance, Roland and Roger stumbled upon the chance to obtain a cache of silk stockings, they pooled resources in order to buy it and sold them off by the pair at a serious markup. From the Vichy government, both Roland and Roger received a small monthly "refugees' stipend" by virtue of not being able to go home to Mulhouse. Still, with increasing bravado, Roger traveled to outlying agricultural regions and returned with sacks of food that brought hefty profits on the Lyon black market. The money he made, for example, when he managed to come by a large wheel of Gruyère that he sold by the wedge carried them both for a number of weeks. Roland pawned the gold Baume & Mercier wristwatch that had been his proud father's baccalaureate present, then seized upon any *petit métier* or odd job he could find in order to claim it again. He sold chocolate truffles made by the cousin of a friend of a friend, and besides grading papers for Janine's employer, he rewrote a thesis for a Chinese graduate student struggling to put his ideas into French. "Anyone can live well with money," Roland would observe. "The art is in living well *without* money."

For those who suffered the barren routine of deprivation, however, it gradually spawned tension, envy, suspicion, and hatred. Consumers reviled as greedy and opportunistic the very suppliers on whom they depended. City dwellers accused the farmers of jacking up prices, farmers resented those in the city for hoarding resources, and everyone jealously eyed what others were getting. The wealthy who managed to acquire things beyond the reach of less fortunate neighbors were despised with more vitriol than even the Germans. They turned themselves into targets for denunciation based upon the clothing they wore, the magic deliveries that arrived at their doorsteps, and the smells that wafted from their apartments like a tantalizing essence of privilege.

. . .

In June, with classes over, Roland opted for a simple life, after he and a tall and brawny Algerian Jewish friend encountered a woman selling a kayak. Though the price was steep for their means, the two young men impetuously bought it together and managed to get it to Saint-Germain-au-Mont-d'Or, a town on the Saône north of Lyon.

From there they paddled to a small, uninhabited river island, pitched a tent, and decided to spend the month of July camping under the stars. They kept bicycles tied up on shore for trips to seek food, and they padded their diet with little fish they caught on a string, grilled in the open, and popped whole and crunchy into their mouths. While friends occasionally rowed out to visit the campsite where they presided like indigenous kings, they spent most of their time swimming, kayaking, lolling on the banks of the Saône, and baking themselves on their own island fiefdom. Janine was never able to get there, and she counted the days until his return, even as his eager departure delivered the message that, where she was concerned, a casual friendship suited his needs.

In the weeks he was gone, Janine tried to forget him and went so far as to agree to be introduced to a young rabbi who, Mimi insisted to Sigmar and Alice, would represent an excellent match. Aiming to cut a dashing impression in equestrian garb of fitted jacket, jodhpurs, and boots, the rabbi called at the place Rambaud in order to meet Janine and her parents. Sigmar gaped, astounded, as the young man straddled his chair, having flipped it around so that the back of it rose between his splayed thighs like the head of a horse, and then held forth for over an hour.

"So this is a rabbi?" Sigmar subsequently mused aloud, shaking his head as he summoned to mind the dignified Rabbi Zimels of Freiburg. He would have rejoiced to see his daughter marry a rabbi, but this one seemed a self-impressed fop, and Sigmar concurred with Janine's decision not to invite his further attentions.

At the end of July, Roland returned to Lyon slim and dark, his hair grown long and his skin kissed gold by the sun, even more impossibly handsome than Janine recalled. *Basané*—tanned by the sun. That was how his friend from the island described him, and that was how she would think of him always, his skin smooth and sleek and lacquered the golden color of honey. Captive to the physical longing his grace and beauty always aroused, she worshipped him like a primeval totem. She felt complete only when near him. Roland became her reason for being. Like many others of her generation, she was under the spell of a feminine model learned from her mother, a desire to serve and worship her man. And in her it was charged by the potent force of an aesthetic attraction that held her entranced.

Once Roland was back in the city, Janine reverted to searching for him in the usual places—the cafés, the bookstores around the place Bellecour, the stalls that lined the quay of the Saône under the sheltering branches of chestnut trees, and along the stretch of the rue de la République where she knew he strolled in the late afternoons. She risked getting home late to linger in front of the Opéra, where he would have to pass by on the way to his building. But their impromptu talks, generally occurring in front of his friends, were rarely of any personal nature.

Roger came home to their room one day that August to find Roland writhing in bed, wet with fever, near delirious, and groaning in pain. His pants gaped open, and his trembling fingers were clutching his abdomen, stiff and distended. His clothes and sheets were sodden with vomit. Roger ran for help, and when he returned hours later with a doctor in tow, Roland was unconscious. Emergency surgery confirmed the diagnosis of a ruptured appendix, with pus contaminating the abdominal cavity leading to virulent peritonitis. Even after the operation, there remained serious potential for developing sepsis, a bacterial infection polluting the blood, which often proved fatal.

Each day, Janine rushed after work to Roland's room in the Clinique Vendôme, though her parents believed she was spending time with Malou. At his bedside, she stroked his hot brow with cooling compresses, attempted to talk, held his hand, straightened his pillows, and fervently prayed for his recovery. She read to him without really knowing whether he heard her and tried to coax him back to life. She came prepared with political stories, news of the war, and gossip of friends. She watched him sleep, massaged his shoulders, and worried about the weight he was losing. Yet as he slowly roused to awareness, and the doctor said he should try to eat solid food, Janine despaired of her failure to find any dish tasty enough to entice him.

"I can't assure you he's out of the woods," Dr. Pesson conceded. "He's an extremely sick young man, and it's too soon to tell which way this will turn. But it would help if we could build his strength to fight the infection."

So began Janine's career as a nurse, a role for which she had amply studied in Gray and which she would play long into the future. She quizzed the doctor and learned the importance of fluids to boost circulation; she searched the city for sources of glucose and paid for it out of her own meager salary. Miraculously, soon Roland appeared to rally a little, and her joy in her hospital visits gradually mounted, as they provided the chance to be at his side. For the first time, she knew every day where she could find him, and she made use of his weakness to anoint him with love and such tender attentions that the closeness she had strived to achieve since the day they first met now, at last, in intimate quiet started to flourish.

Still, her happiness in his budding response and her understanding of how it had happened inexorably touched off moral self-doubt. Was she secretly pleased that this brush with death had so helplessly placed him into her care? In the disconnected hospital room, as removed from life as a prison cell, she had made herself essential to him. Guilt invaded her most precious moments: when he smiled at her with thanks in his eyes, kissed her fingers, or held her hand. When she wished they might stay, forever together, alone in that room. When she caught herself hoping he wouldn't recover and leave her too quickly, before she had taught him to love her and want her. She agonized that God would punish her for it, that to teach her a lesson about discovering joy as a by-product of another's pain, Roland would suffer a relapse, perhaps even die. But that horrible fear evolved, she saw, from an equally horrible, selfish conception. Why would God use Roland as an expendable tool for teaching *her* something? Was *she* that important?

As Roland's condition slowly improved and she saw him return her gestures of love, her fear dissipated. Still, five weeks passed after Roland's emergency surgery before Dr. Pesson delivered a cheery prognosis with an avuncular clap on his young patient's shoulder. "Well, my friend, you're saved," he announced. "Frankly, I thought you were finished. But it looks like you're lucky—you're going to make it."

Less apparent was how much he had changed, as the awareness of death lent him some of the wisdom of age. The life of casual friendships and carefree good times had lost its attractions. Beyond gratitude for Janine's dedication to his recovery, in the closeness of hours they had shared Roland had surprised them both by falling in love. How could he help but respond to her kind ministrations? And if, when he saw her approaching, he sank a little lower in bed—wan, parched lipped, and slightly disheveled—who could blame him for not wanting to look too much better for fear that it might slacken her care?

Over weeks of talks and peaceful silences alone with him in his room, she grew dearer to him than anyone else. Having come from a home where conversation generally meant bridging the gaps between courses at dinner, he luxuriated in hearing her stories and bathed in the calming alto tones of her voice. So she ransacked the suitcase of her experience for the most compelling memories to rouse him and nudge him back toward the land of the living, the place where he would love her robustly and never find cause to leave her again.

When Roland was well enough to be released from the hospital, the doctor nonetheless advised a rest in the country. Not allowed: climbing four long flights to the room he shared with Roger. Reluctantly, Roland agreed to spend a month at the home of a family friend in the western suburb of Ecully, which left Janine distraught. Almost two years had passed since their first separation, in the panic-whipped days when war was declared, and that parting had stolen him from her. This time, when Roland left Lyon, thin and frail, Janine feared that the man who came back would again be the one who had readily left her before to spend a month self-sufficiently camped on an island—a man content to travel alone. A man she had already seen in her dreams: a man in a kayak, his skin shining gold in the light of the sun, paddling past her, waving to her as she stood by herself on the banks of a river.

It was an image she carried back from her nights and tortured herself by bringing to mind, a vision of how she would lose him again. How helplessly she would watch him float by! She would cry to him over the rippling waters, but there were already so many cries in the world that hers would be lost and drown in the clamor, and she would watch him vanish into the distance.

"*J'attendrai*," she would whisper the words of her favorite song, whose lyrics comprised a promise to wait. With its echo of loss and unfulfilled longing, this tune would drift above the course of her years and battle forever the onrush of time that carried Roland farther and farther into the past. Even so, her love would remain perpetually with her, like a star whose glittering beam continues to journey into the present, long after the spark of its life is extinguished:

> *J'attendrai, le jour et la nuit,*
> *J'attendrai toujours ton retour,*
> *J'attendrai . . .*
> *Le temps passe et court en battant tristement,*
> *dans mon coeur si lourd,*
> *Et pourtant, j'attendrai ton retour,*
> *et pourtant, j'attendrai ton retour,*
> *j'attendrai.*

> I shall wait day and night,
> I shall always await your return,
> I shall wait . . .
> Time passes and runs and sadly beats
> in my too heavy heart,
> And yet I shall await your return,
> and yet I shall await your return,
> I shall wait.

THIRTEEN

A TIME OUT OF TIME

WHEN ROLAND RETURNED TO LYON at the end of September, the greatest challenge was finding a place where he and Janine could be alone. On the single occasion he attempted to bring her up to his room, simply to sew a button onto his coat, his concierge indignantly ordered them back to the street. Yet appearing together in public was not without its hazards, as well. One afternoon, the young rabbi whose courtship she'd spurned spotted Janine walking arm in arm on the street with Roland, and he rushed to tell Mimi what he had witnessed. The picture the rabbi painted for her, the evident physical closeness in the way the young couple touched and talked and looked at each other, propelled the unhappy woman up the Presqu'île to report to her uncle. Wings of

Roland after his return to Lyon from
recuperating in Ecully

envy sped Mimi's arrival, so that Sigmar and Alice had already heard an ample report of Janine's unsanctioned romantic outing on the arm of a stranger even before she walked in the door. When Sigmar inquired where she had been, she pretended a crisis had detained her at work, a lie that enraged him. As punishment, he directed his eighteen-year-old daughter straight to bed with orders not to place a foot on the floor for three days, except to go to the bathroom.

He relented the following evening, but only because an oil painting in a thick gilded frame, hanging directly over her bed, slipped from its nail. The noise brought him running to find that her head had crashed through the canvas, ripping a crater into the landscape. Still, he refused to meet Roland and forbade Janine to become involved with a non-Jewish man. It would only lead to heartbreak for he would never permit her to marry out of the faith, Sigmar warned. In any event, he added, she knew very well they soon would be leaving so that separation was inevitable.

Unexpectedly, that last rationale helped to make her mother an ally. "Ach, puppy love," Alice pronounced with a tolerant sigh. She agreed to meet Roland during one of her husband's trips to Marseille, and impressed by his charming manners and respectful demeanor, she could not see the harm in allowing the pair to spend time together. In view of Sigmar's plans to emigrate, the relationship, for better or worse, would necessarily end. Alice would not dare to challenge Sigmar about it, but she agreed to a mode of silent acceptance, as long as Janine was careful not to invite her father's suspicion by coming home late or making a public display of herself.

Janine was not permitted out in the evenings except for very special occasions when Alice helped to cover her absence because Roland had splurged on seats at the Opéra or tickets to hear a favorite performer. The couple grew misty together, holding hands through *La Traviata*, and sat transfixed before Charles Trenet, the jazzy, blue-eyed *Fou Chantant* or Jester of Song, who attained wild acclaim through the widespread demand for something uplifting. For the most part, however, Janine and Roland found their time with each other restricted to weekends and late afternoons, when they sometimes went to the movies on the rue de la République, always eager to catch a new film with Tino Rossi, the ebony-haired Corsican heartthrob who had popularized the song "J'attendrai" that they now adopted as theirs. Far more often, they walked and talked, followed their interests through secondhand bookstores, and watched daylight dwindle in their preferred cafés—le Royale or le Tonneau—contentedly sipping cups of Bovril. They were "dancing on the edge of a volcano," as Roland put it to her, enjoying the moment, blinding themselves to the inevitable.

As they strolled through town, they paid little attention to threats against Jews—TO KILL A JEW IS TO AVENGE A SOLDIER—scrawled in chalk on buildings and walls. Rather, they tried to find places to relax their guard about being noticed by someone who might report them to Sigmar. Roland took her exploring the city's concatenation of hundreds of obscure, covered passageways known as *traboules*, which permitted the cognoscenti of Lyon to weave through buildings from street to street without being seen. These internal alleys were originally designed to enable silk workers to shield the delicate fabrics they carried from dirt and bad weather, and later would help hunted members of the Resistance elude the Gestapo. In hidden, decoratively sculpted interior courtyards between the *traboules*, standing against slim Renaissance pillars or under groined vaults of stone gothic arches, Janine and Roland found shadowy corners for sharing their love in the only privacy available to them.

In the movie theater they hid in the dark in the last row and snuggled together under the coat that Roland brought along regardless of weather. Their hands and fingers went on adventures, sneaking past buttons and sliding through zippers, cautiously edging down uncharted ridges of muscle and bone, and into the warm, hidden places where once again they found one another. Wordlessly, they dissolved in kisses and imagined a future more glorious than any film on the screen. Though consumed with desire, they lacked a place to succumb to temptation, even had they both been prepared to reject the prevailing sanctions against premarital sex.

One afternoon, they ventured into the Boîte à Musique in the passage de l'Argue, a covered arcade between the place de la République and the place des Jacobins. Above the long, narrow bar, the second-floor hallway was lined with a half dozen doors that each opened into a small cubicle where a faded sofa, a lamp, and a table provided a décor dictated by function: couples with no other space to spend time alone rented the closetlike rooms by the hour. When they entered the boîte, Janine was too embarrassed to climb the stairs with Roland, so he went up first, and she followed five minutes later. Upstairs, they were amused to discover that the door of each room had a small opening cut into the center, covered by a sliding wood panel, which permitted the waiter to pass drinks discreetly to the patrons inside. When the waiter knocked to alert them to open the service window, both Janine and Roland rushed to the door to peer into the hallway. At that moment, the panel slid open in the door facing theirs, and they found themselves staring directly into the face of the patron in the opposite room, who apparently thought the knock was for him.

In one paralyzed moment of disorientation, Norbert and Janine stared at each other across the narrow breach of the hallway. Neither brother nor sister could muster speech under the mortifying circumstance that called upon them to acknowledge each other. Norbert's glance darted back and forth between Roland and his sister, an older brother's possessive sense of honor and outrage ablaze in his eyes despite his having been caught in the exact same position of compromised virtue. With Norbert still gawking in disbelief, Roland slid their panel back into place, and as soon as they judged the coast to be clear, they relinquished all plans for sexual intimacy and hurried back to the violet twilight of the place Rambaud, for fear Norbert would reach the parents before her. By getting home first and holding her tongue, she was able to strike a pact of secrecy and see it prevail.

"What in hell were *you* doing in a place like that?" Norbert hissed to her later. To which she replied, unusually brazen, "I guess I was doing the same thing as you."

"But it's not the same!" Norbert countered.

"Oh, no?" she successfully bluffed. "Why don't we ask for Father's opinion?"

. . .

Late that fall, anti-Jewish measures grew increasingly harsh, with the staggering fine of one billion francs imposed upon the Jews of France for their purported involvement in the killing or wounding of

German officers in the Occupied Zone. Bombs felled synagogues in Paris, and the Germans arrested and interned one thousand prominent French Jewish professionals around the capital. On October 23, under orders of *Reichsführer* Heinrich Himmler, head of the Gestapo and the *Waffen-SS*, Jews were forbidden to emigrate from Germany or any area of Reich occupation. At the end of the year, the threat level soaring, Vichy announced that *all foreign Jews* who had arrived in France since January 1, 1936, would be rounded up and consigned to forced labor battalions or internment camps. If the Pearl Harbor invasion on December 7, 1941, and the U.S. declaration of war raised any spirits in France, Roosevelt's prior refusal to enter the conflict in Europe, along with America's closed-door policy toward refugees, gave Jews little hope that Uncle Sam would come to their rescue anytime soon.

Less than two months later, in late January, when the rule went out to regional prefects to pursue the internment of all foreign Jews, Janine was seized by terror when, heading off to work one morning, she saw French police loading Jews on a truck. Fearing her parents had been arrested, she ran back home and raced up five flights of stairs to their silent apartment. She rang the bell, but nobody answered. Over and over, yet no one responded. Breathless and sobbing, she pummeled the door with her fists and cried for her mother, and then she collapsed against the wall in the hall, too drained to move until she heard a noise at the door and Alice poked out, still dressed in her nightgown with braids askew.

"*O mein Gott!*" Alice exclaimed, as she dropped to the floor at Janine's side. "What's wrong? Are you hurt? Are you sick? Why aren't you at work?"

"I thought you were taken!" Janine wailed. "Why didn't you answer the door? I was ringing and banging! On the street . . . I saw them forcing Jews on a truck! I was sure they got you and Father!"

But Alice and Sigmar had simply stayed in bed, the only place to hide from the cold in their unheated apartment. From that moment on, Janine would board the bus to work every morning wearing the new double-breasted, fur-trimmed brown suit and matching brown coat that her parents had bought her in optimistic anticipation of leaving the country. To ensure their daughters would travel in style, they had taken another loan from Maurice and pooled their accumulated textile rations to have outfits made for the girls. That both chose dark fur-trimmed suits to descend well dressed in the unaccustomed heat of Havana proved how little they knew about its climate, as well as how quickly they hoped to move on to New York. With the fresh understanding that any Jew in France faced instant arrest at any time, Janine grimly determined to wear these fashionable new clothes to work every day so that wherever she landed, she would look like a lady when she arrived.

Over the previous months, Sigmar had been quietly pursuing escape with newly desperate, fear-stoked obsession. It was only good fortune that having blindly waited in Europe for far too long, he finally sought the permits they needed a half step ahead of the effective enforcement of new regulations. His goal was to get all requisite permits approved in time to qualify for a sailing planned for mid-March. Tentatively, HICEM had their places reserved on the *Lipari*, a ship leaving from Marseille for North Africa; from there, another vessel chartered by the Joint out of Lisbon would take them to Cuba.

In late December he had gone to a Lyon notary's office with two Jewish friends—one from Freiburg, the other from Mulhouse. Both had to attest that they knew who he was and where he was from, in order to help him obtain a document to take the place of a birth certificate, which he could not hope to acquire from Germany. A week later, because being "stateless" they lacked valid passports, he had brought the family before police officials at the Préfecture du Rhône to apply for temporary safe-conduct passes permitting them to travel by train to Marseille and from there to leave France. On January 3, he had gained exit visas that would expire in three months; two days later, the Cuban consulate had granted them permits to land on the island as "tourists"; in late February, they obtained stamps of approval to pass through Morocco; and on Saturday evening, March 7, 1942, a cable from one of the rescue agencies arrived on their doorstep bearing the news that they were cleared for departure the following Friday. They were told to report to Marseille a day before sailing to obtain further visas from the Préfecture des Bouches-du-Rhône permitting their boarding the *Lipari*.

Although Herbert would eventually sponsor more than one hundred refugees for entry into the United States, he could not persuade the Goldschmidts, Marie, or Bella to let him arrange passage and visas for them. Maurice and Mimi were stubbornly fixed on remaining in Lyon, both insisting the persecution that targeted foreign-born Jews would not really apply to those who were native-born French. Besides, Maurice confessed, he was afraid of the water, had not learned to swim, and therefore could not bring himself to travel by ship. Marie

Janine's safe-conduct pass, dated January 2, 1942, served in place of a passport, valid only for one trip to Cuba via train and ship.

and Bella, of course, would not think of leaving without the rest of Marie's family. On March 8, Maurice loaned Sigmar $500 for traveling money, a sum that Sigmar duly recorded, along with his own reminder to calculate interest, in the notebook where he scrupulously listed the many debts he had been forced to incur since fleeing Freiburg.

Unprepared for instant departure, the family had trouble coming by trunks for packing their things and faced the prospect of hurriedly selling Sigmar's piano and the furniture they had succeeded in moving from Freiburg to Mulhouse, to Gray and Lyon, only to give it all up in the end. With no possibility of transporting anything more than clothing and some lightweight personal items, regret was numbed by the frenzy of action. The barrenness of the French marketplace enhanced the value of everything they were leaving behind, yet for simplicity's sake, they struck a deal for the lot, only to have the promised buyer, exploiting their weakness, fail to show up with the payment in time. Thus, in the last moment they were obliged to close the door on all that they had left in the world without the money they anticipated. In their last hasty check around the apartment, they even forgot the crates of valuables they had used to support the mattress on which Norbert slept and so unwittingly abandoned a treasured assortment of family heirlooms. At least documents, letters, and photographs were carefully packed.

Shrouded in grief as the rest of the family buzzed in fretful preparation around her, Janine barely had time to absorb the enormity of the loss she was facing. Throughout the months of Sigmar's fruitless travels to arrange their escape, she had persuaded herself it never would happen. She had rejected the prospect, declined to discuss it, blocked the image even from nightmares, and assured herself that should the day come, she would insist the family travel without her. She was eighteen years old and eager to make her life with the man she loved. But even as she told herself this, a practical voice argued against it. In the confrontation between self and soul, she knew she lacked the resolve to break from her parents at this perilous time. Recalling the morning she feared them arrested, she knew that she might have to protect them. Who knew what conditions awaited in Cuba? They needed her and, she had to admit as her thoughts reached this point, she doubted that she could manage without them in the labile and increasingly menacing climate of a Europe cruelly ruled by the Nazis.

If she stayed in France, where and how would she and Roland be able to live and support themselves? She could not be with him without getting married, but neither could she imagine presenting themselves in a French city hall expecting someone to marry them now—a foreign Jew and a displaced Alsatian ripe to be nabbed for use by the Germans. Would it even be fair to expose Roland to the growing dangers of wedding a Jew? He might well be suspected of being Jewish himself: his boyhood circumcision posed a threat they had already discussed, as stories of fearsome *Hosenproben* conducted at the point of a gun filtered over the line from the Occupied Zone.

As the week rushed by, she agonized over the question whose resolution would taunt her forever—to stay or to leave—as if she had free choice in the matter. She counted the days with the same bitter foretaste of inevitable hunger with which she had learned to squirrel her rations, already knowing there would not be enough. She changed her mind over and over again. She packed her things, gave up her job, and acted, if only for the sake of her parents, as if she fully intended to emigrate with them. Meanwhile, every cell in her body protested against it. Roland himself worried aloud about his power to protect her if the Germans decided to retake Lyon, so in the end, fear had the last word.

Janine went through those final few days with the same strange eyes that drank in the city when she arrived. But this time the distance with which she surveyed the places around her devolved from the effort to fix them in mind. She felt herself an invisible person, her own ghost, seeing it all as if she were gone. Unengaged in the swirl of everyday life that continued unchanged, she imprinted it all in sadness and longing at a frozen and lonely remove from the world. She felt jealous of every girl she passed in the street, seeing the possible face of a rival who would comfort Roland and then steal his love.

That Tuesday, after her last day at work, Roland showed up outside her office on the place Jules Ferry and announced they were going together to buy her a ring, an enduring symbol of their commitment to marry after the war. For one delirious hour, choosing a ring that pledged his future to hers, she freed herself from the specter of leaving that had blackened the days since the cable arrived. Together, they selected a square-cut stone that aspired to resemble an aquamarine and mirrored the crystalline blue of her eyes. The stone was set in a modern wide band of silver—nothing showy or complicated—as simple and clear as their love for each other. While the jeweler inscribed Roland's name and the date inside the band, another ornament caught his eye: a brooch composed of three little poppies, enameled in blue, white, and red to symbolize the French tricolor. It was the flag of the country where he would be waiting for her, and before she could stop him, Roland emptied his pockets for patriotism's token, as well.

"*J'attendrai.*" He whispered the words of their song in her hair as he attached the floral pin to her jacket and then slipped the glittering ring on her fourth finger. "*Moumoutte,*" he murmured, his term of endearment. "*Chérie.*" He opened his arms and clasped her against him, pretending that nothing could force them apart. "*Jour et nuit, j'attendrai ton retour.*"

That night, not having the means to reciprocate by buying a present, but wanting to leave something for him to remember her by, Janine searched through her things for the only two items of value she had: a pink-gold heart-shaped charm with her German initials, *HG*, that she had received from an aunt when she was a child, and a garnet ring that Alice had had made, and the same for Trudi, out of a pair of their grandmother's earrings. Janine knew they were things Roland couldn't use, but she gave them to him along with her prized autograph book as a deposit—proof that after the war she would return to redeem them with the gift of herself for the rest of her life.

On Thursday, March 12, the family went in a horse-drawn cab to the gare des Brotteaux for the train to Marseille. Edy's wife, Lisette, planned to board the train farther south in Valence, where she was living in hiding, in order to see the family before they sailed and to spend a parting night with Janine. No one expected Roland to be there, but he and Roger, along with one of Norbert's girlfriends, were at the station when the family arrived. Janine's eyes were swollen with weeping, but instead of the wrenching departure she dreaded, Roland strolled casually by while the parents were busy exchanging farewells with Marie, Mimi, Maurice, and Bella. Curiously, he did not stop to greet her, but flashed her a wink, squeezed her arm, and whispered, "*Pas encore.*" You won't leave me yet. Then he walked down the track and mounted the train a few cars behind the one the family boarded.

An hour after the train pulled out of the station, with Sigmar and Alice lulled to sleep in the rocking compartment, Norbert beckoned his sisters to follow him through the cars to look for their friends. They couldn't stay long for fear the parents would wake up and worry, but they scribbled the name of their hotel in Marseille and arranged to meet in the city that evening after Alice and Sigmar had gone to bed. Then they returned to their own seats to watch the soft fields of France roll behind them and fall into memory, and the chestnut and plane trees begin to give way to spears of dark Mediterranean cypress.

"*Never in my life do I remember to have passed a day as sad as this Thursday at Marseille, and I still hate that town for that awful day I spent there,*" Janine would later write in a journal. "*It was only on our arrival there that we fully realized that the next day—only twenty-four hours later—we had to leave France for good.*"

Scanning the crowd to catch sight of Roland after debarking the train, she came out of the Saint Charles Station with her family and found herself standing at the top of a terraced mountain of steps that cascaded sharply down to the street, flanked by verdigris art nouveau lampposts and white statuary. From the crest of that hill overlooking Marseille, she stared in awe for the first time at the sweep of the sea endlessly stretching into the distance and understood with fresh despair the vast chasm that would divide her from Roland.

The sprawling city was laid out beneath her, and on an opposite hilltop over the harbor, the gilded Notre-Dame de la Garde, crowned and cradling her infant son, kept watch on the Mediterranean waters. Pink limestone formations patched charcoal hills surrounding the city, and down past the end of the principal artery of the grand Canebière, antique flesh-colored forts, built from the stone chiseled out of those hills, stood in defense of the narrow Vieux Port. There, at the foot of the city, bustling streets embraced the notorious harbor on three of its sides, and the fourth one opened into the sea. The family wandered the streets toward their hotel, twisting through a warren of tiny alleys north of the port, so steep that many were laddered with steps. Come darkness, Janine worried, what if Roland could not find the place where the Jewish rescue agency had booked them rooms for the night? It was in the vice-ridden, decrepit tenement section, the Quartier du Panier behind the seventeenth-century city hall that crouched in faded glory like a worn-out whore at the side of the harbor.

That evening, after an early supper, Janine and Trudi went back to the room they shared with Lisette, hoping their cousin would fall asleep quickly so they might slip out undetected to meet their friends. But they should have known better. Though Edy had since left Switzerland to join her in Valence, Lisette was delighted to be with Janine again and fully intended to talk all night. Out it poured: a dizzying array of observations and theories, feelings and stories, jokes and poems, philosophies regarding the war and the plots of the Germans and the hope of resistance and the fate of the world and the clash of the sexes, Dostoyevsky and Schiller, and the human condition and the cretins in Vichy and the state of the theater and Hindu art and the pretentiousness of her mother-in-law and the treachery of Marshal Pétain, and the folly of faith and the absence of God and anything else on which she had definitive views.

And so, as their reunion unfolded, sensing her friend would never tire and fall asleep, Janine finally had to reveal to Lisette that she had actually planned to sneak out to spend her parting hours with Roland. It amounted to a rejection that neither woman would ever forget, and Janine mourned her choice at the same time she made it without hesitation, berating herself but helpless to do anything but swallow her shame and beg Lisette not to alert the parents once she had left. Then she folded her beautiful custom-made blue silk pajamas from Freiburg in a paper bag and crept out the door with Trudi behind her.

The six young people met on the street near the hotel and walked the Vieux Port until they found a brasserie open for *moules marinières*, a tricky dish for Janine to eat with only one hand, the other one being attached to Roland. With bloodred, fruity but potent concoctions called PGK—Amer Picon, grenadine, and kirsch—they toasted reunions after the war, and three times again with table wine. Breaking away on their own after dinner, Roland and Janine strolled arm in arm around the tight U-shaped harbor, where a flotilla of boats lent the illusion that in the voyage of life, anyone could set a free course and at a self-chosen hour slip back into port and return to land.

The hotel where Roland had rented a room was even more sordid than the one where Lisette was left to stew on her own. On a rickety bed in a seedy flophouse far better known to sailors and hookers, smugglers and addicts—by the light of the moon that danced through the windows—Janine and Roland hoped to seize a single precious night of their own, a time out of time at the outskirts of war. But the room was cold and dank, the radiator silent and dead. Janine's blue silk pajamas remained in the bag as Roland drew her onto the bed, and they fumbled for buttons, caressing each other, kicking off shoes and throwing off coats. More than anything she had wanted before, she wanted now, needed now, to give herself to him. The imminence of separation haunted the moment, and she was determined to prove there was nothing she would withhold from him now. This was no time for coyness or feminine wiles, for innocence, for fear or hoarding of love she might never again be able to share. No matter what the future might hold, she needed her first experience to be with Roland. She urged him on: her lips traveled the length of his angular torso, and she kissed the glossy, welted abdominal scar that had stitched them together. She teased his desire and could not understand why Roland pulled away at precisely the moment she was most open to him, boldly decided to know him as part of herself.

But he was determined to prove his love through restraint. It was marriage he wanted, not sexual union rushed on the brink of an anguished good-bye. Roland would not let her leave with any suspicion that sex had been his main purpose, when instead his most ardent desire was to make her his wife, to sacralize what they meant to each other. He had set this inviolable rule for himself even before their train left Lyon. He told her this: it seemed morally reprehensible to him—in a squalid room, at a terrible hour—to become her first lover, only to part the very next day. The rupture of leaving would only be harder, not to mention the risk of making her pregnant. Using a condom would be crude and demeaning, he felt; it was a device to use with a prostitute, not a shield to employ with the woman he loved. And so he was chilled to imagine her nauseous and seasick, alone on the ocean, bearing his child, afraid to confess the truth to her parents, beyond the reach of his protection or even adequate medical care. All these worries lent him resolve. And so, instead, he tenderly held her, her head on his chest and the pulse of his heart. He kissed the auburn tendrils fringing her brow and smoothed her hair, he painted dreams of their future together, and he urged her at last to close her eyes and rest for a while. . . .

"WO SIND SIE?" A man's voice, shouting in German, pierced her sleep. "WHERE ARE THEY?" The voice came again, louder this time. She reached for Roland.

"My father!" she gasped. She was instantly sure that Lisette—how oddly out of character for her!—must have woken Sigmar to tell him Janine had sneaked off, and he had somehow tracked them to this hotel. Now he would be climbing the stairs. She already heard the heavy tread of his feet on the steps, and she lunged for her clothes, strewn about the floor near the bed. She was terrified of his finding her there, even while she reminded herself that no punishment he could ever devise could match the one she already faced in leaving Roland. Still, she dreaded meeting her father's eyes, dreaded his disappointment and loss of respect, and dreaded the voyage looming ahead, trapped with him on a ship where his punitive silence would prove impenetrable. Years would go by, and still this night would burn in his mind.

From the street below, beams of headlamps flashed in the window. She heard car doors slam, German voices, sharp and demanding, and then the ominous thud of boots on the stairs. Roland's eyes were wild. He spun in a circle, assessing the options, and then rushed to the window. As he yanked the musty curtains apart, Janine peered down and saw three black Citroëns, the preferred vehicle of the Gestapo, blocking the cobbled street before the hotel.

"That's not your father out there. It's the Germans!" he whispered. "They must be searching for Jews in all these stinking dives in the port! Merde, we've got to get you out of here now!" He turned from the window and flung open the door to the hallway. But the exit was jammed by an onrush of nightmares

*forcing them back: thundering boot steps, pounding fists, moaning and weeping,
breaking glass and splintering wood. Roland drew her across the room, where a
second window facing the bed opened onto the roof of the building next door, a
drop of only a couple of feet. He threw back the shutters, opened the window, and
crawled onto the roof, gingerly testing the sloped surface under his feet. Then he
reached back to help Janine climb out of the room. From a sitting position, they
inched higher up the slippery tiles of the roof, away from the window, to avoid
being spotted.*

*"Stay behind me," he told her, "and keep perfectly quiet." He turned up her
collar to keep her warm, stroked her cheek with the back of his hand, and laid
a forefinger over her trembling lips, a warning to silence. But she was already
speechless.*

*In spite of her terror, the view from the roof brought tears to her eyes with
all its twinkling, ephemeral beauty: the starlight skipping over the water, the
shadowed terrain of the morning moon, the glow of the searchlight brushing
the clouds from the medieval watchtower at the mouth of the harbor. She saw
herself riding the breezes with white-winged gulls, as they landed on sills to peek
into rooms where bureaucrats slept and refugees tossed. Far in the distance, bell
buoys pealed their lonely alarums over the waves that ran to Morocco. Ropes
beat the masts of all the weathered boats in the harbor. An icy wind swept off
the water. Janine shuddered, clung to Roland, and buried her face in the back
of his coat. The travel, wine, passion, and fear had all combined to drain her
completely. Despite the precariousness of their rooftop perch, she fought to try to
stay awake. . . .*

In the hazy mist where memory and history blend into each other,
where what one imagines was true becomes more real to the heart
than what actually was, the events of that night in Marseille were
recorded. Personal history was sketched forever in memory's colors.
Even nightmares took on a truth of their own that overwhelmed dates
and facts regarding the war at that moment. That Marseille was then
unoccupied—Germany almost eight months away from seizing control of France as far south as the Mediterranean coast—was a truth
completely obscured for Janine by the trauma and pain of leaving
Roland. Or rather, the Nazi assault that would cleave them apart from
each other was translated into a dream of such terrifying immediacy

that it seemed the Gestapo was already there in Marseille, doing its worst.

Out of fear or eternal remorse for having yielded to reins of prudent restraint, Janine tumbled into the web of a fiction in which choice played no part in how they passed their last hours together. She came to believe that she and Roland spent most of the night perilously suspended in air, cheating arrest on top of a roof, while cheated of time for sharing their love. This dream was the tale she felt to be true, the one she remembered, and the one that she told and retold over the years. For her, the reality would be forever distorted. As a result, for all my life before I delved deeply into the facts of the war, this story was part of the magic and romance surrounding my mother. Dazzled, I fully believed her imagined account: made brave by love, as a girl she hid on a roof at the edge of the sea in the black of night in the middle of war with the man she adored guarding her from the grip of the Nazis. This would later become the only one of her stories my researched disproved.

At the first hint of dawn, when Roland kissed her awake and out of her dream, Janine was confused to find herself curled up beside him in bed. His voice was urgent as he roused her to return to her own hotel room before her parents discovered her missing. They rushed back together with the rosy halo of the rising sun just peeping above the pink limestone hills surrounding the city, fishermen checking over their tackle, and wraithlike cats sliding through alleys and pawing through garbage to pick out their breakfasts. Janine clung to Roland in tearful embrace on the street, but to her astonished relief, he firmly rejected any farewell.

"*Non, ma chérie, pas encore,*" he insisted again, and he promised to meet her at the *Lipari*'s pier.

Quietly, she slipped inside the hotel, and Roland detoured past the quickening quay, heading back to his room for a few hours' rest. It was then he noticed a vendor unpacking her flowers at a stall on the street, and he stood and stared for that one extra second that encouraged the woman to entreat him to buy.

"Fresh mimosas! A gift of the springtime!" she sang out the words, lifting a bunch of the golden-tipped stems of fertile Provence and waving them toward him with a hearty grin. Like Persephone's herald, mimosa came into flower at the end of winter, proof that the earth had not been forgotten. "Give her mimosas, and your girl is sure to remember you always," the vendor suggested, inclining her head to inhale their sunny perfume. "Mimosas, you know, they stand for remembrance."

. . .

The quai de la Joliette, with its capacious piers for large ships plying the Mediterranean Sea, was slightly northwest of the narrow Vieux Port and built at the edge of the Panier district, whose wanton streets sang sirens' songs to incoming sailors. Compared to the picturesque confines of the central Vieux Port, jammed with pleasure craft and small fishing vessels, Joliette provided the harbor with muscular piers for the serious shipping of cargo and people. Here Roland came to wait for Janine, his arms full of mimosas, and in his pocket, the letter he'd written three nights before in his room in Lyon, pledging to find her after the war. Their moment of parting would be too public and painful for everything he needed to tell her, so he had written it out—a contract of sorts.

The wharf was swarming with people, those departing and those to be left, with the ship's crew and porters and official inspectors checking papers and baggage, and rescue workers from the Joint and HICEM to help ensure that all those entitled could board. There were disputes and tears, fracases over glitches in papers, missing stamps of approval, questionable visas, names inexplicably dropped from authorized lists. And of course there was the usual frenzy, as families were split in the mayhem, struggling to hold on to each other as well as their baggage in the surging crowds that converged toward the ship. In the pandemonium, Roland finally found Janine, lagging behind the rest of her family, lugging her suitcase. He had dressed in a white shirt and tie and his suit and his long overcoat in order to make an impression on Sigmar, in case the chance arose to be introduced. But if Sigmar and Alice noticed him or witnessed his meeting Janine and their ardent farewell, they didn't let on but rather left them alone for some minutes.

"Mimosas stand for remembrance." Roland murmured the street vendor's promise into her hair as he gave her the flowers, pointillist puffs of bright yellow blossoms with leaves like dark feathers. He slipped his letter into her pocket and urged her to wait to read it until the ship was at sea. When he opened his arms and clasped her to him, she was weeping too fiercely even to speak. He lifted her chin, wiped her tears, and tried to breathe hope and courage into her spirit with one hard, enduring kiss.

"*J'attendrai, ma chérie,*" he told her, attempting to smile. "*Le jour et la nuit, tu sais. J'attendrai ton retour. Toujours.* I love you always." Oblivious of all the noise and turmoil, they held each other against the void of letting go. But before Janine could answer, Norbert appeared at her elbow. It was time to board, and Sigmar was chafing. The two young men hugged one another. Then Roland cupped Janine's face between his hands to memorize every dear feature, and with one last searing kiss, he entrusted her into the arms of her brother to be led away in sobs to the gangplank.

Now Roland dashed back down the pier toward a stand where he'd noticed rowboats for rent. Paying for one, he rowed toward the *Lipari*'s side, fighting the wind, and was able to spot Janine's brown coat at the railing, where refugees pressed for a parting glimpse of the crumbling continent they were leaving behind.

"*Moumoutte!*" Roland called from below to get her attention. "*Chérie! Janine!*" He stood up in the boat, incongruous in his white shirt and tie and overcoat, waving to her and calling her name. She gaped down at the water, overcome by a torrent of laughter and tears.

"Sit down!" she cried. "*Mon Dieu,* I'm afraid you'll tip over!" Through her smile, she blanched to consider all the more terrible things that might happen to him in the time she was gone, without her even learning about it.

"Excuse me, mademoiselle, perhaps you would like me to take a picture?" The man beside her was holding a camera. Many months later, when he was finally able to give her the snapshot, her fellow passenger would pen his own caption in French on the back: "*seul sur la mer,*" alone on the sea. That photograph, though small and blurry, tucked in her wallet, would forever preserve her last view of her lover, thin and grave.

It was past three o'clock when the *Lipari* pushed away from the quay, with the sun already floating toward the horizon. Roland was sitting alone in the rowboat, blowing kisses and waving to her. As the *Lipari* moved out past the jetty toward the cold open sea, Janine buried her face in the sweet mimosas and knew she could not stand to watch them wither and die. So she broke off a single stem for her buttonhole, and then, leaning over the railing in tears, dropped the flowers stalk by stalk into the water, as if marking a path to find her way back. The bright flowers spun on the waves that carried them toward Roland's little boat, but his oars couldn't keep pace, and the *Lipari* carelessly left him behind. It was, Janine realized, exactly the way she'd imagined it that previous autumn, after she had nursed him to health. Her golden lover was drifting away, but instead of waiting alone on the banks of a river, now she was moving in the other direction. Until all that was left was a tiny, bobbing pinpoint of love, gold as the dots of mimosa that flickered around him, she stood there and watched, her thoughts riding the vow of their favorite song.

J'attendrai. I shall wait. Always.

FOURTEEN

DARKNESS ON THE FACE OF THE DEEP

ON MARCH 13, 1942, seven vessels sailed from the port of Marseille, but the daily listing in the city's commercial newspaper, *Le Sémaphore*, reported the destination of only six. For the seventh, the *Lipari*, discretion seemed vital. A French steamship built in 1921 and registered in the port of Le Havre, it had 105 first-class, 39 second-class, and 84 third-class passenger cabins, in addition to refrigerated cargo compartments down in the hold. But on March 13, in place of fish or bananas, of wine, wheat, or dates, the *Lipari*'s cargo walked on board and consisted of almost five hundred Jews, a fact no one was eager to advertise because their survival hung in the balance. For them, there was danger involved in just raising the anchor and getting away, and still more in the prospect of drawing the interest of German submarines presumed to be prowling Mediterranean waters.

The destination the *Lipari* withheld from the public: Casablanca. There the refugees would transfer to a Portuguese freighter from Lisbon, chartered to take them across the Atlantic. The trip would prove longer and sail closer to the brink of disaster than any who embarked that day could have imagined. But for each, this escape was miraculous, the result of arduous negotiations and detailed arrangements handled

Marseille's commercial newspaper, Le Sémaphore,
listed seven vessels sailing from port on March 13, 1942,
but the destination of one, the Lipari, *was not revealed.*

Le nouveau paquebot *Lipari*, de la Compagnie des Chargeurs Réunis.

Cliché Labbé

The steamship Lipari, *commissioned in 1922 out of Le Havre*

on a case-by-case basis by rescue organizations working through Lisbon, Marseille, and New York. Indeed, the full extent of their good fortune was yet to be known, for these passengers would be among the very last Jews to slip out of France. Thousands of other desperate refugees who made their way toward Marseille seeking escape would soon find themselves trapped. In the region of lavender fields and sunlit towns whose names conjure dreams of art or vacation—Arles, Aix-en-Provence, Saint Rémy, and Cassis—they waited, hungry and fearful, in makeshift camps that were French holding bins for transports to Nazi death camps in Poland.

On March 27, just two weeks after the *Lipari* sailed, the first French deportation took 1,112 Jews on a three-day journey to Auschwitz from the camp of Drancy in the suburbs of Paris. The Nazi leadership had adopted a "Final Solution of the Jewish question," defined as "the complete annihilation of the Jews," at the Wannsee Conference the previous January. It called for exterminating what they estimated as eleven million Jews in Europe, including those in undefeated or neutral countries. Now, to achieve Hitler's goal, the Germans demanded French help in arresting, interning, and deporting Jews from all parts of the country.

In response to Berlin, the French decided first to offer up stateless Jews found south of the line along with foreign or stateless Jews still in the northern Occupied Zone. The quota of Jewish bodies to be supplied to the Germans had to be filled, and under a *loi du nombre*, a law of numbers, any life spared meant the inexorable sacrifice of somebody else. On June 27, the Germans ordered fifty thousand Jews to be supplied from the Unoccupied Zone. Under terms of the armistice that required France to turn over any former Reich citizen upon demand, the Vichy government—with Prime Minister Pierre Laval now in effective control—absolved itself of any obligation to provide foreign-born Jews with asylum. But three days later, Adolf Eichmann, head of the central German security office branch for Jewish affairs, more fully revealed the scope of the Nazis' Final Solution when he personally carried new orders to Paris: *all* Jews in France, foreign *and* native, would henceforth be targeted for deportation. Citizenship no longer offered protection to Jews.

The impact on French emigration proved drastic. Already in February, a month before the *Lipari* sailed, the Germans widely reissued their previous ruling that forbade the emigration of Jews from the Occupied Zone without prior approval from Himmler. (As chief of the dreaded SS, Himmler was responsible for implementation of the Final Solution.) In the Unoccupied Zone, Vichy's aim of deporting foreign Jews first, before French citizens—"*pour commencer*," to begin, as Laval would express it—swiftly led to a similar crackdown. On July 20, Vichy's Interior Ministry suspended exit visas previously issued to all foreign Jews except those from Belgium, The Netherlands, and Luxembourg. Quickly thereafter, on August 5, Vichy's aim of deporting foreign Jews first produced a stringent order to regional prefects. With few exceptions, the order directed that *all* foreign Jews who had arrived in France after January 1, 1936, be promptly sent to the Occupied Zone and that any exit visas they held be summarily canceled. The following month, Laval explained the directive by saying, "It would be a violation of the armistice to allow Jews to go abroad for fear that they should take up arms against the Germans."

As a result, more than two-thirds of the 75,721 Jews deported from France would ultimately prove to be foreign born, despite the fact that they accounted for only half the Jews then in the country. Few of those seized would survive the ordeal to the end of the war. Three-quarters of the deported were arrested *not* by the Germans but by French policemen, while besides the deported, another four thousand died or were killed while still in French camps. More than half the dead—almost forty-two thousand, mostly foreign—were deported from France in that same year, 1942, that Janine and her family escaped from Marseille at the very last conceivable moment.

That July, a notorious operation involving nine thousand French police produced the arrests of nearly thirteen thousand Jews around Paris. The so-called Vel d'Hiver roundup was named for the sports stadium where those arrested, including more than four thousand children, were held for five punishing days with meager amounts of water and food before being deported to face execution. The following month, the pace of arrests sharply picked up in the southern department of the Bouches-du-Rhône, where many deported already held emigration visas in hand. On August 11, a convoy from the camp of Les Milles near Aix-en-Provence took adult German and Austrian Jews with last names that began with the letters *A* through *H*. Thousands from other French camps were forced onto trains in the following days, while French-run dragnets on August 26 and 27 snatched 6,584 more Jews from throughout the Unoccupied Zone for convoys headed to death in Poland.

Even evading capture in France, the Günzburger family's flight to freedom would have been blocked in Morocco had they left any later. That summer, shortly after they sailed from Marseille to Morocco and from there on to Cuba, Joseph J. Schwartz, the Joint's charismatic European director, cabled the rescue agency's New York office from Marseille to report: NEW DIFFICULTIES HAVE ARISEN WITH REGARD MO-ROCCAN EXIT VISAS EVEN FOR THOSE WHO ALREADY HAVE FRENCH EXIT VISAS THUS MAKING IT DOUBTFUL WHETHER ANYBODY WILL BE ABLE DEPART CASABLANCA.

As obstacles mounted, Schwartz rushed for help to the American chargé d'affaires in Vichy, S. Pinkney Tuck, who said he had already objected to Laval and other French leaders, and there was nothing more he could do. Schwartz reported Tuck's resigned observations back to the Joint in New York: "Washington is fully informed of every detail and the French Government knows our reaction to the inhuman steps which they are taking," Tuck had told him. "I do not believe that anything can be done by anybody for the time being. The only language these people understand is force."

Quickly the situation grew worse. PRACTICALLY IMPOSSIBLE EVEN JEWS FRENCH NATIONALITY OBTAIN EXIT VISA, Schwartz wired New York on September 11, and the trend he noted was soon formalized. On November 8, the Vichy government called a total halt to granting exit visas, as the Allies launched Operation Torch, attacking the Moroccan and Algerian coasts. The landings—which Churchill optimistically hailed as "the beginning of the end" of the war—met French resistance in Casablanca, and Pétain broke off diplomatic relations with the United States. American fighters and warships engaged with French fighters protecting French warships, submarines, and transports, and as fire swept through the harbor of Casablanca, the *Lipari*, on which the Günzburgers had escaped just the previous March, was destroyed.

Three days later, on November 11, under Hitler's orders, the *Wehrmacht* stormed over the Demarcation Line and swept south to the sea. Operation Anton, the Nazi code name for the seizing of France, met no armed French opposition, despite its clear violation of the 1940 armistice between the two nations. Unchecked by Vichy, the Germans easily grabbed the rest of the country and conclusively sealed the routes of escape for all Jews still caught inside France—the foreign, the stateless, and the French citizens—leaving them equally subject to being deported. Within a month of taking Marseille, Hitler ordered the immediate deportation of every Jew still to be found south of the line.

By January 1943, the Germans unleashed Operation Tiger, a massive roundup throughout Marseille that included—besides Jews—Communists, petty criminals, and others condemned as undesirables. It was the first step in a Nazi plan to demolish the historic port district in order to root out resisters already traced to anti-German guerrilla actions and to control the area in advance of a possible Allied attack from the sea. When they finally came, on May 27, 1944, American bombing raids on Marseille killed more than two thousand, mostly civilians, and also leveled much of the city where Janine and Roland had shared their last night.

This, then, was the menacing world that Janine escaped when she was forced to board the *Lipari* for Casablanca, leaving Roland behind. That she loved him so much, while understanding so little of the dangers involved in remaining in France, would color her future and cloud her memories of that fateful day. Instead of embracing the last-minute chance to survive, at the age of eighteen, surrounded by madness and evil for almost a decade, she viewed leaving as exile, because the only place she felt safe in the world was within Roland's arms.

· · ·

Janine stood fixed at the *Lipari*'s railing as the last sea-tossed golden mimosa drifted away, the last curious gull wheeled back to shore, and Roland—capable of rowing no farther—finally turned his boat toward the pier. Twisting his treasured ring on her finger, she tried to find solace in its solid reality there on her hand, as if it might guarantee they would be reunited. With everything that mattered to her rapidly shrinking into the distance, she felt enraged. Yet she was not the passenger who cursed aloud. Rather, the male voice that startled her out of her own dark reflections expressed a view she could not bear to hear.

"*Merde à la France!*" She spun in surprise to see several bearded Orthodox Jews, diamond dealers from Antwerp, standing beside her. The speaker's native Polish accent saturated his acquired Belgian French, as once again he swore, "*Merde à la France!*" Shit on France! He was wearing a long black coat and broad black hat that he clutched to his head to keep it from blowing away, as he reached over the side and spat in the sea. "The cowardly French are no better than Germans, only less honest," he contemptuously remarked to his fellows, who took his words as a cue to follow suit and spit in the waves.

Janine studied the man—his grim, black attire, his bony frame and narrow hunched shoulders, his skeletal fingers hooked over the railing—and meanly observed that he looked like a crow. His attack on France, with Roland by now just a dot on the water, clawed at her heart. In him she saw the embodiment of all her problems: he was one of those Jews who attracted suspicion wherever they went and incited hatred from the rest of mankind. Why should her existence be shaped and confined by people like this, who scoffed at the need for winning acceptance, when all joy in her life had solely depended upon remaining in France, yes *belonging* in France like anyone else?

Four years. Almost four tumultuous years had passed since their leaving Freiburg, and now they would have to begin all over again. But she didn't know Spanish, and she certainly didn't know what to expect from this destination called Cuba that sounded barely civilized to her. And what if Roland forgot her this time? Senselessly, she turned her despair on the stranger beside her. "*Vraiment*, you spit on the French?" she confronted the man. "I, for one, would much rather be staying in France than be sent into exile here beside you!" He stared, speechless, as if he couldn't believe such hostile words had come from her mouth.

With that, realizing she had best be alone before she lashed out at somebody else, she moved off and tried to focus her sights on the shore. High above the clay red rooftops of the ancient, sprawling maritime city, she could make out the gilded Virgin and Child atop Notre-Dame de la Garde. Roland had said he would climb the hill to the basilica's terrace after the *Lipari* sailed in order to keep her in sight as long as he could.

"Keep your eyes on the top of the hill," he had told her, "and know I'll be there." Janine fixed her gaze on the church and tried to pretend they could see one another. "Wait for me," she whispered under her breath. "Please, *mon chéri*, please wait for me, or come for me soon."

When the evening sky turned gray and cold, she grudgingly withdrew from the deck and found the stairs that wound down through the ship. Off-limits to her were the impressive common rooms—the bar, the library, the spacious salon—with patterned carpets, inlaid tables and Louis chairs, heavy draperies, potted palms, bronze sconces, and richly paneled wood ceilings and walls. Not for refugees either, the first-, second-, and third-class passenger cabins. Instead, their place on the voyage was the dark, cramped, and windowless hold. A space designed for packing freight, it now held more than two hundred double-decker beds set up in rows. Curtained partitions divided the sexes and a tin basin hung from each bed to accommodate the needs of the seasick. In addition to Jewish refugees, the hold carried

Roland watched Janine's ship sail out of sight from the plaza of Marseille's nineteenth-century basilica, situated at the city's highest point.

red-capped French colonial soldiers returning home to Africa, their wartime service no longer required. Those assigned to the hold were permitted one exterior deck to congregate, while the ship's fine common rooms were mainly reserved for the use of higher-ranking military personnel traveling in the passenger cabins.

Reaching the hold, Janine found Alice and Trudi nowhere in sight near the beds they had claimed by planting their things—upper bunks for the girls and a lower for Alice. She assumed they were trying to give her some time to herself. Her parents had shown no sign they noticed her anguish in leaving and had not even questioned the ring on her finger. To confront her about it would open the issue of why she'd pursued a romance with Roland in overt defiance of Sigmar's objections. Relying instead on distance to end it, the parents kept silent, and Janine herself would never dare broach the topic with them, either then or, for that matter, anytime later. Relieved for the moment not to be bothered, she climbed into the top bunk of the bed next to

Trudi's—a plank covered with a rough straw mat and bedding limited to one black, foul-smelling blanket—and then, hiding her head in her arms to muffle the sound, she wept until she felt empty. At last, following Roland's directive, she decided to open the long envelope he had slipped in her pocket just as they parted.

With it she found a small, useful gift of a new handkerchief that coaxed her to smile as she noticed the bright embroidered scene in one corner. It was a childlike view of a jaunty French cock singing the start of a better tomorrow as it summoned that day from over an ocean. A half circle of sun arose from the water wearing a radiant crown of yellow stitches. Beneath the rooster, embroidered letters spelled the name of France's Resistance leader, DE GAULLE, still in refuge across the Channel in England—a political message expressly designed to wipe away tears. Janine pulled the coarse blanket over her legs and tore open

The brightly embroidered handkerchief that Roland gave to Janine

the seal of Roland's envelope to find twelve neat, handwritten pages. In the dim light of an ugly bare bulb that hung from the ceiling, she started to read, carefully savoring each precious French word.

Lyon," it said at the top of the page, dated three days before. "*This Tuesday evening, the 10th of March, 1942. To my darling Janine, so that she will always believe in me and to help her wait for better days.*" Roland's letter continued in part:

When I first knew you three years ago, you were still young, and I myself did not know more about love than the word. The affection that I had for you would soon fade with the war but I treasured a memory of you.

Roland's letter to Janine

Later, when we met again in Lyon, I did not retrieve this memory, and the idiotic principles that I had adopted during a year of war turned our meeting into a banal adventure, one more sorrow for you, one more remorse for me, because all the same I was aware of my cowardice. You must know, however, that I never completely forgot you. In Villefranche, I thought of you from time to time, but never without a pang of anguish and disgust for myself. It was necessary to have last summer together for me to discover the young woman you are. Everything I lacked the courage to say, I now will say here. I ask your pardon, Janine, because you loved me and as a result, there was a great deal I caused you to suffer.

Happily for me, I fell sick and if my operation brought mainly ennui, it also succeeded in bringing me close to you, and since then, I could love only you. But one is forced to believe that actions and their consequences do avenge themselves. Scarcely have I found you back once again than you must flee, but now you are not alone in suffering, and destiny sends me a just punishment for all of my weakness.

Still, we share a love that is strong enough to triumph over all obstacles and to arrive at its most perfect expression in marriage and a life together. I consider you from this present day as my fiancée and future partner. You ask only to belong to me. We must wait for that reality. Our sole enemy is time! Whatever the length of our separation, our love will survive it, because it depends on us alone. I give you my vow that <u>whatever the time we must wait</u>, you will be my wife. Never forget, never doubt.

Believe in the fulfillment of our happiness, believe in it with all your strength, all your will, all your love, and our test will end as we desire. Time will change nothing. I am sure of you, be equally sure of me, and we will have overcome half our pain.

You will tell me that it is a long time, two years without seeing each other. But there is no reason to think that our separation will actually last that long. The war may end in Europe in a few months, and nothing will stand in the way of regular correspondence and telegrams. In any case, the hostilities will end by winter. And as soon as normal communications are reestablished, our separation will be less difficult.

Please believe, *ma chérie*, it is absolutely untrue that you might not be able to return to Europe. One way or another, as soon as the war is over in Europe, even if it is lost, you will come back to France. If you can't get permission to stay, you can get tourist papers, and that will be enough for us to regularize our situation and for you to become my wife. Under the worst hypothesis, if the war is lost and you are forbidden entry to Europe, I can obtain a permit to reside in or visit the USA, which will enable us to pursue our most cherished plans. There is no reason to worry about this. I give you my word that <u>I will come to find you</u>, and no law could forbid a foreigner from coming to a country if his intention is only to marry the woman he loves!

All that remains now is the matter of your family. No one, *ma chérie*, can force you to marry a man you don't want. Don't let yourself be discouraged by anything your family will tell you. It is normal for parents, only wanting the best for you, wishing and believing that they are acting to secure your future, to try to make you marry the man they choose. It is normal that they should combat in you that which they dismiss as puppy love. It is for you to show them enough ferocity, enough energy, to make them understand that you will create your own happiness.

With time, your parents may also try to sow doubts as to my love for you. They may not want to believe that I still love you and that time will have changed nothing in me! Have faith in me and do not let yourself fall into despair over these arguments. The foundation of our love and the fulfillment of our happiness depend upon <u>mutual trust</u>. Don't ever forget, *ma chérie*, that you have my complete confidence, you have it completely, and that I count on you <u>for all of life</u>. I give <u>you my word that we will be married</u>.

You see, *ma chérie*, fate has sent us a test so that our love will achieve its full greatness. You are everything for me, and I do not want to speak here of all my pain in letting you leave, going so far from me, but know that if I had to lose you, nothing good would come of my life. You are my goal. And this reward, do you see, *ma chère* Janot, I want to merit it. I must make something of myself to deserve you and deserve at the same time my own happiness. I would like you to realize the entire sum of love and of tenderness that I have for you and that I do not dare to let you know for fear of frightening you. But this love can do much in a life. It is love that influences everything else. Guard this love for me, *ma chérie*, and believe in me. You are now my fiancée; remember that when you see me again, it will be to become my wife, never to leave me again. Already I am entirely yours.

I embrace you, *ma chérie*, with absolute faith in you and in the future. Reread these lines on the days when nothing goes right in the hope that they may be able to give you a bit of courage and convey all the dreams I can put in a kiss. Receive all my kisses, the very little ones and the most profound and the most passionate, and guard them well until the day when we see each other again. This love is a precious deposit that I leave with you. May you be able to return it to me intact and without blemish on the day you come back. And then, you know, we will never be alone in struggling, because in addition to those we love, there is God in whom we both believe, and when one is sincere and true, God never abandons those who have heart. He will lead me back to you, you will see. Of that I am sure. And the most beautiful day of my life will be the one when I will be able to embrace my little *Moumoutte*, never to lose her again.

He signed it *ton Schatsy*, using the nickname she had given him, derived from *Schatz*, the German word for "darling."

For the next several days, Janine lived belowdecks, drenched in sadness. In the dark of the hold, she lay with Roland in her memories and tried to pretend he was lying beside her under the blanket. For the first time she noticed how long months of limited rations had outlined her ribs and how her abdomen dipped like a basin between the bony peaks of her hips. But the hunger she felt was only for him. She tried to call up his smell and his taste, the pulse of his heart, the warmth of his skin, the soul in his eyes. It was not enough. *A baby*, he'd warned, resisting desire that night in Marseille. But how she wished that a part of Roland were growing inside her, traveling with her, linking them always, their love enduring through all generations by way of their child. Why had she let him deny her that blessing? She lay for days with her knees curled up to her chest and allowed Alice to believe seasickness had paralyzed her, while Trudi attempted to lure her on deck. But Janine would not move. She lay there and wept, consoling herself with promises of love she engraved in her heart:

We share a love that is strong enough to triumph over all obstacles. . . .
You are now my fiancée; remember that when you see me again, it
will be to become my wife, never to leave me again. Already I am
entirely yours. . . .

One night, as she lay in the dark and gave in to her tears, she jumped
in alarm as the curtained partition, stretched across the width of the
hold, suddenly opened next to her head. She found herself staring
into the shining eyes and ebony face of a Senegalese soldier whose
bunk was behind hers. His gleaming teeth flashed a friendly smile in
the night, and she was mortified that her noisy misery had been disturbing his rest. Gently, he reached an arm past the curtain and placed
an apple next to her cheek. "*Ne pleurez plus,*" he urged her. Don't cry
anymore. "You must eat and get up. Things will work out." Before the
end of the week, the chivalrous soldier would give her a thin metal
ring wrapped inside a note asking her to become his wife.

The *Lipari* traveled along the coasts of France and Spain and past
Barcelona before turning south to cross the Mediterranean Sea. Without incident, it reached North Africa and stopped in Algiers, but the
refugees were not permitted to disembark. "*We had to stay for two days
on board the ship in the harbor, seeing the town not far away, and the crew coming and going,*" Janine later wrote of the journey. "*I thought that Moses
must have had the same feelings as we had, when he could see but not enter the
Promised Land, and when we arrived three days later at Oran, the same thing
occurred. It was inhuman.*

"*From Oran to Casablanca, our ship was accompanied by five little warships,
which had to protect us,*" she added. They studied the waves for signs
of U-boats lurking under the water, and minesweepers scoured the
oceans before them. "*We practiced safety drills several times in case our ship
should be attacked. I had waited to see the famous Straits of Gibraltar, but the
sea was very rough, and long before we reached that place, I felt more sick than
ever and could not leave my bed.*"

Another night, asleep in the lower berth of the bunk beside Janine's, Alice woke up and shrieked, as a set of false teeth fell from
above, landing square on her face.

"*Mes dents, mes dents! Qui a volé mes dents?*" Who stole my teeth? their owner demanded, scrambling down to search Alice's berth for the teeth she had dropped. The woman's voice was indignant, no theft beyond imagining now.

"*Gott im Himmel!*" Alice exclaimed, her heart racing, after her bunk mate had climbed back to bed. "Those teeth landed right on my nose! That scared me to death!"

"Why? Did they bite you?" Janine inquired, her anger inspiring a joke that surprised even her by making her giggle. It was the first spark of life to enter her voice since she'd boarded the ship. Yet as silence descended again in the hold, Janine lay awake in the groaning darkness and wished she could take back the words that now seemed unkind. She was acutely aware of the rustle and sighs, the breathing and snores of all the people, her mother among them, trying their best to escape into the illusion of dreams as they maneuvered through the fears of the night.

The following morning, Janine ventured on deck and started to meet a few fellow passengers, but still she spent most of her time staring at two tiny pictures of Roland pasted inside a three-inch, blue spiral notebook that substituted as a new autograph book. The first was a formal portrait, Roland in a suit, white shirt, and striped tie, with his glossy, thick hair slicked back from his forehead and a very solemn look on his face. The handwritten entry on the opposing page was undated:

La soeur	The sister
L'amie	The friend
La tendresse	The tenderness
L'amour	The love
Toutes sont parfaites en toi	All are perfect in you
Et je ne sais laquelle aimer le plus	And I do not know which to love most

The next page offered an informal snapshot of him, grinning shyly and wearing his coat, standing along the banks of the Rhône in Lyon, a bridge in the background. Roland had written the message accompanying this picture just the day before she sailed from Marseille, when she objected to his having termed her a *sister* and *friend* in his

Roland's first entry in Janine's little blue autograph book

Roland's second entry, written the day before Janine's departure, pledges lifelong love.

earlier entry. She needed far more romance than that to take away with her, and he complied:

> To erase that which I told you one day when I did not yet dare pledge my love, I ask you here to preserve our love intact until the happy day when you will be able to become my companion for life.

Before leaving the ship, another young man, having noticed her devoted attention to her little blue book, asked to inscribe a message himself: "*For the day when your sad blues have been drowned, I dedicate to you this little word.*" At the top of his page, he had pasted half a French postage stamp that showed the face of a girl gazing into the distance, with a single word over her head: "*Espoir.*" Hope.

. . .

"*We would have liked to stay at least a week at Casablanca and see this town so famous in France for its beauty,*" Janine would later write of her trip, practicing English as a student in Cuba. "*Instead of this, we had to leave our ship at four-o'clock, just cross the wharf and go on board the* San Thomé, *which had arrived the same day from Portugal.*"

The Joint's Lisbon office had chartered the *San Thomé*, like others before it, in neutral Portugal, the only country that still had available ships. The agency had to guarantee payment for filling each berth and was contractually obliged to pay for the trip in full before the ship left Morocco. It paid half when the *San Thomé* set out on the voyage with some 110 refugees embarking in Lisbon, and the balance before it left Casablanca, where 448 passengers boarded. There, in addition to the *Lipari* travelers, it had taken on passengers from the *Ville d'Oran*, a cramped freighter for animals that had carried refugees, along with more than one hundred sheep, across the Mediterranean from Marseille eight days ahead of the *Lipari*'s sailing.

Some of the *Ville d'Oran* group, interned in Casablanca while they waited for the *San Thomé* to arrive, powerlessly watched their visas expire and were separated from family members with still-valid papers who had to continue the journey without them. Those left behind could not renew their visas in Morocco, and as they stood on the docks tearfully waving farewell, no one could say what would happen to them. It seemed all too likely that they would be sent back to France with almost no chance of escaping again.

Jewish relief agencies paid the Portuguese approximately $400 per adult passenger and half fare for children, a total for the ship as a whole of $192,607 (the equivalent of well over $2.6 million today). At the HICEM office atop the rue de Paradis in Marseille, a staff of seventy-eight people had helped secure visas and fix travel arrangements. By the end of that month, the Joint would report that together with HICEM, from January 1941 to May 1942, they had helped almost eight thousand refugees get out of France. That November, after the Germans invaded Marseille, the Nazis would transform HICEM's villa, turning a haven of hope into a house of torture for hundreds of Jews and Resistance fighters whose only escape would be death.

The refugees who managed to board the *San Thomé* constituted Babel afloat—Germans, Austrians, French, Poles, Dutch, Belgians, Czechoslovaks, Russians, Latvians, Luxembourgers, Bolivians, Romanians, Yugoslavs, Spaniards, and Swiss—though records would list many others as "stateless," aliens officially stripped of citizenship. Most were Jews who had been targeted for deportation and all that implied, but there were also those who had volunteered with the French Foreign Legion during the war, only to be denied permission to reenter France after it fell.

There were non-Jewish German political refugees fleeing the Reich, as well as a contingent of refugees from the Spanish Civil War. Volunteers from dozens of countries, they had joined the International Brigades on the Republican side six years before, unsuccessfully battling the Fascists in Spain. Many of them were scheduled to leave the ship in Veracruz, the *San Thomé*'s next port of call on the way to Havana.

Also on board, among a coterie of artists and intellectuals, was a forceful woman reputed to be the daughter of the late Spanish novelist Vicente Blasco Ibáñez (author of *The Four Horsemen of the Apocalypse*). There was a Russian sculptor who came close to sparking a fistfight with Sigmar, a most unlikely brawler, when he suggested that Janine might agree to pass the time modeling in the nude for him because his wife had watched her undress in the hold and reported she had a very fine figure. There was a Viennese actress who taught Janine about the transformative magic of makeup and light, a Spanish aesthetics professor and poet with a nobleman's profile, and a firebrand German Jewish communist who would return to Germany after the war with lofty ideals for rebuilding the nation.

In short, it was an unlikely assortment of careworn souls who met traversing the oceans of war, all cut adrift from their past social circles and thus free to interact with each other in a circumscribed time and place that cast them as equals. Money alone was no passport to safety, nor was its absence a bar to making the voyage. As far as the Jews were concerned, the Joint Distribution Committee and HICEM raised funds through philanthropy and from refugees' families abroad to ensure that no one who held appropriate visas would be denied rescue solely because he or she could not pay for a ticket.

Though the *San Thomé* had been built as a freighter, the passengers' comfort had not been ignored. There were lounge chairs on deck, and Portuguese waitresses served food more ample and varied than most of the passengers remembered enjoying in years: bread, milk, sugar, coffee, and meat—even the basics were luxuries to them. There were a few sinks and limited makeshift toilet facilities, generally clogged. But there were also large laundry basins set out on deck, and groups were welcome to make use of the lifeboats to gather in private. As the days wore on and people began to know one another, a Frenchman carried an old fur bedspread up on the deck. He invited other young people to stretch out with him under the stars on "*la pelouse de mes ancêtres*," his ancestors' lawn, as he charmingly called it, almost as if he could claim a new home, sacred space, wherever he laid it. The ocean itself was eerily empty, never another ship within view, as danger and cost discouraged most vessels from making the voyage.

At least compared to the *Lipari*, Janine found conditions on the *San Thomé* a happy surprise:

The new ship was very comfortable, white and clean, five o'clock tea was served, flowers stand on the tables, the holds in which we had to sleep were white, the beds were of white wood, the straw-mats covered with white sheets, and although we had no saloon [salon] in which to spend our days, at least we had some chairs on deck, which in some places was covered. We had become very modest during our voyage, so that these things, which we would have disdained before, now really enjoyed us.

But this joy swept away. As the ship was very small and we were almost 600 persons on board, it was impossible to be even one moment alone. Moreover, being no more accustomed to have such rich food, so many butter and grease, in a few days many of us felt very ill. People began to quarrel, one day for a chair, the next day for a spoon; but we still were not on the end of our endurances. The more we approached the South, the more we began to feel the heat. We were obliged to spend our days on deck, exposed the whole day to the sun and during the night sleeping just under the engines, we nearly couldn't support the heat. It was terrible. Moreover, we couldn't extinguish the light during the whole night for the case of accident, and the noise of the engines disturbed us very much. So we decided to make our beds on the deck, an idea that did not work out very well. The nights were so humid and cool that at once we caught very bad colds. Moreover, the deck was cleaned every morning at 5 o'clock so we were obliged to get up early. But although this solution was not very fine, we liked it better than to sleep in the cave.

Finally after two weeks, we sighted land, which the captain told us was Jamaica, where we had to leave the ship and spend three days in a camp. Before we could land the ship was inspected and of course the travelers also. From the time we had left Marseille this was the first part of the journey that we could enjoy. It was a wonderful day, the sun was just rising behind the hills forming the backbone of the little island of Jamaica. It was the most marvelous moment in our trip. Our ship quietly entered the harbor of Kingston backed by the Blue Mountains, and not far away we already could see the little houses of the town. We all were very glad to see land again and how beautiful it was—we almost forgot that we had still three weeks more to travel before we could arrive at our destination.

Janine stood enjoying the sight of the colorful colonial harbor as the *San Thomé* drew into Kingston, when Sigmar caught her off guard by grabbing her chin to study her face.

"The British are very conservative," he snapped, his face white and taut in spite of the weeks they had spent in the sun. "Lipstick will give them the wrong impression of you. Take my handkerchief and wipe it off immediately."

Who could foresee how his family's virtue and value now would be judged as they landed on this Caribbean isle? He scarcely knew who he was anymore. In vain he pawed at his pocket for a cigar. Beneath him, native Jamaicans bent in the sun to secure the *San Thomé*'s ropes to the cleats on the quay, and British officers carrying clipboards talked with the captain. Warily they eyed the hundreds of refugees amassed on deck in somber woolens and dark hats that advertised their foreignness. It was the officers' unpleasant duty on this Easter Sunday, April 5, 1942, to explain to the stressed and weary passengers that they would have to debark and be moved to a camp about a half hour away so their credentials and baggage could be inspected. The British were worried that German spies might have infiltrated these newest arrivals and needed adequate time to clear the ship for traveling onward.

Orders were issued matter-of-factly, but as not all the passengers understood English, there was a good deal of multilingual chatter on deck as the instructions were informally translated, person-to-person, with varying degrees of accuracy. The gist was this: passengers would have to leave their belongings behind, save for a change of clothes and toiletries for a couple of nights. When they returned to the ship, they would find everything just as they left it. Customs and immigration officials would be searching each person who filed off the ramp, inspecting their visas and asking them to declare any money and valuables in their possession.

How could they know, these British officials at empire's outstation, that to the refugees' minds, this routine inventory would undercut pride? Lost, stolen, long since abandoned were homes and businesses, paintings and pianos, bank accounts, stock, insurance, furnishings, jewelry, cars, cash, and any and all other wealth they had once possessed. Schadenfreude lent truth to rumors that flew through the group that the British subjected the diamond dealers from Belgium and The Netherlands to the most invasive sort of personal searches.

The Günzburger family was waiting on line for the bus to the camp when an officer tapped Janine on the shoulder. Her parents watched in alarm as he led her away, explaining he needed to ask her some questions. The Orthodox Jew she had insulted on the day that the *Lipari* sailed from Marseille had reported her emotional outburst in favor of France, which raised concerns regarding her sympathies now. Did she still maintain that this chance to leave France represented *exile* to her? Did she really imagine, as a Jew, that she could conceivably be better off there? His rhetorical questions still hung in the air when one of the British inspectors who had been searching the ship entered the office and placed a thick envelope on his superior's desk. With horror, Janine recognized Roland's parting letter—her most treasured possession. Testimony to the discipline with which her parents had reared her, she had obediently left it behind with her things in the hold.

"No! No!" she exclaimed. "Please! You must give that back!" She lunged for the letter while she struggled to say what she needed in English. "That is only for me!" Silent tears of frustration rolled down her cheeks.

"I understand your sentiments, but we shall have to examine this," the officer said as he flipped through the twelve densely packed, handwritten French pages, his caution punctilious at this critical checkpoint. When he came to the last page, with writing that extended all the way to the bottom, he had to rotate it to read the signature, which ran sideways along the paper's left margin in larger script than that of the text. He frowned at the name and then at the envelope, which offered no indication of where and when the letter was sent. "Who gave this to you? *Schatsy*, is it? A German name, if I'm not mistaken. Whoever that is, he certainly had a great deal to tell you! I'm afraid I shall have to order a translation of this, and that will take time, obviously."

No explanation and no amount of begging and blushing, of tears and pleading would induce the official to return it to her. All correspondence found on the ship, her letter included, would have to pass scrutiny by censors, he said. While she did not appear a dangerous person, the risk of permitting an Axis spy to enter undetected into Allied territory was simply too great, given the current state of the war. If her loyalties lay where they belonged, with the Brits and the Yanks, she would surely approve of every safeguard. The letter, he said, would be waiting for her, under her name at the main post office, poste restante or general delivery, when she got to Havana. But she would have traded an arm to take it with her.

"By the way, young lady," the officer added before he dismissed her to join the family and get on the bus, "in future, I'd advise being more careful about the sorts of things that you say. These are difficult times, and words can be weapons."

Three days later, almost all the 500-odd refugees were returned to the ship to continue their journeys to Mexico, Cuba, or the United States, depending upon which visa they held. Thirty-three remained in Jamaica. There were 235 bound for Mexico, 280 for Cuba, and only 10 for the States: American visas, most coveted, were the hardest to get for Jews fleeing Europe. Many of those on their way to Havana did not plan to stay there, but hoped to continue on to the States as soon as they could.

On April 16, more than a month after leaving Marseille, the *San Thomé* reached the port of Veracruz on the Gulf of Mexico. Unexpectedly, thirty-seven former fighters of the International Brigade from five different countries, all scheduled to disembark there, were forbidden to land. There were threats of shipping the former Loyalist fighters back, and they were terrified of returning to Europe. Negotiations sputtered on for ten days as all the passengers miserably languished, until finally money changed hands. The Mexican Central Jewish Committee, supported by the Joint, agreed to post bonds, which proved crucial to winning the refugees' entry. In the interim, though, some daring young men even dove off the boat and into the water, viewing the prospect of creeping ashore as preferable to facing the risk of being hauled back to the Fascists in Europe. Bored with waiting, Norbert taunted his parents that he was planning to jump off as well.

But the long delay, even while fraying the refugees' nerves, inspired the locals to organize parties, which was more to his liking. Night after night—attracted, perhaps, by the allure of young foreign girls on the ship—handsome Mexican harbor policemen with pistols strapped to their waists boarded the *San Thomé* with musicians. Cheap local cane liquor called *aguardiente* may have helped to make the passengers friendly, and the music of *sones* lightened the mood. Steamy tropical nights sweated the notes of marimba and bamba played on harps, tambourines, and four-stringed guitars plucked with picks fashioned from cow horn. The Mexicans danced with young Europeans and tried to teach their dazzling footwork to people who, having run for their lives just weeks before, barely even knew where they stood or whether they ought to celebrate yet.

On one of these evenings, the *San Thomé*'s attractive Portuguese captain, Antonio Bravo, having noticed Janine, invited her to dine with him in his personal quarters. He was at least two decades older than she, nearly bald and not very tall, but with a strong cleft chin and bright blue eyes, he cut an elegant figure in his well-fitting white uniform with its high collar, brass buttons, and epaulets. Sigmar was flattered the captain had singled her out, and as he calculated that such a connection might somehow prove useful, he urged her to accept. But did he stop to consider that after cold and lonely weeks on the ocean, shepherding refugees over the waters of war, the captain might seek something more from a beautiful woman who dined in his quarters than polite conversation? Certainly not. In good German fashion, Sigmar took in the title, the gold braid that adorned the captain's square shoulders, the sense of authority that Bravo exuded, and he determined it quite safe and proper that Janine should go. Naïvely, he could not conceive of liberties taken, not under the eye of her very own father.

"My, such an honor!" Sigmar reflected aloud. "My daughter invited to dine with the captain!"

For history's sake, Janine brought along her little autograph book, in which the captain obligingly pasted his picture and also penned an inscription in English: "*I think every time the best and lovle* [lovely] *girl on my ship.*" But the invitation would not be repeated, nor would she have accepted again. As they sat and talked on his deck after dinner, the captain took hold of her hand and without any warning urgently clasped it between his legs, where her fingers encountered a limp little bird. It attempted to flutter, but she yanked back her hand and ended the evening, realizing that nothing was ever as simple as her parents believed, nor could she ever tell them about it. It seemed too much to expect them to withstand the shock of her broaching a sexual topic. The captain's behavior nonetheless marked the start of a new education. Without Roland at her side, she learned the language of strangers' desires, which totally changed her views about men and affected the way she would one day teach me about them: skeptically, with mistrust and with warnings about all of the ways one's heart might be broken.

· · ·

As the *San Thomé* crossed the Yucatán Channel and drew closer to Cuba, the passengers read in the sun, played chess or cards, studied Spanish, debated the course of the war, and tried, if only for the sake of their children, to envision a new life with something resembling optimism. But for one couple, obsessed by memories of a similar trip three years before that had ended in nightmare, nervousness mounted. In May 1939, Arnost and Camilla Roth and their young son had sailed on the ill-fated *St. Louis*, almost all of whose 937 passengers were unaccountably barred from landing in Havana and then unconscionably shipped back to Europe. Most of them Jews who hoped eventually to settle in the United States, they had purchased Cuban landing permits in Germany at inflated prices through a racket headed by Colonel Manuel Benítez, Cuba's corrupt immigration director. What they did not know, however, was that eight days before they set out, infighting among unscrupulous officials, in addition to political pressure against admitting more Jews, had led Cuban president Federico Laredo Brú retroactively to cancel permits and visas for all but twenty-eight of them.

When the *St. Louis* entered Havana's outer harbor on May 27, 1939, it was not permitted to approach the dock and was shortly ordered to leave Cuban waters. Frantic telegrams to President Roosevelt and other world leaders proved unavailing. No country would offer asylum. Even with the *St. Louis* anchored off Miami Beach, the combined forces of anti-Semitism and isolationism chilled the American State Department, which refused to relent. To spare the imperiled Jews from returning to Germany, the Joint finally arranged—posting a cash guarantee of $500,000 (equal to almost $7 million today)—for France, Belgium, The Netherlands, and Great Britain each to admit a share of them. Still, when war broke out the following year, only the 287 accepted by England were safe from the Nazis, and a quarter of the rest ultimately perished in internment or death camps.

Among the group admitted to France, the Roths had sailed again for Cuba, now on the *San Thomé*, relying on assurances that the island's immigration restrictions had changed since their last diverted and harrowing journey. Inevitably, though, their story spread through the ship, terrifying the travelers holding visas for Cuba who had missed or forgotten the shocking headlines of three years before. As the *San Thomé* moved toward Havana, the refugees restlessly counted the days and waited to land, while a new specter of horror haunted the ship.

On Sunday morning, April 26, almost six weeks after the refugees sailed from Marseille, the *San Thomé* arrived at the tip of the port of Havana where the great Spanish fortress, the Castillo del Morro, has stood for centuries facing the sea, guarding the city and watching for pirates. But on that spring day, in a place far removed from the violence of war, the "pirates" were already ashore—mercenary Cuban officials looking for plunder under cover of law. Their attack on the refugee ship came by way of a special decree signed by the Cuban president, General Fulgencio Batista, on April 16, just as the *San Thomé* was dropping anchor in Veracruz.

While Cuba had already provided asylum for six thousand Jewish refugees up to that point—five thousand six hundred of them having arrived just within the previous year—now, abruptly, Batista cut off the island to those seeking safe harbor. It seemed the tragic experience of the *St. Louis* would be repeated, as his new regulations effectively revoked permission for the *San Thomé* refugees to land in Havana. They blocked entry to all natives or citizens of any enemy country and, moreover, of any country being occupied by an enemy power. (Although Cuba did not engage in the fighting, its government

four months earlier had declared war on Germany, Italy, and Japan.)
By denying admission to refugees not only from the three Axis countries but also from any part of the globe the Axis occupied, Batista's
decree banned refugees from virtually all of Europe and good deal of
Asia. Described as a measure aimed "to avoid infiltration of enemy
aliens into Cuba," the decree resulted in only 40 *San Thomé* passengers free to debark. Among those barred from entry, subsumed under
the law as possible enemy spies, were 147 women and children. Just as
in the *St. Louis* fiasco, the new law made no exception for refugees already at sea and heading for Cuba with visas in hand. To the contrary,
the third provision of the new decree spoke directly and negatively
to their situation: "All visas granted prior to this decree to persons
who have not yet entered Cuba and are included in the above named
restrictions, are hereby annulled."

The Joint jumped into action even before the passengers learned of
the crisis ahead. The agency sought help "on humanitarian grounds"
from the American State Department and the President's Advisory
Committee on Political Refugees; from the Polish, Czech, and British
embassies; from top ranks of the Catholic church and Cuban officials.
The American embassy in Havana cabled the State Department that
"while the decree's ostensible purpose was to prevent entrance of possible Axis agents," it seemed the real purpose involved "an attempt
to extract more money from Jewish relief societies" eager to see the
refugees land.

Meanwhile, Cuban newspaper accounts compared the *San Thomé*
to the *St. Louis* and begged that mercy be shown to the beleaguered
"Hebrews."

"It would be a cruelty to have refugees turned back to the Axis-
controlled nations," wrote *El Crisol* on April 18. "In this moment of
drama and horror for humanity, all those persecuted by the Nazi-
fascist monster are worthy of the respect and consideration of all free
men."

The paper *Finanzas* lauded the Batista government for guarding
against the entry of enemy spies, yet it also denounced the injustice
of voiding visas that Cuba had previously granted to the "unfortu-
nates" already at sea. "Let not our Cuban government permit another

spectacle such as that of the *St. Louis*; let it for the last time permit the disembarkation of this boatload of Hebrews who have fulfilled all the requisites of immigration before the issuance of this decree," it suggested. If they are not permitted to land, "they will have to be returned to their ports of entry to be at the mercy of the fiendish Gestapo torments." Still other editorial comments spoke in favor of granting the Jews permits to land on the grounds that they were "people of means," likely to "add to the wealth of the country."

For ten nerve-racking days, the *San Thomé* waited in limbo outside the harbor. Although there was no way for them to know, on April 19 the United States had rejected the Günzburgers' applications for visas, so admission to Cuba was essential for them, as it was for most of the others on board. The Joint brought fresh supplies of food and water onto the ship and held meetings with a passenger panel that struggled to find an end to the impasse. The refugees' panic and fear mounted each day, much like the garbage and excrement that overwhelmed efforts to maintain hygienic conditions on a ship that had now been at sea three times longer than initially planned. The course of the talks with Cuban officials was the only thing on the passengers' minds, and rumors spread through the ship like a virulent plague.

Casablanca! A fate overheard. God, no, the passengers wailed, was it possible the Cubans would actually ship them back there? In the face of despair, the understanding arose that the situation might change if only they could raise sufficient funds for a meaningful bribe. Janine would always remember that the figure demanded was $100,000— equivalent to almost $1.4 million today—but few of the refugees had any substantial money with them. There were, however, those who had diamonds. And Janine would also remember that the Orthodox Jewish merchants from Antwerp whom she had scorned at the start of the journey were the ones who helped pay for the passengers' lives.

In a special bulletin when the crisis was over, the Joint would announce that for two weeks it had "worked incessantly" with Cuban officials and "interested public-spirited persons" before receiving a call at eleven forty-five p.m. on May 5 with the news that the Cuban government would admit all the *San Thomé* refugees still out in the harbor. Of the twelve thousand refugees who had sought shelter in

Cuba since Hitler took power, these were the last, as the decree of April 1942 shut the doors of the island for the duration of war. Sizable bribes bought sanctuary for the persecuted who came in those years, helping to add to the staggering fortune that Batista took with him when Fidel Castro's revolution forced him from power and required *him* to flee in the following decade.

"The nature of the problems which confront us in the Cuban situation do not permit us to give them publicity," a confidential Joint memorandum noted that June. "You can readily understand that much that is done must go unsung." But in a subsequent report it clearly explained that Colonel Benítez, Batista's director of immigration, had "conducted a thriving trade in the sale of illegal landing permits," and that refugees, once admitted, then became vulnerable to "squeezes" from other officials "using the threat of expulsion from Cuba." When refugees lacked funds to pay, the burden fell on the Joint.

The resolution of the *San Thomé* story as presented for public consumption, however, in the *Havana Post*, *El País*, and other newspapers ascribed Cuba's decision to admit this last boatload of Jews to an Allied agreement to help weed out any Axis agents hiding among them. American and British officials resolved the crisis by offering "to 'cooperate with the Cuban Government' in checking over the refugees' documents, to determine whether they are political refugees in good faith or not," the *Havana Post* said. It reported that the refugees, guardedly viewed as enemy aliens, were being transferred to the Tiscornia Immigration Station to await thorough investigation of their papers before being released into civic Havana.

Havaner Leben, a Yiddish-language newspaper founded in 1932 to serve a large, settled Jewish Cuban population stemming from earlier waves of European immigration, explained that the American and British ambassadors had also promised to help verify which of the *San Thomé* passengers would eventually be able to proceed to the United States.

On May 7, on behalf of the Joint, its honorary chairman Paul Baerwald sent his thanks to Batista. "Your Excellency," he wrote, "the lofty spirit of humanitarianism displayed in your action illuminates the dark chapter of man's inhumanity to man. We beg to assure you that we are deeply appreciative of the hospitality of Cuba to these refugees and to the others now in your country."

For those aboard ship, admission to Cuba at last put an end to unspeakable years of terror and loss, grief and despair that they had suffered in Europe under the Nazis. Whatever came next, at least they were safe. For Janine, however, throughout the bleak, restless days that still lay ahead—like the ones endured on the *San Thomé* while waiting to learn if the currents of war would save or destroy them—there was really only one thought in mind. One reason to land. She needed to get to the Havana post office and reclaim the letter whose promise of love would carry her over the borders of time, both back to Roland and ahead to still happier dreams of their future together.

FIFTEEN

INCOMMUNICADO

ALMOST TWO MONTHS after leaving Marseille, the *San Thomé* passengers disembarked in Havana. But as soon as their uncertain feet regained solid ground, the weary travelers were forced onto boats once again. The destination was no longer whispered: Casablanca. Not the teeming port they had left behind in Morocco. Rather, it would turn out to be a sleepy fishing village of the very same name, reflecting the fact that a white house—*casa blanca*—stood on the shore near its pier. Still, that did not alleviate the refugees' fear and confusion, when instead of being released into the Cuban capital, they were ferried across the Bay of Havana, a channel so narrow it looks like a river. Landing in this unknown Casablanca, on the northeast side of Havana harbor, they were crammed onto buses that lumbered on unpaved streets past humble tin-roofed shacks and up a very steep hillside. At last at the summit, the refugees were shocked to be herded into a spartan detention camp called Tiscornia, which would serve as their home for as long as the Cubans decided to hold them.

In years to come, curiously, many of these refugees would remain baffled about where they were taken. Apprehension and unfamiliar surroundings so distorted their sense of the quick boat ride of less than a mile, from Havana across the sleeve of the harbor to the opposite shore, that it would loom in memory as long and mysterious. As a result, they would mistakenly claim that Tiscornia existed on some other island off Cuba's coast. It was Cuba's Ellis Island, they contended, a place removed from the mainland. From the vantage point of the camp, Havana had sparkled, a distant glimmer of freedom over the water. Once released from its confines, they had never returned. A small street sign on a rustic alley, Callejón Tiscornia, now provides

```
                    REPUBLICA DE CUBA
               DEPARTAMENTO DE INMIGRACION
          TARJETA DE IDENTIFICACION DE PASAJERO TURISTA
             (IDENTIFICATION CARD OF TOURIST PASSENGER TO CUBA)

Nombre del Pasajero  Gunzburger  Janine
Name of Passenger
Nacionalidad                    Nombre del Vapor
Nationality                     Name of steamer
Manifiesto No.  4               Partida No.  25
Manifest No.                    Line No.
Puerto de procedencia del pasajero  Casablanca
Port of origin of the passenger

AVISOS :  1—Esta tarjeta deberá ser conservada por el pasajero para su identificación en Cuba.
   2.—Transcurridos 60 días de la llegada del turista, y sin prejuicio de lo que disponen las Leyes
       sobre inmigración, deberá inscribirse en el "Registro de Extranjeros".
   3.—El portador se obliga a no desempeñar empleo ni trabajo de ninguna classe en Cuba.
   NOTICES :  1.—This card must be retained by the person to whom it is issued for purposes of
       identification during permanency in, and departure from Cuba.
   2.—Upon arrival in Cuba the person to whom this card is issued agrees to comply with and conform
       to the Laws of Inmigration, and 60 days after date of arrival must register at the "Registration
   3.—Bureau for Aliens".
       The border also agrees not to engage in pursuit of work or employment in any shape or form,
       during his or her, permanency in Cuba.

Firma del pasajero              Sobrecargo
Passenger's signature           Purser
```

The tourist identification card provided to Janine aboard the
San Thomé *for debarking in Cuba*

the only indication of where the camp stood. Even in Cuba, its role in the war years has been forgotten.

The site, however, is easily reached today not only by ferry, but also by car through a short tunnel crossing under the rocky tip of the harbor where the forts of El Morro and La Cabaña, looking out to the ocean, once comprised the most powerful Spanish defensive position in the New World. Here, in colonial times, a large wood-and-bronze chain was stretched across the harbor each night to block foreign ships from reaching Havana. Guards at the massive fortress of La Cabaña sounded a cannon to signal that the harbor was sealed, preventing those already in port from sailing away under cover of dark.

. . .

On July 31, 1942, the New York–based immigrant newspaper the *Aufbau* publicly pleaded for mercy and justice on behalf of 450 refugees from Hitler's Europe, the Günzburgers among them, still confined at Tiscornia after almost three months. The detainees included 250 passengers from the *San Thomé* as well as 200 from an earlier sailing arranged by the Joint. Passengers from that ship, the *Guinée*, also a Portuguese vessel, had been interned since April 9, about a month longer than the *San Thomé* group.

As of 2004, the street sign on Callejón Tiscornia provided the only indication of where the detention camp for Hitler's refugees stood. The camp had been replaced by Cuba's Instituto Superior de Medicina Militar.

"The captive refugees are surrounded by silence," the *Aufbau* reported. "Every once in a while they hear rumors that their liberation is nearing, only to find out that what looked like a transitory period is developing into a state of permanence. They live without comfort, in overcrowded quarters, inadequately nourished, exploited by individuals who sense an opportunity to enrich themselves. Their spirits are low; they brood over their undeserved fate and find no answer."

An internal report of the Joint's Relief Committee condemned their condition with stark facts: "The facilities are entirely inadequate" for a population it described as including 88 children, 66 elderly, 168 women, and more than 100 men. "The great majority of the refugees live in dormitories in groups of 120 to 125 each; men and women are separated from each other so that there is no privacy of any kind." Noting that the refugees could not understand the reasons for the indiscriminate internment of babies, children, the sick, the feeble, and the aged, the report warned, "We feel very strongly that there is a serious danger of a general breakdown of health and increasing signs of camp psychosis."

Passengers from both ships were being held subject to "case-by-case examination," the Joint in Havana explained to New York headquarters. "Rumors have been circulated to the effect that there were Nazis among these groups. To the best of our information, these are unfounded." But getting the refugees freed from the camp involved complex financial, diplomatic, and political issues, and the American State Department, demanding "the most complete investigation of each of these cases," seemed less than eager to help speed the process.

Initially promised release within days—*sí, sí, mañana, mañana*—the refugees gloomily waited with no sign of progress. For the Cubans, meanwhile, detaining these lost Europeans was proving highly profitable. The émigrés took no pains to disguise their goal to get out of Cuba and head for the United States the instant that their visas came through, so Batista's regime was less concerned about building long-term relationships with them than with making the most of their stay on the island. The Cubans imposed camp fees of $1 per person per day, in addition to medical fees and so-called extraordinary fees that together amounted to $45,000 (equivalent to more than $600,000 in current value) by the start of July. At the rate they were paying the Cubans, families like Sigmar's could have supported themselves both better and longer on their own in Havana, but the grossly inflated camp fees quickly devoured any money they had. "It is leading them into bankruptcy, no matter how well-to-do they may have been at the start," the Joint reported. Along with detainees who could afford to contribute, the Joint was covering fees for half of the refugees, those deemed penniless, because the Cubans made paying the fees a precondition for eventual release.

Compounding money problems was the camp canteen, charging exorbitant prices in a monopoly market. The Cuban music that tumbled from loudspeakers over the camp and filled the store with upbeat, rhythmic songs of the tropics—with mambos and rumbas, drums and trumpets—failed to blot out the extent of the scam. Without competition, the bodega charged at least double the price for everything it sold to the inmates, who could barely subsist on rations alone. Camp doctors themselves advised refugees not to eat the meat or the fish served at meals because it was spoiled. Alarmed by the sight of refugees starving, the Joint distributed money to shop at the canteen for those who had nothing, and also sent in bottled water, 1,000 oranges, mangoes, bananas, or pineapples daily, 450 eggs, and sometimes sardines for the adults, as well as butter and milk for the malnourished children.

As weeks went by, the detainees banded together in a committee and elected leaders to deal with the Cubans and handle their interests with the Joint. Incensed by the canteen's blatant price gouging, they organized boycotts with pickets, and their activism lifted their spirits; for the first time in years they effectively managed to wield influence and push prices lower. Food, however, was just one of a long list of troubles. Physically weak and emotionally spent, trapped in crowded and unhygienic conditions, many fell victim to heat, lice, bedbugs, and illness. Lacking the extra money required to stay in the clinic, those who were sick remained in the dorms, where crowding barely left space to walk between beds. The *San Thomé* group sparked an epidemic of a flulike disease that the doctors described as "seasonal grippe," while whooping cough, enteric fever, hepatitis, and accompanying jaundice claimed many others.

PATIENT EXPIRED was the sign that Trudi only half jokingly hung over a rope, trying to set up a makeshift quarantine around the metal bunk bed where Janine, stricken with hepatitis, lay moaning, yellow, and nauseous. But others quickly came down with it also, including an infant of just seven months, who sickened and died. "It goes without saying that such a child might have been saved under proper conditions," the Joint concluded, despairing of the state of the camp. Yet because the child and his mother had shared a bed close to her own, Janine would not stop blaming herself for being the proximate cause of his death.

While the ill were not quarantined, the refugees' contact with the rest of the ailing, war-weary world was so sharply restricted that the Joint summed up their status with one grim word: "incommunicado." At the very moment they desperately needed to find out the fate of relatives elsewhere, make new arrangements, and reach out to friends or family already arrived in the United States for aid in securing visas and loans, they were kept isolated.

"Despite the fact that all mail is carefully censored all the way," the Joint reported, the Cuban Ministry of Communications prohibited the delivery of critical mail, which might have provided important news, much-needed money, or documents that would help verify the refugees' backgrounds. Nor did the Cubans permit the inmates to send any mail, a situation that punished Janine particularly, as her heart had been fixed, from the day the British in Jamaica confiscated Roland's precious letter, on getting it back and writing to tell him where he could find her. More than sickness and bugs, heat and boredom and inedible food, her inability to make contact with him over so many months remained the overriding cause of her torment.

What if he'd been picked up in Lyon as an Alsatian? Already, the Germans might have him. Might have sent him to Russia. He could have been killed! She couldn't bear to wait any longer to get to a post office, and so, when a tooth flared up, she begged the camp doctor for permission to make a trip to a dentist, never expecting to be kept under guard by two policemen throughout the time she spent in the city. She returned to Tiscornia minus a molar, but with her letter to Roland still in her pocket, as her minders would not allow her to send it. Nor would they let her attempt to retrieve any mail from Roland that might have been waiting for her, poste restante in Havana, as the British had promised.

Her only hope was to smuggle a letter out of the camp with someone she trusted, someone permitted to come and go freely. Her range of choices included just one, Sigmar's cousin Max Wolf, a shrewd businessman who had managed to sail from France to Havana with his wife and children months earlier and had been held at Tiscornia for only a number of days. He was now living in a spacious apartment not far from the Malecón, where cooled by sea breezes, he could look north to his future over the Florida Straits and plan a path to profit on Wall Street. Meanwhile, having urged Sigmar to follow his route of escape to Cuba with the ultimate goal of reaching New York, he dutifully came to visit by ferry from Havana each week.

A heavyset man, Max invariably arrived at the gate exhausted and huffing from his arduous climb from the dock to the camp bearing food, cigars, and the latest newspapers. Once past the guards, with his face florid below his straw hat and under the shadow of his stubbly beard, Max would collapse in a chair in the open-air pergola under the trees that the refugees used as their common salon. Janine would watch him, quietly transfixed, as the floor gradually darkened around him, soaked by sweat that dripped down his legs and pooled at his feet.

His wife, Emma, never made the trip to the camp, but she regularly baked buttery pound cake and sweet fruit tarts for her husband to carry up to their friends. Her son Erich, on the other hand, often came to visit Janine, and it was the fondest desire of both fathers that their offspring might someday marry each other. Even in Lyon, he was the rival who most vexed Roland, knowing the power of Sigmar's approval. Erich had come there to see the family on several occasions and before leaving France had inked a declaration of love in Janine's little blue autograph book for the open appraisal of any reader, including Roland:

> Was this the same Hanna of earlier times whom I had never bothered to notice in Freiburg? She has become a superb young woman! Now I cannot fail to appreciate her calm, decided, and serious character, and I realize too late my enormous stupidity in having left such a charming person so quickly. What more natural than for me to want, by any means, to return to Lyon to see her again and to find her as adorable as ever and to treasure an unforgettable memory of her?

Indeed, it was Erich whom Roland had in mind when he wrote in his parting letter to Janine that while it was normal for parents "to try to make you marry the man that they choose," she should always remember that no one could force her. Still, it was not beyond her, after months of unavoidable silence that nevertheless grieved her heart almost as much as rejection, to seek to make Roland jealous by way of the letter she was hoping to send him. She therefore frankly included the news that Erich Wolf was also in Cuba and had been regularly—yes, devotedly—making the strenuous trip to the camp in order to court her. But how she could manage to mail it was far less clear.

One day as Uncle Max took leave of her father, heading home to Havana after a visit, Janine caught up with him near the camp gates. She felt emboldened by having noticed him sneak out letters for Sigmar and Alice, who had been urgently writing to the American relatives of their old friend Meta Ellenbogen. Upset by rumors that their Freiburg tenant had been among those deported to Gurs, but was now being held in a transit camp near Marseille, they hoped her American cousins might swiftly gain her release by helping secure a visa and passage. So, Janine reasoned, if Uncle Max was willing to skirt Tiscornia's rules and mail letters for Sigmar, perhaps he would mail her letter to Roland. Then she went further. Not only did she beg Max to post her letter to France, but she also gingerly ventured to ask to use his Havana address to receive a reply, since she could not receive any mail in the camp.

Monsieur Roland Arcieri, 27 rue Puits Gaillot, Lyon, France. Max perused the envelope she handed to him, raised his eyebrows and studied her face.

"*Nur ein Freund, Onkel,*" she quickly assured him, only a friend. He said nothing, folding the letter into his pocket, where she hoped it would not become too wrinkled and sweat-stained before it reached the hand of her love. When she unexpectedly saw her letter again the following week, however, this time in the hands of her father, its crumpled condition was the least disturbing aspect about it. Uncle Max had opened the letter, read it, and furiously brought it straight back to Sigmar, whose dark eyes behind his bifocals popped with rage.

"'*Erich comes here to see me, but he is the same foolish boy he always was!*'" Sigmar quoted the letter, her hurtful description and indiscretion having embarrassed him terribly in front of his friend, whose loyalty seemed a godsend in this odd, forgotten spot on the planet. "How could you let yourself write such a thing? What possessed you to risk letting Uncle Max read such a nasty comment about his own son? And after all of his care and kindness toward us!"

Sigmar punched at the air, tore the letter into a scattered puzzle of meaningless pieces, and totally sidestepped the propriety of Max's violating Janine's privacy by reading her mail. She silently fumed, not daring to speak. How could the man be so lacking in morals and pride as to admit to snooping and then bring back the letter to share with her father? The gall—imagine acting aggrieved and indignant instead of ashamed!

"As for Roland, you must forget him," Sigmar asserted, somewhat more calmly. "*Fertig*," finished. "There is no point even thinking about him. *Dummes Zeug*," just stupid nonsense, he muttered. "He is not one of us. You can't ignore that. The world doesn't, either. There is a war and an ocean between you. Even if Erich is not the man you're ready to marry, you will make a new life and meet many others when we get to America. But if you can't be more careful, what with writing to France in the middle of war, you'll get us locked up here forever! Don't dare try something that foolish again. If the Cubans find out, they'll think you're a spy. And the next time you see Uncle Max, I expect you to apologize to him and make some excuses."

To soothe his nerves he pulled out his cigars, the single delight that coming to Cuba had thus far afforded, after years of enforced abstention from smoking. Dourly, Janine stared at the package. Sigmar termed his favorite cigars his "*Lieblinge*," his darlings. How peculiar—Janine hadn't really noticed before—that the brand was called Romeo

The box cover of Sigmar's favorite Romeo y Julieta Cuban cigars

y Julieta. Their names on the box were written on a pink ribbon above a picture of the romantic Shakespearean balcony scene. Roses and bougainvillea encircled the couple in a bower of blossoms, but their faces were already wearing tragedy's masks. Juliet gazed with ineffable sadness and longing into the hopeful face of her lover as if she already knew their future was doomed.

Life in the camp proceeded that summer with no sign of release, and the refugees tried to organize constructive activities: morning exercise classes in the pergola; lessons in English (some taught by Norbert), Spanish, and Russian; school for the children and evening lectures. The Orthodox Jews also established a prayer room above the bodega to hold services, while in the shaded tranquillity of long afternoons, bearded men bent over tables outdoors to study the Talmud, a scene that created an image of peace and continuity for those who simply lingered to watch them. But with the boredom and unremitting heat of the summer, frustration lit fires beneath restive young people, impatient for ways to spice up confinement.

"*Lisel! Komm schnell!* I can't wake up Norbert!" Sigmar came crying for Alice in alarm outside the women's dormitory one morning, having woken to find their son unconscious. Norbert had joined a group of young men who broke into the clinic the previous evening to get drunk on rubbing alcohol, which just made them sick. Others channeled their energies more purposefully into organizing political action. Fritz Lamm, a Socialist activist, then thirty-one, whom Janine had met aboard ship, took to the soapbox to call on the young to stand up to the Cubans and militate for release, if for themselves only.

"The older generation has already lived their lives!" Janine would always remember his impassioned appeal. "Let the older ones stay and wait in the camp. We young must demand our freedom now to get on with our lives, or else we will have to take matters into our own hands! The time is now!"

When the outspoken utopian placed an inscription along with his picture in Janine's autograph book, he addressed her in a similar vein. "Needless Fear!" he titled his page, writing in German with its capitalized nouns that seem to dress up the vaguest pronouncements with the dignified luster of aphorism. "No one can seize Freedom and Fortune from you as long as both lie within you, and both lie together with Hope and Memory."

Many who gathered to hear Lamm's orations admired his insistence on action, and, returning to Germany after the war, he would gain public attention as an idealistic social thinker. But within the camp there also were those who resented Lamm's divisive proposal to demand freedom for just part of the group, giving rise to consternation among older inmates who did not appreciate being discounted.

This prompted Charles H. Jordan, the hardworking Joint representative in Havana, to send a special report to his New York office observing that the Tiscornia refugees were sunk in a "very depressed state of mind." He added: "I am afraid that they are becoming very impatient and inclined to follow the leadership of some of the more aggressive people who believe that the policy of waiting for action on the part of the authorities should be changed for a policy of action on the part of the refugees themselves—which expresses itself, at this point, in internal incidents."

While working for the detainees' release, Jordan had been assiduously trying to better the conditions in camp, assisting with food and medical aid, and eventually persuading the Cubans at least to allow for the delivery of mail and money sent to the refugees in care of the Joint. On top of the inflated expenses of life in Tiscornia, the refugees were each expected to show a $500 bond and $150 in "continuation of voyage money" as a condition of winning release. An extremely high sum, for the Günzburger family of five, for example, it would translate to more than $45,000 today. While there were efforts afoot to get these requirements waived, the Joint simultaneously worked through the National Refugee Service in New York to contact the inmates' American relatives and urge them to help out with loans.

In regard to Cuba, however, Joint officials pronounced themselves shocked and discouraged by what they viewed as "abnormal" indifference on the part of the local Jewish community, among them fifty American Jewish families, in the face of the troubles afflicting the refugees. They found the community of more than ten thousand local

Jews disorganized, lacking in leadership, and uniquely tightfisted in response to pleas for philanthropic assistance. In a report tracing most Jewish settlement in Cuba to Eastern European refugees who had arrived in the 1920s, the Joint charged that although those immigrants had become financially successful on the island, they had failed to develop an appropriate sense of concern for the newcomers, many in need. "There is the perennial antagonism on the part of the East European Jew to the Western Jew," the report explained, while "the American Jews as a whole seem to resent the refugees' entrance to Cuba, and are not at all keen on helping, whether financially or otherwise."

In an interview that September in *Havaner Leben,* Jordan spoke even more bluntly, declaring Havana "the only place in the world" where the local Jewish community had failed to help the Joint in its mission. "The local Jews who have lived here many years do not have any feeling about helping the refugees," he said. "The Jews the whole world over, everywhere on the whole earth, know their duty, except the Jews in Cuba."

The Joint went so far as to conclude that not only had wartime immigration turned into a "rich source of graft for Cuban government officials and employees," but also that several members of the Havana Jewish community were themselves involved in these rackets, while the rest remained passive or wasted their energies in aimless infighting. With unproductive lay members, the Cuban branch of the Joint, founded five years earlier, depended almost entirely on Jordan himself. To help him negotiate with the government, Jordan therefore hired a prominent local attorney and politician, Jorge García Montes—later Cuba's prime minister—and their combined endeavors achieved major improvements to the refugees' lot.

Key among them was a change in the law that had required all refugees to renew their transit or tourist visas monthly, a difficult and costly process. Now all the Jews who had fled to Cuba to escape Hitler's Europe gained resident status valid until the end of the war. This effectively stopped the graft in the Immigration Department that was bilking them tens of thousands of dollars per year in fees and bribes just for the right to renew their expiring visas every thirty days. With this guaranteed stability, those refugees who had arrived in Havana somewhat earlier and were living in the city could find jobs.

A more challenging problem involved the special situation of the three thousand five hundred German and Austrian Jews whom the Cubans regarded with extra distrust. Like those German Jews who had sought safety in France before the outbreak of war in 1940, only to be slapped in French prisons under suspicion of being Nazi spies, these refugees found their allegiances questioned. Even before the *San Thomé* landed, the Joint planned to persuade President Batista to certify the German and Austrian refugees as "loyal aliens," based on a careful review of their individual credentials and backgrounds. Toward this end, according to a confidential Joint report, García Montes sent the Cuban State Department a "memorandum detailing the persecution of the refugees, their denaturalization by the German government, and the actual feeling of the refugees toward the totalitarian countries."

The consulates representing the other nations whose refugees were interned in the camp had sent officials to see their former citizens and seemed prepared to offer them the moral guarantees the Cubans required as another precondition, besides money, for winning release. The American consulate in Havana, as well as other American and Cuban government agencies, had investigated all the passengers, but detainees from Germany and Austria had no way to obtain the requisite moral stamp of approval. On July 19, grappling with their lack of a consulate to vouch for them, eleven German men in Tiscornia, Sigmar among them, hit upon the idea of enlisting support instead from the international fraternal order of the B'nai B'rith. In desperation, they wrote via the Joint in Havana to the *Grossloge* or grand lodge in New York, beseeching the B'nai B'rith—like a government of a people dispersed—to provide the character references the Cubans demanded.

No longer citizens of any country, they wrote as "international brothers" and offered the only credentials they had: their former faithful membership in the German lodges of the B'nai B'rith based in the cities where they had lived. And so they listed themselves, each former German reduced to identifying himself through a lodge now destroyed in a city where he no longer belonged: Sigmar Günzburger of the Breisgau Loge in Freiburg, Otto Nussbaum of the Kaiser Wilhelm Loge in Bremen, Alfred Kahn of the Carl Friedrich Loge in Karlsruhe, and so on, all of the men, from Plauen and Stuttgart, Augsburg and Saarbrücken, where going to meetings of the B'nai B'rith had been part of their roles as upstanding Jewish community leaders. They explained their arrival in Cuba on the *Guinée* and the *San Thomé* and pleaded for help in winning release from the "bitter torture" of a continued detention behind barbed wire, an imprisonment they did not understand after so many years of suffering under Hitler's oppression.

"*Warum wir hier sein müssen, wissen wir nicht,*" they wrote. Why we must be here, we do not know. . . . "While the refugees of other countries have the protection of their consulates, we feel completely abandoned. It would be an enormous relief for us lodge brothers—who in better days always tried to help others—if our American brethren would take some interest in us. Please let us know quickly that we can depend on you."

The B'nai B'rith could do little more than forward the letter to the Joint's New York office. On October 6, a Joint official also updated headquarters on the situation, which by then had dragged on for more than five months. Cuba was about to begin releasing those who qualified, insofar as they would not become a financial burden to the country and they could present official guarantees of their moral and political backgrounds.

"The passengers of the [*San*] *Thomé* have been investigated by the American consulate in Havana as well as by other agencies of our and Cuba's government. To the best of our knowledge, all of these are unobjectionable and loyal to the cause of the United Nations," wrote Robert Pilpel, a top Joint official. "Those who are nationals of the United Nations countries, Poland, Russia, Czechoslovakia, Luxembourg, Belgium, as well as the Swiss and French, number about half those in Tiscornia, the balance being made up of some Austrians and for the most part, Germans. After all these months, the reasons for their extremely prolonged detention remain unclear and ununderstandable. Only now is there a prospect for the release of some whose consulates in Havana are prepared to give a moral guarantee."

Those without consular representation in Havana could face problems, he noted, especially the German Jews, deemed stateless as a result of having been denationalized by German government decree on November 25, 1941.

The High Holidays passed that fall without the buoyant sense of spiritual cleansing and rededication that Janine and others had hoped to recapture in a new world. Prayers for forgiveness of sins, for peace and redemption failed to lighten the hearts of the people whose vision of escaping from Europe had never included hard months of detention. They searched their souls and past behavior, prayed for the blessing of purposeful lives, and extolled the burden of chosenness as if generations had not already paid everything for it.

On Yom Kippur, the Day of Atonement, Janine observed the obligation to fast. But in the parching heat of Cuba's September sun, her craving for water became so intense that in brushing her teeth in the communal bathroom that morning, she permitted a drop to slide down her throat before she piously spit out the rest. Guiltily, she cast around to see if anyone noticed. But the One who counted, she knew, saw everything. She told herself that her indulgence had been an accident only, yet knew in her heart she had done it on purpose and that punishment was inevitable—especially as camp doctors had warned against drinking tap water, contaminated with dangerous microbes.

That evening, after Yom Kippur services, Jordan sat down with the refugees at Tiscornia to break the fast. The next day, the Joint official reported bitterly to New York that although the local Jewish community had tried, this time, "to do the job as they understood it best," the religious observance had been "most inadequately arranged and created a great deal of dissatisfaction all around." But whatever the holiday may have failed to deliver in spiritual terms, it shortly appeared that prayers were answered.

Just ten days later, on Friday, October 2, Jordan called the Joint in New York with good news that Cuba's commissioner of immigration had made a "definite statement" that all the detainees would be released from camp by the end of the month. The Cubans planned first to free the Dutch, with the French to follow, and then all of the

others, country by country. Jordan sounded a note of caution, afraid
of predictions, yet there was reason enough to celebrate.

At sunset the following evening, most of the camp assembled in
front of the building that housed the bodega and above it the prayer
room, for which the Joint had provided a Torah. After performing
the Saturday ritual of havdalah—marking the formal end of the Sabbath and greeting the secular week as they doused a braided candle in
wine—Tiscornia's Jews burst into a memorably festive observance of
the annual holiday of Simchat Torah.

Under the laurels and eucalyptus, men took turns clasping the sacred scroll in their arms and, as tradition required, carried it in *hakafot*
or joyful procession around the building—seven times, singing and
dancing—past the hedges of crimson hibiscus and the exuberant tan-
gles of bougainvillea. The children too went spinning and jumping,
the little ones waving colorful paper flags they had decorated over
the previous days and marching with candles. The flames leaped with
the children and flickered like fireflies in the deepening dusk, men
whirled and stomped and voiced praise to the heavens that stretched
above the high royal palms, and Jews at Tiscornia affirmed their faith
in a God who had brought them from the cellars of death to rejoice
in the hope of a fresh beginning. Even those like Sigmar, Jews of more
contemplative faith and natural reserve, not given to dancing, watched
and prayed with an added measure of feeling that day, after so many
years of terror and chaos.

Camp releases began shortly thereafter. On October 14, 1942,
alarmed that they alone might still be confined while the others went
free, the eleven German members of B'nai B'rith wrote again to New
York, pleading for help. "We are afraid that our cases might not be
handled particularly benevolently," they said, this time in English.
But the next day, the Günzburger family was among a group suddenly granted permission to leave. By way of supporting background
as to his morals, Sigmar's files would prove to contain a report sent
from Paris six months earlier, in which the French Justice Ministry
confirmed that he had no criminal record. By the start of the year, all
but thirty-five refugees had won their release, and on February 2, 1943,
the last five detainees walked out of the camp in search of new lives.

"This closes the Tiscornia situation for the passengers of the *Guinée* and the *San Thomé*," Charles Jordan typed his report to the Joint. "*In other words, there is nobody left in Tiscornia.*" The last sentence he added in ink and by hand, almost as if he needed to shape the words with his fingers to feel the reality, the blessing of freedom, he had worked to secure for so many people.

SIXTEEN

LEBEN IN LIMBO

WHEN SHE WALKED DOWN the splendid Paseo del Prado, with its long center island of trees that stretched toward the ocean, Janine felt like a goddess. A goddess of love or of beauty, or, perhaps, given the way the men eyed her hips, a fertility goddess. Habaneros sprang into her path, whipped handkerchiefs out of their pockets, and crouched to wave them just inches above the sidewalk before her, as if they had only been waiting to clean and to polish the granite in advance of her step. "*¡Ay, qué linda!*" they murmured, clicking their tongues. "*Ay, señorita,* to be worthy of such beauty as yours, the street itself must be wearing a shine!"

Months aboard ship and in the open air of the camp all through the hot summer of 1942 had left Janine slim and tanned, and sunlight had gilded the tobacco-hued curls that wound to her shoulders. Her blue eyes were wide as they took in the vibrant scenes of the city, the pastel-colored porticoed buildings; the Paseo's bronze lions and wrought-iron streetlamps mounted on marble; the chic boutiques selling alligator purses, jewelry, and perfume. Especially, she admired the fashionable strollers, whom she carefully studied in order to learn how to fit into this place, whose cosmopolitan style and colonial charm had so very pleasantly caught her off guard.

"*¡Ay, señorita hermosa, de dónde es usted? ¿A dónde va?*" Oh, pretty young lady, where are you from? Where are you going? "*¡Vamos juntos!*" Let's go together! Men in short-sleeved tropical guayaberas tossed questions like roses to draw her attention, trailing her steps. But on this particular morning, instead of sternly evading their greetings as she kept walking, she smiled and she laughed.

Clutched in her hand was a bundle of letters she had just retrieved, not only that most precious letter the British surprised her by sending from Kingston exactly as promised, but to her delight, numerous new ones—months' worth of letters from Roland, all waiting for her in care of the Havana post office. Surely, he must have believed she had gotten them sooner! She imagined his worry over never receiving any reply and headed toward the Malecón, where she could sit on the seawall and enjoy them in peace. If she closed her eyes, the sound and spray and smell of the ocean might let her pretend she was back in Marseille, back in his arms, hearing his tender words in her ear.

Years later, except for the treasured original one, my father would destroy all these letters in a futile attempt to rip their author out of her heart. I can therefore only imagine their fervent expressions of love and desire and how Roland's pledge of reunion and a lifetime together carried her dreaming over the water and allowed her to hope that nothing had changed. Though the words on the page have been lost, Janine would always remember that she devoured the letters in order, according to date, and that Roland had started the first by quoting their favorite verse from Lamartine:

"Un seul être vous manque, et tout est dépeuplé." Missing a single person makes your whole world empty.

. . .

On October 27, 1492, the first few Jews in the New World, presumed to have sailed with Columbus to escape Spain's Inquisition, spotted the island of Cuba, where they soon landed. Four hundred and fifty years to the day later, another Jewish refugee who crossed the ocean to flee Europe, Sigmar Günzburger, purchased from the Cuban Defense Ministry the requisite foreigner's registration booklet that came with strict warnings to report any address changes within ten days of moving. For his own life in the New World, he gave his first name as Samuel and dropped the umlaut (ü) from Günzburger. Yet in the black-and-white mug shot pasted into his booklet, No. 352202, he remains European, formally dressed in a suit, white shirt, and striped tie, and his glance is deflected. Gone, the resolute glare of the man in the family portrait taken in Gray. The picture here is one of

The Cuban Defense Ministry's foreigner's registration booklets, including fingerprints, for Samuel Gunzburger, sixty-two years old; Alice Gunzburger, fifty; and Janine, nineteen.

submission. He gives in to the photo and fingerprinting, allowing his thumbs—*derecho* and *izquierdo*, right and left—to be pressed against a pad of black ink and rolled onto a page like a hustler caught committing a crime. Now as I study the booklet, the eyes in the picture refuse to meet mine, and so I place my thumbs against his, as if some warmth of life might seep through the paper and permit me to feel his hand through the years.

The address that Sigmar provided authorities when his booklet was stamped on October 27, 1942, was a place he was lucky to find within days of being released from Tiscornia. A three-bedroom flat in the manicured upper-middle-class section known as Vedado, it was beyond the hubbub of central Havana and just a short walk from the Moorish–art deco palace of the Hotel Nacional. There, a glittering clientele of Hollywood idols, foreign dignitaries, and American industrialists had worked on their tans, sipping minted mojitos and pink foam daiquiris on seafront patios under the palms, even as Mafia gangsters raked in the dollars from its casino and cleverly greased the government's wheels.

Never before had Sigmar so easily moved into a region described as "off-limits," the meaning of *vedado* in English. The name derived from the fact that in the 1500s it was forbidden to build there, a practical rule designed to preserve an unobstructed view of the ocean and of pirates sneaking up on the beaches from over the waves. Having gone on to become a landscaped neighborhood of broad streets, grand mansions, and jagüey trees dripping thick and eerie aerial roots, it was and remains today one of the finest residential parts of the city. That Sigmar could rent there and live in Havana not richly, but modestly and cautiously well, was thanks to Herbert, who helped with loans, as Maurice and Edy had extended in France.

The family's new apartment, in house number 855 on Calle 25 between A and B, came furnished in French provincial décor and was on the second floor of a three-story building with only two apartments per level. Each had a large open terrace facing the street and glassless windows fitted with dark brown shutters to keep out the sun. From the living room, adjoining the terrace at the front of the building, a narrow hallway ran between the kitchen and dining room to the quiet

Moisés Simons, standing (L) at the piano, with his orchestra in the mid-1920s

of the bedrooms, shaded by trees in the garden out back. Off the hall, there was one green-tiled bathroom with a tub and bidet. A bridgelike balcony looking onto a yard connected the small galley kitchen to the kitchen of the apartment next door. This was a convenient place for the maids of each household to chat in off-hours, domestic help being so cheap and easy to find that even refugees on limited budgets indulged in hiring Cuban servants.

Their landlord, Moisés Simons, was one of the country's most beloved musicians, and he lived with his pretty French-born wife in the ground-floor apartment. Simons had made an international name for himself in 1930 with a lilting hit song, "El Manicero," which introduced Havana's humble peanut peddlers to the rest of the world. It had probably been recorded by then in more versions than there are notes in the tune. So why would a composer of such success and renown rent space in his home to Jewish refugees during the war? It continues to be a source of conjecture whether Simons—ostensibly Catholic of Spanish descent—might have actually been Jewish himself or else, perhaps, had Jewish forebears. Information about him is scarce, and while it remains unclear how or why he left Cuba for Spain at such a dangerous moment, Simons is known to have died at age fifty-six in Madrid in 1945, some say after a period of hard labor as a captive at Buchenwald.

During the year that Janine lived in his house, she took pride in her landlord's musical fame and in learning to sing his most popular song, in a style called a *pregón*, drawn from the tunes of the *pregoneros* or wandering peddlers who enticed customers as they sang out their wares. "El Manicero" was inspired by a vendor of *cucuruchos de maní*, paper cones of roasted peanuts, whose jingle Simons heard outside a bar in Havana. Legend had it that he composed his lighthearted masterpiece on the spot that night, setting notes to dance on the back of a napkin. From there they took flight as a worldwide sensation.

Not far from the house where the Gunzburgers lived above the musician, a pair of prim English sisters ran a private girls' school where Sigmar enrolled his two daughters. It was reputed to have a strong English program, and in tribute to England's patron saint, its founders had named it St. George's. The school catered to the elite of Havana, Cuban or American girls who lived in Vedado and the still swankier suburb of Miramar, with landscaped *palacios* close to the ocean. It prepared them for life in the best social circles, whether they married in Cuba, left for the United States, or divided their time between the two spheres, traveling abroad with affluent husbands.

Nowhere in sight were the bare-breasted girls with flowers in their hair, girls in native costumes of grass skirts and beads that Norbert had teased his sisters they would have to adopt. Instead, despite the heat of that tropical autumn, Janine and Trudi were taken aback to discover classmates with prosperous fathers in the tobacco, rum, or sugar business who dressed for the elegant chill of Fifth Avenue. Yes, these were girls who might parade in style equally well in downtown Manhattan or under the wide palm-lined Fifth Avenue running through Miramar. Here, Cuba's landed gentry and pedigreed industrialists danced in black tie and silks at embassy parties or luxuriated at one of the so-called Big Five country clubs, whose membership was so tightly restricted that even Batista (born out of wedlock, an impoverished mulatto) was never accepted.

Now with nostalgia, Janine remembered the uniformed smocks that her Mulhouse lycée had required its students to wear over their clothes. That was a time when she herself would have preferred to show off her custom-made outfits, but she had long since outgrown the designs of the Freiburg dressmaker. She tried to blend in among Havana's rich daughters, impeccably clothed in pleated plaid skirts, Shetland sweaters, pearl chokers, and saddle shoes. Chauffeurs drove these girls to St. George's each day, accompanied by maids who carried their book bags from their cars to the school and then returned to help them back to their cars each afternoon. Privileged as most of them were, however, the Cuban girls vied to be friends with Janine and Trudi, who took care from the start to let it be known that they were *French*. To be known as German with Hitler's war still raging in Europe would not win them favor, while being French lent them allure that more than made up for their refugee status. Their classmates openly argued over the pleasure of driving them home and also took them to dinner, to parties, and to lavish oceanfront clubs. Sometimes they even provided the sisters with handfuls of nickels, sharing the naughty excitement of the slot machines that spit unearned winnings all over the floor.

Among other girls new to St. George's were a few who had also been in Tiscornia with them and talked of returning to Europe after the fighting. But the student body generally looked north for inspiration, and the girls' cultural preferences showed a distinct American bias, including Dinah Shore, Tommy Dorsey, Frank Sinatra, Bob Hope, Bette Davis, and Donald Duck. The Cuban girls drank Coke and washed with Palmolive. If most listed swimming as the sport they liked best, it was probably less because of the ocean at hand—sharks and sea urchins being so frightening—than because the school swimming coach, Arturo, was tall, blond, and impossibly handsome. They kept up with the world through *Reader's Digest, Vogue, Town and Country, Life,* and *Harper's Bazaar.* They liked Longfellow, *Gone with the Wind,* Lucky Strike's "Your Hit Parade" radio program, and suitors who attended Yale. Some may have dreamed of college themselves, or even of business careers, but their futures after leaving St. George's tended to be more domestic. Members of the class of 1944, for example, reported a year after their graduation to be contentedly busy with lessons in tennis, art, French, music, knitting, and sewing, while the most outstanding student among them was taking a secretarial course.

"The modern girl is well able to look after herself," a former Tiscornia friend of Janine's would declare in a graduation speech at St. George's one year after the end of the war. "Her opportunities for independence are vast, but still she feels that her greatest happiness may be found when she is 'the worthy wife of a worthy man,'" and, far from losing her individuality, and her woman's rights, she may gain in power. Is it not said that 'the hand that rocks the cradle rules the world'?"

Nineteen years old when she entered St. George's, Janine was placed with younger students for English and Spanish, but advanced quickly enough to earn a diploma by the end of the year. With enthusiasm, she wrote about school in a letter to Hannchen, her Eppingen cousin, then in New York. The letter was part of a school exercise, and Janine wrote it in her blossoming English:

You know that when I left France, I never thought to enter in other time a college. But when at the end of six months we finally could leave Tiscornia, father told us that the best thing to do would be to go at school, even if I would not like it so much. At first I was very unpleased of this idea, but then I understood that it is the only way to learn English and Spanish. So I tried to find a school, and I really had good luck because St. George's is a marvelous one.

Our school is a very nice house, with a little garden before and little flowers help to give us an impression of kindness, and you find it just the same insides. Teachers speak with us like friends and however are respected and everybody works. We learn a lot of interesting things and I only realize that I lost a lot of time during the three years of war, which had us obliged to change our schools three times.

The girls are very nice, but I could tell you many things of the difference of spirit of these girls and the French girls. They have such a different education as we have it in Europe. They see the world from an other point of view; they don't know what is poverty, distress and even don't realize that we are in war. Of course it isn't their fault, they never see such things nor feel them. Consequently their interests are not the same as ours. We think in the happy end of the war, in American visas, in learning to speack English and Spanish, or we worry about our family in France. I think I don't need to tell you about this. You also must read in the news-papers all the evil the Nazis do in France. Naturally these happy girls can't care about all those things, so as we also before the war were mostly occupied with dances, dresses and other joys. Nevertheless, I like them all very much and often go out with them. I only tried to explain you that due to the differences of interest we can not make a friendship here, so as for instance I had it with Malou.

Twice a week we go swimming with the college and we have a very good swimming teacher. You see that even the sport is not forgotten. Besides this I go from time to time to the movie, I still like it very much. But the pastime I prefer is to stay at home, reading good books; for you must know that our school has a wonderful library, where you can find all kind of books you like. Now I think you can understand why I wrote you that I am relatively happy and don't want to leave Havanna very soon.

The parents are very well. Father spends his time reading the whole day, he nearly lives in his books and tells us always about the marvelous persons of the books. He is very much pleased of our college and he takes great interest in our work. He really is often astonished to see us studying so much and he is very glad to see that finally we receive of the "culture" he missed so much in an education.

The only thing I am very anxious about is that my English is still very defective; like you can see in writing I make a lot of mistakes, but so much more in speaking. But I still hope that in several months I shall learn it better.

But now I really must finish my letter. Please answer me very soon again. Today it isn't a letter I wrote you. It is nearly a narration of my schoollife.

Writing was emphasized for the St. George's girl, and write Janine did, in Spanish, French, and English, laboring over biographies and book reports, historical analyses, geography projects, and personal essays exploring her feelings—not always as fully adapted to the immigrant life as her letter to her cousin sought to project:

I would be so happy to see a day of winter and to do the sports I so much enjoyed in Europe. I would so much like to see the high mountains covered with snow. I would love to hear the bells ringing and stop in a field to pick flowers and cherries and apples and pears and what other fruit Europeans have. It is the truth that man is never content with what he has, but always looks for other things until he receives them and begins with another fantasy.

Sometimes her choice of subject hinted at yearnings she could not express. As mail from Roland ceased to arrive after the Nazis overran France that November, for example, Janine wrote about a fictional postman who found personal joy in the job of transmitting love: "*It is for me every day a new pleasure to see a mother or a fiancée smile happily, receiving a letter from their dearest one.*"

• • •

With Norbert's formal education behind him, he began work as a novice cutter in one of the new diamond companies that refugees from The Netherlands and Belgium were launching in Cuba. Being new to the country, this industry was one in which refugees were granted work permits, and so thousands of men and women trained to cut and polish rough stones from South Africa. Proximity and favorable American trade regulations facilitated their import to Cuba for cutting and their export back to New York for market. Novices in Cuba perfected skills in cutting eight-sided stones predominantly used in jewelry settings. Trainees practiced, however, on gems so very tiny that when Norbert loudly despaired that he had lost one and it would cost him, it was futile even to bother hunting for it. Only by luck, at breakfast days later, did Janine happen to notice the extra gleam in his eye, where, lodged in the corner, the little diamond was found to be hiding.

Between work and play, Norbert was rarely at home. Had the Nazis not come to power in Germany, his future as an underling in the family business—caught between his demanding father and his irascibly fragile uncle Heinrich—would have been determined for him. Now he regarded losing his eventual share of their company as an acceptable price to buy independence. His frustrated boyhood efforts to win Sigmar's approval weighed less heavy in Cuba: free of school and the duty to help his father with work, no longer pressured to burnish the family image, he escaped the scrutiny he had always detested. Consequently, with dollar bills lining his pockets and no shortage of female admirers, he was, at twenty-two years old, soon the only family member to enjoy Havana as the lively tropical playground it was. Invariably, when telephone number 8809 rang in the front room of the apartment, it carried a girlish voice asking in mellifluous Spanish, *por favor*, to speak with Norberto. When he was in, Norbert would dash to answer it first. But bathed and scented, handsome and carefully dressed, he was more often out, allowing Sigmar to answer requests for his son with three clipped Spanish words—"*En la calle!*" Out in the street! Out on the town!

Sigmar spent much of his day on the Avenida de los Presidentes, which, like the Paseo, featured a parklike median strip sweeping down to the sea and marble benches under the trees. Here he focused on reading *El Mundo,* the liberal newspaper, trying his best to teach himself Spanish. At home, beneath his windows, he heard the call of the lottery vendors selling numbers and the seductive illusion of life-changing riches. But a man of his staunch frugality was never tempted to gamble, nor would he accept any money from Norbert, so that living in limbo meant constant worry over finances. Besides the family debts he recorded on the lined pages of one student notebook, in a second notebook he listed in German all daily expenses, from potatoes and pickles to laundry and paper. Warned of thieves who dangled fishing rods through open windows to hoist men's trousers from bedroom chairs in dark of night, Sigmar slept with his money under his pillow. And more than once—the maid having blithely stripped his bed in the morning and shaken his sheets over the side of the terrace—he scurried downstairs to crawl through the bushes to hunt for his cash. With each week that passed, he became ever more eager to get to New York, to pay off his debts and plan for the future.

In the steamy spring of 1943, Janine returned home one evening to find her father angrily sputtering. Sigmar's head shone with perspiration, and he gnawed a cigar as he paced the floor of checkerboard tile. "*Hasch du mal so was gehört?*" Have you ever heard anything like it? he was saying in dialect to Alice as he reviewed the discussion they'd had with the visitor who only moments before had left the apartment. Alice sat quietly fanning herself with a piece of paper folded in tight accordion pleats. She had lingered too long that afternoon with Emma Wolf in a café where the fierce sun had burned her fair skin through the window. Now red blisters painfully pocked her arms and her legs.

Perhaps Janine had passed their guest on the sidewalk? Sigmar asked. His name was Sokoloff, the brother of Herbert's wife, Estelle. As promised back when Herbert first pushed the idea of refuge in Cuba, Mr. Sokoloff was willing to use his official connections to help speed up their American visas. But his conversation left Sigmar outraged. He was shocked that their guest, whose wedding ring was plain on his finger, had shamelessly sat at their table over coffee and cake, extolling his girlfriend.

"'My *amie* is beautiful,'" Sigmar quoted him, recalling that Sokoloff had used the French word for a female friend. "I'll help you get to my *amie*. She's not far from here. You'll spend a few days, and then you'll move on to New York." But could Sokoloff really imagine that Sigmar—no matter how impatient he was to get to the United States—would coolly condone such an illicit liaison? That Sigmar would knowingly take his own wife and daughters to be houseguests of a married man's mistress? It was simply *verrückt*. Crazy.

"I'd prefer to stay right here in Havana than have to lie to Herbert and Estelle when we get to New York," Sigmar fumed. "What in God's name could the man have been thinking, to come here and brag about his mistress to us? Unbelievable chutzpah! And then to suggest *we* pay her a visit!"

Janine listened in silence, then broke into giggles.

"This is funny to you? You are laughing at *me*?" Sigmar attempted to summon the bulging-eyed glare that proved so threatening when his children were young.

"Papa, I think you're mixing up your English and French," she more gently suggested. "M-I-A-M-I." She pronounced the word slowly. "*Miami*, not *mon amie*. *Miami*, Florida. It sounds like your Mr. Sokoloff is arranging for us to leave for the States!"

. . .

On July 13, 1943, Margaret L. Hannan, principal of St. George's School, wrote and officially stamped a letter that listed the courses Janine had taken, with the superior grades she achieved, and recommended her as college material:

> Her progress in English was remarkable, yet her work showed that she possessed knowledge far in advance of her ability to express that knowledge in what was to her a new language. She was tested by examinations of the standard of New York College Entrance Examinations and gained credits in Medieval History (91%), French 3 years (98%), Spanish 4 years (94%). Her English work was very good, but she still needs practice.
>
> We feel sure that as soon as Janine has more practice in the English language, she will find no difficulty in qualifying for the university of her choice.

Janine proved a good "mixer" in school, and took part in the swimming competitions for which the school entered.

Her conduct throughout has been excellent. We wish her all success.

Miss Hannan peered above the rimless glasses that always perched near the end of her nose as she extended the letter, shook Janine's hand, and inquired into the family's plans. "We are all very sorry to see you go," she said. "But you must promise me one thing: when you get to the States, please don't ruin all the work that we've done by picking up that thoroughly dreadful American English!"

Six days later, the vice-consul of the United States signed and approved Sigmar's affidavit in support of the family's immigration visas. Norbert, though, decided to remain in Havana. He persuaded his parents that he was better off working there than being drafted into the American Army and shipped back to Europe. His experience in the French Foreign Legion had sharply curtailed his previous zest for fighting the Germans. Knowing Norbert, Sigmar and Alice also suspected the influence of a saucy Cuban señorita, but since they could not dispute that he was safe and content with life in Havana, they sadly relented to his staying behind.

On his affidavit, Sigmar was obliged once again to define himself as a refugee: "*I was born on December 29, 1880, at Ihringen, Germany. I am a citizen of no country, formerly Germany,*" he stated. "*I am unable to obtain from the authorities of the government to which I owe (or owed) allegiance a passport valid for travel to the United States.*"

Photos of Sigmar, Alice, and the girls were affixed to the form, and each of them signed, Janine writing her name as *Johanna Dora Gunzburger,* thus ending her travels under almost the same name as she began them in Freiburg.

On August 10, they left for Miami. Before Janine and Trudi nervously boarded the plane for the first flight of their lives, Norbert kissed them on both cheeks and rewarded them with his most disarming grin. Then he enfolded both his sisters in his arms, and with their three heads huddled together, he gave them a little parting guidance. The musky scent of his favorite cologne found its way to their hearts

REPUBLIC OF CUBA
CITY AND PROVINCE OF HABANA
EMBASSY OF THE UNITED STATES OF AMERICA   S.S.

Before me, Thomas J. COLE.......... Vice Consul of the
United States of America, duly commissioned and qualified,
personally came Samuel Gunzburger........   who, being
duly placed under oath, deposes and says as follows:

My name is Samuel GUNZBURGER   and my present
home and address is calle 25 No.855; Vedado,La Habana,Cuba

I was born on December 29,1880   at Ihringen, Germany
I am a citizen of no country Formerly Germany

I am accompanied by:

Wife_Alice Heinsheimer____   June 19,1892
         (Name)   (Date of birth)

         Eppingen, Germany
         (Place of birth)

Minor children:
Name   Place of birth   Date of birth

Gertrude;_____   Fribourg,Germany   January 1,1925;

Janine(Johanna)   Fribourg,Germany   Sept. 5,1923

I am unable to obtain from the authorities of the Government
to which I owe (or owed) allegiance a passport valid for travel
to the United States, and therefore submit this affidavit to be
used in lieu of a passport in order to proceed to the United States.

Samuel Gunzburger

Subscribed and sworn to before me this 19th day of July 1943

Thomas J Cole

Vice Consul of the United States of
America.

Description:
Height 5'3
Complexion fair
Hair grey
Eyes brown
Marks baldheaded

Service No.   unnumbered
Fee NIL. To be used in connection
with application for a visa.

*Sigmar's affidavit of July 19, 1943, for use in lieu of a passport for the
family's travel from Cuba to the United States*

as they felt the warmth of his words in their ears: "Before you take off,
you mustn't forget to check for the parachutes under your seats," he
counseled. "You'll definitely need them in case you have to bail out."

This time there was no glint of a misplaced diamond to draw their
attention to his mischievous eyes, and so they panicked to find their
parachutes missing when they got on the plane and made fools of
themselves. And that was not the only surprise of their journey.

The two sisters landed at the Florida airport proudly wearing identical light blue gabardine suits, with slim, straight skirts and mandarin collars. Just as Alice had done in leaving Freiburg and Lyon, she had insisted that each of her daughters have one new traveling outfit, custom made for arriving in style, first impressions being so very important. Both of her girls wore their hair with parts on the left and curls to their shoulders. And while Trudi's hair was a little bit lighter and she had brown eyes and the faintest dusting of Alice's freckles, and Janine had blue eyes and broader shoulders, they might very easily have been taken for twins, dressed as they were in the same clothes, wearing the same bright smiles of anticipation.

"*Was werden da die Leute sagen?*" What will the people say when they see you? Sigmar had playfully asked when they dressed for their trip, just as he had when they donned their Passover best as children in Freiburg. But to their dismay, as they walked in their new finery through the Miami airport, the American people said nothing at all. No whistles, no winks, no clicks of the tongue, no appreciative comments from men who rushed by, which, after more than a year in Cuba, came as a shock.

"I'm sorry to tell you I think we left something important behind in Havana," Trudi observed to her sister. "And I don't mean Norbert."

"What's that?" Janine stopped and put down her suitcase. In fear, she surveyed the terrain of the past, scarred by losses, and she braced herself for an additional one, as yet unmarked.

"Our looks," Trudi grimly replied.

SEVENTEEN

HÔTEL TERMINUS

ALL OF ROLAND'S INNATE RESOLVE to avoid any type of regimentation could not ward off the Vichy government's summons in April 1942 to don the khaki shirt, dark green tie, and matching beret of the *Chantiers de la Jeunesse*, or worksites for youth, and fight for his country by chopping wood to make charcoal. Aiming to stiffen the backbones of France's young men through duty in quasi-military units organized after the army had fallen, the *Chantiers* established hundreds of campsites in the Unoccupied Zone and told Roland to report to Rumilly in the lush alpine woods of the Haute-Savoie near the Swiss border.

Yet so sure was he of worming his way through a loophole that he traveled to camp on the day of induction, just a few weeks after Janine left Lyon, carrying only a toothbrush. Indeed, a painful hernia resulting from his appendectomy the previous summer sufficed to win him a two-month reprieve, and he was sent home after just one night with instructions to go for hernia surgery—promptly ignored. Two months later he was called up again. This time, he won no sympathy from Vichy officials bent on improving the virtue, vigor, and virile demeanor of the country's young men so as to combat what Marshal Pétain denounced as a "decadent" culture and blamed for the ignominy of France's condition.

"Eh, eh, no dice." The induction officer wagged a rigid government finger when Roland invoked the pain in his gut the second time he was summoned to spend eight hard months in a forest learning the discipline of following orders. Like untold thousands of draft-age young men, he would be armed with an ax, a pick, and a shovel and be forced through the monotony of physical labor to embrace the patriotism of Vichy's National Revolution. If the *Chantiers*, while modeled on

scouting, managed to harden a cadre of men with the potential of one day forming a new French army, Vichy officials quietly agreed, that would also be a result to be valued.

For Roland, life could have been worse. In Alsace, both men and women between the ages of seventeen and twenty-five had for more than a year been forced into the Reich Labor Service, and later that summer, the region's young men would be drafted into Germany's armies. It was also that June, in a radio speech expressing his hope to see Germany triumph in Europe, that Prime Minister Laval announced a deal he made with the Reich to send three French workers over the Rhine to factory jobs for every French prisoner of war the Germans released. Under the terms of this purported relief plan, called *la Relève*, Laval aimed to minimize the political damage of 1.5 million French soldiers still being held in Germany's prisons, despite Vichy's groveling collaboration with Hitler. Even so, the three-to-one ratio meant that 4.5 million French workers would have to volunteer to serve in Germany in order to bring all the prisoners home.

That July, among new restrictions, Pétain's government officially excluded Jews from the dubious pleasures of the *Chantiers*. This allowed Roger to stay in Lyon, where a record outpouring of anti-Vichy protesters took to the streets on Bastille Day. Roland, however, knew nothing about this public unrest, with no radio or newspapers at the camp, which was expressly sited to be cut off from the world and the lure of insurgent political action. Rather, days started and ended with nationalistic flag ceremonies and loyal pledges of faith in their leaders. In the snow-topped, craggy face of Mont Blanc, a place naturally suited to humbling the soul and pointing one's efforts to loftiest purpose, Roland was exhorted to work for the glory of God, Pétain, and country. This he would do by bending his back in the collection of wood on the Semnoz Mountains and by learning to value such simple joys as being marched down the slopes, past the occasional remote chalet or docile herd of grazing cattle, for the once-weekly treat of taking a shower.

Within a matter of weeks, glory or no, it was obvious to Roland that he had the wrong job. The camp orderly's lot seemed far more appealing: to provide basic first aid for accident cases, to look after the sick in the camp, and to escort those in need of professional medical treatment down the mountain to visit the doctor who ran an infirmary based in a farmhouse. "*Il faut développer des choses,*" one must develop things, he ruminated over a plan. And so, reporting sick on account of his hernia, he pursued a friendship with the camp doctor and managed to shift to the post he wanted. Ultimately, he even persuaded the doctor to send him to the hospital in the picturesque lakeside town of Annecy for hernia surgery at government cost, on government time. There, lying alone and helpless in bed, recalling the sweetness of weeks when Janine had nursed him to health through her love, he would cower beneath the heart-stopping drone of British bombers that cut through the night on their way south to bomb the Italians.

The following March, Roland was released from his tedious tour of forestry duty. By then, Hitler had seized full control of France, and at a moment when no one was safe from the eye of suspicion, on December 27, 1943, the Germans demanded the ouster of the French general who had launched the *Chantiers*. Within days, the general was thrown into prison—first in Germany, then Austria—accused of lending support to the growing Resistance. That spring the Germans ordered the *Chantiers* disbanded. Then they harnessed the unarmed scouts to forced-labor battalions tasked with building the *Atlantikwall*, a massive system of bunkers and minefields stretching from Norway to the French-Spanish border, to block any northern Allied invasion.

. . .

With the second German occupation of Lyon in November 1942, the Gestapo set up headquarters in the swank Hôtel Terminus at the gare de Perrache, the railway station near the southern end of the Presqu'île. From there they could keep a close eye on the network of trains that crisscrossed France. In this 1906 art nouveau jewel—a decorative wonder of elaborate wood paneling and wrought iron, stained glass, sculpture, and neo-Impressionist murals by award-winning artists— Klaus Barbie, notorious as the Butcher of Lyon, established his offices upon arriving in town to head the Gestapo. On the fifth floor of the lovely hotel, while clerical workers went about their business as usual, he and his henchmen pursued the cruel interrogations of Resistance fighters and Jews, for which Barbie would face criminal charges more than four decades later.

Yet in the same hotel, on a different floor, valiant members of the Resistance burrowed into the French railway system and secretly worked to sabotage the aims of the Reich. And here, naïvely blind to the dangers swirling around them, Roger Dreyfus and Roland Arcieri eagerly accepted employment with the French railroad, the Société Nationale des Chemins de Fer Français—for Roger to avoid being deported to whatever mysterious eastward destination that meant for a Jew, for Roland to evade being forced to fight or toil for the Germans.

Roland had been shocked to discover upon his return from the mountains that Germany's relentless demands for hundreds of thousands of added French workers now placed him directly in line to be called. Unable to fend off Germany's soaring manpower demands, Laval had announced a compulsory program, the Service du Travail Obligatoire, requiring all French men between the ages of twenty-one and thirty-five to register for Reich employment. Even worse for Roland, Laval ordered *all* of those born between 1920 and 1922 to surrender immediately for two-year terms of forced German labor. Only those in a few essential job categories were exempted, among them miners, agricultural workers, police, and railway employees.

With his birth date of December 27, 1919, Roger slid out of the category of conscripted workers by the slimmest margin of only five days. But facing extra risk as a Jew and ousted for the same reason from his science studies at the university, he was quick to accept when a friend who worked as a railroad engineer found him a job as a *Dolmetscher* or interpreter in the offices based at the Hôtel Terminus. When Roland returned from the *Chantiers* that spring of 1943, Roger arranged the same post for him. At a hub where 3.5 million travelers would pass that year, the two young Alsatians were put to work translating communications between French and German railway officials.

The railway system, or SNCF, nationalized in 1937, became an unparalleled focus of the Resistance as the Germans forced it to transport troops, munitions, goods, conscripted French workers, and Jews condemned to death in the camps. Clandestine fighters in the

Resistance who worked with the railroad tried to delay or derail trains and slipped information on train schedules to saboteurs who set bombs on the tracks to blow up locomotives. They relied on trains to aid the escape of those hunted by Nazis, and to deliver letters, contraband, and underground newspapers. Reich officials were well aware that French railway workers engaged in sabotage and threatened the death penalty for any involved. Still, in the end, the SNCF reported that from the time of France's defeat in June 1940 to July 1944, there were 249 derailments achieved by resisters in the region of Lyon and thousands in other parts of the country.

Even after Resistance leader Jean Moulin was betrayed, arrested, and murdered that summer of 1943, the tide of defiance continued to mount. Ragged bands of self-styled saboteurs or guerrilla fighters, forming the Maquis in the countryside or the more urban Franc-Tireur Partisans in Lyon and elsewhere, attracted increasing numbers of volunteers to fight the Germans instead of submitting to work as their slaves. As evidence of their secret warfare, in August, over the course of one night, Roland was obliged to translate twenty-eight cables from French into German, all reporting sabotage somewhere on the lines. Hour after hour, all through his shift, he nervously faced the Germans at Lyon-Perrache, angry as hornets, as he brought them fresh accounts of railroad subversion.

Every day was tainted by terror of being found out, Roland as Alsatian, Roger as a Jew. In case he needed to disappear quickly, Roland procured a set of false identification papers listing a birthplace outside of Alsace that defined him as unequivocally French. His landlady, a civil servant with disdain for Vichy and—more important—valuable access to government forms, fashioned a safer alternate identity for him. With humor, the name that she chose for the handsome young man whose girlfriend had fled and left him alone was Jean Moine, or John the Monk.

But even false identity papers could not provide sufficient protection on the Sunday afternoon in the fall when Roger's girlfriend appeared in panic at their door to tell Roland that the Gestapo had come in search of their friend. They had ransacked her room and grilled her with questions, and she'd told them she thought Roger had gone out of town. He had, in fact, boarded a train the previous day on one of his regular trips to the country to visit his parents and brother, waiting out the war in seclusion; less benignly, he would also buy food on the farms to resell on Lyon's black market. With so many types of employment now blocked to Jews, and with his father, unlike Roland's, barred from resuming his prewar business in Alsace, Roger's petty black marketeering provided the family with crucial income. Despite Roland's warnings, Roger refused to give up his outlawed trade, and he went so far as to sell to the Germans, discounting the threat of their turning against him. Roger was due back that same afternoon, and Roland rushed to the station to warn him not to come home to the room they shared or to go to any other habitual haunt where the Gestapo might be planning to trap him.

In the waiting room, Roland paced the floor, compulsively checking and rechecking his watch. Then, checking himself, he decided it best to appear more relaxed and assured. He waved to the occasional co-worker who spotted him there on a day he wasn't scheduled for duty. Still, he made no attempt to invite conversation that might distract him from what he needed to do. The minutes crawled by in a torment of worry. And little by little, as Roland considered why the Gestapo had come for Roger, he felt suddenly certain that *he* must be a target as well. For who could say whether his friend had been sought because he was Jewish, Alsatian, a minor-league black marketeer, or suspected in some subversive scheme to aid the Resistance through work with the railroad? Based on his own circumcised member and any contraband found in their room, whatever pretext the Gestapo employed for seeking Roger's arrest might just as well apply to him too!

Roland scanned the crowd of strangers around him, leery now that he might have been followed. Near the door to the tracks, he picked out a pair of pale-faced men with dark suits and fedoras but no discernible facial expressions who were standing alert, smoking, with their backs to the wall. When the lonely wail of the train pierced the air like a mourner's keen—no carefully plotted derailment that day to cheat expectations—the two men crushed their cigarettes under their heels. The regular churning beat of the wheels came closer, grew louder, closer and louder. The two men stepped forward, and Roland dashed past them, out to the tracks. Brakes squealed, wagons groaned to a halt. There was a last wind and a powerful shudder, and then the silence that followed the mighty mechanical sigh of the beast. It rolled over Roland like the sound of surrender. The doors opened, passengers spilled onto the platform, and Roland lunged toward them, parting the crowd with his elbows to find Roger. To save him.

"*Ah! c'est gentil!*" How nice! Roger stopped in surprise, set down his valises, and beamed at his roommate. Before Roland could whisper a warning, he froze at a snarled command behind his back: "*HALT!*" The two broad-shouldered Nazi agents shoved him aside and seized hold of Roger and his bags, undoubtedly filled with black-market produce.

Roland stood gaping in impotent horror at the retreating backs of the three silent figures as the agents dragged Roger through the crowds in the station. He wanted to scream, to flee, to wrest his friend from the arms of those thugs. Numbly, he awaited the grip that would claim him next. Then, a desperate gambit, he pretended to look for somebody else, as if greeting Roger had come to pass as coincidence only. He searched the waiting room, knitted his brow, and threw up his hands in a feint of annoyance, a public charade to say that the person he had actually come to collect had missed the train without sending a message. He made a show of rechecking his watch, studied the timetable, shrugged his shoulders, and very slowly strolled out of the station, at every step fighting the urge to turn around and face the future rushing to catch him.

That evening, his landlady managed to sneak him a warning not to return to his room: the Gestapo had been there already and slashed up the place, and she wasn't looking for any more trouble. She told him to move. He went to stay with another Jewish friend in the city and with deep trepidation returned the next day to the French railway office at the Hôtel Terminus across from the station, planning to tell his boss he was leaving.

"*Finito, finito*," he said, after recounting the terrible story of Roger's arrest. But he yielded to his boss's insistence that he would be reckless to give up a job that meant an exemption from forced German labor. Why compare his own situation, his boss asked, to that of a Jew? Still, Roland was sunk in despair over his best friend's arrest and agonized about what would happen to him in the hands of the Nazis. Black marketeering was sure to raise extra charges. Would the Germans realize or care that Roger was only an amateur dabbler where that was concerned? How long would they hold him? And where? Roland was plagued by memories of how Roger had raced for a doctor while he lay unconscious two years before, a ruptured appendix spewing infection. Without Roger's quick action, Roland would have died. To abandon Roger in an equally menacing hour made him feel like a traitor. A coward. There had to be someone who knew how to free him, yet Roland's contacts in the Resistance offered no hope. They just shook their heads and advised him to keep his mouth shut, or else he'd wind up sharing a cell with Roger, wherever he was.

Near the end of the following week, Roland was summoned to interpret for a group of German and French railway officials, two *Wehrmacht* men, and a Gestapo agent, as they walked down the tracks to inspect a special train parked in the yard. Horrified to see that all its windows were covered with bars to secure the wagons for transporting captives, Roland studied the train with dread in his heart, now understanding that prisoners like Roger would ride these cars to hellish places. Even then, Roland could not foresee that most of the prisoners forced onto the trains at Lyon-Perrache would never be freed to come home again. When the group of inspectors turned back toward the hotel, content with the railcar modifications, the Gestapo agent summoned Roland—"*Sie, Dolmetscher! Kommen Sie hierher!*"—to walk alongside him. In the bright October sun their own opaque shadows glided before them.

"*Wo haben Sie so gut Deutsch gelernt?*" the agent inquired. Where did you learn to speak German so well? "Do I detect a hint of an Alsatian accent? *Nicht wahr?*" Not so? His smile was icy as he paused to offer Roland a cigarette and intimately cupped his hand around a match in order to light it for him. "Where are you from? Tell me again, what was your name?" For the next half mile, as they walked together back down the track, the Gestapo man peppered Roland with invasive questions—pointed, poisonous, and too polite. He probed his past, his credentials, and his thoughts on the war and the Jewish-Bolshevik menace in Europe, with his inquiry coiling around to the same repeated personal issues by way of back doors until Roland grew certain the agent was trying to trap him.

"Take my card," the Nazi concluded when they returned to the station. "Do not make the mistake of failing to call me when you have something to report."

That afternoon, Roland quit his job at the Hôtel Terminus. Through a connection in the Resistance, he soon found another job that exempted him from forced German labor, doing office work for a petrol firm. Roger was less lucky. After several weeks at Lyon's Fort Montluc, the prison where the Nazis held thousands of Jews and resisters for deportation and torture, he was loaded onto a train to Drancy, the crowded and squalid transit camp on the outskirts of Paris. An enormous U-shaped complex of utilitarian five-story buildings, Drancy had been designed to house a low-income French population, but was taken over for use as a camp even before construction was finished. Inside, it was almost devoid of electricity, water, or toilet facilities, but it was soon well provided with guard posts, floodlights, and barbed-wire fences nine feet high. By late 1943, French police continued to serve as its guards, but SS *Hauptsturmführer* Alois Brunner was the Nazi official in charge of the disease-ridden compound, which eventually served as a last miserable French residence for sixty-seven thousand of the seventy-six thousand Jews deported to death camps from France.

There were three thousand inmates when Roger arrived, just two months short of his twenty-fourth birthday. As part of induction, and with the detailed bookkeeping designed to win approval from their German mentors, the French Interior Ministry police, on page four of Drancy notebook #16, recorded what they took from his person: "*Received on October 29, 1943, from Monsieur Roger Dreyfus, no. 7271, of 27 rue Puits Gaillot, Lyon—the sum of 100 francs.*" There was no accounting for the balance of days they robbed from his life.

. . .

Lyon's Centre d'Histoire de la Résistance et de la Déportation, the museum and research center where I found Roger's records, occupies a building formerly used as a Gestapo headquarters, located on the

The three Goldschmidt children shortly before their deportation to Drancy and Auschwitz (L to R): Elie-Jean, eighteen years old; Jeanine, sixteen; and Jacques, fourteen

avenue Berthelot, just over the Rhône from the gare de Perrache. It was here too that I found ledger entries that finally answered painful questions as to the precise fate of my mother's cousin Mimi in Lyon. She was forty-one when she was interned at Drancy with her three children and Aunt Marie's loyal attendant Bella Picard, on November 9, 1943—exactly five years after *Kristallnacht* and eleven days after Roger's internment.

"*Reçu de Mme. Goldschmidt, Emilie née Cahen, 99 rue de l'Hôtel de Ville, Lyon, la somme de trois cent dix* [310] *francs,*" a police official duly inscribed in ledger #20, page 27. Bella is recorded as having been carrying only ten francs, a poignant reflection of her lower status. In a peculiar contortion of societal values, the Drancy chief of police observed the niceties of convention, not forgetting in these fateful ledgers to add the honorific *Madame* or *Monsieur* or the traditional identifier of a maiden name.

The research center also located a picture from Serge Klarsfeld's memorial tome, *French Children of the Holocaust*, depicting the three Goldschmidt children, posed in the sun and clothed like dolls in party attire. Jacques, the youngest, appears about four—with knees

French police record of 310 francs "received" from Mme. Goldschmidt, Emilie née Cahen at Drancy on November 9, 1943

as delicious as little round apples—dressed in dark velvet shorts, a matching jacket, a round-collared white blouse, spotless white kneesocks, and white ankle boots. His sister, Jeanine, not quite eighteen months older, is a miniature lady in a box-pleated dress topped by a jacket and a broad-brimmed hat that casts a shadow over her features. Elie-Jean, three years older than his little brother, stands off to the right and grins for the camera in long pants, a nautical shirt, and sailor's beret. Like three living gifts, they all wear outfits adorned by bows at their necks. The caption reads as follows:

> Jeanine Goldschmidt was born on June 23, 1927, in Lyon, where her brother, Jacques, was also born on December 8, 1928. Their elder brother, Elie-Jean, also born in Lyon, had just celebrated his 18th birthday on November 8, 1943, twelve days before their deportation to Auschwitz on Convoy No. 62. They lived at 99 rue de l'Hôtel de Ville in Lyon.

On the day that I left the research museum with the Drancy records and this photo in hand, I wandered alone, shaken in spirit, across the pont Galliéni over the Rhône to the gare de Perrache where Roger was arrested, up the Presqu'île, and past the bloodred earth of the place

Bellecour. Nearby, at number 99 on what had been the rue de l'Hôtel de Ville and is now rue du Président Edouard Herriot, I stopped before the beautiful entry of the building where my cousins had lived. The central panels of the wooden door still bore intricate carvings of fruits and flowers, and above the arched doorway, a bearded devil still lurked under the white marble bench where cherubs sat and played with a bird. A prayer of mourning filled my heart for family members I never had known because they were murdered before I was born: frozen in time, Jacques, Jeanine, and Elie-Jean forever remaining children to me. I lingered there, trying somehow to connect with their presence, and when a young and pretty North African woman walked to the door and unlocked it, I asked for permission to glance inside. My cousins had lived there during the war, I told her, and when I mentioned their name, she insisted I join her upstairs to speak with her husband.

His family, she said, had spent four generations in the same apartment next door to the Goldschmidts, so he was fully aware of the tragic events of the past. Like me, Marc-Henri Arfeux, thirty-nine at the time of my visit, a writer and teacher, had not known the Goldschmidts. But he, too, had grown up hearing about them, such that both our lives were touched by the ending of theirs. His mother had been a friend of Jeanine Goldschmidt, the two girls being apart in age by only a year. And his great-uncle, André Laverrière, had actually spied through his peephole into the hallway to watch in anguish as agents of the pro-Nazi French *Milice* banged at the Goldschmidts' door when they came to seize the family in the first black hours of October 29, 1943.

As luck would have it, Mimi's husband and mother were saved from arrest that night because both were in the hospital: Maurice for hernia surgery, Marie with heart palpitations. Curiously, the *Milice* left the building without taking Bella. But the following morning, the doting woman could not stand to think how her precious Mimi and the children she loved as if they were hers had been yanked from their beds into the chilly night air without being allowed to take along so much as their coats. Heedless of personal danger, Bella hastened to pack up the family's warm winter clothes and delivered them to Fort Montluc. It was then that officials took a good look at the sixty-four-year-old

Jewish housekeeper, checked her name in their records, and seized her as well.

Further details came from Marc-Henri's mother, Monique, and Pierre Balland, a retired shirtmaker who had known my cousins and still lived in the building, indeed in the same top-floor apartment where the young Jeanine Goldschmidt had regularly come to spend afternoons with Pierre's childless wife.

"The Goldschmidts were denounced," said Monsieur Balland, hale and trim at almost ninety. "Was it jealousy? Who knows? Madame was always *le feu dans le bâtiment*," the fire in the building. It was clear that someone gave the *Milice* or the Gestapo their names, he said, and that others in a position to save them had failed to act. A second Jewish family in the building, refugees from Poland, had been warned about the impending raid in time to get out and quietly left a few days beforehand, thus surviving to return to Lyon after the war. Monsieur Balland stared at the floor in discomfort as he explained that, based on some latent enmity between the two families, the Polish couple had not shared with the Goldschmidts the alert to leave. It was rumored that Mimi had sent them away empty-handed when

Emilie "Mimi" Goldschmidt in 1940

they sought a contribution from her for a fund to help impoverished Jews escape from the Nazis. Whoever turned over the Goldschmidts' names presumably had not mentioned Bella Picard, Monsieur Balland suggested, theorizing as to why the agents initially failed to arrest the housekeeper, although she was Jewish.

Monique Arfeux fought back tears as she recalled how the Goldschmidts had waved off entreaties to escape from Lyon, Maurice refusing to give up his business, and Mimi spurning the wisdom of hiding her children in the country. The morning after the raid, she said, her uncle André rushed to the hospital to warn Maurice and Marie not to come back because the Gestapo was taking over their home. Hesitantly, afraid of giving offense by speaking ill of the dead, Madame Arfeux and Monsieur Balland intimated that Mimi had imprudently turned herself, and therefore her family, into a target. At a time when the *Milice* and the Germans were hungry to round up Jews who caught their interest, the Goldschmidts not only dismissed the need to hide or even to lie low, but also had failed to ward off resentment that led to condemnation and finger pointing.

In days that followed the Goldschmidts' arrests, the Gestapo and the *Milice* destroyed all that they found in the Jewish apartments. Photographs and personal papers lay in the street, and for fear of the Germans no one dared touch them. Maurice, broken in spirit, survived until Lyon's liberation on September 2, 1944, alone and in hiding, and then wandered home to his vacant apartment. According to Monsieur Balland and Madame Arfeux, once he returned, Maurice spent all of his days hounding relief agencies to search for his family, while becoming the victim of ruthless hucksters who promised to find them. Strangers arrived and moved in with him. Opportunists devoid of conscience or pity claimed to have seen his wife or his children. One swore to have spotted Elie-Jean at Auschwitz III, digging in coal mines, while another remembered Jacques in its quarries; still another said he had seen Mimi herself, a feeble skeleton in line at a roll call. Someone had glimpsed her in the Buna synthetic rubber factory that I. G. Farben built at the camp in order to profit from ever-replenished ranks of slave labor.

These tipsters fed on Maurice, clawing for shelter and money. Day after day for almost a year, they goaded him to wait for his family at the gare de Perrache with photos in hand. Each day with fresh optimism, accompanied by one of a changing cast of nefarious guides, Maurice rushed toward the travelers who climbed off the trains, certain the moment would finally come when the people he loved most in the world would wave to him from the crowds on the platform and fling themselves into his too-empty arms. In a fever of madness, he met the trains and showed his pictures to anyone willing to stop and rifle through memory's permanent nightmares. Thus the man who escaped the fate of his family became a ghost, haunted by ghosts, lost to the world in his search for the others.

That fall, his mother-in-law Marie sent word to Sigmar in New York that her daughter, three grandchildren, and Bella had been deported the year before, and that she and Maurice were still struggling to maintain faith that they would return. Marie herself had succeeded in reaching Valence to hide with Lisette and Edy, who had both been working within the Resistance. Once the Germans were driven out of the region, the Cahens were able to retrieve their two sons and two daughters from the tiny mountain village in the Vercors where a rescue agency had sheltered them for more than a year. Because the name Cahen was recognizably Jewish, Lisette had equipped the children with a new French last name: with customary, if ill-advised, wit under the circumstances, she had dubbed them Cacheux, from the word *caché*, hidden.

Visiting the little Cacheux children the previous summer, Lisette had found them badly malnourished and had rushed to Lyon to ask her sister-in-law to take the children into her home. Mimi agreed to accept the oldest child only, not the three others, and Lisette, incensed, rejected the offer. "I'd prefer her to starve to death with her sister and brothers than to have her here living with you!" Lisette hotly retorted. "I shudder to think what she'd learn." But in the end, her disdain for Mimi, who would welcome one child and reject her siblings, unexpectedly worked to save Lisette's daughter, when two months later, the *Milice* raided the Goldschmidt apartment and deported the family.

After Lyon's liberation, Maurice came south to visit his in-laws, and seeing him shattered, Marie took it as her duty to go back to the city and care for him. But soon she, too, was seduced by whispering devils that clamored around them, selling unfounded hope. Marie shared her sorrow across the Atlantic, sending her brother Sigmar an anguished series of densely written postcards and letters. Despair filled her pages and spiraled the edges in a barely legible scrawl. She begged him to help obtain information, possibly through the American Red Cross, and poured out her message of pain many times over:

> You have surely learned of our great and terrible tragedy. My dear Mimi, the three children, and my poor Bella were arrested on 29 October 43. We have had no news of them since Drancy. They are surely in Poland or in Upper Silesia. What I suffer, you can believe, is more than terrible because we don't know where our poor children are. . . . One despairs above all at a time when it is so cold. Do you think perhaps Herbert can do something? I have already written to him. . . . If only one knew where they were. Nothing now for more than a year! It's totally hopeless. There is such misery in the world.
>
> It will truly be the most sacred of moments when the good Lord will liberate them. Maurice suffers horribly. I cannot speak. God give us strength! How often I think of my dear Sigmar who wanted to take us away with him! How right you were to leave! If only God will protect our dear deported ones and preserve them in health. My time is filled with prayers that I hope God will hear. Write to me. Think of me. I kiss you with my whole heart. Your sad sister, Marie.

Again and again, she wrote to Sigmar seeking advice and describing Maurice's frantic attempts to search for their loved ones, as he continued to do until after the war, when all five names turned up in the lists of the dead. Only then did he learn that his wife, three children, and Bella were deported on Convoy Number 62 that pulled away from Bobigny station near Drancy just before noon on November 20, 1943. The transport approved in Berlin by Adolf Eichmann had included one thousand two hundred Jews crammed into freight cars. Among the other prisoners was Roland's friend Roger Dreyfus; also among them was Jacques Helbronner, widely known as "the Marshal's Jew" for his friendship with Pétain, along with his wife, Jeanne; another was

Madeleine Dreyfus Lévy, the granddaughter of Alfred Dreyfus. Of no known relation to Roger, Madeleine had been arrested in Toulouse in early November on charges of working for the Resistance.

The train crossed the border north of Alsace on a journey that ended at Auschwitz in Poland, missing 19 prisoners who had managed a daring escape on the first night of travel. In an icy rain, on a platform patrolled by SS guards with dogs, the remaining 1,181 prisoners were separated from their belongings. Quickly selected for immediate death were 895 deportees, with the remaining 241 men and 45 women assigned to hard labor. Of those, all but 29 men and 2 women from Convoy Number 62 would perish before the end of the war.

. . .

In the fall of 1944, Norbert left Cuba to come to the United States to be with the family at Sigmar's sixty-fourth birthday at the end of

Norbert in his American army uniform, stationed in Germany after the war

December. But only weeks after his arrival, as he'd predicted, he was drafted into the American Army. Dispatched to Camp Blanding in Florida for basic training with an infantry unit, he was then assigned to an intelligence branch that valued his fluency in French and German. On the day in late April 1945 when Norbert shipped out, Janine and Trudi saw him off at the pier on Staten Island. True to form, he railed against leaving his latest girlfriend, this one an American, but any fears of going back to war were quickly assuaged by his enormous good fortune of debarking in Europe on May 8, the very day the Germans surrendered.

It had only been a matter of days since the arrest of Pétain, the execution of Italy's Fascist leader Benito Mussolini, and the suicide, in his Berlin bunker on the last day of April, of a crazed Adolf Hitler. He had skirted defeat and certain capture by choosing to shoot himself in the mouth. With his last written words, the leader who plotted a Thousand Year Reich had blamed the Jews for provoking the war, causing millions of deaths and appalling destruction. Aides found the Führer's mangled corpse beside the slumped form of his poisoned bride, Eva Braun, whom Hitler had finally married in the dark morning hours of the previous day. Then, in a macabre, self-prescribed Viking funeral— a wordless ceremony amid the roaring bombardment of Red Army shells—they were both laid to rest in a bed of flames.

Never one to miss a party, Norbert arrived right in time for the great jubilation, free French kisses, and small opportunities for silent revenge. And the following fall, when a few days' leave gave him the chance to strut through Freiburg, resplendent in his American uniform, and then to visit Lyon, a friend told him that Roland was still there, living alone now in a one-room apartment. When they met, Roland recounted the trials of the past three years: how he had narrowly escaped arrest by the *Milice*, dodged bullets and bombings in the liberation, and served with the Allies in a revived French Army during the months between the rescue of Lyon and final triumph over the Germans. Filling a low-level clerical job with a tank regiment at a barracks in Lyon, he had been tasked with tracking food and supplies for the troops in his unit. At that point, he still knew nothing about Roger's murder.

In the champagne exuberance of victory, the madcap gaiety sweeping the country, the two young men—Norbert twenty-four, Roland twenty-five—celebrated an end to the terror.

"You can't walk on one leg!" Roland proclaimed after they downed a first drink together. Concurring in the need for a second round, they jovially continued from there.

After that meeting, Norbert fired off a devastatingly harsh letter to Janine, defaming Roland and insisting that she break off with him. What was his motive? Perhaps Norbert had already discovered the blond, German Protestant girl he would later fight his parents to marry and wanted to deflect Janine from upsetting them by also choosing a non-Jewish partner. Perhaps Sigmar had influenced Norbert's message to her. Or maybe Norbert was merely being protective, judging Roland unworthy to wed his sister. These questions persist, unanswered. And while the truth of Norbert's damning report was never confirmed, there can be no doubt as to the brutal hurt it inflicted. No bomb could have wreaked greater damage in assaulting Janine's most cherished dreams for the future.

In years to come, however, Janine managed to expunge this letter from her memory entirely. She therefore never blamed Norbert for playing a role in her decision against returning to France, which she always regretted. Instead, she ever after condemned herself for permitting her fears to overpower the resolve of her love. Norbert's cruel letter remained hidden away in a neglected archive tucked in a closet, completely forgotten in what Janine persisted in calling, despite her marriage, her "Old Maid Box." Things saved but too painful to open. It was almost as if, not having married Roland, like a reclusive, ill-fated Victorian maiden, she would preserve the fragments of her one true romance tenderly wrapped in ribbons and cobwebs.

All in one paragraph, typed in French in an italic font on blue airmail paper, Norbert's letter was written from Freiburg on November 16, 1945. The voluble, pompous gush of his words and the paternalistic pose that he strikes are fully his own, along with the switches to capital letters. But my translation does not reflect the numerous French grammatical errors that add to the sense of its having been written with the drunken bravado of a soldier on leave, a soldier with a conquering army, puffing his chest in a beaten country where his memory of persecution was raw.

My dear sister Janine,

I have just received your letter of 3 November 1945 and I am hurrying to respond by return mail. You tell me that you believe me sufficiently intelligent to understand that your relationship with Roland is not a flirtation but something more serious. Then you say that you think me senseless, because I have paid little attention to this affair. Well, my dear, I believe rather that it is because I do have sense that I have acted in this manner. I know you, and I know your thoughts, and I therefore had no intention of making you angry by giving you my ideas on this subject. I remember, however, having made allusion to the fact that while everyone else in the world tries to establish himself to become something, Roland is still the eternal student. But perhaps I have overestimated your intelligence, and you did not understand what I was trying to say. I will therefore tell you again now in French. Roland is a good guy, and I would be delighted to have him as a pal to share a good time. But Roland does not have two cents, and still he spends his time in cafés, in restaurants, in bars, and is the man known on the rue de la République to many women, while he pretends to love only you. Visiting for just a few days, I have wanted to preserve a friendship with him, and for that reason I have taken an absolutely neutral position with him where you are concerned. You probably know as well as I that for the moment, it will be impossible for him to go to America. I admit, however, that it would be absolutely possible for you to return to France. Therefore, here is the conclusion: IS YOUR LOVE FOR RO-LAND GREAT ENOUGH FOR YOU TO ABANDON YOUR PARENTS? TO LEAVE THE USA AND RETURN TO A COUNTRY WHERE YOU KNOW NO ONE? TO RETURN TO A COUNTRY WHERE THOSE YOU DO KNOW WILL SCORN YOU? DO YOU WANT TO MARRY A MAN WITH WHOM YOU WILL STARVE? OH WELL, IN THIS CASE YOU HAVE MY BENEDICTION. Make your application, take the risk as to whether he will marry you or not, and you can rent yourselves a little attic room on the rue des Roses, and you will be happy. To be fair, I can even tell you that Roland appears to be interested in you, and I suppose that this is all that matters to you. What else would you like me to tell you? That we went out on the town together, that we had a great time, that we spent the night with two girls we picked up and brought to his room, that he's had a girlfriend, that he has a terrible reputation, and that we only talked about you for 30 minutes? To give you a fuller picture, I can add that not only do I fail to realize that you are no longer a child and that this relationship is not a simple flirtation, but I can assure you, and this is my most sacred decision, that in the event you return to Europe and marry Roland, I WILL ONLY HAVE ONE SISTER, AND WITH YOUR HONEYMOON TRIP, YOU WILL SAIL OUT OF MY LIFE FOREVER.

He closed the letter without signing his name, but with an expression in German modeled on the fictional Indian warrior Winnetou he had adored as a child, an absurdly imperious declaration that could have thundered only from an unassailably powerful chief with muscles rippling, hatchet gleaming, and feathers cascading over his shoulders:

"*Ich habe gesprochen.*" I have spoken. "*How!*"

Two years later, Janine would marry Leonard Maitland.

EIGHTEEN

THE LION AND MISS AMERICA

THE MAN WHO WOULD BECOME my father was twenty-eight years old in October 1946 when his blunt and practical older sister, Mona, arranged for him to meet Janine on a blind date in New York. Janine, five years younger, was working in a Madison Avenue endocrinologist's office, where Mona arrived as a patient and instantly noticed the doctor's lovely assistant.

"What a shame she's a shiksa. If she were only Jewish, I'd fix her up with my brother," Mona remarked to the doctor and nodded toward Janine, who stood in the hallway dressed in white. "He's a cross between Gregory Peck, Gary Cooper, and Cary Grant. It's only because he's been away in the war that he's still unattached." Leery of matchmaking schemes, Janine glared at the doctor to keep silent, but he cannily lured her into the open.

"Oh well, she's meshuga, anyway," Dr. Morton replied. The Yiddish word for "crazy," provoked just the reaction he anticipated.

Leonard Laurence Maitland

"Why would you say that?" Janine blurted out, her rubber-soled nursing shoes squeaking on the linoleum floor as she plunged back into the examining room. "Have I given you reason to say that about me?"

Mona turned in surprise. "Meshuga? If she's really a shiksa, how did she just understand what you said?"

"*I* never said she wasn't Jewish." Dr. Morton chuckled in self-satisfaction. "*You* did."

Leonard Maitland called Janine that same day and insisted on coming to see her that evening. And although she had dreaded meeting a stranger, Janine needed only one glance at the man at her door to be thankful that being revealed as a Jew finally managed to work in her favor. Her only problem that evening as they sat and talked in the living room proved to be getting Trudi to leave them alone because, as Mona had promised, her new date was entrancingly, movie star handsome. Well over six feet tall with glossy black hair, a strong cleft chin, arresting blue eyes, and a deep, mellifluous voice, he had a ruggedly masculine demeanor. Janine mistook for confidence his brash attempts to be seductively charming. In time, his true nature would reveal itself as less self-assured, if all the more inscrutable.

About that young man who ardently courted Janine I myself would learn rather little. For while my childhood was wrapped in a tapestry woven from my mother's riveting stories about her life and its perils in wartime and her star-crossed romance with Roland, my father was guarded about his past and his feelings. I know he had once aspired to write the great American novel, focusing on rail-riding hobos. That touring the South in search of a college football scholarship, he ran out of money and spent a hungry night in jail for stealing apples from an orchard. But I was seventeen before I discovered he had been married before, a youthful mistake he sought to keep hidden. And ironically— while my mother's family had spent almost a decade dodging the Nazis in Europe, hiding in plain sight while never disguising their Jewish background—it was my father, the quintessential American, who changed his name by way of court order in 1941 to avoid anti-Semitism he feared would hinder career advancement. Prejudice limited options for American Jews of that period, and because he could readily pass as

Christian and had little feeling for any religion, he discarded a name
that made him a victim. He claimed to have found the name Maitland
by throwing a dart at a map of the world on the wall of a bar where he
was drinking with friends. It was a town to the north of Sydney, Australia, and he thought it had the right sound for the restricted domains of
engineering and business he wanted to conquer.

The name Maitland, actually Scottish, is thought to have found its
way to Australia with a prisoner shipped to distant exile from Britain.
Leonard never set foot in Australia—or Scotland—although he could
jauntily mimic the accents of both, and quite a number of others as

*Len's parents and sister: Bernard, Fanny, and three-year-old Mona
Friedman in 1911*

well. He was born in Manhattan on October 11, 1918, the son of a Russian Jew, Beresh Friedman, who had fled the pogroms and poverty of Eastern Europe after the 1905 Revolution. A self-reliant, humble, and taciturn man, Beresh initially struck out by himself for Argentina and then London, before trying to make a fresh start in the United States. He left Ellis Island renamed Bernard and went to work in New York as a tailor. It took some years before he had saved enough money to pay passage for his violet-eyed wife, Fanny, a baker's daughter from a Polish shtetl, and their daughter Mona. Their only son was born in New York after the couple reunited, which accounted for Mona's being eleven years older and inclined to take charge of how he was reared. She took credit for having gone on her own to the city registrar's office to change the name her immigrant parents had given her brother: within days of his birth, she crossed out their choice, Louis, and dubbed him Leonard Laurence, which sounded more American to her.

Bathed by classical music on the radio, Bernard gave his days to constant labor. Yet he remained poor to the end of his long life, by which point, a widower for seventeen years, he had lost his eyesight to glaucoma and the strain of countless invisible stitches. He worked from the family's ground-floor apartment on 84th Street on Manhattan's Upper West Side and exercised his political views through membership in the Workmen's Circle, a Jewish labor association with Socialist leanings. Appreciation counted for more than pay on a job, he maintained, and he fretted over custom-made clothing and the lesser challenges of alterations while barely charging enough to earn any profit.

A loner, an atheist, and a privately bitter, cynical man, Bernard proudly recalled his glory days in the czar's army, a sentimental view of his youth that his avowed socialism left undisturbed. In fact, ever after, that dusty Russian door to his past was the only portal through which one might lure him into discussion. In the arduous life that had followed for him, his keen intellect was always stymied by the conditions that forced him to sew for a living. The tailor vowed to chop off Len's fingers before he would sanction his taking up scissors or thread, yet there was no risk of that. Father and son could not get along, the language of music being the only one they amiably shared. What little money Bernard ever spent on himself went for standing-room tickets in the dizzying topmost balcony of the Metropolitan Opera, and at home he would whistle an accompaniment as Len, a powerful bass, sang their favorite Italian arias. But Bernard cast a permanent shadow over their relationship with a sardonic prediction about his son's future.

"Hair will grow in the palm of my hand before you make anything of yourself!" Bernard habitually chided him. The Old World method of spurring a child to greater achievement rankled, and Leonard never forgot or forgave it, such that in the end, like an omen foretold by the blind Tiresias, my grandfather's curse indirectly affected us all. Leonard's own assessment of his success could never equal what he seemed to need to prove to his father, and as the years passed, resentment spawned cold criticism—of his father, himself, and then other people. Confronting his father's limitless challenge, he assumed a combative stance in the world and could never quite put his anger behind him.

In 1940, Len was studying engineering at New York University when he disappointed his family by marrying—too young, at just twenty-one—a non-Jewish woman four years his senior. It was an impetuous elopement largely spurred by his zeal to escape his parents' bleakly cluttered apartment. There, patterns and pins, thick bolts of fabric, all the detritus of the dressmaking business overwhelmed the musty confines of rooms where the whirring of Bernard's old sewing machine stopped only when clients came in for fittings. For an extended period, Mona with husband and son lived there as well, making for an airless, irritable environment that Leonard detested almost as much as he loathed his parents' stifling immigrant culture.

The new couple moved to a studio apartment near NYU in Greenwich Village, but before long his bride's manic spending habits plunged Len into debt. Required to sacrifice college during the day in order to work full-time as a draftsman to pay for her lifestyle, he gave up his coveted place in the college choir and shifted to night school at the university's Bronx campus. After classes, to cover their bills, he worked a second job as an assistant to a department store window dresser until the man's sexual advances forced him to quit.

He had a scientific, analytical mind and insisted upon objective reasoning and factual research in regard to every issue in life. "Don't make assumptions," was the major lesson he took from his studies and later on drummed into his children, providing my basic training for journalism. When he graduated with a degree in mechanical engineering in 1943, with war raging and color blindness preventing him from fulfilling his dream of becoming an Air Force pilot, both logic and the lure of the sea led him to the Merchant Marine, which had issued an urgent national call for skilled engineers. He joined the effort that helped win the war through the greatest sealift the world had seen, ferrying fuel, ammunition, planes, tanks, trucks, jeeps, and other crucial supplies over mine-infested foreign oceans to American and Allied troops in the fighting.

Though news of their losses was a well-guarded secret during the war, the Merchant Marine suffered a higher casualty rate than any branch of the military, with thousands of volunteer mariners killed or injured on hastily constructed Liberty and Victory ships, under lethal attack from land, sea, and air. By act of Congress in 1936, merchant seamen were considered military personnel in times of war, yet they were deprived of the GI benefits awarded all other veterans to attend college, buy homes, and start businesses. A pledge to remedy this injustice died unfulfilled with President Roosevelt. Sporadic efforts at redress still falter in Congress more than six decades later, even though most war-era mariners are now gone. Indeed, many former mariners would die of service-related lung diseases, haunted by memories of Victory ships where the asbestos used to insulate pipes floated like snow in the engine rooms.

For secrecy's sake during the war, mariners were not permitted to know their destinations in advance, and even discharge certificates listed each voyage only as "foreign." But Leonard later described perilous missions to the Philippines, Guam, Hawaii, France, England, Italy, Africa, as well as the Soviet Union, with American ships slipping past Axis defenses. From his Soviet visits, he brought back a small wooden cigarette box inlaid with silver, a book on Stalingrad written in Russian, a memory of loudspeakers spewing Marxist dogma over the streets, and a lifelong horror of what he decried as the soul-crushing evils of communism. From walking the decks on cold, rolling northern seas, he adopted a sailor's stability-seeking, wide-legged stance and loose-kneed, rubbery gait. From war-whipped oceans, serving a chief engineer whom he hated, he came home a lieutenant with a misanthrope's credo: "Never educate a sucker, and when your boss is a bastard, don't undertake to do any more than you are specifically instructed to do." But he gave his doctrine lip service only and always demanded the most from himself, as well as from everyone around him. His shipboard nickname, "L-square," or L^2 for Leonard Laurence, also fell by the wayside, later replaced in the minds of his family by "Leonard the Lion" for the way he restlessly paced in a cage of domestic convenience, exuding dynamic, ferocious potential.

As to his first youthful marriage, what commitment existed quickly died a victim of war. Between sailings in November 1944, Len discovered that during his absence his wife was openly living in Queens with a lover. Rejecting entreaties to take her back, he divorced her in 1945 on grounds of adultery, shipped out again, and resolved that he would never remarry. With his discharge, just two months before meeting Janine in 1946, he landed a job as a manufacturer's representative for a sales engineering firm and went on the road. He took on New England and the cold reaches of New York State, a lonesome young man carrying heavy sample cases to sprawling factories in nondescript towns. He almost enjoyed the challenge of sales, the validation that came when he could charm and persuade, educate or downright bully hesitant customers into placing orders with him. But he found little pleasure in his travels, only long, empty miles leading to puny commissions, solitary dinners, and an endless string of barren hotel rooms.

He described his complaints about work in the many letters he wrote to Janine, though in the earliest months of their long-distance courtship he mainly endeavored to make her jealous. Their meetings were full of the banter that marked their early correspondence. He found Janine a challenge. He thought her "exotic." Over sodas in what he mockingly called "the Orange Room at Nedick's," they teased each other and planted suspicions that may have sparked passion, but also left both of them feeling exposed and at risk.

On yellowed stationery imprinted with drawings of old, imposing upstate hotels—the Onondaga in Syracuse, the Van Curler in Schenectady, the Cadillac in Rochester, the Arlington in Binghamton—it is easy to recognize the insecurity behind the youthful salesman's sexual swagger. "*I trust that this correspondence finds you in good health,*" he wrote her, "*and bubbling with poisonous enthusiasm for me.*"

> January 7, 1947—These towns are really not very much fun, forcing one to create his own diversion. Naturally your correspondent is not lacking in fortitude in these directions. If you find me lacking in detail anywhere, you can assume that I have been a dirty bastard, as usual. . . .

> January 23, 1947—If this traveling of mine doesn't stop pretty soon, I will be in much trouble as I will probably have a femme fatale in every city I go to and that is not good because it makes for a very restless state of mind. . . .

> January 27, 1947—I had a miserable time Friday night, but I had a wonderful time on Saturday. During the afternoon, I took my rifle and another chap and we went off and did some target shooting until it was almost dark and then quite by accident some girl got me a blind date and a very nice time was had by all, even me. . . .

Janine tried to get even, writing back letters—sometimes in French, just to annoy him—in which she made up theater dates, parties, and dancing with other dashing escorts in such specificity that he believed her. When she showed up for a date one evening wearing a thin gold anklet, his pride was outraged. Such an intimate token could only have come from some other suitor! How dare she wear it when she was with him! He grabbed her leg, took hold of the chain pasted under her stocking, and managed to rip it straight through the nylon, snapping the anklet's tiny links. She kept the pieces but never had it repaired and never admitted it was a gift from Trudi. "Well, that certainly shows some interest," she mused, unsure whether she ought to feel pleased or upset.

As weeks and months passed and she grew closer to Leonard, Janine tried to block out thoughts of Roland and to put him behind her. In the time since Norbert's meeting with him in Lyon after the war, Janine never received the one thing she yearned for: a plea from Roland to come back to him. Had he really forgotten their sacred vow to marry each other? Had he been changed by the war, or had he just fallen for somebody else? Day after day, she prayed to receive a letter from him. And when God failed to answer, she resorted to magic or bargains with fate. If I walk home from the subway by way of Cooper Street instead of Broadway today, I know I'll find a letter from him. If I make myself do the laundry first, before even looking at the mail, there'll be a letter for me today on the table. If I don't let myself think about him even once all day long, I'm certain to find an envelope from him. Day by day, once the war ended and regular mail delivery from Europe resumed, Janine's grief and loneliness grew as no letter arrived and her hopes for Roland dripped slowly away.

Painful questions consumed her, and she confided her heartbreak to her cousin Herbert. Over a string of Saturday lunches near his apartment on Madison Avenue, she confessed her longing to go back to France and become Roland's wife, or at least to see him again and determine the truth of whether their love for each other endured. Her friend Malou, now married and working as a dentist in Marseille, had written Janine with just that advice:

> I am of the opinion that you have certainly both evolved and a period of reacquaintance will be required. But it is imperative that you go see Roland again before you do anything else. You might ruin your life with useless regret if you should abstain from seeing him now.

Reluctantly, Herbert offered to lend her money for a steamship ticket across the Atlantic, but Janine worried how she would repay him. He had loaned her $10 in pocket money for her first week of work, and when she politely offered repayment from her first modest salary check, despite his wealth he had not turned it down, if only to teach her the value of money. How would she manage a much larger debt after getting to France? Beyond that, Herbert's willingness to grant her a loan was more than matched by his pessimism when it came to assessing the hazards of going:

How could she know for sure that Roland would want her? Had she fully considered what her leaving New York would do to her parents? Certainly they depended on her, as they struggled to build a new life in a world so unfamiliar to them. On the other hand, how would Roland support her in France while he had yet to finish his legal studies or prepare for any fruitful career? If things didn't work out, where would she find the means to return to the States? Was she prepared to spend the rest of her life in a bad situation, in view of the fact that the Gunzburgers had never been people who indulged in divorce? How would she cope if she regretted her choice but had no way out?

All this had been in the back of her mind during the years before meeting Len, as she casually dated the occasional man, not away at war, who was presented to her in a life of routine, largely confined to the dull social wasteland at the northernmost reaches of Manhattan. This was not at all what she had envisioned when she and Trudi persuaded their parents to abandon plans to settle in upstate Buffalo near Aunt Toni and Uncle Heinrich, whom they had visited directly upon arriving from Cuba. (Celebrating Janine's first American birthday, Sigmar's brother presented her with *The Brothers Karamazov* in German.)

No, it was the razzle-dazzle, vibrant life of midtown Manhattan that Janine and Trudi had dreamed of exploring while waiting for war's end: skyscraper canyons, Broadway theaters, swanky shops, and enticing people. The life that they had expected to find would glitter like mica in city sidewalks, twinkling in the glow of streetlamps or in flashing lights of carnival neon, proving the myth of streets paved with gold. Instead, Sigmar and Alice had followed the German Jewish refugee influx to Washington Heights, the so-called Fourth Reich, and to Inwood just to the north. The far end of Broadway at 204th Street, eight miles north of Times Square, where Sigmar was lucky to rent a small two-bedroom, one-bath apartment—not without paying a $500 bribe to the superintendent to get it—disappointed his daughters by being quiet and dark, with none of the glamour of the fabled city they had so long imagined.

Beyond that and much worse for Janine, despite her high grades on New York college entrance exams and the opinion of her Havana head-mistress that she would qualify for any American university she chose, she had been obliged to abandon the sort of medical career that had been her goal since childhood. Even as Sigmar jokingly called her *die Medizinerin*, the medical student, he proved unwilling to underwrite the long and costly studies required for her to become a doctor. Rather, he believed that his daughters' best prospects depended on finding af-fluent husbands. And while he failed to consider that Janine's chances of marrying well might have been boosted by going to college and medical school—if only because she would meet more young men with promis-ing futures—Janine never dared to press him about it.

Pursuing her interest as best she could, Janine thus resigned herself to becoming a physician's aide and attended a medical trade school. It was a place, coincidentally, where one of Alfred Dreyfus's grand-daughters turned up as a classmate, her father Pierre earning a liv-ing by lecturing to American audiences about the Dreyfus affair. For Janine, a scholarship helped pay tuition, and she worked after class as a secretary in the school office. But the daily drudgery of school, bologna sandwiches at a lunch counter, work, and evenings with her parents left her eager for change, especially after Trudi became se-riously involved with a man, Heinz Rawitscher, whom both sisters remembered from Freiburg.

Two years older than Norbert, Heinz had first met the girls in the 1930s as members of the Bund Deutschjüdischer Jugend, one of the so-cial groups organized for young German Jews excluded from joining their Aryan classmates in mesmerized ranks of Hitler Youth. The sis-ters recalled Heinz as a very good-looking fellow—a dapper dresser with regular features and a friendly, placid demeanor. His family had owned a department store, the Kaufhaus Modern, at the center of town. But during the Reich, the family store was Aryanized, Heinz's father died, and in 1944 the Nazis murdered his mother and sister.

Heinz had saved himself by leaving Freiburg for nearby Basel at age sixteen to learn the trade of an auto mechanic in Switzerland, hoping a skill would speed an American visa. Three years later he bravely moved to New York on his own, adopting a new name, Harry Rawlings, for his new country. One of the few eligible men not caught up in the war, having been spared the draft for medical reasons, Harry visited the Gunzburger girls shortly after they came to the city. A few days later he sent a postcard saying that he had enjoyed seeing the sisters again and eagerly hoped to continue their friendship. That Saturday at eight p.m., he wrote, he would be waiting under the clock at the Biltmore Hotel.

"*Here's hoping that one of you will show up!*" Harry invited indiscriminately. In response, Trudi opted to meet him—just as well for Janine, who found his inclusive approach to them both unappealing. For her, romantic interest required a challenge. It was not in her nature to value a man too easily won, and this, by the time she met Len, made him all the more intriguing to her. As with Roland, her desire was piqued in direct proportion to her efforts to win him. If Len was soured on marriage—he never intended to marry again, he frankly warned—well, she would work to make him want to propose! The fact that he was uncommonly handsome and irresistible to other women only added zest to the chase. He was forceful, witty, and insatiably curious, and he gave the impression he could conquer the world. He was a man to rely on, a take-charge guy who would always protect her.

After all she had learned in Europe of evil and madness, she found appealing his soaring trust in human achievement and the boyishly optimistic idealism that he seemed to claim as an American birthright. Moreover, for Janine, the fact that Len was American born carried its own significant value. The person she always met in the mirror still felt—as Hannah Arendt similarly grumbled to her former lover Martin Heidegger in Germany, years after she had fled to the United States—like a "girl from a foreign land." By the time Janine considered marrying Len, she was determined to shed her foreign accent, along with the hated refugee label. If she couldn't return to France and Roland, she wanted to *be* American, to be married to an American and cultivate American friends. She wanted finally to begin her life, to claim her role as a citizen and belong where she lived. She was suddenly sick to death of waiting for an impossible dream. And if Leonard's modest *ostjüdischer* background displeased her parents, as she knew it would, part of her relished the prospect of retaliating for their rejecting Roland strictly because he wasn't a Jew.

As she balanced her fantasy life with Roland against the idea of marrying Len, Janine made the selfish mistake of telling her new suitor about his past rival, a confession with permanent impact on the course of their marriage. Even now, she cannot explain her motive beyond that she thought making him jealous would only help to stoke his desire. But after hearing enough about the first man in her life and about the pain she had suffered when forced to leave him behind, Leonard wanted to see his rival's picture. Then he decreed a "tearing-up party" aimed at expunging Roland from her heart. It was an event so traumatic, so engraved in her mind, that Janine never forgot the tan skirt and green turtleneck sweater that she wore on the night of the ritual destruction, five months after they started dating.

They were sitting on the couch in her parents' living room when Sigmar emerged from the kitchen with a knife and an apple. "I always eat an apple right before going to bed," he observed, signaling Janine that the hour had come for her guest to depart. But after Sigmar retired to the bedroom, Len insisted she bring out the box in which she'd saved Roland's pictures, as well as the letters he'd sent her in Cuba. Inspecting them all, Len then demanded that she destroy them. Perhaps he was right, she reflected. Perhaps now, almost five years since leaving Roland, it was time to wrest free of the past and move on. This would hurt, but it also might help.

"Are you in bed yet, Hannele?" Sigmar called out from the bedroom. But she ignored him, her eyes fixed upon Leonard as he began to ravage the box on the coffee table. One by one, he had her tear up all reminders of the man she had loved since her first teenage years. What she did with regret at first slowly caught hold, providing at last the relief of catharsis. Fueled by years of unexplored rage and pent-up desire, she ripped through the face she adored and silently cursed him for every day she had rushed for the mail without ever finding the letter she needed. *Assez, genug,* time enough, she thought fiercely. Rip. *Bastante.* In every language she'd learned on her travels. Enough,

enough. Rip. Too late now. She tore straight through his face and stared at her hands as if they belonged to somebody else. Here, the dark eyes. She remembered his habit of blinking them both tightly shut, as if looking for some interior peace, and how that had felt like rejection to her. Now her own eyes were welling with frustrated tears. Rip. She tore that piece in half one more time and studied the ragged fragment in her left hand, just a flattened shred of his magic smile.

She remembered his lips in the Lyon movie theater, where their own hushed adventure was far more exciting than anything flickering on the screen—hiding in darkness, finding each other. How she had thrilled to the touch of his hands on her skin! She remembered his kisses, kisses that drifted slowly and gently and others that were hot and demanding, that seared her neck and traveled along the curve of her cheek toward her own waiting mouth, wanting him and waiting for him. *Always* waiting—waiting and waiting for far too long. In Mulhouse and Gray, Lyon and Havana, and now in Manhattan. Rip, rip, rip, rip, rip. The pile of torn paper and photos mounted before her, a scattered mosaic transformed into love's funeral pyre.

Len's dark, shining head was bent over the box as he rummaged through the shards of her past like an antiques dealer at a second-rate tag sale. But then she spotted her dear and final shot of Roland adrift on the sea in his small rented boat, snapped from the *Lipari*'s deck on that last unbearable day she was pulled from his arms. Still in the box, too, was the twelve-page letter Roland had slipped in her pocket—her arms already so full of mimosas—at her anguished departure from the quai de la Joliette in Marseille. No! No! That precious picture, that beautiful letter, both were treasures she had to preserve.

"Would you like something to drink?" she suggested offhandedly, occupying herself by picking up bits of paper and snippets of photos that littered the carpet. "There's juice, or I think Father might even have an open bottle of white wine in the icebox." But uncharacteristically, she made no move to get up and serve him, so Leonard stood, hesitated, and then went to the kitchen. In his absence, she wiped her eyes, took the snapshot, and dropped it behind the brown brocade couch. "There are glasses in the cabinet across from the icebox," she called toward the kitchen, hoping that Len wouldn't detect the catch in her voice. Then she seized the thick envelope, Roland's promise for their future together, pushed it behind the couch as well, and sighed with relief as she heard it graze the wall and slip to the floor.

"*Whatever the length of our separation, our love will survive it.*" She had long since memorized Roland's predictions and sacred pledge. "*I give you my vow that whatever the time we must wait, you will be my wife. Never forget, never doubt . . .*"

· · ·

That March, Janine clipped a Dorothy Dix column from the *Daily Mirror* and sent it to Leonard, stapled to a sheet of white typing paper on which she had inked only three words: "*BEWARE!!! Brother BEWARE!!!*" The columnist offered guidance on marriage that Janine passed along:

> Son, when you think about getting married, how much serious con-
> sideration do you give the matter? Do you try to use as much intel-
> ligence in picking out a wife as you would in buying an automobile?
> Remember this: That the success of every marriage depends more
> upon the husband than it does upon the wife, for the man does
> the picking and he is responsible for the kind of a girl he marries;
> whereas the woman has to take what she can get, and very often he
> isn't her taste at all. So give as much real thought to selecting your
> wife as you do to buying your new car.

The answer Len sent back to her on March 27 was written as if to the columnist, care of the newspaper's "*Eros Department.*" It began by confessing, "*Your provocative article left me in a state of considerable di-lemma,*" and wound up expressing veiled concern over Janine's prior broken heart:

> The model I expect to get this spring is very nice and I think it
> can be looked upon as a great bargain. It has many interesting gad-
> gets which although not new or of radical design seem to be in
> properly functioning order. It is neither a sport model nor fancy
> or luxurious but seems to combine those features of solid com-
> fort, stability, graceful contours and simplicity that appeal to sane

judgment. . . . She takes the bumps beautifully and eliminates all fears of possible dangerous roads ahead. The motor purrs like a kitten when idling languorously, the transmission goes into high gear without difficulty and the brakes are almost too good.

The other day, however, I learned from the creator of this wonderful device that before going completely nuts over it, I should consider carefully the effects an accident has had upon it. Closer, more deliberate scientific examination revealed that it had suffered extensive damage. . . . It is necessary that I come to a decision soon as someone else may take up my option but I find myself agonized into a state of despondent perturbation, as is evident from the foregoing considerations. I appeal to your sage advice in the hope that you will be able to assist me in the expedient solution of this pressing problem.

In response, Janine concocted a scheme designed to encourage Len to propose. I was shocked as a child when she told me about it, as was he, in fact, when eventually she confessed it to him. In the long run, my mother later concluded, "I fooled myself also by acting so rashly. I didn't know the man I married."

The trick made use of the fact that Aunt Marie had arrived from Lyon that spring to spend several months in New York. Still mourning the deaths of Mimi, Bella, and her three grandchildren in the slaughters of Auschwitz, Marie had sailed to the States on the SS *Mauritania* yearning for solace from her brothers Sigmar and Heinrich and her sister Sara in Cleveland. When Janine asked to borrow her return steamship ticket to play a little joke on her boyfriend one night, Aunt Marie was amenable, if somewhat surprised.

"I've booked passage back to France," Janine announced to Leonard, coyly flashing the ticket in the hope her unexpected plans to leave the country might prompt a proposal. She counted on him to remember Roland.

"You would go without me?" Len asked, every bit as taken aback by the news as she had intended. He reached for her hand.

"Yes, why not? There's really nothing to keep me here," she replied.

"Well, I'll go with you," he said. "I'll get some time off."

"Out of the question. Can you picture what Father would think of our traveling together, not being married?" She shook her head and laughed at the prospect.

"Okay, then let's get married."

"You'd better take awhile to think about that," she advised, her conscience getting the better of her.

"No need. I've decided."

"Well, in that case, I guess we can stay right here," she said, placing the ticket back in her purse. "We'll need to find a place to live, so how would we pay for that kind of travel?"

The next morning, Janine returned the ticket to Aunt Marie and announced her engagement, subject, of course, to her parents' approval. But she was not inclined to wait long. While her twenty-fifth birthday was still more than a year away, she dreaded reaching the traditional milestone when an unmarried woman in France might receive a symbolic Sainte Catherine's bonnet, signifying her status as "spinster."

Indeed, on my own twenty-fifth birthday, my mother fashioned a primly delicate Sainte Catherine's bonnet for me. She trimmed it with artificial sprigs of flowers in pink and lavender, and with mischievous glee wrapped it in tissue paper inside a silver Bergdorf Goodman box that she ceremoniously placed on my bed. To this day, I can summon the speechless upset I felt when I removed the ribbon and opened the unexpectedly promising gift—Bergdorf's not being the place my cost-conscious mother generally shopped—but her message managed to work nonetheless. Perhaps she had already sniffed a nuptial wind, but only two months later I married—an immature union that quickly dissolved. Still, *both* my parents admitted regarding my being divorced as preferable to never having been married by then. Unwed by twenty-five? They concurred that such a sorry impression of being passed over could only scare away other suitors who would not understand my still being single.

In Janine's case, sibling rivalry added further pressure in the spring of 1947, when Trudi and Harry Rawlings announced plans to marry. Survey results from the late 1940s showed that 62 percent of Jewish men who fled to America from Germany chose wives who were also German Jewish refugees, but in regard to my aunt and uncle, I prefer to cite the Freiburg legend: it warns that any native who stumbles into the mountain-fed waters of one of the city's many foot-wide canals is certain to marry another Freiburger *Bobbele.*

Trudi's wedding was set for June 15, 1947, and Janine did not look forward to living alone with the parents after her sister moved out. On Saturday nights when they had company coming and Leonard was traveling on business, Alice encouraged her older daughter to hide in her bedroom rather than be seen by their friends who would cluck about her lack of a date.

"I'll understand if you choose not to come out to greet my guests," Alice would say, her tone empathetic. "I'll just tell them you're not feeling well."

And yet, Alice's opinion of Leonard was muddled. Overwhelmed by the young man's good looks, bluster, and kindness to her, she could not but admire what a *"schöner Mensch"* Janine had captured, even though his alien lineage gave rise to distress. "How can you marry a man when we don't even know the family background?" Alice fretted over genetic hazards. "What if insanity runs in his family? How do we know? *Wirklich*, we know nothing at all." She proclaimed herself to be mystified by him, wishing aloud that his head were "transparent" so she might "read" just what he was thinking—a wish I confess I frequently shared. But he forever remained an alluring enigma, a complicated, mercurial man with a brilliant, eager, principled mind, yet a soul that held back, a man who craved the validation of love, but could never quite learn to give or accept it.

Sigmar also regarded the match with mixed feelings. Leonard had labored to polish his college German and made concerted efforts to entertain Sigmar in his own language, which was easier for him with his hearing failing. And although Sigmar regularly looked forward to his political and business talks with Janine's lively American suitor, when Len asked formal permission to marry his daughter, Sigmar mounted surprising resistance.

"C'est un prince!" He's a prince! Aunt Marie roused her spirits to be the first in the family to argue for Leonard. But Sigmar demanded to see Len's divorce papers and then voiced doubts that Len was Jewish. Out of embarrassment, Janine locked herself into the bathroom

as Sigmar probed his background. First her father placed a yarmulke on the young man's straight black hair and stood back for some moments, gravely appraising the total effect. It was almost as if he expected the prayer cap to send him a signal that the head where it sat was not, in truth, entitled to wear it. When Sigmar added a prayer book to the tableau and told him to read it, Len opened the volume from the wrong direction, thereby disclosing his unfamiliarity with the Hebrew right-to-left format. Finding out that Leonard *Maitland's* parents were Fanny and Bernard *Friedman*—yes, Jewish, but humble immigrants from *Hinterberlin,* east of Berlin—equally dimmed Sigmar and Alice's views of the marriage. The sense of superiority with which German Jews had long regarded their Eastern European brethren outlasted even Hitler's efforts to destroy all Jews, irrespective of origin or social status.

"You make your bed, and you will lie in it," Sigmar warned Janine on the day he granted grudging permission for them to marry. But if Sigmar's misgivings eventually proved not entirely unfounded, the reasons for troubles between the couple would differ from any he had predicted.

. . .

Janine does not remember her marriage that summer as a particularly joyous event. Planning a wedding so soon after Trudi's, she shrank from burdening her parents with a second costly, grand celebration. So when Estelle and Herbert offered to host an afternoon wedding at their posh country home on Long Island at the end of July, Janine was pleased to accept. With weddings barred on the Sabbath, that would have placed the ceremony on Sunday, July 27. But for Janine, of course, that date, always portentous, was out of the question, and so she set it for July 28, a Monday, which limited the guests who could spare the time from work to attend. Even Norbert, the instant life of any party, was missing, still with the army in Germany. To fill out the guest list, Herbert and Estelle invited their own country club friends, and the bride and groom felt awkward marrying in front of a crowd of indifferent strangers.

Logistics aside, factional conflict flared over the bridal gown. Ever practical, Janine eschewed white: she wanted something she could

*"Because God Made You Mine"—Janine and Len marry
at the Winters' summer home in Sea Cliff, Long Island on
Monday, July 28, 1947.*

wear again and decided on blue, but when Leonard's decisive sister
directed her purchase of a navy blue taffeta dress with a deep dé-
colleté, Estelle ruled it out. "*You're* the one getting married here, remember?" Estelle said, dismissing what Mona termed "stunning" as
too risqué and eccentric for a virginal bride. Instead, Estelle dressed
Janine far more demurely at her favorite Park Avenue dress shop in an
off-the-shoulder pale blue chiffon gown with a fitted waist and a flowing skirt of tiny pleats. To that Estelle added a floral tiara, her own
graduated pearls, and white lace gloves that climbed past the elbows.

The only music was the bridal march played on a phonograph, "Because God Made You Mine." Janine had thought its lyrics meaningful

in view of the historical forces, a half century of persecution, which had drawn her and Len from two thoroughly different worlds to exchange marriage vows in an American garden. But with Sigmar virtually deaf to the music, he could not march in step to its purposeful rhythm. Instead, he propelled his daughter in her silvery sandals down the grassy aisle to the chuppah of leaves, the Jewish ritual wedding canopy symbolizing a new couple's home. Long, silky ribbons fluttered behind Janine's compact bouquet, as father and daughter breezed past the meager standing assembly of guests. In the wedding pictures, Sigmar looks stern in his double-breasted, pin-striped gray suit, Janine almost mournful at points, the festive, white-blossomed tiara holding her veil incongruous with her far-off expression.

"Oh, my God, what am I doing?" Janine asked herself in panic, simultaneously squeezing her father's arm in a useless effort to slow his gait. There are so many ways for a couple to part, but for Janine and Roland, free choice had played no role in their separation. And so even there, on her wedding day, with her first passion never willingly renounced, it still remained—a dream as elusive as a butterfly that hovered above the vows she would take. She sensed Roland there, the love of her young and innocent years, before war had taught them how time and events could conquer resolve and shatter even those goals that served to sustain them.

"May your love burn as brightly as these candles!" This was the blessing invoked by the rabbi, as he joined Janine to Leonard before a draped wicker table bearing two lit silver candelabra. But a strong gust of summer wind suddenly extinguished the flames. In her trailing ice-blue chiffon gown, as light as a kiss, Janine shivered and stared at the tendrils of smoke swaying like ghosts above six blackened wicks. Leonard had already placed the wide gold band on her finger, and she remembered that inside both of their rings, there were three words engraved: *à toi toujours*, yours always. It was a promise written in French but exchanged with an unimagined American husband.

That night the newlyweds first drove Alice and Sigmar home to Inwood in Len's lumbering 1935 black Buick convertible, dubbed "Jackson," and then headed toward the luxurious Hotel Pierre on Fifth Avenue and 61st Street, where Janine had fantasized spending her wedding night. Embarrassed to pull up in his wreck of a car, she insisted Len park it several long blocks away. Indeed, while Jackson would carry them off on a honeymoon trip and return them safely to her parents' door, that would prove its last mile, as it thereafter refused to start up again.

Exuberant stalks of white gladiolas standing stiffly bunched at attention saluted Janine in their room at the Pierre. They were Len's favorite flower, "the biggest bang for the buck," he thought—tall, showy, also long lasting—and he would buy them for her for the rest of his life. She never told him that the flowery totems seemed vulgar to her,

Gladiolas for every birthday—this one in Glen Head, Long Island, 1949

rigid and lacking in grace with their discrete bursts of gaudy beauty. After Len's death, out of nostalgia, Janine would begin to buy them herself. But she eyed them warily on their first night together, uneasy about the life she was starting.

Later, when she finally emerged from the bathroom in her frothy white peignoir—having delayed by washing her stockings and every other bit of underwear she might reasonably hope to dry overnight—her new husband had also changed into immaculate white pajamas with navy blue piping. He sat at the window waiting for her, patiently gazing out over the dark, wooded expanse of Central Park. With a fresh rush of pleasure, Janine admitted to herself that her husband did resemble, as Aunt Marie put it, a magnificent prince surveying his realm, a man even she should be happy to marry. Len heard her step, turned his head, raised his dark eyebrows appreciatively, and beckoned her closer to listen to the roar of the lions pacing their cages nearby in the zoo. He tenderly drew her into his arms.

"Oh, I thought that was you roaring," she said with a smile, stroking his hair.

"Well, I was roaring too," he said. "Any self-respecting lion would roar, given the length of time I've been waiting."

The next day, before the newlyweds set out on their honeymoon trip, Janine insisted on making a detour to bring the gladiolas to Alice. They drove on to spend a few happy days at a rustic Adirondacks resort named Paradox Lake and then headed to Montreal. From Canada, the honeymooners each wrote to Sigmar and Alice, Len rhapsodizing about his new wife:

> Janine is by far the most beautiful girl here and as I look at her I think she should be Miss America herself—she seems to get prettier, healthier and more self-assured and serene with each passing day. When I watch her do little things for us both and see how pretty and nice she is, I am sure that she is certainly the most wonderful wife in the world and I can't believe that I was so lucky and that this is all true.

Yet how strange can life be, the mysteries that fix our paths and plot destinations? Janine and Len began their life as a couple exploring the same city where Roland would arrive less than two years later when he sailed from France determined to find back the woman he wanted to marry.

NINETEEN

LOVE LETTERS

I CAME INTO THE BOOK of life almost two years after my parents married, disadvantaged, as are we all, by not knowing what occurred before. Who can grasp that as a child? Unsuspecting, we fall into the plot of time and try to piece the past together. We puzzle over mysterious scars, we catch the scent of doubt in the air, and we stumble over relics of dreams that litter the intimate family landscape. Years go by before we discern our place in the story, yet as we open our eyes on the dawn of our lives, we may imagine the world begins with us.

The day that I entered the tale I am telling was one of the very few times in life I managed to show up anywhere early. Shortchanged at only eight months, I was ejected into the world prematurely, which apparently left me feeling aggrieved. I would later have to hear many times how I flailed and kicked so furiously in my bassinet that the nurses resorted to binding my legs together in the attempt to stop me from bruising myself. Then and there, they warned my mother that it appeared she would have a somewhat difficult case on her hands.

Did that sour professional view worsen the mood she was in the following day when my father failed to arrive until afternoon to visit us both at the hospital? He bounded into her private room sporting a novelty tie with a proud announcement splashed in yellow on a burgundy background: "It's a Girl! It's a Girl! It's a Girl!" the tie squawked the news in a pattern of print from collar to belt. But that was not all. He arrived with a dozen fragrant gardenia corsages, which he proceeded to pin on all the nurses on the obstetrics ward. By the time he returned to my mother's bedside, the florist's box with its waxed layers of green tissue paper was empty: in a flush of munificence, Len had given all the creamy flowers away, neglecting to save a corsage for his wife. Thus it began. The first battle I witnessed between my parents evolved from my father's needy compulsion to enchant other women.

"By all means, take those too." Janine pointed to a lavish display of long-stemmed red roses, a gift from Norbert, still based in Germany. "I'm sure there must be some nurses you missed. You could always try a different floor." Later that night after Len went home—and before a nurse extolling his charms wheeled me off to sleep with my newborn peers—my mother and I indulged in a solid postpartum cry together. They were not the last tears my father would cost us.

. . .

A basic premise of my parents' marriage was my mother's refusal to leave her parents. Having failed to leave them for Roland, nothing could make her move away once she'd married someone else. When Herbert offered Len a job, Janine insisted he turn it down because, while it was a leg up to a great career, it involved a six-month posting to Japan. No, she said, not possible even temporarily for her to leave New York. Reluctantly rejecting Herbert's offer, Len continued in the engineering salesman's job that cast him as a wandering peddler. And again, six years later, when Janine went with him on a business trip to California, in deference to her feelings Len sacrificed a lucrative opportunity that would have meant their moving to Los Angeles.

"*The people here keep telling me what a remarkable husband I have, and they offered him a very important job in the factory, which he would love to accept,*" Janine wrote home to Trudi. But the company president told her that Len had turned it down out of his "respect" for her attachment to her family—"*born out of the troubles we went through together.*" She confided to Trudi, "*I didn't realize he was that understanding.*"

Janine was working now for Mount Sinai Hospital's chief of cardiology, and when it came to household chores, Len initially took upon himself both the laundry and the gritty cleaning. Every Monday evening, he celebrated their Monday wedding with another anniversary present, and at the end of their first year, he gave his bride his handmade voucher—a *Gutschein*, as her parents termed it—for the belated purchase of a diamond ring. It was an offer she did not accept because she knew that he could not afford it. Happily, he plunged into the family circle and answered now to "Leonardle," the *badisch* nickname Alice gave him in token of her growing fondness. So, for the time being, he took it as a fine arrangement when he and Janine found their own apartment literally steps away from his in-laws. Amid a serious postwar housing shortage, they, too, paid the superintendent's $500 finder's fee to rent a place across the hall from Janine's parents. A penthouse on Fifth Avenue would not have pleased her more.

From the start, Janine and Trudi with their husbands spent their time together, and they were several sets into canasta on a sticky summer evening one year after they had married, when Trudi shared alarming news. She had taken Alice to the dentist that afternoon to see about a painful canker sore, and he had raised the possibility their mother's lesion might be cancerous.

"God, no!" Janine burst out. "I'd better get pregnant quickly! If something happens to Mother, I'll need someone to love!" She tossed out these words unthinkingly, like easy discards from a well-planned hand, and Len pretended not to hear her. Afterward, the devastating impact of her statement hit her, and she felt guilty, even as her goal remained. By summer's end, while fears for Alice proved ungrounded,

Trudi with Lynne (L), and Janine with Leslie

Janine and Trudi both were pregnant, and ever locked in rivalry, they conceived just weeks apart, so that Trudi's daughter Lynne would be born merely twenty days ahead of me.

"What goes through a man's mind, driving seven hundred miles home without having earned a cent?" Arthur Miller wrote of the salesman's plight in the year that I was born. In my father's case, his letters from the road in March 1949 voice the ache of exile from his cozy home and distance from his pregnant wife. "*Ich bin ganz allein in der großen Welt,*" I am all alone in the big world, he wrote to Janine from Hudson, New York, repeating words he knew that she had used in childhood, writing home in misery from her prescribed confinement in the Alps. "*I'm very lonesome without you and can't wait till I get home to you again,*" he bewailed from Syracuse. "*It's awful not to be near enough to call you during the day, and the nights are intolerable.*"

Finding my father's needy, youthful letters only after he had died was a wrenching revelation to me. Even now, I read them with overwhelming grief of loss. How I wish I might have known this tender, ardent, open man.

Syracuse—My dearest, I think of you constantly and pray that you are all right—I miss you so terribly that it makes me sick sometimes. . . . It makes me so nervous and uneasy to be away that all I can think of is getting thru and getting home. . . . My darling, I love you so much and I want you with me always . . . I've been a good boy and haven't even done anything bad—you'd be proud of me. But I have no desire for any one but you. . . . Take me in your arms tonight. I need you, and I'm loving you with all my heart. Len

He called her almost every day and shared his schemes to organize his business stops, scattered in far-flung towns around the state, in order to steer home to her as soon as possible. "*More and more,*" he wrote from Utica, describing his new outlook, "*I realize that family life is really the most important thing and can't wait to get home to start it again with the girl of my dreams.*" Longing for her robbed him of necessary patience to study for his state engineering license test, he fretted, even as he also worried over racking up sufficient sales to justify his trip expenses to his boss. "*I'm shaking oak trees*" in hopes of knocking loose potential business, he wrote, but the market was so bad that "*each sale, no matter how small, is like pulling teeth—impacted molars.*"

But the letter that most captured me was one that showed how poorly Leonard understood the rival he was battling. What was Janine thinking when she shifted to her husband the anthem of her first romance? "J'Attendrai" was the secondhand love song that Len sang aloud in his hotel room to fill the cold space of his solitude. He could not have known the song belonged irrevocably to another man or that its words of loss and longing would conjure up Roland for her.

I miss you muchissimo and wonder how the devil I sleep at all without you. I've been so *allein* that I keep talking to myself nights to keep up a conversation and then sing "J'Attendrai" to you for an encore. A few more days of this and I'll be as nutty as a fruitcake so please don't mind if I seem a little peculiar at first when I return. I'm a-lovin and a-worshippin that girl of mine—you know who she is—yes, Hannele, and please tell her if you can. All my love and a thousand hugs and kisses, Len

When I read the letters of that eager, boyish husband, I see him on a marital minefield, like the "wide open flats" of the windy corporate campuses he described, but this one rigged with potent memories of an unseen rival. Len, Janine, and Roland—each betrayed by love and war.

• • •

In the fall of 1948, Sigmar and Alice left the city for a few weeks' visit with Heinrich's family in Buffalo. This annual pilgrimage and a two-week summer stay at a lake in the Catskills—he reading, she knitting—were the couple's only forays from the confines of their small apartment where their daily lives were governed by routine and economy. Already sixty-two when he reached the States, Sigmar had not attempted to get a job. Instead he worked at learning stratagems of stock investing—this notwithstanding the fact that his prospects for growing capital were significantly diminished when the great inheritance he had anticipated in America proved much smaller than expected. His original large bequest from one wealthy older brother had dwindled throughout the many years he couldn't claim it or direct the way it was invested. And the widow of another older brother who had died childless many years before, leaving a vast estate and similarly generous bequests to his siblings, had managed to circumvent the will to her advantage. Yet when Sigmar's surviving brothers and sisters sued to win their lawful shares, he refused to go along with them.

"*I* should sue my brother's widow?" Sigmar demanded with incredulity, denouncing his siblings' lawsuit as an ugly tactic, regardless of her assets or greedy machinations.

What money Sigmar gained from the first inheritance went to repaying with interest all his debts to Herbert, Maurice, and Edy, and the balance he endeavored to invest. Every day he went to Wall Street to learn beside his cousin Max, who was trying to become a broker. In the risky ventures of the market, though, Sigmar's belated apprenticeship proved more costly than profitable. He watched, now in helpless indecision, then in loyalty to those few stocks he termed his "darlings," as the value of his holdings fell. In that context, calling home one day from Buffalo, he told Janine to search his files to verify the purchase price of shares that now seemed poised to plummet even lower.

The blinds were drawn and everything in tidy order in her parents' second-floor apartment when Janine, then ten weeks pregnant, sat down at Sigmar's mahogany keyhole desk in the living room. Above her head, a large framed picture of President Franklin D. Roosevelt reflected her father's gratitude to his new country. After years of living with the visages of Hitler and Pétain leering at him everywhere, Sigmar had uncharacteristically sent away for this poster-sized artistic tribute to FDR, believing, with many Jewish refugees, that the patrician wartime president had done his best to rescue them. (That Roosevelt had failed to open the gates of immigration to Europe's victims anywhere near as widely as he could have, or that his administration had refused to accede to Jewish pleas to bomb the railway lines leading to Nazi death camps, were facts not yet known.)

In years to come, Janine would not remember whether the financial statement Sigmar needed had been difficult to find, obliging her to expand her search of his private files, or—she acknowledged the possibility—it was random, audacious snooping that broadened her explorations. Either way, like Pandora, she would regret her curiosity, when drifting from the broker's statements, her eyes picked out a telegram from the International Committee of the Red Cross. It announced that a Roland Arcieri had enlisted help in France through the Red Cross Tracing Service to determine the whereabouts of a Janine Günzburger in New York. In the event this message reached her, the Red Cross instructed her to get in touch—promptly, please.

In an instant of total joy she forgot the sorry waste of tortured years, forgot her husband, forgot the child nestling deep inside her, and she responded to the wondrous fulfillment of her greatest wish: finally, finally, Roland was calling out for her! At last, after all her years of patient waiting, here was clear-cut proof of Roland's enduring love. Yes, with the urgency of a telegram, her lover was crying out to her.

In a fever of excitement, she studied the telegram for directions on responding. But when had it arrived? She read it again, flipped it over, hunted vainly for its envelope, but no date could be found. Why had no one shared this with her? A cloud of dark suspicion slowly slid across her heart. Months or even years could well have passed since this telegram arrived. She struggled with the realization that its burial among Sigmar's papers was proof that he had purposely concealed it. The ground tilted underneath her feet. The father whose steely dictates she had always feared, but whose honor she had never doubted, had acted with unconscionable deception.

A wave of nausea seized her. She fought for breath, her legs felt weak, and the room began to turn: Roosevelt, so solemn in his business suit, the violets with their velvet buds uncurling on the windowsill, Lindt chocolates in a porcelain dish that Alice offered every guest, the *Aufbau*'s latest issue folded on the coffee table, a cut-glass ashtray next to Sigmar's reading chair—all these ordinary objects now seemed sly and slippery. Like painted scenery on a stage, her parents' gemütlich living room disguised a disappointing world of secrets and duplicity. She gripped the corner of the desk. An unaccustomed sense of rage and violation overcame her, and she did not know what to do with it. Her thoughts went racing backward in useless search of explanations to make forgiveness possible.

Did this mean there had been letters too? Obviously so! Her love had written, begging her to come to him, and not receiving any answer, Roland could only have concluded that his letters failed to reach her. Why else would he have turned to the Red Cross Tracing Service? But hadn't Norbert given him her address when they got together in Lyon? Then surely he had written her! How terrible for him, through years of doubt and silence, to be misled into believing that she had forgotten him. With eager fingers and frantic determination to understand the truth of things, she ransacked every drawer of Sigmar's desk, certain that if he saved the telegram, he must have saved the letters too. Surely, the telegram was proof that Father would not have dared destroy them. But there was only that one telegram, saved from the incinerator by its officious pedigree, the sort of communication, she recognized, that no true German like her father, mindful of proper record keeping, would carelessly obliterate. Suspended in time—with a past that now demanded reevaluation, a present that no longer seemed of her own making, and a future robbed of honest choices—Janine spent hours on the floor of her parents' living room, debating where to go from there. No point in raising the issue with Father. He'd cite his rights—no, his *obligation*—to protect his lovesick daughter from the dangers of pursuing an ill-advised relationship. Sigmar would not admit to doing wrong, and it would only drive a wedge between them. And so, respectful of his authority and still devotedly committed to winning his approval, she worked to squelch the anger to which she was entitled.

Beyond that, she numbly granted, she could hardly bring the issue to the open without involving Len and showing him how much Roland still mattered to her. Why hurt her husband now and taint their marriage, when she couldn't leave him anyway? For how could she sail back to France anchored by an unborn child? She was fixed to the spot by the growing weight of me within her womb. The golden moment when she might have set a different course was as lost in clouded history as an intercepted telegram hidden in a file drawer.

At the end of 1949, Janine would be cruelly tested once again when her first employer, Dr. Morton, forwarded a letter that he had just received from Montreal. It was written by a stranger with a graceful hand, dated Christmas Eve, misspelled her name, and included no mention whatsoever of Roland. All the same, Janine instantly recognized his part in it. Most amazing, Roland seemed to know that she had married (perhaps via Edy and Lisette and the busy rumor mill of Mulhouse) and yet was looking for her anyway. He had already crossed the ocean! He was already on his way to her.

> Dear Sir,
>   A friend of mine just arriving from France for a trip in Canada and the United States would like to get in touch with an old acquaintance: Miss Jeanine Gunsburg.
>   Miss Gunsburg was working for you a year or two ago, and we only know that she got married since then.
>   You are the only person to whom we could ask any informations connected with the name of her husband and her new address.
>   If it is possible, would you kindly send me back those few informations at the address below. Thanking you in advance for all the trouble.

If not for me, she would have run to him. My mother often told me so, and she still remembers the silent torment of longing to write back to Roland's friend, though she knew it was too late. Incapable of absconding from her marriage with me *or* without me, she could not allow herself to write to Montreal. She passed her days in a fog of unspoken anger and sadness, desperate to reply, but stymied by the fear that if Roland arrived to visit her, she could never let him leave again. Any contact would be too dangerous. Her dream had come in search of her, and now she had to hide from it.

I have always shouldered a sense of accountability. At a moment when she might have grasped the freedom to take her chances with Roland, it was I who held her captive. Any wonder that beside my fascination with her romantic story, I felt an overwhelming need to protect the mother I adored—to make her *happy*, which would often pit me against my father. I needed him to help me validate the choice

Janine and Leslie

she made; instead, as time went by, he would insist upon pursuing an agenda all his own.

• • •

In that same month that Janine forbade herself from replying to Roland's intermediary in Montreal, Norbert came home from Germany for Sigmar's seventieth birthday and brought the parents devastating news of his aim to marry a German woman he had met five years earlier, shortly after landing back in Europe on VE Day. He had met his intended wife while working as chief investigator for a Special Investigations Section of the United States Military Police stationed north of Frankfurt, and he knew his parents would be horrified. After all, what could be more difficult for them, more humiliating before their friends, than for their son to bring home a German Gentile war bride? Like Janine before him, Norbert was torn between the one he loved and duty to the family. But throughout his visit, he kept his plans a secret both from her and Trudi, and the parents peculiarly kept it from his sisters also.

After he went back to Germany, an emotional exchange of letters between parents and son smoldered for many months, with Norbert's reading like the ravings of a youth at least a decade younger than his twenty-nine years. Madly, he waffled back and forth in a show of turmoil and confusion, confessing that his prolonged stay in Germany *"was not uniquely due to my love for my work or certainly not for my sympathy for Deutschland."* Rather, he had struggled unbearably to weigh *"sentimentality against reason,"* and as emotions had finally prevailed, he wanted permission to marry the woman of his choosing. Evidently pained, he outlined his dilemma to the parents, even as he promised not to marry without their blessing:

> Is it better to be unhappy without her but with you; or with her, but not with you? . . . In your answer, please do not threaten me with a thousand possible things. . . . I could never be happy in a marriage that goes against your will. If I could ever be happy by submitting to your possible disapproval, only time will tell.

Ever after, Alice preserved Norbert's letters along with drafts of the replies that she and Sigmar, with heavy hearts, labored over wording. Theirs show harsh phrases crossed out and sympathetic inserts composed in the margins. The stakes were high. Sigmar and Alice feared losing their only son, and Sigmar well remembered his own older brother Hermann, who had disappeared completely after marrying outside the faith. Hermann had emigrated from Germany when Sigmar was a youth, but was so afraid his marriage to a Protestant in London would crush his parents that he changed his name to Gunn and ceased all contact. Until their last breaths, Simon and Jeanette remained tormented over him. Many years later Hermann resurfaced in New York. For Sigmar, however, the grief his parents suffered was not forgotten; rather, it guided his pen to write cautiously to Norbert. He feared an unyielding attitude about his son's intended bride might encourage Norbert to settle permanently in Germany, instead of returning home to make his life with the family in the States.

All the letters were in German, with Norbert's typed on army paper. At the top, by hand, a mistrustful afterthought, on one of them he penned a warning to his sisters not to pry: "*NUR FÜR PAPA UND MAMA!*" And he closed another writing, "*With a thousand greetings and kisses, your loving-and-hoping-you-have-the-same-feeling son and brother (though this is not my sisters' business), Norbert*"

Remarkably, while debating the situation, none of Norbert's letters or his parents' answers ever mentioned the name of his bride-to-be or told anything about her—Dorothea Ostheim, who would turn out to be a petite and pretty blonde of twenty-seven. A feisty, sensible, and unpretentious person, she had been a member of the Bund (the girls' equivalent of Hitler Youth) and had worked in the war years as a secretary for the *Wehrmacht.* Only later would it be learned that her parents had been divorced, her father was dead, a sister had committed suicide, and her only surviving brother was an unrelenting anti-Semite. Alice wrote her son to plead against the marriage:

Dear Norbert,

Your letter makes me realize that you were sent away from home too early and for too long, forced out of your milieu and obliged to live with people with a different outlook on the world, a different life and feeling. Only once back here would you probably see that while you may have had an understanding girlfriend there, she is not the right wife that you need. It is always the same with you, as you always think you love someone whom you don't want to leave, and then each time you forget her and end up happy that it's over. . . .

You are not, as you say, a child anymore. You alone are responsible for what you do and don't do. If *you* think that all conditions are present for a happy and worry-free future, we cannot stop you. We here in America certainly feel differently than you over there; none of all the refugees here will forget Dachau and Auschwitz or the outrage of how we were regarded and treated. It is too much, dear Norbert, to expect people to have sympathy for our accepting a German Aryan girl into the family. . . .

With much love, your Mama

Sigmar advised in writing that he had seldom heard of a "*successful intermarriage that ended up happy,*" and avowed that Norbert's choice of

bride came as "*a great shock to me and the biggest disappointment of my life.*"
But he nonetheless went on to capitulate resignedly:

> . . . You are now of an age when a man has a right to choose his own
> course and far be it for me to want to influence you in your deci-
> sions. If after thorough reflection you are still of the opinion that
> your planned union is absolutely necessary for your life happiness,
> we want to put absolutely no obstructions in your way, and I hope
> that the relationship between us and you and our family will in no
> regard be changed by this marriage.

That Sigmar censored his feelings is clear from the sentences he
struck out in composing his final version:

> But you cannot force us in any way to accept a Christian German
> woman as a member of the family. And I personally do not know
> if I can ever overcome the resentment I have against such a union.

Still, before marrying, he urged his son, "*Come home and take the necessary time and distance to think this over once again, thoroughly and unin-
fluenced by us or by anyone on the other side of the great waters.*" He closed,
"*Fervently, your Papa.*"

That December, Norbert and Dorothea quietly married in Germany.
Sigmar and Alice sent a wedding gift of $2,000, an enormous amount
of money for them, the equivalent of more than eight times that much
today. Pledging to make Norbert happy, Dorothea wrote to thank the
parents for their generosity and understanding:

> I can well imagine what it cost you to give your permission, and es-
> pecially because I know the reasons for your reluctance, I am doubly
> grateful to you. . . . Many thanks for your dear letters, which confirm
> to me that you have accepted me as a daughter. I am very happy
> about that—I can't describe it in words. It is so wonderful to know
> that I am welcome with you and I am convinced that this will make it
> much easier for me to adapt to life in the United States. I pray every

day that it will not be much longer before I can get to know my new parents. . . .

Many loving greetings and all good wishes, your Thea

It would take a year before Norbert could win approval from immigration authorities in Washington for his German bride to follow him to New York. He spent months engaged in lobbying and paperwork to surmount restrictions and cope with stringent postwar immigration laws. By the time Norbert's wife arrived, Janine felt so disturbed about the impact of this marriage on her parents—who struggled within their refugee community of friends and family to reflect the proper mix of acceptance and disapproval—that she refused to allow herself to compare Sigmar's acquiescent attitude toward her brother with his autocratic intervention in her own romantic life. Instead of harboring resentment against Sigmar or even Norbert—in view of the vitriolic letter he had sent from Lyon warning her that in marrying Roland she would lose her only brother—Janine embraced her new sister-in-law with kindness and friendship. Indeed, it was Janine who became her guide in creating an American persona, which included the seemingly obligatory name change as Dorothea reentered life as Doris.

For Sigmar, however, the coup de grâce in this affair came when Herbert invited Norbert to come see him to discuss his future. That his son might build a fine career with his prosperous nephew had been Sigmar's eager hope ever since he landed in America. There was, moreover, historical justice to it. Sigmar had launched his nephew in the steel business that had made his fortune, and now Herbert could reciprocate for Norbert. But on the morning in 1951 that Norbert arrived in Herbert's Manhattan office with a fresh haircut, shined shoes, a new suit, and buoyant expectations, his older cousin kept him waiting for more than an hour and then dealt with him summarily.

"I believe your father generally reads *The New York Times?*" Herbert inquired after asking about his parents' health.

"*Ja, jeden Tag, jede Seite,*" Norbert replied brightly, every day, every page.

"Good. As I understand you want a job, I suggest you check the want ads in the Sunday edition," Herbert said. "Under the circumstances of your marriage, that's the best that I can offer you."

To their credit, Sigmar and Alice never allowed their German daughter-in-law to know their frustration and dismay over Norbert's marriage. For her part, Doris formally converted to Judaism and wore a gold Star of David on a chain around her neck, even when she went to work for a German top executive in the American corporate offices of Mercedes-Benz. When her only child became a bar mitzvah, a beaming Sigmar stood at his blond-haired grandson's elbow to recite the Torah blessings.

As long as he lived, Norbert demonstrated devotion to his parents by visiting them every Friday night, always by himself. It was a ritual for which his parents invariably prepared by setting out fresh bottles of Seagram's Seven and ginger ale beside a pack of cigarettes, and only after he went home would they shake their heads in worry over his indulgence in habits so detrimental to his health. Among them, my uncle would include an ever-hungry taste for women. Yet his marriage to Doris would endure, in spite of his succumbing to sexual adventures that rarely remained a secret and always contained a titillating hint of danger by way of jealous husbands threatening violent reprisal. Working in the linen supply business in New Jersey, as he and Harry would later go on to do, Norbert would more than once nervously confide to Janine that given the range of potential retaliation he might face, the most extreme vengeance—"a rub out"—would actually be preferable to him than lesser alternatives he could imagine.

In view of my grandparents' belief in the value of a common background to guarantee a happy marriage, it is interesting that among their three children, Trudi was the only one to wed a Jew from Freiburg, and hers the only union to end in divorce, albeit a friendly one in middle age. All the same, arranged through intermediaries with little thought of romantic love, Sigmar and Alice's marriage was unquestionably the best of all, lasting through adversity and more than fifty faithful years.

"Thank you," Sigmar would say to Alice on his deathbed at the age of ninety-two, exactly thirty years from the day in 1942 that they had sailed from Europe. "You have been my darling *Hausgeist*," he told her, the spirit of his home. "In spite of everything we went through, we've had a wonderful life together. No man could have a better wife."

Alice and Sigmar in the New York apartment where they arrived in 1943 and spent their lives, Sigmar to the age of ninety-two and Alice to ninety-five

TWENTY

FROM THE DYCKMAN HOUSE
TO OUR NEW HOUSE

THE ORANGE-AND-BEIGE BRICK BUILDING where I lived surrounded by my mother's family until the age of almost nine remains virtually unchanged at 680 West 204th Street, one quiet residential block west of upper Broadway in Manhattan. Here, beyond art deco double doors with a wrought-iron sunburst fanning over etched glass panels, there were Gunzburgers in four apartments during most of the 1950s. Our own place was on the second floor and prized in my opinion for having Sigmar and Alice just across the stucco hallway. Three flights directly overhead, my Aunt Trudi's daughter, Lynne, was my dearest friend and constant playmate. And my brother, Gary, born when I was four, was just a month apart in age from Uncle Norbert's son, Stanley, whose family lived in an apartment two floors above our own. My mother and her sister even rigged a primitive communication system between their two apartments with a coffee can they operated on a pulley system from their kitchen windows. Every part of life was shared, and the closeness of our circle made this the period that we would treasure as a golden age.

Just outside the secure cocoon of family, soft-spoken German Jewish refugees recreated to the best of their ability a European world at the quiet northern tip of the planet's most exciting island. And to me it always seemed as if their insular community had adopted as its center the Dutch colonial farmhouse that still presides, kitty-corner to our old building, overlooking Broadway. What a curious delight—the Dyckman House, an obscure city-owned Manhattan landmark and a solid anachronism on a hillock above the modern street, surrounded

Janine (L) and Trudi at the Dyckman House benches on the corner of Broadway and West 204th Street circa 1951

(L to R) Harry and Trudi, Norbert and Doris, Len and Janine out to dinner in New York, 1951

by retaining walls of rough-hewn fieldstone. It spoke to me of other times as wistfully as the refugees who sat conversing on the painted benches that lined its walls. Three centuries after the arrival in the New World of the neighborhood's first intrepid German immigrants, it seemed as if the Dyckmans' ghosts had summoned refugees of Nazi Germany, inviting them to treat that green and pleasant corner like the cobbled marketplace in *Deutschland* each one had left behind.

In that enclave nestled between the Henry Hudson Bridge to the Bronx about thirty blocks north and the George Washington Bridge to New Jersey about thirty blocks south, Sigmar and Alice and other German-speaking émigrés endeavored to restore the civilized traditions of the land that had been home. By unspoken prearrangement, they met at the benches near the Dyckman House on daily walks throughout the area. Men in formal overcoats tipped their gray fedoras to ladies wearing velvet hats with black net veils. Politely they took care to draw off gloves to shake each other's hands. "*Guten Tag, wie gehts?*" The *badisch* dialect of the Black Forest had migrated—as so many languages before and so many yet to come—to city streets that gleamed with the patina of acceptance.

Colorful Spanish signs describe a new array of upper Broadway stores these days. Gone now are the Irish bar, the Italian market, and the Chinese laundry whose grim, efficient owners starched the plain white shirts of Jewish refugees and handed them receipts with indecipherable pencil reckonings. Gone, too, are the sounds of German that filled the neighborhood when my cousin Lynne and I learned to roller-skate to the penny candy store on 207th Street to agonize over ten cents' worth of choices or to the corner soda fountain for ice cream cones, pretzel sticks, and Golden Books with American stories that no one knew to tell us.

My mother's stories were far more complex and disturbing. Early on, she held me spellbound with tales of danger and romance in far-off places. Knowing she had crossed the waters from a distant land called France, I believed that I could see it on the Palisades across the Hudson River, where what impressed me as the Eiffel Tower was actually a radio transmitter in New Jersey. While it was German that I heard all day, my mother insisted on evoking France as the scenery of my imagination. My favorite treat was therefore lunch at Nash's, a Dyckman Street bakery where a mural in the dining room recreated a Parisian café on the rue de la Paix. As we ate our hamburgers and potato chips, I felt drawn into that Paris scene of tiny tables where waiters wearing aprons and mustaches balanced trays of demitasse for sophisticated ladies in fancy hats, fishnet hose, and cinched-waist dresses. Long-legged poodles posed languidly beside them, flaunting ribbons on their pom-poms.

In the real world, long blue numbers tattooed the inner forearms of the European women who picked out cookies for us from the trays of Nash's bakery counter. And the real-world parties I witnessed in the afternoons involved quiet German couples who took turns hosting one another for *Kaffee und Kuchen* in their small apartments, happy to find familiar faces capable of mirroring the people they had been. In this brand-new land of supposed assimilation, these refugees rediscovered separation and tried to recreate a stolen world. As they draped their best linen cloths over folding bridge tables set up in their living rooms, Alice and her friends recalled with mute regret their abandoned gilt-edged china, thin Czechoslovakian crystal, and monogrammed silver, all chosen for their weddings and meant to last a lifetime. Now they set Swiss chocolates on paper doilies, dressing up the dishware that they never expected to be anything but serviceable. Converting grams to ounces, they drew passable Old World *Linzer Torten* and buttery pound cakes topped with powdered sugar out of ovens whose unfamiliar Fahrenheit settings heated their anxieties. Still, they contented themselves by reviving their recipes, their language, and their manners as they shared tips on filing claims for German reparations and tried to reintroduce themselves with American identities, if only to each other.

Aging émigrés tentatively built new lives in a land devoid of memories, relying on their own newspaper, *Aufbau* (founded in 1934 for New York's German Jewish population with an advisory board including such intellectual luminaries as Thomas Mann and Albert Einstein), to enable them to read in their own language about their generation. I still remember them: Gretl, Marcel, and Jacob, Max and Emma, Frau Burger and Frau Dreyfuss, Herr Meyer and Herr Kaufmann—the latter being my mother's former Freiburg Hebrew teacher, who re-appeared in Inwood, inexplicably retaining his power to make her squirm. Like newly hatched birds fallen from their nests, they seemed frail and small, yet valiant. Yes, even now, theirs are the faces I remember when I hear a German accent that provokes a sense of intimacy stretching back to childhood. In those accents of the Reich, I hear the echoes of survivors. There is nostalgia in the love that a certain kind of German voice, with history in its undertones, always calls to life in me.

Sigmar spent the decades after his arrival in New York in his own private war with Germany, all of it on paper. His scrupulous efforts to calculate and verify his losses for *Wiedergutmachung,* or reparation claims, against the German government dragged across the years. He also struggled to obtain equitable compensation for the business and the Freiburg home given up to private opportunists whose payments, however undervalued, had been lost to him in blocked accounts in German banks. For the remainder of his life, as if it were his paying job, Sigmar sat almost daily at his desk, drafting letters and appeals that recounted his losses and expenses over six hard years of hiding and escape. He put the total cost of flight alone, not including the assets he relinquished, at 82,781.50 Reichsmark, for which the postwar German government initially agreed to reimburse him only for the inconsequential train ride across the border from Freiburg to Mulhouse in 1938. Much as he needed money and pursued his claims on paper, making handwritten copies of everything he sent, never once did Sigmar venture back to Germany to press his campaign personally with the acumen and expertise that would have been required.

In his written appeals, Sigmar mostly directed his attention to the transactions involving the two German brothers, Albin and Alfons Glatt, who had snapped up the Günzburger brothers' "non-Aryan" building supply business for a token of its true worth. Norbert's negotiations proved unsuccessful when he first went to see them in 1946, and Sigmar's nephew Edy, practicing law in Mulhouse, gained nothing from them either. Now Sigmar wrote to tell the Glatts that time had come to reevaluate the situation. Why, the Günzburgers' warehouse at the railroad tracks in itself had cost 36,000 Mark a full twenty years before they had been obliged to sell it to the Glatts for *half* that price! The Glatts had obtained the company's furnishings, cars, and trucks at ridiculously unfair prices, and there were aspects of the business—such as its long-established base of customers and its rights to purchase scarce materials based on seniority—for which, contrary to usual business practice, the Glatts paid nothing. In all good conscience, Sigmar argued in his letters, the Glatts ought to pay the balance of what the business had actually been worth: they should either compensate the Günzburgers for having preyed upon their weakness under Hitler, or else give the business back.

In reply to such entreaties in 1949, the Glatts wrote Sigmar, insisting they alone had saved the business, while also voicing interest in coming to a compromise:

Very Esteemed Herr Günzburger!

We were so happy with the visit of your son. In the past years we often wondered where fate had placed you and where you spent the war years. We are very pleased to know that you and your family are doing well. I imagine your son told you how we are doing, but I wish to add a few details.

In the first two years after we took over the business, we had to work very hard to manage to get the business off the ground. Once we achieved that we were very busy throughout the whole war. Because all the male personnel were drafted, we were forced to work many more hours than normal. For instance, we spent every Sunday working.

The difficulties of transportation were enormous. Our trucks and personal cars were requisitioned. We enlarged the warehouse at the railroad tracks. We enlarged the business on the Rosastrasse considerably and started to sell screws. We took very good care of that particular part of the business and it developed well.

On November 27, 1944, however, the whole Rosastrasse establishment was destroyed [in Allied bombing] and with it the warehouse, offices, and apartment and furnishings of Herr Albin Glatt. Lost on the same occasion were all our files and paperwork and accounting as well as everything that was in the safe. . . . We racked our brains, but had to rely especially on the honor of our customers. It was impossible to avoid a loss, particularly since many of our clients were hit the same way and many died in the attacks. The railroad warehouse was hit by bombs several times and each time we tried to repair it. . . .

We spent the next six to eight months digging through the ruins of the Rosastrasse in the hope of finding anything that could be slightly usable. It was unbelievable how there was nothing to be gotten, but here and there we would find a complete fitting or a pipe or something of that kind. In that way we collected every charred nail and every melted screw or fitting we hoped to be able to reuse. The iron sheeting business was completely dead as we did not receive anything from October 1944 to the beginning of 1946. At the railroad warehouse we had to be very careful as there was always a risk of robbery and indeed several times people broke in and stole materials.

Beginning in 1946, the deliveries of material began to return, and by the end of the year, the business achieved a very strong upsurge.

For the last two months, business has been weakened, however, and the way the clients pay is terrible. We have to watch closely and constantly monitor what is happening. . . . I assume you are aware that the profits are pretty well absorbed by taxes. . . .

Personally we are more or less okay. Unfortunately, we both have lost our wives. Albin's wife died in the beginning of 1945, Alfons's wife in the beginning of 1948. . . .

Your son has wanted us to respond to the demands presented through Monsieur Cahen. We suggested a personal discussion and asked Monsieur Cahen to come here, but his busy schedule has made that impossible. . . . We would of course prefer to come to an understanding with you personally as we believe we would achieve faster results that way. . . .

With friendly greetings, the Glatt Brothers

In October 1949, empowered to act on behalf of his father and uncle, Norbert, still stationed in Germany, went back to see the Glatts again and naïvely settled for 40,000 Deutsche Mark, then equal to $10,000.

Still far below the value of the company, it represented total payment for the business in the heart of Freiburg and the warehouse on the railroad tracks, as well as inventory, vehicles, accounts, and an established base of customers. Sigmar and Heinrich soon despaired that by depending on Norbert, with his youth and inexperience, they had once more permitted the Glatts to get the better of them. Indeed, two years earlier, the French military government had enacted a sweeping restitution regulation in their zone of occupation, including Freiburg, stipulating that victims of Nazism were entitled to get their assets back. To make matters even worse, Norbert had gone so far as to sign a waiver of restitution rights that eliminated the chance of further public compensation from the state.

At the same time, Sigmar and Alice were both kept busy writing to family and acquaintances in Europe and contemplating pleas from former associates who begged the Jewish couple to vouch for them in connection with official denazification proceedings under way in postwar Germany. Nazi sympathies that once appeared expedient now tainted reputations, endangering social standing, employment, and professional advancement. Thus Sigmar's former Freiburg accountant, for example, wrote for help, as did the wife of the German military man whose family had lived rent-free in the Günzburgers' basement before Hitler came to power. Writing from Bonn in 1951, their former tenant, Frau Nagel, bolstered her appeal to Alice with snapshots of her daughters, describing them as cheated by the casualties of war of the likelihood of finding mates, and of her son, pictured in 1943 wearing a German Army uniform with tall black boots and a medal on his chest. As ever, Alice kept a handwritten copy of her reply to Frau and Herr Nagel:

> It is actually very difficult for me to answer your letter. So many sad and awful memories were reawakened—memories of a time when we were frightened and demeaned, times that took so much from our lives and that we would happily forget. Here, in America, thank God we are well and after our long wanderings we have found in this country a new homeland and bread, and for that we are very grateful. But until we got here we knew hard and painful years, and

it is a miracle that we all found each other once again. Already in France, our flight to cross the demarcation line from the Occupied to the Unoccupied Zone was made possible by a worthy German officer. That in itself was a gift from God. If we had not been able to escape at that time, we would probably be among the six million who were gassed. Many of our closest relatives died that way. Also poor Fräulein Ellenbogen with her brother and sister-in-law.

Alice closed with a pointed observation:

I am happy your son came home safely from the war. I felt scared for him. At his age, with his enthusiasm and his zest for the Thing, he was surely in the front rows of the battle and an eager Wehrmacht soldier. It must have been hard for you. It must have not been easy for you either, dear Herr Nagel, to repeatedly change your lifestyle and your livelihood. How much misery there is in this context among the refugees you cannot begin to guess. All those people lacking money and knowledge of the [English] language have no choice but to accept the most unbelievably lowly jobs. This is a misfortune of our times that has spared no one, but rather it has hit all mankind.

The change of "lifestyle and livelihood" that Alice so empathetically mentioned in her letter in regard to Herr Nagel was something she understood firsthand. In coming to New York, she had found her sister Rosie living in a dismal railroad flat in a walk-up building in the South Bronx, renting out a room to a boarder. Rosie's husband, Natan Marx, once the proud proprietor of the family business in Eppingen, was earning $40 a month washing dishes and pots in a sweltering hospital kitchen in Brooklyn. (A heart attack would kill him in 1949 at the age of sixty-two.) Their daughter Hannchen, sixteen years old when they immigrated at the end of 1938, had been helping to support her parents by working for $28 a month as a live-in maid in the Bronx.

Spared such hardships that other refugees encountered, Sigmar and Alice lived lives of small routine. On days that Sigmar did not go down to Wall Street trailing Max, his business activities consisted of devouring the financial pages of *The New York Times* in the mornings and *The Herald Tribune* in the afternoons, which provided little more in terms of social engagement than a regular impetus to walk to the newstand. Several times a week, he met with Max to play their favorite German card game. On very rare occasions, he and Alice splurged on tickets to the Metropolitan Opera—especially for Wagner—or to Carnegie Hall for a master pianist playing Chopin or Beethoven. But their experience in America was generally confined to Inwood, where they were content with the close proximity of family and other German Jewish refugees who shared their simple gratefulness to be alive.

With his grandchildren in the building, Sigmar mellowed, and the stern authoritarian that Janine, Trudi, and Norbert remembered fearing in their youth was replaced by a kind and doting patriarch—"Bapa," adored by all. He taught me how to read from the pages of his newspapers, inspiring my interest in journalism. And he never missed an opportunity to lead me, humming, in stately bridal march down the length of his apartment, culminating in a solemn ceremony in which he placed the golden paper band from his cigar like a wedding ring upon my finger.

Almost as soon as Alice and Sigmar moved into the building, their next-door neighbor, a schoolteacher named Lou, started to give them English lessons. For homework, Lou had them fill lined composition books with page after page of random statements and spontaneous thoughts that roamed disjointedly between the political and personal. Sigmar in ink and Alice in pencil, they diligently practiced writing in English and wound up creating haphazard journals as both voiced feelings they normally stifled.

From Sigmar:

> Everybody has his deal of misfortune. It is better to live in the present than always to remember times past. Many refugees arrive without a single dollar in their pockets. The moment I could leave Europe I was a very happy man. Great nations should work for peace but keep the sword always sharpened for their defense. History will judge our generation as foolish, making wars one after another and destroying millions of people and the prosperity of the countries. Going to the stock market is a hazard. I should like

to give all war criminals to the judgments of the Russians. A ruined Europe is all what the war left.

And Alice:

A person who travels from one country to another for religious reasons is called a Pilgrim. The Jews are not welcome in any country. To speak a foreign language is hard for older people. Mistakes are human. Life is hard especially in our time. It is very helpful to have a good dictionary. There will be joy and laughter and peace when the world is free. I wish I were able to support the poor. I spend most of my time in the kitchen. It is a long time since I left my home. Old furniture is better than new furniture. I owe my home and my freedom to this country. I will never return to Europe.

As it happened, despite her resolve, Alice would travel there twice, overcome by longing to visit her brother in London. On her first solo trip, in 1957, en route to see family in Zurich as well, she stopped in Freiburg, gravitated to the Poststrasse, and checked herself in to the Hotel Minerva. It was now being run by the Schöpperles' daughter, Rosemarie, and her husband, Friedrich Stock. While they were polite, it was upsetting for Alice to see how the ivy-draped premises of the Minerva had swallowed her home—the place where all three of her children were born and where she'd enjoyed the properous early years of her marriage.

Across the street on the Rosastrasse stood Sigmar's former business, now called Eisen Glatt. That afternoon, Alice went to gaze in silence at the department store once owned by Trudi's husband's family. "Nebbish!" she wrote home, summarizing sad emotions of disbelief on the back of a postcard that showed the Minerva. She mailed it before she climbed the stairs and went to bed that night, but hours later, unable to fall asleep in Germany as a paying guest in what should have been her own home, she packed her things and called a taxi to take her across the border to Mulhouse. Never again would Alice go back to Germany. Or France.

When she reached Mulhouse late that night, she went directly to the Hotel du Parc, among the city's finest, and asked in English for a room. But in the empty lobby at that hour, Alice overheard the hotel clerks make fun of her: "*Quelle idiote! Avec cet accent alsacien, elle ne parle aucun mot de français?*" What an idiot! With that Alsatian accent, she doesn't speak a word of French?

"No, not an idiot," Alice retorted in French with the bravado of her girlhood as *die freche Lisel*. "Just an American."

* * *

In the land of my early childhood, no disrespect to Alice, it was my father who stood apart as the sole American. He was the man to count on for directions and information and who drummed up conversation to keep Sigmar entertained. He worked to master French and German, learning lengthy lists of foreign words and complex rules of German grammar to translate for his in-laws, editing their correspondence for proper English usage. In language and self-confidence, know-how and personality, he had no equal. On Sundays, when he played tennis near the Harlem River with Trudi's husband, Harry, he competed in raiment I took to be symbolic—a classic tennis sweater that Alice knitted for him with thick white cables and stripes of red and blue around the sleeves and V-neck. It seemed a costume meant for him alone, an entitlement of birth and nationality, especially as my uncle never had a sweater like it, with its bold tricolor citizen's assertiveness. My American father wore that sweater like the flag, and I was proud to be his daughter.

It was rare, however, that my mother or my brother and I got to spend much time with him. Mom had given up her job when I was born, and we spent long summers in a rustic rental on a lake, where Dad could get away to join us only on weekends. But our familial city life was replicated in the country also, for Trudi and Harry and Norbert and Doris also rented lakeside houses just steps away from ours. On Friday nights, the men drove up with string-tied ziggurats of Nash's baked goods and a week's supply of dirty laundry for their wives to wash and iron, and they returned to the city early Monday mornings.

For the rest, Len was often driving out of town on business trips that continued to leave him lonely and disconsolate and determined to reach beyond his salesman's route and salary. When he was home, he repeatedly debated with Janine the wisdom of striking out in business for himself—a conversation complicated by his being optimistically impetuous, while she was highly risk averse and all too well acquainted with the randomness of danger. Based on agreements with two industrial manufacturers to represent their products in East Coast regions, he quit his job, founded his own company, calling it Unisco, and rented office space not far from the apartment. Energized and instinctively a boss, he grew in stature and authority as he began to hire employees, even as they bristled under his perfectionism. Still required to travel, he lamented in letters from the road how hard it was to build sufficient sales to raise the level of his commissions from 2 percent to 5 percent, and so he logged even longer hours, working nights and weekends.

Though I seldom got to be with him, I loved him wholeheartedly and wanted nothing more than his attention and approval. For his part, he was driven to make me fearless and competitive, a process he regrettably began by pitting me in rivalry with my cousin Lynne, my alter ego and the friend with whom I spent almost every waking moment. Together we walked to P.S. 98 on 211th Street and back each day, traversing subway tunnels rather than crossing over Broadway, with its crush of traffic that our mothers thought more dangerous than the underground passageways of the Independent line. Often we were even dressed alike, in Madison Avenue finery passed down from Herbert's daughters. Without exception, I always got the blue dress and my brown-eyed cousin the identical in pink, our mothers continuing

*Leslie (L) and Lynne, cousins
and constant playmates*

the eye-color-based assignment that Alice had employed in outfitting her girls like twins many years before us.

Despite our closeness, my father contrived to set up constant contests, the first of which was based on height. Almost weekly, he placed us back-to-back to judge which one was taller, and I stretched as high and straight as possible, hoping to measure up for him. With his hand weighing on my head, I strained to roll my eyes behind me to check the outcome, but Daddy's disappointment was invariably palpable, impelling me to offer him consoling explanations as we rode the three flights home from Lynne's apartment together in the elevator.

"Lynne's three weeks older!" I offered hopefully. "Are you sure you pressed her hair down?" All explanations he waved away, complaining that I would *never* grow to match her height unless I started eating more.

Determined as he was to make me strong and self-reliant, he was frustrated to have to battle a range of childish fears that were no doubt fanned by the apprehensive worries of our Nana and our mothers. For them, the experience of war and persecution seemed to leave a residue that clouded every day with the possibility of ending in disaster. My father, however, had no patience for limitations he regarded as irrational: he could not abide my fear of dogs, and when we went to an amusement park, it exasperated him to see me shrink away from

Gary and Leslie at a fair on upper Broadway in New York City in 1956

any ride more dizzying than the Ferris wheel. My delight in spending precious time alone with him was inevitably tempered by anxiety that lacking nerve, I'd let him down.

On wintry Sunday mornings, for example, when he took me to an outdoor ice rink to teach me how to skate, I begged him to hold on to me, but he insisted that I skate alone and struggle to catch up to him. He skated backward. He held his hands out, urging me to come to him, but he never made that possible: his method of instruction depended on his taunting me, slipping ever out of reach. The closer I got to him, the faster he backed away from me, beckoning, retreating, enticing, rejecting. Effortlessly, gracefully, he glided off into the distance, mingling with strangers, admiring agile girls in skating skirts spinning pirouettes for him. I inched across the ice with clumsy, frozen baby steps. I was frantic to keep sight of him, with his flashing can-do smile and nods of encouragement. Rigid on the ice, I wanted only to be enveloped in the warmth and safety of his arms, but he was always unattainable.

Worst of all were nighttimes when the lonely darkness of my room was enough to keep me up, on guard, afraid of formless demons that crouched lurking in the shadows. How I yearned to claim my mother's gentle solace in those nights that sleep eluded me and the hours crawled on implacably, with slowness that tormented me. And so I started creeping out to her, night after night, until finally, fed up with intrusions, my father warned of punishment more fearsome than my nameless fears if I so much as dared to step a foot beyond my bedroom door.

Even so, the night arrived when I could not endure remaining in my room in bleak, fear-riddled solitude. Inspired by the dish and the spoon that perennially scampered off together in the picture on my bedroom wall, I decided to run away. I lugged a heavy dining chair across the foyer in order to climb up, reach the bolt, unlock the door, and tiptoe out of our apartment toward the shelter of an older generation that understood escape. I prayed my grandparents would be home, I hoped they'd hear the bell, and I wondered if they'd summon my parents or welcome me, a barefoot refugee in a flannel heart-print nightgown, desperate for asylum.

Well, you'd think the kaiser's daily birthday party had been bubbling behind their door! Sigmar's brother Heinrich and his wife, Toni, had arrived a few hours earlier by train from Buffalo, and so a world away from the silence I had fled, there were blazing lights and conversation, Nash's chocolate oak leaf cookies, Nana's special pound cake, her lemon meringue pie laced with homemade whipped cream, and a platter of green grapes beside a bowl of water. My grandfather was nursing a cigar, and he and his brother were sipping German wine. I was delighted to see that it was Schwarze Katz, for then I knew that Bapa would give me the little black plastic cat that came tied around the bottle's neck.

Peering in disapproval over wire-rimmed glasses, my great-aunt Toni pursed her purple lips in a wrinkled ridge of condemnation. "How is this she sneaks away from home in the middle of the night, without her parents knowing?" she demanded. "Lisel, you cannot go along with this. Take her straight back home again." My heart sank. But welcoming the opportunity to make an independent stand against her overbearing in-law, Nana fed me cookies and then took me in to sleep with her. She changed into a long white cotton nightgown with her initials embroidered on the collar, a remnant of her trousseau. Then, removing hairpins, she unwound the barely graying braid that I had never seen in any other style but coiled around her head. Soon we nestled in her mahogany twin sleigh bed on square European pillows, under downy claret-colored comforters, and we compared the peculiar shapes we saw in the darkness even with our eyes closed.

I focused on the swirling shapes of white and gold and black that swam across my eyelids, patterns changing faster than I could describe them. "*Ja*, I see just the same," Nana assured me. "Everybody does." But by then my shapes had altered, and I struggled to pin them down. Fireflies! Bumblebees! Tiny dots of red and blue! Flashing silver fireworks! "*Doch*, the same," she said. Her bare arm pressed close to mine, cool and hairless, the skin beneath the freckles as smooth and pale as moonlight. Guiltily, I doubted her. If my own description barely matched the thing that I was seeing, how could either of us know whether anything we saw was actually the same at all? Nana's breath came soft and regular, so I guessed that she was sleeping now, while a few feet away from me, Bapa's snoring filled the silence of the night. For the first time, though, it didn't seem to bother me to be the only one awake. I scanned the room for monsters; I sought out old familiar witches writhing in the drapery, but they all had disappeared.

The next morning, frantic that I was missing, my father was furious to find me being coddled with his in-laws, and the next time I tried absconding in the night, he nabbed me in the act. Before I managed to unlock the door, he came tearing down the hallway from his bedroom, scooped me off the chair, and threw me back in bed. But in truth I don't recall his being very angry. Not himself a man to knuckle under to authority, he may have secretly applauded the audaciousness involved in my defying him again.

. . .

In the spring of 1954 my mother overlaid the nubby, cherry-red upholstery of her living room couch with a lightweight floral slipcover reserved for warmer months and planted herself in front of her Zenith television set, rooted to the spot by the Army-McCarthy hearings. With morbid interest, cigarette in hand, she followed the evildoings of yet another ruthless demagogue who manipulated hatred and suspicion, fanning fires of persecution—this time of alleged Communists in the United States military. She didn't miss a minute of that snarling drama. Meanwhile, at a very early age, I, too, was drawn to sit before the Zenith, in my case riveted by the *Million Dollar Movie*. The same film played several times a day, each day for a week, so that by the end, moved to tears and knowing every line by heart, I would kiss the actors each good-bye behind the glassy screen. Indeed, watching them over and over only made me more devoted to my favorite movies, and in retrospect I realize that they shared a common focus: a pair of star-crossed lovers in a hopeless situation.

The two films I liked best of all illustrated for me what havoc may result when a reasonably happy couple meets a third exciting character. In *Mr. Peabody and the Mermaid*, a married, middle-aged, upper-crust Bostonian falls passionately in love with a siren of the deep, and although he seems callously prepared to abandon wife and daughter to live forever with his fantasy, he has to give her up. In the final scene, the mermaid disappears alone, deep within the grottoes of a black-and-white Caribbean.

Yet nothing could compare with the romantic classic *Casbah*! At its close, the beautiful French heroine takes off from Algiers, stricken that her lover, the dashing jewel thief Pepe Le Moko—having stolen her from her fiancé—has not joined her on the airplane as they had planned. We see her through the little airplane window in gorgeous, grieving profile. Just beyond her view, Pepe lies bleeding on the tarmac, fatally shot in the back by the police while rushing to escape with her. With his last strength, the handsome thief reaches out in longing and despair toward the fleeting vision of the girl who is flying off without him. Her plane lifts into the air, and the heartbreak written on her face tells us she assumes that Pepe's failure to make the flight means he has abandoned her.

These were the scenes that would play in my mind's eye when my mother later confided to me the story of her lost Roland. But *Casbah*, with its subplot of an earlier love that Pepe cruelly casts aside, also served as a cautionary tale. It taught me to be leery of the too-inviting smiles of women whose cheeks bloomed roses and whose voices kissed the air with music when encountering my father. It was a situation that I recognized within our very building when I was seven years old and returning from the park with him. Dad was wearing his tennis sweater with white shorts and sneakers when a pretty dark-haired woman with long and shapely legs beneath a frisky, pleated tennis dress rushed across the lobby to join us in the elevator. He flashed a rakish grin and held the door for her. Her name was Jean, and I knew her as my mother's friend from the benches along the Dyckman House. She lived in our building with her husband and two young daughters, and to Alice's annoyance, she'd already conquered Sigmar as a courteously vocal, though innocent, admirer. But Jean had not yet met my father.

"Is *this* your daddy?" she patted my hair and cooed, not troubling to hide her interest. "You have to introduce me, honey. I'm always looking for a tennis partner!" I studied her animated face in the mirror of the elevator as she turned her charm on him. I was anxious to get us out of there, but when we reached our floor, my father blocked the door and paused to talk.

"Why, I can't believe you're Janine's husband and that we've never met before!" Jean trilled. "No wonder she's been hiding you!"

Returning home that day, we found my mother sitting on the carpet, intent upon a sewing project. Gary was in his playpen, and Louis Armstrong was crooning on the phonograph, "Jeannine, I Dream of Lilac Time," a record Dad had bought for her. She had taken apart one of her best cocktail dresses, a deep blue taffeta with silver polka dots, and cut it down to fit me so I could wear it as Queen Esther in a Purim play at Sunday school. Mom had sacrificed her lovely dress and spent the afternoon resewing it by hand and adding silver sequins that winked across its bodice. I gaped at it in wonder, overwhelmed by my mother's generosity and handiwork. Yet schooled, perhaps, by the *Million Dollar Movie*, I also felt uncomfortable. It somehow felt disloyal to have witnessed that elevator scene without telling her about it, but I lacked language to define the special spark that electrified the atmosphere when Mommy's friend encountered her very handsome husband.

· · ·

For the better part of two years, the quest to find the right suburban house at a price they could afford was the sole objective of my parents' weekend travels through a region whose limits were defined by a twenty-minute radius of 204th Street. But I took comfort in believing the day would never come when—my father dreaming big and my mother always reining in—they would agree on how much they could spend and thus find what they were looking for, allowing us to move. Dad was adamant about climbing up in life and out of Inwood, though Mom was anything but eager to leave her family behind. She had made a significant mistake, however, in giving Alice a key to our apartment, and Nana used it freely, intruding on Dad's privacy. Meanwhile, his business was doing well enough that he had bought a building for it in that northern region of New Jersey that Mom had finally identified as the suburban area closest to her parents. Now he was insisting that they find a house nearby.

Even I couldn't quibble with the fact that we were cramped in our apartment with its little kitchen and single bathroom, especially since

my mother had hired a full-time housekeeper who slept in the bedroom I already shared with Gary. Still, the thought of leaving my
beloved grandparents; and Lynne, my closest friend; and Trudi, like a
second mother; and charming Norbert, the comedian, was too horrible to contemplate. And the prospect was only made more gruesome
by the tedious process of looking for a home.

Week after week, the only thing that seemed to change was the ball
game on Daddy's car radio as we drove from house to house in Bergen
County. Crossing the Hudson gave my father the opportunity to extol
the genius of the George Washington Bridge as a marvel of suspen-
sion engineering and often to indulge in full-throated renditions of
"Ole Man River," Paul Robeson–style. But it ended forever my ability
to picture Paris perched atop the Palisades. The radio transmitter I
had fantasized as the Eiffel Tower turned out to be planted firmly
in Fort Lee, whose Champs-Elysées was an unattractive commercial
stretch of Route 9W.

In each house that we visited, my mother attempted to drum up
my excitement by showing me the room that was soon to be all mine
and telling me to plan how I would like to decorate it. But regardless of how I mentally placed the furniture, we rarely returned to the
same location for a second look, which never left me disillusioned.
No matter what, I didn't want to move to any house beyond a Spald-
ing's throw of my favorite house, the Dyckman House. I was therefore
stunned when suddenly they bought one—a new split-level in Englewood Cliffs on an unpaved street with half-built houses and empty
lots for sale. They put down their deposit on the same day they went
to see it—a day when, tired of seeing houses, I had stayed behind to
play with Lynne—so my bedroom there came without my dreams
installed.

My parents each had different views about it.

It's really time we move now, so this will be our starter house, my
father thought.

I will never pack my bags again, so this is it, my mother vowed.

My own feelings were expressed in an anguished note I slipped
beneath the door of my aunt's apartment on the morning that we
moved:

Dear Trudi,

I can't stand leaving you. Oh no! I won't leave you what'll I do? Please buy the house next to us. Please.

Love,

Leslie

When we crossed the Hudson River from Manhattan on that day we pulled away from the shelter of our building and the protective circle of the family, I was going into exile in a foreign land. It gave me an entirely new appreciation of my mother's story, of all the times she'd had to leave her home not knowing what would happen next. Then eight years old, I identified completely with how she must have felt on the day she crossed the Rhine, relinquishing her childhood. I realized that my life would never be the same again. In leaving In-wood, I, too, was moving to America.

TWENTY-ONE

THE OTHER WOMAN

THE OTHER WOMAN WHO infiltrated my parents' marriage and undermined my father's relationship with everyone who knew him was an iron-willed Russian Jew whose abhorrence of communism had prompted her to abandon her home and family in St. Petersburg at the age of twenty-one in order to pursue a life of freedom in America. Like my father, Alissa Zinovievna Rosenbaum had been determined to shed her past and so changed her Jewish name, but she never quite could lose her smoky Russian accent. Nor did her appeal for Dad, remarkably, have anything to do with her sexual attractiveness.

An intense and compact woman with large and hungry eyes and short dark hair that capped her like Athena's helmet, she was in fact older than my father by thirteen years. But from the moment in 1958 that he read her massive manifesto, *Atlas Shrugged*, the novelist-philosopher who had renamed herself Ayn Rand became his goddess. As another of her disciples later wrote of her psychological seductiveness, she "spiritualized" the secular, and my atheistic father rallied to the banner of her so-called Objectivist philosophy and its icy credo of rational egoism with the all-consuming fervor of fanatical religious faith.

With his smoldering good looks and a slide rule in his pocket, Len embodied the Ideal Man that Rand worshipped through her novels: the romantic hero as thinking individualist, motivated by self-interest, battling conformity. Yes, the very incarnation of her own Howard Roark (the defiant protagonist of *The Fountainhead*, an architect played in the iconic movie by Gary Cooper) was seated at her feet in a Manhattan lecture hall in the person of my father, who became her avid student while in his early forties.

How to understand that this man of fiercely independent intellect and spirit could lose himself within what amounted to a cult? That he could swallow whole not only Rand's general philosophy of life, but also a range of judgments that prescribed his opinion on almost everything—from psychology and politics to literature, art, and music—and demanded his contemptuous rejection of anyone espousing views that she did not endorse? What unspoken need for meaning or approval did Objectivism fill for him—a midlife, midcentury, fledgling industrialist, first-generation American whose native optimism and personal ambition impelled him to insist that man can and must create himself?

He viewed everything through the prism of her Self-adoring worldview: "My philosophy, in essence," she wrote, "is the concept of man as a heroic being, with his own happiness as the moral purpose of his life, with productive achievement as his noblest activity, and reason as his only absolute."

Lofty principles aside, conflict raged within our house when it came to applying Randist doctrine to the realities of life. It branded altruism as anathema, elevated selfishness to virtue, and shrugged off social responsibility for poverty and suffering. While it denounced the collective, the ideology Dad parroted seemed to border on the fascist, envisioning a super cadre of elite, right-thinking, steely individualists, men who refused to yield to any force on earth except Ayn Rand. She insisted on being hailed as the greatest human being who ever lived and the "supreme arbiter" of all morality. Incredibly, my father was bewitched.

He had come upon Rand's work thanks to an employee who presented him with a copy of *Atlas Shrugged* the Christmas after we moved to New Jersey. With Unisco installed in its own building, Dad began producing metal nameplates for machinery, finally branching out from sales to manufacturing. Now, in his ambition to build an empire, Dad found Ayn Rand cheering for him as "the highest type of human being—the self-made man—the American industrialist."

"The words 'to make money' hold the essence of human morality," she preached, and so he worked most nights past eleven and on Saturdays as well. He reveled in his factory, toying with machinery, tackling engineering problems, enjoying the precision of production, inhaling without regard the toxic chemicals and metal filings that compounded the assaults upon his body already waged by the asbestos he had lived with in the war. With his employees, as with his children, insisting on perfection, Dad proclaimed they didn't have to like him as long as they respected him. Still, in the silent, isolated space where his feelings burned, he held to a mythic vision of oath-pure loyalty and was stunned to find that his training incited treason instead of gratitude. Though several key employees quit, taking with them customer lists and knowledge of his product line, and then mounted competition, he never tried to modify his exacting style of leadership. Instead, each betrayal added to his sense that he stood alone in warfare with the world.

We arrive in life an empty slate, Ayn Rand told him. Nothing is inborn, but anything is achievable. Not just intellectually, but physically as well, Leonard now embarked on a rigid program of self-perfection. In the early 1960s, long before bodybuilding gym rats became ubiquitous, he started working out with heavy weights he set up in the basement. True to form, he exercised with scientific exactitude, didactic mission, and unrelenting discipline. Regardless of how tired he was, near midnight he descended to his lair and through the early morning hours, even in our bedrooms two flights overhead, we could all appreciate his groaning efforts. Forcing out his last repetition of every set of exercises, Dad would drop his massive barbells clanking to the floor. The storm windows rattled in their metal frames. The house shook on its foundation.

"Hit me!" he'd order at the kitchen table, rolling a sleeve or lifting his shirt to expose ready targets of unyielding flesh—bulging biceps or his chiseled abdomen with its well-defined six-pack. He insisted I punch him, a demand that I hated. "Harder, harder!" he urged. "What's happened to you? Don't be a sissy! Can't you put any more force behind it?"

The joke underlying his bellicose posing was that he neither required nor indulged in physical force to defeat his opponents. Yet time and again, he would volunteer to demolish the knave who dared to upset us, be it a boss, a teacher, a friend, or a neighbor. As a matter of fact, we never saw him get into a brawl, but he defiantly relished the concept of it, and from the safety of home he made boastful threats with the zesty enthusiasm of some teenage gang leader.

"Did you *tell* him what I'm like?" he would earnestly ask—flexing his muscles, baring his teeth, his jaw sliding forward—regarding any imagined combatant. "How I could destroy him?" This he would ask with an innocent, hopeful look on his face, wanting nothing more from a wife or a daughter than to be idolized and daily acclaimed her one perfect hero with all of life's answers.

Unhappily, most of Dad's answers came undiluted from Ayn Rand, and he soon began to proselytize on her behalf with everyone he met. Through years to come, I would witness his philosophical interrogations with my stomach tied in knots. He ambushed unsuspecting visitors and held them victim to his grilling, even high school boys who came to pick me up for dates and unguardedly agreed to sit down for a chat. All the more within the family, he pressured us unceasingly to accept her every word as Truth.

Dad hired Mona's son, Ken, a lawyer by education, to work for his company and was quick to convert his nephew into an Objectivist of equal fervor. He was frustrated when his attempts with Mom and me proved less successful. On any weeknight that he made it home for dinner, he took advantage of our time together to lecture on Rand's precepts, igniting hot disputes. Starting around the age of twelve, I'd be drawn into the discourse by the intellectual challenge of it, never quite accepting that a difference of opinion on topics so abstract as the meaning of existence or the nature of morality would signal disrespect and turn the battle fiercely personal.

"Don't argue with him," Mom advised, ever seeking peace. "Just do what I do, pretend that you agree. I sit and nod and let it all go in one ear and out the other, while I think of something else."

On weekends, however, every social outing became a nightmare for her, as Leonard's dogmatism invariably led him to disparage and offend anyone who mistakenly believed that Objectivism might be the starting point of mutually enlightening debate. Publicly, she tried to hold her tongue, yet after they came home, late into the night, I would strain to overhear the quiet, mournful rumble of her voice as she chastised and lamented his intellectual arrogance and his rigid, alienating promotion of Ayn Rand. As she spoke, I knew she was mentally scratching another couple off the list of people willing to make plans for another social evening and another contentious round of Dad's philosophizing. Friends were hurt by his disdain, she warned, hating how he snapped, "You're wrong!" at anyone who disagreed with him.

As a result, if the first decade of my parents' union was lit by the happy glow of extended family, the next was plagued by raw dissention introduced into our home by Rand, whose own personal life was roiled by her widely publicized adulterous affair with her youthful protégé Nathaniel Branden. Still, in the arena of sex and love, as in all else, Rand laid out definitive expectations for her followers. Her heroines were "worshippers" of man—of the sort of *Übermensch* who made them yearn to yield in sexual submission, like maidens in some bodice-ripping period romance. On the other hand, she said that ideal man must have a woman "who reflects his deepest vision of himself," a woman whose surrender allows him to experience his sense of self-esteem: "There is no conflict between the standards of his mind and the desires of his body. . . . Love is our response to our highest values—and can be nothing else."

Where did this leave Janine? Having experienced the results when an all-defining "ism" captures a society, she recoiled from a philosophy with tentacles that wrapped around all aspects of our lives. She couldn't go along with it, nor would she agree to attend Rand's Objectivism lectures with my father until it was too late and he had found another woman to take the seat beside him, sharing private communication on the pads where he took notes. A slim brunette with bitten nails, she was divorced from a magazine photographer and lived alone with two young sons. Len had hired her as his office manager, and she was ruthless in angling for a more important title.

"*BETSY*," she inked her name in his notebook in thick letters during one of Ayn Rand's lectures where they sat together; and then again, coy and delicate, all in lowercase: "betsy ellen chase," a last name that seemed fitting. Amid his notes on "pseudo-self esteem," "psycho-epistemology," and "integrated consciousness," Len listed on his pad a half dozen possible titles for her within his company, ranging from Secretary-Treasurer to "Master of Arms @ Love."

"What's the difference between Vice-Pres & Exec. Vice-Pres?" she jotted back.

"You are a good looking dish tonite," he scrawled to her in his notebook during another lecture, then scribbled over his words to hide them, like a teenager flirting with a classmate behind the teacher's back in algebra.

In a lecture on sexuality, he took copious notes on neurotic "indiscriminate promiscuity" in the pursuit of self-esteem. "Mr. Promiscuous" was the Randist label for the man who is "unable to achieve sustained sexual happiness" with a woman who reflects his own highest values, but is ever on the prowl for new and varied conquests. "'I need constant approval, constant re-assurance,'" he placed the thought in quotation marks, as if that made the man at issue someone else. But he filled the back of the page, a little sheet of graph paper, with an emphatic warning to himself:

"ALWAYS KNOW WHAT YOU ARE DOING!!!!"

. . .

Moving to New Jersey was like settling in a foreign country in ways that I had not imagined. Now, in my small public elementary school, the war and persecution that had brought my mother to America seemed utterly removed from my classmates' experience and curiosity, as did the Inwood neighborhood, which I missed terribly. I felt alone, and walking home from the bus stop every day, I kept my fingers crossed and whispered little prayers that my mother's car would be standing in the driveway when I reached our corner, my sign that she was there for me.

To alleviate my desolation over leaving my cousin, my mother had bought a trundle bed for my beautiful dusk-blue French Provincial room so that Lynne could visit us on weekends. It hardly seemed possible to own my new suburban life unless I could share it with my lifelong friend, and it caused me sorrow beyond telling to watch our closeness evaporate. Weekend after weekend, I begged her to stay over, but even when I managed to persuade her to accept, she unfailingly canceled by Friday afternoon, preferring to stay at home. After fluttering with excitement throughout the week in anticipation of her visit, I felt crushed each time that in spite of the fun I'd promised her, Lynne would not be coming after all!

"Cripes, get over it!" Dad would chide me, sitting at the kitchen table eating roasted peanuts from the lid of a Planters jar and sipping the one extra-dry Beefeater martini he allowed himself each night. "It's *your* fault for still expecting her!"

By now, Trudi had a baby boy, Michael, and their family left Inwood, too, moving north to Riverdale, where they overlooked the Hudson River from the Bronx. But since this meant I no longer saw my cousin even when I visited my grandparents, our separation and my sense of loss only grew more painful.

In the isolation of our house, so different from our family-filled apartment building and the cozy hubbub of the nearby benches, I found my mother. Suddenly deprived of my constant companionship with Lynne, I needed her. My mother, too, separated for the first time from her parents and her siblings, with my father unavailable, turned to me. We soon developed an extraordinary friendship. There was nothing we couldn't tell each other, and the bond of trust we shared was one that we maintained even as we gradually made friends of our own ages. Now as then, I cherish our closeness as among my most important gifts in life.

When did I learn about Roland? Actually, like my brother, Gary, I cannot remember ever *not* knowing about the Great Romance our mother was forced to leave behind in Europe, though I am often told it is unusual for a mother to be so open with her children. Still, it was only after I turned thirteen that she permitted the story of her first true love to carry overtones of irremediable remorse. Until she felt betrayed, she may have described her marriage to my father as a different type of life from the one she would have lived had war not intervened, but never as the wrong one. Then suddenly, things changed.

As I approached my thirteenth birthday, I hoped to mark it by becoming a bat mitzvah. But my atheistic father opposed it, and my grandfather Sigmar became his unexpected ally because his traditional

Jewish views did not include extending the religious rite of passage to females. So as a secular compensation for the religious ceremony I had wanted, Dad proposed celebrating my "coming of age" by taking me to the Metropolitan Opera to introduce me to the music he loved. For me, of course, it was not the same, though I was touched and delighted he had thought of sharing opera with me.

Dad groused about the opera schedule: my first exposure to the art form should be something colorful or romantic with opulent costumes and scenery like *Aida* or *La Traviata*. Instead, the performance for which Mom was able to get tickets would be heavy and austere— Richard Strauss's *Elektra*, based on the tragedy by Sophocles and legends of the Trojan War, presented in one perturbing act and sung in German. I nonetheless looked forward to this rare outing alone with both my parents, Dad generally so elusive in my daily life. And having developed an avid interest in Greek mythology, I myself was pleased by the selection. Indeed, as things evolved, the gods themselves could not have chosen more aptly, given this opera's archetypal themes.

Elektra is the story of a daughter and a son caught up in the passions of their parents' adulterous relationships and grievances, a tale of suffering and guilt, of vengeance and murder and filial responsibility. As a memorable rite of passage into the adult world with all its stern realities, it taught me that secrets and infidelity can destroy a family from within. The fateful story of Elektra and her devotion to her father suggested that it was natural for children, with their sharp sense of justice and loyalty born out of love, to take sides and seek retaliation for a wounded parent. Its message soon proved timeless.

On the afternoon of my birthday celebration, my father called home profusely apologetic to tell us we would have to go without him because some foul-up with an order and a delivery deadline required him to work all night. The outing felt ruined. At the end of the performance, sitting beside an empty seat, my sadness was only deepened to see Elektra fall lifeless to the ground, a crazed victim of her own emotions and thirst for blood, doomed with both her parents. But when the lights came up, Mom gamely tried to resuscitate a festive note.

"Let's call Daddy at work and see if he can take a break to join us for a late dessert," she offered, as we drifted arm in arm into the neon night and the glittering buzz of Broadway. Our original plan had been to go to Sardi's, my favorite treat and the best place for spotting actors enjoying after-theater suppers, but I readily agreed to try to lure Dad from his work to someplace closer to his office. As Mom encased herself in a glass-walled phone booth on the sidewalk, I stood admiring the glamorous crowd of opera patrons swirling out into the city. When next I glanced at Mom, however, I was stunned to see her weeping. Tears were running down her cheeks, an unfamiliar sight, as she fumbled to retrieve her coins and dropped them in the slot to make another call. It seemed she got no answer, but when I tried to open the phone booth's folding door and ask her what was wrong, she mutely pulled it shut and shook her head, dabbing at her eyes with an embroidered handkerchief. With the third call, someone answered—I could hear her speaking German, the habit in the family, so frustrating to us children, when grown-ups needed code—and I could tell that she was talking to her brother, Norbert.

Drenched with fear, I had no way to guess why she sat there crying. The familial tragedy that had swept across the stage with costumed figures drawn from legend had devolved into this real-world drama, also in German, with my mother sobbing in a cage of glass on a busy city street. Was Daddy sick? Had there been an accident? I had yet to understand how her position in that phone booth, exposed in pain to any passerby, would later seem an emblem of her public humiliation in the face of Dad's duplicity.

With little conversation we were soon driving along the Hudson River and across the bridge, and then we veered off course as Mom headed for my father's office in Ridgefield. But the one-story stucco factory proved dark, and the parking lot was empty. She left me in the car as she went to try the doors and peered into his office window, but everything was locked.

"I bet Daddy finished earlier than he expected and just went home!" I said when she returned, the explanation seeming obvious. "Why are you so worried?"

"I already tried there," she responded flatly, eyes fixed upon the factory door.

In fact, when we reached our house Daddy wasn't there, nor would he appear for several hours. If my mother had been deceived, I felt, then so had I. If she had been rejected, then so had I, on what was meant to be my very special night.

That summer Gary and I went off to camp, and in her lifelong quest for stability, afraid of ultimatums, Mom tried to close her eyes to the problem with her husband that was only growing worse. She had her dark hair fashionably cut and streaked with blond, but since her efforts to save her marriage stopped short of embracing Objectivism, Dad seemed to feel entitled to pursue a woman who shared his ideology. Miss Chase apparently endorsed the life of "rational self-interest" that Rand insisted was essential, and soon Dad was wooing her transparently, heedless of our feelings.

He decided, for example, to give my brother's bicycle to Miss Chase's son. Despite Gary's protestations, Dad told him he'd outgrown it and insisted on buying him a bigger one. Then he announced that he was giving Mom's station wagon to Miss Chase, and he told Mom that she could buy any other car she wanted. Who could have imagined our sensible, cost-conscious mother pulling up in a new sleek, silver Thunderbird convertible sports car? It had black leather bucket seats and a black cloth roof that retracted automatically, vanishing into the trunk at the push of a button more smoothly than Dad had slipped away on the night of my birthday. The price tag was punishing.

But on the day that autumn when my mother found Grace, the housekeeper, passed out on the floor of the living room and frantically called my father's office for help in what appeared a medical emergency, Betsy Chase crossed all bounds.

"I'll send you Ken to deal with it," Miss Chase answered curtly. "Len is busy." When she hung up on my mother without so much as putting my father on the line, it was my cousin Ken—devoted to Janine and no fan of Miss Chase's—who finally set my mother straight.

A few days later, Mom told us that Daddy would be moving out at her request. My father asked to speak with me, but I refused to see him and hid in misery in my room. Uncle Norbert brought a truck to the house to help my father move his things to the garden apartment in nearby Leonia where he was going to live with Miss Chase and her children. Mom had loaded up big cartons with pots and pans and sheets and towels, magnanimously setting aside an assortment of furniture for him to take along as well. In his pile were his riding boots, his tennis racquet, and his ice skates—items he so seldom used that the fact that he was taking them fortified our impression that the breakup would be permanent. I pictured Daddy racing on the ice between Miss Chase's sons and was sure they skated with more confidence than I did.

With Dad and Norbert loading the truck, Mom decided to distract us by taking us to the movies, where she retreated to a phone booth to talk with Trudi. By the time we headed home, I had convinced myself we'd find him, as usual, sitting in the kitchen nursing a martini and waiting for Mom to cook him dinner. But no, like his office on the night of my birthday seven months earlier, the house was still and dark. It felt altered and vulnerable. Before, the dynamic energy of my father's outsized personality and the crackling, pulsing life force of his restless spirit pervaded the atmosphere like the hum in the heating ducts. Now the silence of his absence was deafening.

. . .

My father's place in the bed he shared with Mom was never empty in the time that he was gone. That's where I was sleeping. Whether by her invitation or by my own initiative, we spent every night together, holding hands. Although strong and over five foot seven, my mother seemed instantly diminished and, more than anything, I wanted to protect her—an overwhelming job assignment for a thirteen-year-old girl, herself suffering with feelings of abandonment. I also carried a secret sense of guilt. I agonized that the nighttime fears that had prompted me so often to invade the private space behind my parents' bedroom door had fueled my father's hunger to find another woman, a woman who wouldn't tolerate children's interruptions. What clearer proof could anyone require that I had come between my parents than the fact that *I* was sleeping now in my father's place? Desperate to restore my mother's happiness, I wanted to become like the hero in a fairy tale who slays the evil dragon and escorts the damsel in distress to a magic golden castle where all conflicts are resolved.

In the quiet of late nights in her bedroom, her muffled tears and anguished sighs inspired me to coax my mother to talk about the past. Our magic golden castle was the world of Europe twenty years before, in which she had been loved by another, faithful man. Against the ticking of the pendulum and the half-hourly chimes of the antique French clock in the hallway, I traveled with my mother to her Freiburg girlhood, and I understood her pain at leaving home and lifelong friends when her family fled to France. She took me back to Mulhouse of 1939, frightened near the border on the eve of war, and she permitted me to know Roland, a slender, doe-eyed youth of exquisite sensitivity. Night by night, talking more than sleeping, we delved into her stories as we lay together in the darkness. The unraveling of history was far, far better than any *Million Dollar Movie*, and I relished all my mother's stories, knowing they were real.

I saw my mother as a teen barely older than myself when she caught Roland's attention. I saw them at the party where a game of spin the bottle first emboldened them to kiss, and then along the banks of a green and curling river where they nestled in the reeds and let their fingers wander. Mom hunted through the pages of her memory and invited me to share the romance of her past. Perhaps it was her way of getting even with my father: as Daddy coupled with Miss Chase in a strange apartment, my mother brought Roland to life to spend the nights with us. She nullified the hurt of my father's infidelity by evoking a greater love and a greater loss, turning Daddy into second best, a reluctant compromise. I lay there in confusion, simultaneously feeling angry with my father and disturbingly untrue to him. I deplored his cheating, even as we cheated with the memory of Roland. I wanted my mother's story to have a happy ending: I longed to hear the episode that saw her reunited with Roland, even though that ending might have meant my not existing.

When my closest friends inquired what had happened to my father, the reason for his leaving us, I wanted to protect my mother from any intimation that Dad had found another woman more worthy of his love. So I used Mom's romance with Roland to turn everything around. There was another man, I said. The Nazis robbed my mother of the true love of her life. It hardly seemed to matter that my father had moved out, I said, because my mother's broken heart still belonged in France. She had never gotten over him—Roland, who had loved her absolutely and whom she would have married had war not intervened. In its terrors and its tumult, they had lost each other, but Mom would always be in love with him: enduring, hopeless jealously had made my father leave.

There were other aspects of the story that, being just thirteen, I felt I couldn't tell a soul. Under cover of darkness, my mother had confided that she'd run to meet Roland on her final night in France and wound up hiding on a rooftop in the harbor of Marseille. Who knows where passion might have led them, she admitted, in those terrible brief hours before their separation, if only Nazi agents hadn't raided their hotel? I lay rigid in my parents' bed, amazed at the audacious girl who would become my mother. The dutiful woman who planted geraniums around our patio and fixed cream cheese sandwiches for my lunch box and picked me up from piano lessons had, once upon a time, trembled with her lover in the moonlight glinting off the waves that would carry her to Casablanca.

"But why didn't you stay with Roland and let your family go without you?" I pleaded, wanting to believe that love could conquer all. It was tempting for us both to mourn the losses of the past when the future loomed in jeopardy.

"You know it wasn't safe for Jews in France with Nazis taking over. If it had been up to me, the way I was insane for him, I would have spent my life hiding in an attic with him, but Roland was worried we'd get caught."

"Then how come he didn't go with you?"

"He couldn't get the papers that he needed."

"And after the war, why didn't you go back and marry him?" I needed to know everything, and that remained the crucial mystery.

"I was afraid to leave my parents here without me. But I also thought Roland had given up on me. Bapa hid his telegram and maybe letters, too, for all I know. By the time that I found out Roland was looking for me, I was married to Daddy. I was already expecting you. I couldn't just run off to France and steal you from your father." Beneath the covers, Mommy squeezed my hand. I said nothing for some minutes for fear that I would cry. But I had another question.

"Why don't you go and find him *now?* Now that Daddy's gone away. . . ." I held my breath, fearful of her answer. Trying to be generous, I waited for my world to fall apart, the fate Ayn Rand reserved for altruists. In the silence, the brass pendulum in the hallway vacillated back and forth.

"It's too late now. I'm sure Roland is married. He never had any problem attracting girls." The recollected pain in her voice was washed in sepia. "But more than that, I could never leave you."

By day, I sat on the carpet in my mother's bedroom beside a little walnut two-drawer French chest in which she kept her trinkets, and we examined everything, never growing tired of the comfort of nostalgia. An enameled brooch, a memento of cousin Mimi, was an eighteenth-century maiden dressed in petticoats, watering her flowers. There were class ribbons Mom had worn to school pinned onto a red beret, but she'd never stayed in any one school long enough, she said regretfully, to collect sufficient ribbons to feel that she belonged. I admired her Cuban swimming medal for prowess in the breaststroke. Yet her most important treasures were the tricolor poppy pin and the silver ring with its square blue stone that Roland had bought for her in Lyon as tokens of their engagement. She took off her wide gold wedding band and tried to slide Roland's ring onto her finger, but it only fit her pinky.

"I guess I was much thinner then," she mused. "In the war, nobody had any food. We were always hungry."

"Couldn't a jeweler make it bigger?" I suggested. Mom made no comment but kept it on her little finger. (My father, I knew, had never worn his wedding band, objecting that it "cut off circulation.")

When we finished with the chest, we moved on to her armoire. It was there she found the small black-and-white snapshot of Roland taken by a stranger from the deck of the *Lipari*. He was standing in the rowboat he had rented to follow her steamship out into the harbor, exactly as she'd told me.

"He was very thin then, too," she commented. "See how that coat is hanging on him. But I loved how lean he was. I don't know why Daddy always feels he needs to build big muscles. . . ." Together we studied the old photograph for several minutes before she reached for her purse and tucked the snapshot of Roland behind the others she carried in her wallet—photos of me and Gary and my favorite picture of my father, grinning like a movie star, with the dimple in his chin and jet-black hair.

"I'm sure that Roland's letter must be here, too," Mom said, rummaging through her shelves until she found the envelope. It was the letter Roland had slipped into her coat as they stood together on the pier and he held her in a last embrace in 1942. My French was not yet good enough to translate all that he had written, but Mom put it into English as she read aloud. I supposed that she had memorized it:

"Whatever the length of our separation, our love will survive it. . . . Believe in the fulfillment of our happiness, believe in it with all your strength, all your will, all your love, and our test will end as we desire. . . . I give you my word that we will be married. . . . If I had to lose you, nothing good would come of my life. You are my goal."

. . .

Within a week of Daddy's moving out, he showed up for Sunday breakfast carrying a bag of bagels. I remember retreating very quickly, while Gary and Mommy chatted at the table with him. Listening from the upstairs landing, I heard my father say he was working so late every night that he had trouble getting up on time, which prompted Gary, then nine years old, to volunteer to phone him every morning to wake him up.

"Really, Dad, I'd like to do it," Gary chirped, the innate generosity of his character coming to the fore.

"Hey! That's grand! That would be a super favor," Dad answered in his most ingratiating salesman's tone. I would have liked to pour chocolate milk all over Gary's head and watch it puddle on the wax he slicked onto his crew cut. My brother was pawing through Mommy's kitchen junk drawer for a paper and a pencil to write down Daddy's number, and I was wondering how he would like it when Miss Chase answered the telephone and asked what he was doing, disturbing them at home.

The following Sunday morning, Daddy came to visit us again; then, on a weeknight, he took Mommy out to dinner. To my surprise, she had gotten all dressed up, and her hair and nails were freshly done, but she told me that their meeting didn't mean a thing. Of course there were details in any separation for a couple to iron out. But, oh, no! No, he wasn't moving back, she swore, definitely not! By the end of that next week, however, my father told my mother he wanted to come home. He loved her and needed her and appreciated her even more than he ever had before.

Aside from that, Betsy Chase had revealed herself to be as careless with his money as his first wife, Claire. She had outfitted their apartment down to the smallest knickknack, even buying beach chairs in the middle of December! The farsightedness of her shopping sprees seemed to horrify him. What's worse, he grumbled to my mother, when he scolded her about it, she went wild and started throwing things! Now he needed to come home. He loved us all and missed us terribly. He had already fired Miss Chase from the company, and he swore he'd never see her—not her, not anyone who ever swished a skirt or winked an eye in his direction. From now on, Dad promised, he would be an angel. After all, my mother was the woman who matched his highest standards and reflected his deepest vision of himself.

My father's coming home displaced me from my mother's bed and sent me back into my room, where I struggled to come to terms with warring feelings. I seemed to love him and to hate him, to rejoice at his return and to wish that I could hide from him. The aloofness I'd displayed in their weeks of separation, when I'd stood in loyalty to Mom, now meant I stood alone, the odd one out.

I failed to understand how my mother took Dad back so quickly after all the pain he caused her, and I felt burdened by excessive knowledge—about both Miss Chase and Roland. Miss Chase had disappeared, and I was glad, but what to do about the tantalizing Frenchman whose fate remained a mystery? He languished in my fantasies, calling for attention, and I had to peek to check whether he had kept his place inside my mother's wallet. I wondered what it meant to find him there, even after Daddy had returned.

"Try to pull another stunt like you did with Betsy Chase, and *I'll* go and find Roland," Mom threatened, only half in jest.

"You'd just be disappointed," Dad retorted. "I'm sure you'd learn that I'm the better man. I'll bet you he's a weakling."

TWENTY-TWO

ATLAS

ON SUNDAY, JUNE 27, 1965, my father overcame his slice and hit a drive that sent his golf ball flying like a well-aimed arrow, 195 yards to the seventh green at the Englewood Golf Club, where it struck the pin and plunked politely in the cup, giving him a hole in one. News of the achievement sped around the clubhouse. Someone even thought to call our home to tell my mother to come down, and by the time that Dad strode in—as proud as if he'd landed a rocket on the moon—the Grill Room was abuzz with fellow golfers prepared to help him celebrate. Earlier in the season, ever an optimist, Dad had paid the few dollars it required for "hole in one insurance," which would now kick in, covering his tab for drinks for any fellow member who showed up to toast his feat.

In his striped golf slacks and bright red shirt, Dad was ebullient and handsome and especially delighted that his hole in one had topped my mother's on a different hole only two weeks earlier. From the moment she had scored one with my father looking on, he was hell-bent to catch up, and the fact that his drive was fifty-five yards longer only added to his satisfaction. As he explained it, his powerful and well-directed shot straight to the pin reflected skill, whereas she had merely aced a hole through an uncanny touch of luck.

"Mine was just an intelligent roller," Mom readily agreed, uncomfortable at having made a hole in one before her husband. She demonstrated by example the advice she often gave to me—that it was psychologically unwise to outdo a man in any contest, because the sensitive male ego simply couldn't handle it. But the caption underneath my parents' picture, prominently published the following day in the Bergen County *Record*, summed things up in one snide word: "COPYCAT." The photo showed my parents crouching on a green with two golf balls beside a hole, and the club chairman squatting between them with a hand on each one's back. Mom and Dad are smiling at each other with impeccable eye contact and their profiles to the camera. Thereafter my mother took one look at their picture in the paper and pronounced her husband's toothy smile disingenuous.

"That's his phony smile," she said. "He doesn't fool me for a second. I know he isn't happy sharing the limelight."

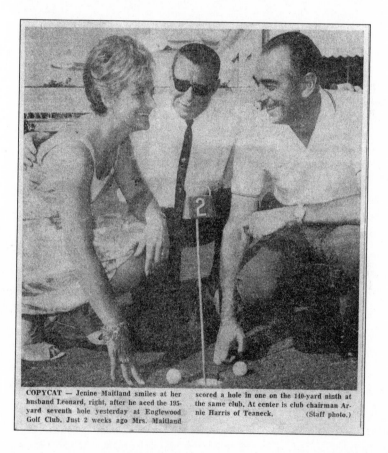

COPYCAT — Jenine Maitland smiles at her husband Leonard, right, after he aced the 195-yard seventh hole yesterday at Englewood Golf Club. Just 2 weeks ago Mrs. Maitland scored a hole in one on the 140-yard ninth at the same club. At center is club chairman Arnie Harris of Teaneck.   (Staff photo.)

But he *was* happy with his feat, and that period was a good one for their marriage. Joining the golf club brought new friends and distracted Dad a little from his ferocious Objectivism. The nature of the club itself, moreover, brought a Las Vegas sort of titillation to their everyday suburban lives. Located just across the river from Manhattan, it was a hangout for

(L to R) Leslie, Len, Janine, and Gary in 1970

celebrities and entertainers who added glitz and glamour, and for well-connected mobsters who brought intrigue and a whiff of danger. Anecdotes about them never failed to make the rounds, and the occasional encounter with a famous or edgy character was fodder for the tables at formal dinner dances requiring closets full of silken evening clothes.

With other couples from the club, Mom and Dad now embarked on their first European trip together. They toured the Continent in a whirlwind, staying in the finest places, but Mom also planned a detour to reconnect with relatives. Most important, she and Dad peeled off from the group to stop for lunch in Mulhouse with Edy and Lisette, the first time Mom had seen them since the war. The visit proved awkward, as Mom's cousin and his wife, listing toward divorce, refused to speak to one another and used their children as intermediaries, even as the family sat together at the dining table. But at a moment when the irrepressible Lisette had my father's ear, Mom seized the opportunity to draw Edy aside and ask whether there was anything he could tell her about Roland. She didn't have the luxury to meander subtly to her point. What did Edy know about him? Had he stayed in Lyon when the war was over, or was he back in Mulhouse? Had he ever married? Did Edy know if he had children? Had he gone on to practice law? Perhaps the two had met in Alsatian legal circles?

Edy scowled and cut her short. "*Laisse tomber! N'y pense plus!*" Edy said. Drop it! Forget about him. "The only thing I can tell you is that Roland Arcieri was ruined by women...."

Janine asked him no more questions. She knew enough about Roland's appeal for women to understand the message. Being married to Roland, she told herself, might well have proved even more tormenting than her relationship with Len. She would have to try to put aside the fantasies she'd nourished, in the event her husband went wandering again, of seeking out the lover whose memory she had conjured to help her through the awful year of Len's affair. When they returned home, Mom sadly confided Edy's words to me. Her dream of someday reuniting with Roland, she said, was one that she had finally buried in Mulhouse, exactly where it started.

· · ·

On a gray November morning in my senior year in high school, Dad wrote out a range of symptoms on a piece of paper—breathlessness, perspiration, weak pulse, hazy vision—and drove himself into the city to see Charles Friedberg, my mother's former boss and the chief of cardiology at Mount Sinai Hospital. We learned the news from Dad's secretary when Mom tried to call him from Newark Airport, as we were about to take off on a tour of colleges that we instantly aborted. Instead, we rushed to the doctor's office and arrived there just in time to hear the verdict: "Shit, man! You've had a heart attack!" Dr. Friedberg exclaimed, studying the electrocardiogram. "I can't believe you lifted weights this morning! And then you went to work and drove here on your own?"

Dad was only forty-eight; Mom was forty-three, and in that awful moment when we first saw Dad as vulnerable, our lives were changed forever. The very picture of virile health and strength, an athlete and a bodybuilder, a man who never ate or drank to excess, Dad had had a heart attack! We were stunned and terrified by what it would mean for him.

"For Chrissake," Dad objected, "I maintain my body like a goddamn temple. There's not a frigging man I know in better shape than I am, but none of them have had a heart attack! Even my own father, who never leaves his sewing table, totally ignores his health, he's already eighty-six and his heart's ticking just fine. It's not fair, damn it!"

Yet Dr. Friedberg said that youthful years of downing quarts of milk at every meal (as Dad had boasted) and eating meat and fats (not to mention his mother's apple strudel) had done the damage. Cigarettes, excessive stress at work, and a tense, hard-driving, type A personality had all contributed. He ordered Dad home to bed until Mount Sinai called to say a room had opened up for him. He should expect to stay there several weeks in a serious attempt to do absolutely nothing but rest and recuperate and try to calm himself. And until further notice, no more driving, either.

We headed home in silence, the first time I had ever seen my mother in the driver's seat with Dad reduced to riding as a passenger. So my father's personality was type A! I had never heard the term before, but felt relieved to learn they had a name for it. Mom was gripping the steering wheel of Dad's long Cadillac as she headed northward to our exit, driving with scrupulous attention to avoid any sort of error that would invite his criticism. But Dad was lost in inner space. He sat there like a toppled general, bound in shackles and cursing careless strategies that had failed him in his last campaign. All at once, the world appeared immeasurably more dangerous. Dad was our protector: he had sworn he was invincible, and on some level we believed him. I felt weak and hollow, and the future seemed a precipice that dropped off every bit as steeply as the cliffs of the Hudson River Palisades, whose craggy edge we traced along the parkway home.

By the time that Dad was ensconced in the hospital, however, Mom had plotted out a different life for him. As usual, she was wise enough not to broach her goal directly, but rather, as she put it, to slip it through "the back door," where he could meet it on his own terms. At the time, he was sitting in his hospital bed, squeezing and releasing a coiled metal gripper, designed to work the muscles of the hand and forearm, which he had prevailed on her to smuggle in to him from home.

"Wouldn't it be crazy if Picasso gave up painting to become a dancer?" she casually put the question to him, forgetting for a moment that Objectivists had scant appreciation for any artist who distorted the noble human form.

"Maybe that would do the world a favor," Dad snapped. "You know Picasso's not my bag. What the hell's your point?"

"Well, then, make it Michelangelo," she persisted. "My question is the same." She was crocheting in a chair beside his bed, where she spent the whole of every day from early morning until midnight and then drove home alone, taking care of Dad much as she had nursed Roland twenty-five years before. "It's tragic if a person doesn't use the talents he's born with. You're a natural salesman, but instead of doing what you're really good at, you've been killing yourself in the factory, and this heart attack is your reward."

The demands of manufacturing created too much stress for a perfectionist like Len, she thought, while breathing metal dust and poison fumes all day were hazardous as well. She therefore wanted him to sell the factory, and inevitably she persuaded him. Whenever it came to the big decisions in their lives together, Dad trusted her advice completely. He would give up the factory that was his source of pride and, with it, the sacrifices it required and the self-destructive cycle of problems with his workers. But a great deal more reluctantly, he would have to abandon his vision of himself as one of Ayn Rand's heroes, those defiantly indomitable captains of industry responsible for running the machinery of the world. Mom's worries for his health, of body and of spirit, required him for the first time to acknowledge his vulnerable humanity. She led him by the hand to a path that saved his life, but it meant he had to walk again in a salesman's pinching shoes.

Within months of his return to work, Dad sold the factory and moved with his secretary into a two-room office suite in a building just six blocks from home. Once again he became the middleman between the thrumming factory fiefdoms owned and operated by other men of business, more lucky or successful—men whose hearts could take it. Instead of making products, he made sales. He worked the phone and traveled through his region, and year after year won the highest sales awards for the companies he represented, brightly flashing his "phony smile" in pictures of the winners.

. . .

Three years later, when Dad gradually became aware of numbness in his fingers, affecting his dexterity and making it difficult for him to button shirts or pick up coins or turn a screw, he seized upon a German word to describe his problem. He had lost *Fingerspitzengefühl*, or "feeling in the fingertips," he said, finding it less frightening to admit this new infirmity in a foreign language. Besides, how could any weakness that sounded so ridiculous actually be worrisome?

Doctors could not identify the cause and advised him to make the best of it. He fashioned small devices that helped him compensate— a hook that pulled his buttons through their holes, for instance. But before long, his racquet met the tennis ball less reliably than usual, and then even longtime partners like Trudi's husband, Harry, avoided playing with him, proffering excuses that were hurtfully transparent. On the golf course, when he lost his grip and his driver started flying from his hands as his golf ball left the tee, it was so humiliating that he decided to stop playing, and my parents quit the club. Membership, Mom said, was not worth the cost for her alone, and anyway, it seemed cruel for her to play when he no longer could.

Instead, on summer weekends, though Gary usually begged off, my parents and I headed for the beach for the best times we ever spent together. Occasionally, we'd enjoy long weekends along the coast in Montauk, but often we made day trips to closer-in Long Island. At the beach, in his daring Speedo bathing suit, my father could pretend that nothing much was wrong. Once we were installed upon the sand, disinclined to waste a potentially productive moment, Dad would stage a public show of calisthenics before tackling a crossword puzzle. We'd pass the hours in harmony and always stay until the crowds packed up and the sea regained its dignity. Then, with his white pith helmet clapped upon his head, sitting in a chair like a bwana on safari, Dad would pop the cork on the bottle of white wine he'd chilled all day waiting for our sunset moment. Mom would feed the squealing birds the scraps we'd saved from lunch—always on the lookout for stragglers too timid or hapless to claim their lot—or she'd sit and rake the sand with long red nails to hunt for shells worth taking home.

Sometimes my parents allowed themselves to be lured into the ocean for one late swim. I'd watch them walking toward the water, Mom tucking golden curls into her bathing cap, and Dad with his long-legged, rolling shipboard gait, increasingly unstable, as if the sea were swelling underneath his feet. Hand in hand they'd plunge into the steel-gray waves. The lifeguards would have left by then, and I'd train my eyes to watch for them as they rose and fell beneath the churning Atlantic waters, heading ever farther out. Frantic and exasperated, I'd squint into the distance as I stood at water's edge, waving my arms and stamping my feet and shouting uselessly into the wind to urge my parents back to shore.

They'd laugh at me when they returned, Mom emptying her ineffective bathing cap, Dad slicking back his hair and shaking water off his body like a giant dog. I never left the beach without doing all I could to linger, wishing I might stop the sun and hold the day forever. Even as we trekked across the sand to the empty parking lot, even as the tide rushed in to reclaim that patch of beach where we had left our marks, I would turn and stare behind me, yearning to imprint the hours and store the blue-gold panorama in the treasure house of memory before the darkness drowned it.

As time went by and Dad's mysterious infirmity did not improve, I wondered whether that might be the reason for his mellowing, particularly when having finished college at the University of Chicago, I announced my hope to postpone a journalism career to study world religions at the Harvard Divinity School. In view of Dad's hostility toward religion, I had expected him to object, but he accepted my decision and even moved me up to Cambridge. He rented a truck and astonished us by donning a sleeveless undershirt as an impromptu trucker's costume. From the driver's seat, Dad honked and waved in collegial greeting to every other trucker we passed along the highway, as he proclaimed his lifelong membership in that fraternity of working men who made their living on the road.

When we arrived at dusk at my apartment building on Prescott Street behind the Fogg Museum, a snafu with the keys barred our entry until morning. But unwilling to leave the truck overnight with all my worldly goods inside it, Dad talked the janitor into lending him a ladder. Then, undeterred by his physical instability, he insisted on climbing up and entering my studio apartment by jimmying the courtyard window in the dark. He worked all weekend to make the small apartment cozy for me—a gift of time and effort he unstintingly devoted every time I moved for the next eleven years until his handicap prevented him from working with his hands and tools. He hung curtains and light fixtures and pictures and towel bars and extra locks on doors and windows and every other amenity or safety feature he could possibly imagine.

That winter, a detached retina sent to him into surgery. He called me from the hospital early on a Sunday morning—the first time I could remember his calling me himself, instead of simply picking up the phone for a minute when I was on with Mom.

"I've been lying here thinking, and it occurred to me that maybe the reason that you're up there studying religion is that you're looking to discover something—the meaning of life, or however you want to put it," Dad began in a tone that also sounded unfamiliar for being hesitant and, to use his favorite word, *respectful.* "If that's the case, I don't know if this helps at all, but going into surgery sort of clarified my mind, and I'd like to share my thoughts with you.

"Be happy!" he said, the engineer's answer as true in his mind as a quadratic equation. "In the end, that's the thing that really matters. Just be happy, dollface. Make the most of life in any way that counts for you. Of all the concepts that we've argued over, you and I, that's the only one I really want to leave with you."

. . .

The first time I saw Carole Gordon she was dancing in a knee-length sleeveless dress, aglow in red chiffon, on the patio behind my parents' house on the day in 1975 that I got married. I was dancing with my father—resplendent in a white suit and light blue shirt that matched his eyes—when she came wriggling beside us and started flirting with him. The deeply tanned and dark-haired wife of a convivial businessman, Carole was a casual friend of Mom's friend Jean, who introduced her to my parents. I remember taking stock of provocatively sculptured calves, a muscled chest, and iron arms, a body that gave evidence to what I'd already heard described as her dedication to tennis. Less impressively, she spoke an exaggerated Brooklynese or a similar Long Island variant that I quickly learned to mimic.

Indeed, I aped her manner and her speech with such dead-on, gum-snapping effectiveness that even Dad was forced to laugh, despite the fact he liked her, and despite the fact he knew my crude impersonation was meant to serve as a signal that I knew what she was up to. He showed restraint by responding in good humor to my less-than-subtle tactics. Yet it didn't take me long to see that Carole Gordon was the effervescent embodiment of the very sort of female my father claimed that men liked best, as bouncy and as fuzzy as a yellow tennis ball. Nor could I fail to recognize that I had trapped myself within a hopeless contradiction: I felt that I could stand it better if my father had been dazzled by a woman I admired, while at the same time I felt relieved not to have to take her seriously, by all accounts a bimbo who could never hope to steal my mother's place with Dad. Meanwhile, Carole connived around me and tried to be my mother's friend. Yes, beneath the guise of friendship, she invited my parents to a lively stream of parties at her well-appointed Scarsdale home and insisted that my father follow—to quote Mom, "like a dachshund at her side"—ostensibly to help her. Certainly, that was a task for which his previous domestic duties did nothing to prepare him, as my mother never gave him any that did not involve a toolbox.

My own marriage, hastened by my parents, ended by amicable agreement within two years. My husband, a television news producer, and I quickly proved unready for permanent commitment. But I was happily living and working in New York, having landed my first job at *The New York Times*, the fulfillment of my lifelong dream, the September after I received my master's in religion. I still don't know whether to credit my new economic independence, the imprimatur of *The Times*, my Harvard graduate degree, or a change in Dad or me for recalibrating our relationship on a more even-handed basis. He kept clippings of my news stories in his breast pocket to show off to friends and customers with the same delight and pride that other men reserved for photos of grandchildren. And when a front-page investigative series I had written on defective subway cars and corruption in New York City's Transit Authority won several journalism prizes, Dad escorted me to a formal awards dinner at the Waldorf-Astoria. It seemed fitting, as it was he who'd helped me understand the engineering of their undercarriages and the significance of stress cracks.

Still, as the women's movement stirred awareness in the country, I found myself reacting with discomfort to the royal treatment Mom bestowed on him, following the example of her parents. While it never disturbed me as a child to see Nana doting slavishly to meet Bapa's every need, Dad's self-centered demands began to seem abusive, since he took it as his due for Mom to wait upon him, even as he often paid her back with inconsiderate behavior.

"Janine!" he called to her upstairs, for example, one weekend when I was visiting and sat beside him at the breakfast table reading morning newspapers.

"Mom's getting dressed," I said. "Is there something I can get for you?"

"No, I need your mother." He raised his voice to carry farther: "Janine!"

"What is it, Dad? I'm sure that I can handle it."

"Janine!" he called again, ignoring me.

Mom came rushing to the kitchen barefoot, clutching at her robe. "What's wrong?" she asked, studying our faces for signs of brewing friction. "I was getting in the shower."

"I'm ready for my coffee now," he told her. I gaped, but he didn't bat an eyelash when he muttered an explanation: "Your mother knows the way I like it."

"Butt out," he'd say when I objected to his treatment of her. "I don't need *you* to tell me how to run my marriage." .

. . .

In February 1976 my parents were in Acapulco on vacation, when Trudi called them with the dreaded news that Norbert was in the hospital, not expected to survive for long, his two-year battle with lung cancer coming to its end. They were on the airplane rushing home when Dad spiked a fever, shivering uncontrollably, and by the time they landed, he could barely walk or move his hands in any co-ordinated effort. With double vision and his usual anchorman's elo-cution replaced by garbled speech, he was admitted to the same New Jersey hospital where Norbert's life was ebbing. There, a nightmare became reality. The elevators ferried us between the rooms of men we loved, in anguished navigation from helpless grief at one bed to nameless fear that hovered at the other, as doctors could not identify the etiology of Dad's symptoms.

The next day, Mom and I were standing at Norbert's bedside when—dressed, handsome, and as freshly shaved and scented as if ready for a date—he died at only fifty-four. Hours later, Mom ar-ranged for an ambulance to transfer Dad to Mount Sinai, the be-ginning of a dismal quest to analyze his illness, a crippling problem temporarily assigned the generic and understated label of "peripheral neuropathy."

Our deep mourning for Norbert, with his ever-engaging personal-ity and love of life, was necessarily layered by our fears for Dad and worries for Alice, who at eighty-four, had lived to bury her beloved only son. Thankfully, as weeks went by, the severity of Dad's symp-toms abated, his vision cleared, and he got back on his feet again. For the next five years he would suffer the same moderate level of functional impairment he had been living with before, though we saw foreboding hints of continuing decline. Still he did not complain, and he wouldn't let his body beat him.

Instead, he decided to create. He bought a piece of land near the beach in the Hamptons and planned to build a house befitting Howard Roark. The forward-looking design was his, with a great open space at the center of the structure, which he insisted be undisrupted by any sort of pillar or bearing wall. I was touched that he planned a balcony off my bedroom as a private outdoor aerie just for me to write, but he had trouble finding anyone who would agree to build the house the way he wanted. Not unlike Rand's fictional heroic architect, Dad so vigorously insisted on the purity of his concept that the ideal pro-hibited the building of the real. On paper, he worked on it for years with an architecture professor from Columbia University, even as his ability to negotiate a beach, with its tricky footing, slipped away. Then once more, he heeded Mother's voice of reason, resignedly insisting it was time to sell the land.

Not long after, Dad acknowledged having trouble climbing the stairs to the second-story office he was renting. Besides that, although he'd hired a salesman to make road trips for him, his income had been dropping, so Mom suggested both for convenience and economy that he move his business into the lower level of their home. The narrow staircase that led downstairs had banisters to lend support, and Dad was well accustomed to descending there each night, as battling mortality he doggedly maintained his rigorous discipline of bodybuilding exercise.

Now, with the business, secretary, and salesman all installed downstairs, Mom began to realize that every Tuesday without fail her husband disappeared. It was not an absence she could miss, because while she had started back to work part-time for a group of local cardiologists, she had Tuesdays off and was generally at home. She noticed that he kept a blanket and a coffeepot and his tennis clothes and racquet in the trunk of his car, and he claimed that he made tennis dates with a Grumman Aircraft buyer. But an overheard telephone conversation clarified the mystery: the reason Dad drove off at eleven thirty every Tuesday morning and did not return until late afternoon was that he was spending the day alone with Carole Gordon.

When Mom confided her terrible discovery to Jean, her friend referred her to a psychotherapist who was brutally stark in summing up her options.

"Put up with it or leave him," he advised. "Just don't imagine for a second you can change him. This has nothing to do with you, or even with his love for you." He suggested that Leonard needed to establish over and over, by way of repeated sexual conquests, that women were attracted to him. With business and health reversals undercutting Len's already damaged self-esteem, it was understandable that preserving sexual power would seem all the more important. "I'd recommend if you can stand it and want to save your marriage," the therapist concluded, "your only option is to look the other way."

But Mom confronted Dad about it. How with any sense of decency could he do this to her once again, after having sworn to respect their marriage when she welcomed him back home in the aftermath of Betsy Chase? She felt mortified and hurt and resentful of the way he took advantage of her, when everything she did was aimed to nurture him. Why, even her decision to go back to work for cardiologists had been calculated to guarantee that he would always get preferential medical attention. But the real problem with his heart, she said, was that he lacked one. His heartless self-indulgence had killed their marriage.

"Leave," she said. "I don't care anymore. Go make your life with Carole."

"Please believe me, I don't love Carole," Len insisted. "You're the only woman I could love. I'm just having a little fun. You shouldn't let it bother you."

And yet, just as in their courtship decades earlier, boasting of his amorous adventures, he seemed bent on advertising his infidelity. Betraying her was not enough. It was as if he had to prove not only to himself, but also to his wife, that there were always other women who fell captive to his charms. Indeed, whatever else it was, Len's brash pursuit of other women appeared expressly meant to make her jealous, whether he was acting in retaliation or shrewdly playing to an innate need of hers for a challenge in romance.

He, too, of course, had ample cause for jealousy, suspecting from the outset that Janine would never love him with the same consuming ardor with which she'd loved Roland. And just as Gary and I had grown up with the story of the love our mother lost in France, it was no secret to our father that everyone else around her came to learn the story also. To know Janine meant to know about Roland. Lost in stolen dreams, wedded in her heart to the Frenchman she had left behind, a love idealized, always perfect, she may have hoarded what my father needed. His unseen rival was unbeatable.

Only later—when I read Dad's letters from their early marriage and met the youthful husband who voiced nascent, hungry love for her—would I sense I had misjudged him. Then, painfully, I wondered at having viewed the shifting balance of their marriage only through my mother's eyes. In all the years she shared with me her grief at Dad's unfaithfulness, I had failed to ask the crucial question: when she allowed Roland to lodge between them, had she established the environment that would send my father wandering? What detours did he have to take to prove that he was lovable?

Or perhaps both of them required the object of their passion to float beyond their grasp. They married relatively young, and the excitement of romance is not easily sustained amid the petty familiarities and bland routines of married life. The sort of passion that fuels myth and drama may require the threat of obstacles to keep the fire alive. Indeed, even Carole Gordon would brazenly declare that she preferred to maintain the illicit nature of her relationship with Len, when my mother, angry and exasperated, held out the alternative.

"I've had enough of all of this. If you want Len, take him," Mom said to her one day, when Dad was out and she picked up the office telephone to find her former friend calling for her husband.

Carole laughed. "No thanks," she scoffed. "I'm quite satisfied the way things are for now."

. . .

By the summer of 1982, my coverage of official corruption and organized crime resulted in my promotion to national correspondent, and I was transferred by *The New York Times* to cover the Justice Department in Washington. There I soon met Daniel Werner, the man who would become my second husband. Curiously enough, like my first, he was a television news producer. In the months that followed, I avoided subjecting Dan to my father's rigorous dissection, wanting to decide my future for myself. So that March, when I told my parents I was engaged to someone they had never met, they were understandably dismayed, yet they shortly got to know Dan and warmly welcomed him into the family. We planned a simple springtime wedding. Before that, however, Dad embarked on a risky trial of plasmapheresis treatments aimed to cleanse his blood cells of excess antibodies thought to be contributing to his worsening neuropathy. The treatments were abruptly halted, however, when Dad contracted life-threatening hepatitis. I had just mailed out our wedding invitations when Jean called to say that Dad was far, far sicker than Mom had let me know. I needed to come home quickly, Jean warned, because it wasn't clear that even Len could beat this one.

Thus again I found him in the hospital, jaundice having turned his eyes and skin a gruesome shade of mustard yellow, and for the first time in my life, I saw him with a beard. The lion lay immobile in the cage of his hospital bed, and as a soaring bilirubin level edged him toward delirium, he barely knew me. My mother, who had tried to spare me frightening news while I was immersed in wedding plans, was again spending all her days and nights at Dad's bedside, sleeping on a cot, and running home for a half hour every morning only to shower and change her clothes. If it was possible to pull a person from the maws of death through superhuman force of will and vigilant and loving care, my mother was resolved to stay the hand of God or slay the hounds of hell in order to accomplish it.

Outside Dad's room with Mom and Gary the following morning, the doctor told us that Dad's liver was so ravaged he wouldn't last the weekend. It was, moreover, information he planned to give my father if he could make him understand. Tears were streaming down Mom's cheeks as she turned to us in horror and tried to speak, yet the only sound that she could manage was a strangulated gurgle.

"I'm sorry, I can't allow you to tell that to my father," I objected to the doctor on Mom's behalf, convinced, as she was, that the grim prognosis would prove more deadly than raging hepatitis. Such hopeless news itself would kill him—the death sentence self-fulfilling. As long as Dad believed he had a chance, I felt sure he'd fight and win, and Gary vigorously backed me up.

Annoyed at being countermanded, the doctor shook his head and shrugged and turned to Mom. "Call me if you need me," he said to her, and he walked off down the hall, his stethoscope swinging like a pendulum.

Returning to Dad's bedside, Gary dragged him into consciousness. Infuriated, he held our father's head up off the pillow and, nose to nose, shouted in his yellowed face: "Goddamn you, don't you die on me! I need you! Don't you *dare* to fuckin' die on me!"

When doctors ordered a transfusion, Gary, whose blood type matched, insisted that the blood Dad got be his, and he showed up every day with protein shakes that he badgered Dad to drink—a process that took hours, Dad sipping feebly through a straw with Gary standing over him to goad him on to finish it.

Within a week, a seeming miracle, Dad had proved the doctor wrong and was winning the war with death. Two weeks later, another miracle: Dad was able to walk me down the aisle by leaning on my arm and on the rows of wooden pews that lined the sunlit Jewish chapel on Fifth Avenue facing Central Park where we held a modest ceremony. Soon after, my parents went to recuperate together at a cousin's place in St. Tropez. Unfortunately, when they returned from France, Mom went through the hospital's itemized bill, which detailed extra charges incurred throughout Dad's illness. And the hurtful thing that undermined the closeness they had reestablished was the statement's revelation that every single morning when she'd left his hospital room just long enough to shower and change her clothes and race right back to him, Dad was on the telephone, groggy as he was, calling Carole Gordon. Fighting death *his* way by rising to romance.

Before long, Dad's diminished motor skills resulted in his totaling two cars in major accidents, one of them on a Tuesday jaunt to meet Carole Gordon, the other on a nearby business trip. After the second one, when his car flipped over an embankment on a highway exit ramp, Mom insisted he stop driving, but that didn't curb his travels. His devoted secretary, Zoanne, now drove him to meet Carole every Tuesday morning and picked him up again in the afternoon. She nonetheless reported these outings to my mother. In addition, Zoanne recounted Dad's daily conversations with Carole, which she couldn't help overhearing in the office space she shared with him.

Carole was a crass and needy fool, Zoanne told Mom. She called the office daily to ask for Len's advice on everything and obeyed without question all he told her. Carole depended on him totally to help her run her life, and even, in the end, when Dad's physical condition deteriorated further, to help her plot the machinations of her next affair. According to Zoanne, Carole had already selected her next lover—a younger man, a tennis pro.

I felt compelled to ask my mother why she put up with all of this. She said she blamed herself for having focused so much time and loving energy on her parents and her children. She also recognized that ever since Dad's first affair, she had not been able to offer him the sort of abject worship he received from Carole Gordon, if indeed she ever had. Yet now, with failing health making him so needy, Mom said that pity prevented her from leaving him. Dad's philandering didn't matter to her anymore, and although she understood the source of it, any romantic love she'd felt for him had been shattered by deception. Life had been so cruel to him, she argued, curtailed by so much illness, that she was ready to believe that he deserved any happiness he'd found. Carole was not usurping anything she needed for herself. In fact, Mom said, it no longer was an issue she even deigned to discuss with him.

To the contrary, come Tuesday mornings, Mom was moved to lay Dad's clothes out for him and help him look his handsomest. She saw it as a question of his dignity. Even with his hair thinner and grayer and his cheeks prematurely gaunt from the unnamed malady that was trying to destroy him only in his sixties, his distinctive looks remained a physical endowment she wanted to preserve for him. When he was ready to depart, Zoanne folded his metal walker—his "horse," Dad called it with warrior's pride—and placed it in her car. For the rest, whatever happened on those outings after Zoanne dropped him off at some unspecified location near Westchester was something Mom was happy not to learn. She was yielding to an enemy, an illness with no name that was stealing him away just as craftily and ruthlessly as Ayn Rand or Betsy Chase or even Carole Gordon.

Intriguingly, Dad himself seemed to apprehend a link between his battle with mortality and the pursuits that lured him from the calm stability of home and marriage. The engrossing pleasure he found in women, projects, or ideas distracted him from the foreboding sense of death that had plagued him always. Four years after his recovery from hepatitis, he expressed this in a eulogy he delivered for his closest friend—Jean's soulful husband, Jack—who had died within a week of being diagnosed with galloping leukemia. Dad was devastated. At the funeral, crushed, seated uncustomarily in a wheelchair, he spoke of suffering a "new sense of numbness" owing to Jack's loss.

"My dear beloved friend, Jack, did not die alone. A vital part of me died with him," Dad said, his deep voice splintered with emotion. "The consciousness that differentiates our species is both a blessing and a curse. Our fears are terrible to contemplate, and we survive in part by our manufactured evasions and diversions. How else could we deal with the ominous invisible?"

TWENTY-THREE

TOGETHERNESS

_____

In the summer of 1989, Mom planned a family pilgrimage to Freiburg and the German towns of Ihringen and Eppingen where her parents had been born, as well as to Mulhouse, Gray, and Lyon, where she had lived in France as a teenager in the war. The idea occurred to her after hearing from her cousin Hannchen that scores of German cities were inviting their Jewish former citizens to come back for reunions, and Freiburg had arranged for such a gathering to take place that October. With inner conflict and trepidation, former refugees would come back to their birthplace from lands where they had built new lives and spend a thoughtful week in conferences and programs designed to introduce them to a very different Germany from the one that they had fled.

It was too late for us to be included on that year's list of official invitees whose travel expenses the city would reimburse. But Mom wondered if it might be possible for us to go there on our own and meet the other visitors, conceivably including former friends of hers. She broached the subject when I was in New Jersey with Dan and our two children—Zach then four, and Ariel two—and my husband encouraged me to go along with Gary and my parents for what was bound to prove a meaningful experience as we traveled to the scenes of long-familiar stories.

Enticing as the prospect was, it seemed poignantly ironic that the most ambitious family adventure we had ever undertaken was one that now required my father to travel with a wheelchair. Except for visits to the zoo with his two adored grandchildren—whom he encouraged to call him "Grumps" in keeping with his flinty personality—he rarely submitted to what he viewed as a public admission of disability and hence refused to invest in a better model than the flimsy castoff he obtained from the local ambulance department. Still, how ill suited it would prove for days spent rolling over knobby European cobblestones was an aspect of trip planning none of us considered. Also not discussed, but ultimately touching, was his unselfish generosity in agreeing to a difficult expedition solely to please Mom, who would not have gone without him.

Better foresight was involved in my arranging to write about our journey for *The New York Times*. The paper assigned photographers in Germany and France to join us on the way, and later, when the article appeared, it surprised me by provoking the largest reader response of my career. Calls and letters poured in from strangers across the country telling of similar experiences, either in the war or on subsequent visits back to places they'd escaped. Of even greater interest, other former refugees who recognized Janine as someone they had known in Europe or in Cuba now reached out to get in touch with her again. Yet most significant for all of us, the newspaper assignment helped to turn the trip into a purposeful mission of fact-finding and rediscovery. It became my impetus for initiating meetings and explorations we might otherwise have missed, had I not been wearing the persona of a reporter bent upon historical research, albeit personal in focus.

So it was in Freiburg that Mom and I were invited to the sixteenth-century Rathaus or city hall for an interview with Mayor Dr. Rolf Böhme and sat in his office with the ghost of my grandfather. Sigmar would have been amazed and overcome with German pride to see us welcomed with honor in the very town that had placed his name on an official boycott list, forced him to relinquish all his assets, and driven him to flee with nothing. A liberal-minded Social Democrat, Mayor Böhme had been instrumental in organizing the visits of Jewish former citizens as part of a broad campaign of reconciliation that included a student exchange program with Israel and the construction of a synagogue on land donated by the city near its glorious cathedral.

The groundbreaking in 1985 coincided with the first reunion, and the new synagogue, replacing the nineteenth-century original destroyed on *Kristallnacht*, opened in 1987. The mayor pointed out that it incorporates a Freiburg *Bächle* in its design, with one of the city's small canals running across the sidewalk to the temple, where Germany's waters bubble up at the open core of a large steel Star of David. In what remained a mystery, he noted, in 1938 the old synagogue's elaborately carved wooden doors were thankfully removed, saved from the fires of *Kristallnacht* and hidden—along with the Torah's silver breastplate—in the basement of a city museum. When the modern synagogue was erected, the original doors were brought back into use for a new Jewish population then numbering about one hundred, the vast majority not German, but people who had moved to Freiburg since the war from Russia or Eastern Europe.

Only five members of Freiburg's original Jewish community returned from the concentration camps after they were liberated, he said. Rare, too, were those who managed somehow to escape the Nazis and then came back to live in Freiburg when the horror ended. Mayor Böhme told us he was well aware that older citizens now felt shame in facing former Jewish neighbors who visited the city in its organized reunions. He was nonetheless committed to what he called a civic responsibility of confronting and atoning for the past. From his desk, he picked up a nondescript black rock that he had taken from Auschwitz a decade earlier, and he slammed it against his blotter with a thud so resolute it had the impact of a vow. "This stone is from the spot where Jews were selected for life and death," he said, as heavily as if the stone encapsulated the weight of Nazi guilt. "It is always here . . . to be conscious . . . never again."

Awed by the unanticipated beauty of Mother's birthplace and its backdrop of deep green mountains, we marveled at the picturesque medieval buildings in the historic core of town that were flattened by British bombers in 1944 and then meticulously restored—an accomplishment of the Marshall Plan and the economic miracle that saw West Germany rise again from the ashes of its ruin. A few blocks from city hall, we went to see Mom's first home at Poststrasse 6, and Dad and Gary waited in our rented van while Mom and I went closer to inspect it. She pointed out her bedroom window, the garden where she had played with Trudi, the Hotel Minerva at the corner (which now looked vacant, out of business), and Sigmar's former office across the street. An EISEN GLATT sign outside a glistening showroom of whirlpool tubs encased in marble provided our first evidence that the Glatts continued to run the construction and plumbing supply company that they had taken over from Sigmar and his brother when it was "Aryanized" in 1938.

"Oh, how I wish I could see the inside of my old home one more time!" Mom murmured wistfully, which propelled me to the wide oak door and a directory of residents. The imposing house where she was born, converted in the war to expand the Hotel Minerva, had evidently since been turned into apartments, and over her protestations that it would be improper to intrude on strangers, I rang a random bell. A buzzer answered, granting access, and Mom came trailing behind me, virtually on tiptoes, peering past my shoulder as I began to climb the winding stairs. On the second floor, the resident who'd admitted us directed us to the landlord. But when we reached that door, the frail blond woman who opened it a crack assumed that I had come to see her son and pointed up another flight. Rosemarie Stock, formerly Schöpperle, failed to notice Mom, nor did Mother recognize her childhood playmate from the hotel next door. On the top floor, a tall young man with sandy hair responded to my knock, an animated smile lighting up his handsome, open features. I expected Mom to explain to him in German the reason for our coming to his doorstep, but she stood shy and mute behind me.

"We're visiting from the United States," I tried in halting German to cover for her silence. "My mother's family owned this house before the war, and she is very eager to have a look inside, if you don't mind. It's her first time back, and it would mean a lot to her."

"*Natürlich!*" Of course! he cried, greeting Mom with the cheery enthusiasm of someone who had spent a good part of his life eagerly awaiting her arrival. Oddly, it seemed that we were keeping to a long-arranged appointment. "Frau Günzburger!" he suddenly burst out, surprising us by using her maiden name, which I knew I hadn't mentioned. He grasped Mom by the arm and drew her into his apartment. "I've waited so long to meet you. I can't believe you're really here!" he said. "I've always wanted to know the truth about what happened. I questioned how we got this house, if your family was treated fairly...."

*Michael Stock warmly welcomes Janine to
her girlhood home at Poststrasse 6.*

Michael Stock, thirty-six years old, exuding warmth and curiosity, insisted we sit down as he rushed to a cabinet for a brandy bottle
and three glasses. "A special occasion requires a toast!" he exclaimed,
relieving Mom's discomfort with such jovial hospitality that, freely
pouring brandy into her glass, he let it overflow the rim. Brandy ran
across the table in a wasted puddle, and he broke out laughing. The
accidental spill appeared to dramatize that the fullness of his welcome surpassed the limits of the possible.

Then, and in greater detail later on that evening when we invited
Michael and his girlfriend, Karla, out to dinner, Mom listened in amazement as he related what had happened on the Poststrasse since her escape. He explained that in 1938, his grandfather, August Schöpperle, had
promptly launched the renovation of Sigmar's home as an extension
of the hotel, but found himself overwhelmed by debt before the work
was finished. Within a year, riddled by anxiety that the war would cut
off local tourism—never imagining that it would actually boost business as the government rented rooms for families whose homes were
bombed—his grandfather hanged himself. August's widow succumbed
to alcohol, and management of the Minerva fell to their daughter Rosemarie, then nineteen and unprepared for so much responsibility. No

surprise, perhaps, that four days after her father's funeral she met the man she shortly married—Friedrich Alois Stock, an athlete in the 1936 Berlin Olympics who had the strapping good looks of Johnny Weiss-muller and was twenty years her senior. By profession a chemist with Schering, in 1941 he was off to war, assigned to duty until the end at a chemical lab, presumably in Poland. Michael said Friedrich would not discuss it, but he suspected that his father had helped produce deadly chemicals of war, including components of the Zyklon B used in Nazi killing chambers. After his return, the family continued operating the hotel until the mid-1970s, and in 1986, eight years after Friedrich's death, Rosemarie sold it—or at least the building at Poststrasse 8 that had housed it from the start. It was then, Michael added, that they moved next door to the Günzburgers' former home at Poststrasse 6, which they had kept, and had it reconfigured into five apartments.

Michael proceeded to show us all around the building, from his newly renovated home in the peaked-roof attic (where Mom remem-bered the birdlike Fräulein Ellenbogen living), to his bright, contem-porary office in the once-dark basement (where Mom recalled their cook storing bins of vegetables), to tenants' flats on other floors. At last, Michael led us to his mother's place.

"I'm glad to see that you survived," Frau Stock told Mom. She in-vited us to sit and talk, but her tone was emotionless and clipped, her eyes alert and darting nervously. Despite a cough so deep and hack-ing it disrupted conversation, she smoked incessantly. Her words lined up like pointed pickets on a verbal fence around the property, in case it should turn out that Mom's impromptu reappearance on the Post-strasse after more than fifty years was sparked by some financial motive. She seemingly suspected that we had come to Freiburg expressly to reclaim the house that Sigmar had been forced to sell her father at a price far below its worth. Michael put its value in 1989 at over $3 million.

"You must have lived very well in the United States on the money my father paid for the house," Frau Stock proposed, dragging on a cigarette that induced another fit of coughing spasms.

But Mom herself was drifting in memories that overlaid this unfore-seen experience in her childhood home like a film of dust, and Frau Stock's probing caught her unawares. "What money?" she retorted, sitting up sharply, stiff with concentrated effort to remain as polite in this uneasy interchange as Alice would have hoped of her. "What do you mean?" Mom asked, knowing Sigmar had relinquished every bit of it to the coffers of the Reich. "Live *well* on the money we got for the house? We were forced to leave with nothing."

"If that is so, then why did *we* have to pay anything?" Frau Stock persisted, querulous and deaf to the resentment infiltrating Mother's voice. "It was hard on my father. Why didn't your father just *give* him the house before you left if you couldn't take the money anyway?"

"Why don't you go and ask the Führer?" Mom snapped, jumping from her chair to end the inquisition. "Whatever sum your father paid to mine, the Nazis grabbed it all."

The following year, meeting with Frau Stock again when I returned to Freiburg for a follow-up research trip, we would sit together side by side in what had been my grandparents' salon over coffee and a sumptuous array of pastry. In 1952, she would tell me, after Norbert had come to see them and cordially discussed the matter, she and her husband agreed to pay 15,000 Deutsche Mark (then worth less than $4,000) in restitution. She wanted us to know that. She added that in 1980, to satisfy a lien on the property in the name of Edmond Cahen that dated back to 1938, she had also sent *him* the equivalent of $5,000. At the point when the Reich was confiscating Jewish assets, I realized, Sigmar's nephew had probably purchased an interest in the building, holding safe his payment for Sigmar in expectation of the family's penniless arrival in Mulhouse a few months later.

"But why did your grandmother leave here anyway?" she asked me. "I didn't understand. Surely, she wasn't Jewish. She didn't look Jewish."

"What does that mean?" I couldn't help myself from interjecting.

"Well, of course, she didn't have a Jewish nose or lips." Frau Stock shrugged, laying down her fork. With her finger, she traced a large hooked nose in the air and mockingly rolled down her lower lip. The moist and pink protuberance recalled ugly racist caricatures on Nazi posters.

Eager to change the subject, I asked her to describe the immediate period in Freiburg following the war. I had pictured dismal years

Rosemarie Stock in her bedroom with her
1934 Hitler Youth track meet certificate

of national humiliation in which the truth about Nazi atrocities prompted worldwide condemnation and a painful imperative to soul-searching among the German people. But through the grimy window of the years, she could see the past from only one perspective, and she translated my question into terms more practical than emotional.

"*Schrecklich!*" she exclaimed. "The peace was harder for us than the war. We had a terrible, cold winter. No heat, no water, no windows, no electricity. There was nothing to eat, but then we had luck because through the hotel, our French and American guests helped us get food."

As time went on, she said, like many of her generation, she and Friedrich never spoke to their four children about the Nazi years, about the Jews or concentration camps. (For the camps, instead of using the actual term *Konzentrationslager*, she used the less evocative and widely accepted two-letter abbreviation: KZ, pronounced *Ka-tzet.*)

"We had no reason to speak about *Juden* or KZ," Frau Stock explained. "The children never asked about such things. It was not interesting. They went to school, did homework, played, ate. Why should I tell them about KZ? *Nein.* You cannot turn back the hands of time. You must look forward."

All the same, before I left, Frau Stock invited me to admire a memento of those years as she led me to a framed certificate that decorated her bedroom wall. Honoring her victory in a 1934 Hitler Youth track meet, it depicted a smiling boy and girl waving Nazi banners, and she was proud to pose for a photograph beside it.

．　．　．

Mother moved through Freiburg in a trancelike state, awash in memories and troubled feelings. She grieved to see her former home chopped into apartments, and she seethed in estimating that Alice—dead two years earlier at the age of ninety-five—had resided more than twice as long in her cramped New York apartment than in the spacious home from which they'd fled. Everything hit her as unsettlingly different. Yet by instinct she directed us to her former school, to the cathedral whose Gothic architecture Dad extolled as an astounding feat of engineering, to the famous university whose thick stone walls were pocked by scars of war, and to the corner where the city's once-majestic synagogue went up in flames. When she and I got lost looking for the new one—planning to meet Gary, Dad, and the rest of the group, including Mayor Böhme, for special Friday evening services—she strictly forbade my asking any stranger on the street for directions to the temple for fear of disclosing we were Jews. Wary of almost everyone we met, regardless of how friendly and accommodating, she puzzled skeptically over their intentions and, moreover, about the city's reasons for dedicating its energy and resources to hosting Freiburg's former Jewish citizens at such well-organized reunions.

"Would you ever consider moving back here?" a German reporter asked her in an interview published in a regional newspaper. Mom paused for a moment and then replied with unusually stunning candor: "Only if everyone old enough to have supported Hitler were forced to leave."

High on Mother's list of obligations in every city that we visited was the Jewish cemetery where her ancestors lay buried. At each one, she bent to find a little rock to place atop the tombstone, a ritual of remembrance. In Freiburg, this meant finding the graves of Sigmar's parents, Simon and Jeanette. It felt strange to realize that their bones had rested in peaceful ignorance throughout the war and persecution that saw their children forced to flee, as also through the decades since, when their graves had gone unvisited. Indeed, it was the first time in half a century that any of our family had gone to see about their up-keep, and Mom had previously worried over their condition. But just as we would learn when we traveled on to Sigmar's nearby birthplace of Ihringen and Alice's of Eppingen, Germany's Jewish cemeteries had been carefully maintained at government expense. Beyond that, in Freiburg, two monuments told the story. One honored local German Jewish soldiers who died fighting for the fatherland in World War I. The other honored Freiburg's Jews murdered in the Holocaust.

Dad wheeled behind me as I paused to take a picture of the tall black marble tombstone that marked the grave of Mom's grandparents, with its German inscription from Psalm 34: "*Though the misfortunes of the righteous be many, the Lord will save him from them all.*" Later, when the photograph was developed, I was aghast to see the image of my father seated in his wheelchair reflected in the tombstone's shiny surface. His figure was as clear as if it too had been etched into the marble beside the names of Simon and Jeanette, and it iced my soul like a fatal premonition.

Traveling on from Germany to France, our expedition did not include an effort to find Roland, nor Mom's devoted friend Malou, nor the helpful André Fick. But near the house in Mulhouse where Roland lived before the war, we visited the family of Lisette and Edy's son, our cousin Michel Cahen. Edy had died in 1987. As for Lisette, she had abandoned her grand provincial home after they divorced in the 1960s, moving with just a suitcase to a room in a modest Left Bank residential hotel on the rue de l'Odéon in Paris.

When we ourselves reached the capital, Lisette's daughter Isabelle took Mom and me to see her, now residing in a *maison de retraite* in a far less lively neighborhood. Lisette's room was crammed as ever with books and little oddities and pictures she'd collected, often from the streets, in a lifetime spent appreciating the world's most droll discoveries. Electric as in her youth, with her own sardonic brand of joie de vivre, she left us breathless with her storytelling, outpacing our ability to record any anecdote in memory before she ran on to the next one.

For Janine and Lisette, this reunion would prove meaningful, supplanting unpleasant memories of their previous time together, when Lisette came to stay with us for several weeks soon after her divorce. Then depressed and drinking heavily, Lisette was critical of everything Janine tried to show her of New York except the United Nations building and voiced nothing but disdain for her friend's suburban lifestyle as a "hausfrau" in America.

By contrast, the meeting in Paris—which would sadly prove to be their last—was brimming with tenderness, as each of them found back what she had valued in the other. Even then, however, though not given to self-censorship, Lisette would tell my mother nothing about Roland. Despite the fact she knew him and that having lived in postwar Mulhouse, she surely had some idea of what had happened to him, like Edy, Lisette would keep forever silent on that subject.

Did Mother search the faces that we passed, hunting for an older version of her first true love in every tall and handsome man, as we strolled together on the rue du Sauvage in Mulhouse or the rue de la République in Lyon, those streets where she'd worn thin the soles of all her shoes, either looking for Roland or walking at his side? I have no doubt she did. But in deference to Dad, she and I avoided mentioning Roland, because even as Mom assessed the changes in the old places she had known, the trip was also prompting a shift in the interplay of personalities in the quadrangle of our family.

Dad acceded to Mom's every wish to stop at sites imbued with meaning for her, and he retreated to respectful silence as she filled in details of the stories of her youth. Tales that we had heard before in outline were gripping as she recounted them again, now on actual location. We journeyed in an atmosphere that reflected our desire to create a perfect interlude. Mom and I were busy delving in her past, taking pictures, taping memories. Dad was marveling at medieval architecture and modern redevelopment, querying construction workers. And Gary was valiantly devoting all his efforts to piloting the van and maneuvering our father in situations that proved trying for him.

Gary had the worst of it. He stood behind our father, arms clasped about Dad's chest and with his legs spread wide for extra balance, as they tried to walk together—two great wooden soldiers lurching forward in clumsy unison. Laboring to keep Dad upright, helping him move from van to chair, getting him into restaurants and restrooms, and supporting his weight on stairways was all physically exhausting, so that my brother, drenched in sweat, fell asleep in public the instant he sat down. Late one night in Paris, however, alone with Gary at a sidewalk table at Deux Magots after our parents had gone to bed, I listened in astonishment as he maintained that Dad's medical condition was actually a blessing. Ceaseless trials had helped Dad develop new compassion for lesser mortals: "The more crippled he's become, the more he's become complete and powerful. He's gone from being a comic book hero to a real hero. I found out that while I never really liked Superman too much, I love Clark Kent."

It was hard for me to take comfort from that analysis. But over the course of the trip, as we each came to terms with one another, it seemed that if only we could climb back in the van each day, finally finding peace in what my mother termed *togetherness*, we might actually continue traveling forever, weaving through the past and future, so lost that even death would not know where to find us.

Six months later, Michael Stock came to New York City with his friend Stefan to compete in an international chess tournament, and Gary, who worked as a lawyer in the city, invited them to stay in his apartment. Several times, Mom had them all to dinner, which was inevitably followed by Dad and Michael testing wits across the chessboard. Then Gary and I suggested Mom invite them to experience their first seder by joining us for Passover. Mom fretted that the focus of the service would make it uncomfortable to share with them, given that the liturgy was fraught with imagery of the timeless suffering of the Jewish people and ultimately of their persecutors. But she yielded to us, and as we invoked the story of slavery in Egypt, escape across the sea, and the Exodus in search of freedom in the Promised Land, our two German guests participated in our rituals. Afterward, Mom was first in pronouncing it an amazing and important evening. "As a celebration of reconciliation, it was unimaginable," she avowed.

Yes, who could have anticipated that Herr Schöpperle's grandson would one day journey to America from Sigmar's former home in Freiburg and read the Haggadah with us, and eat matzo, and dip parsley in salt water to taste symbolically the tears of Jewish captives? Keeping to tradition, we went around the table taking turns at reading, joined that night by German voices. There were moments of unacknowledged awkwardness based upon the passages that fell randomly to them. Yet through it all, our guests engaged unstintingly, even as we read of days "when ignorant and hostile men forced our doors with terror," and the despot who came to mind was as much the Führer as the pharaoh. Michael and Stefan raised their cups of wine as the text directed, and we all declared in unison:

"More than one enemy has risen against us to destroy us. In every generation, in every age, some rise up to plot our annihilation. But a Divine Power sustains and delivers us."

· · ·

That August, my parents came to Martha's Vineyard to meet us on vacation. Dad seemed tired, and it was challenging to get him onto beaches, over narrow trails through grassy dunes that distanced parking lots. The only seaside spot we were capable of managing, not without collective effort, was a small rock-strewn beach on the Vineyard's southern shore where access was easiest, although the surf was strong and the ocean colder than in other places. Each day, aggrandized by the responsibility of their mission, Zach and Ariel scrambled on ahead to clear Squibnocket stones from Grumps's path, as their grandfather painstakingly advanced, moving with his "horse" for balance. Dan and I inched along beside him for support.

Once settled on the beach, I sat with my parents planning our second visit back to Freiburg. They had been invited that October as guests of the city, and once again Gary and I would go with them. This time we would join the official program of discussions that we had largely missed the previous year by going on our own. Eagerly,

Dad proposed extending our German travels by visiting the newly unified Berlin after leaving Freiburg.

Meanwhile, he passed his Vineyard days absorbed in a volume of short stories, a gift from Michael called *The Burning Secret.* It was the work of the renowned Viennese Jewish writer Stefan Zweig, whose books had fed the Nazi bonfires and who escaped Europe in 1939 only to commit suicide three years later. Michael's favorite story, a psychological novella about chess called "The Royal Game," was one Zweig wrote in the last four months of his life, as fatal pessimism overtook him.

My father, however, never gave up hope. One long, hot beach day, he insisted that we help him to the water and, resigned to the fact he could no longer fight the ocean, our crippled Atlas sat with outstretched legs in the pebbles at the edge of the surf. Stoically, he stared into the shimmering horizon that he had crossed years past as an able-bodied seaman on his way to war. Now he sat immobilized, leaning on his arms, braced to meet the stinging waves that crashed against his torso. The surf pounded him with rocks lifted from the rugged bottom, his skin grew red and bruised, and tiny shells and star-bright pebbles tangled in his chest hair.

When at last he had enough, it was a struggle to lift him underneath his arms and raise him to his feet and get him back across the sand. But once Mom had toweled him dry and Dad was re-enthroned, my father gave the children—watching gravely, horrified to see him battered—a movie star's performance. He flashed his blue-eyed crinkled smile, beat his shining chest with two clenched fists, and sang out Tarzan's yodel, loud enough to frighten any beast or demon lurking in life's jungle.

One week later, just in time for Mother's birthday, a large round lump appeared at the base of Daddy's neck. A grossly swollen lymph gland looked like a golf ball lodged inside his throat, but my father's burning secret was a deadly cancer. Like Zweig's, the enemy that attacked him had crept up from within, stealthily evading all of our defenses.

TWENTY-FOUR

CROSSING THE BORDER

I TOUCHED DOWN at Zurich's airport in the white and noncommittal mist of an October dawn in 1990, two weeks after Germany was reunited and Europe was awakening to a world of possibility. At home, it was the opposite, with death already staking claim upon my father.

At his insistence, I was on my way to Freiburg with Trudi (long divorced from Harry) and her partner, Bob, but now I felt consumed with doubt and guilt over having gone away, if only for a week. Discovered in his lung, Dad's swiftly-moving cancer could not be stopped. Our only recourse had been to try to slow it down through potent interventions that Mother quietly opposed. Why make him suffer through lethal chemotherapy, she asked me, only to achieve some painful extra months of fear, waiting for the end? Yet my father wanted life and anything that might prolong it, and Gary and I agreed with him.

We were all three in denial, very nearly giddy with expectations of recovery, but Mother's medical acumen was validated once again when the toxic infusions immediately triggered a major heart attack. Treatment ceased and Dad was sent back home to meet a death that he refused to contemplate. Instead, he celebrated coming home as a kind of victory and daily voiced naïve concern as to why he wasn't feeling better. In contrast to his heart attack of decades past, his recuperation this time seemed much slower, he objected, blocking any reference to his graver underlying illness. Death was never mentioned in his hearing, and while secretly we yearned to share our feelings with him, his doctor's counsel muzzled us.

"Don't force him to confront what's happening until he broaches it himself," the oncologist instructed firmly. "He'll be the one to tell *you* when he's ready to discuss it."

Throughout September I ferried back and forth between my own home outside Washington and my parents' in New Jersey. I was desperate for a meaningful connection with my father, yet he expressed no interest in talking at a deeper level. His only concession to this latest, most threatening diagnosis was that he did not feel strong enough to travel, so he and Mom and Gary canceled plans to return to Freiburg. However, as this reunion, the city's sixth, was expected to be its last, they urged me to go ahead with Trudi, who had also been invited. I had scheduled interviews in Germany to write another story, and at any rate, Mom pointed out, even if I didn't go, my place would be at work in Washington, and with Dan and Zach and Ariel. I couldn't hope to spend every minute at Dad's side.

To console myself, I arranged to fly to Germany from New York and to stay in New Jersey for a week beforehand in order to be with Dad on October 11 for his seventy-second birthday. The only present I thought to give him was a framed photograph of his two grandchildren—the closest thing that I could find to actual immortality. When it was time for me to go, it seemed that even he, in his own gruffly macho way, attempted to enrich the most casual of farewells:

"Have fun, doll," Dad said, impatient with my extra hugs and kisses when I left him at his desk. "Take care of yourself. I love you too. I'll see you next week. Now just stop being a pain in the ass and get the hell out of here before you miss your plane."

. . .

Almost everything turned troubling on my second trip to Freiburg, beginning with the fact that our hosts had failed to book me in the same hotel as Trudi. Alone in the city where my mother had been born, as my father's life was ebbing, I haunted half-strange streets cut adrift in history. The American descendant of my great-grandparents' thirteenth child, I traced the silent footsteps of my forebears confused in my identity. And as I wandered through the town that had beckoned me through all my mother's stories, I allowed myself to morph into her younger self. A girl with chestnuts in my pockets, I was crossing the Colombi Garden, where doves perched high above the pansies, and running up the stairs of Poststrasse 6 to find Alice at her knitting, schmoozing over coffee with tiny Fräulein Ellenbogen.

At night, inside the brooding, lonely confines of my dark hotel room in the town's historic center, my narrow bed became an oarless raft on which I lay awake, unmoored, tossed through space and time. I fought against the undertow of two terrifying waves: one that rolled into the present from a very different Freiburg of the *Nazi-Zeit*, and another that was rising in the distance far across the ocean, carrying my father ever closer toward oblivion. Every thirty minutes the insistent pealing of the bells from the great spire of the cathedral drowned the silence of the night, denying me the balm of sleep as they tolled his passing hours.

By day, I ran about the city in a frenzy of reporting that helped to keep my mind off Dad and also helped me justify my journey. I had thought my aim in this reunion would be to interview other Freiburg refugees—from Israel, Australia, other points in Europe, and North and South America—who might share experiences and feelings for a longer piece I planned to write. Now I knew I had already internalized their story as if it were my own. I understood the bittersweetness of their return—being welcomed back with honor and apologies even as their losses put them on their guard.

I found myself more interested in hearing from the Germans. In meetings the city had arranged with political officials and civic and religious leaders, with students and with teachers, they spoke about their goals for reconciliation and the need for constant vigilance against the lure of hate. Their words were inspirational, revealing how the postwar generations, born in innocence, grappled both individually and collectively with the burden of their history.

"My parents were responsible," said Kristiana Wettling, for example, a language teacher who had gone to visit Auschwitz several times. "I don't feel guilty, because I was not living then, but I do feel *responsible*, because I am a German, and the brutality was always done in the name of the German *Volk*. I am working with a group that is tracking down survivors of the concentration camps, and so far we have identified thirty-three thousand people. I give one month of my salary every year to send them help."

Mayor Böhme's press secretary, Walter Preker, who would become a lasting friend, arranged for me to interview Dr. Hans Schadek, then chief archivist of Freiburg. Among other things, I hoped to verify what happened to the two women who had lived with my grandparents before they fled to Mulhouse in 1938. Dr. Schadek, an expert on Freiburg Jewish history, was waiting for me with documents from the archives, dating back to our family's arrival in the city from Ihringen in 1889 and proceeding through the years of Hitler's reign. With a sigh more encompassing than words, he handed me a list of the city's deported Jews, and I was chilled to find the name of Meta Ellenbogen— the first official proof we'd seen of how she'd disappeared. The roster described her *Schicksal* or fate with a single word: *Verschollen*. The term means missing, lost, forgotten, or presumed to be dead. Auschwitz. August 17, 1942, at the age of fifty-seven. Not knowing of her deportation to Poland, Sigmar had continued his attempts to save her from afar for three more years.

Therese Loewy was number 202 on the list of the deported, although the death of the widow who came to live with my grandparents and gave Sigmar piano lessons was marked a suicide. This was something I needed to pursue. Thanks to Walter, I met with Hugo Ott, a University of Freiburg professor and preeminent scholar of Martin Heidegger who had written a book about Frau Loewy's death. Professor Ott's study of the widow of Alfred Loewy, Heidegger's former mentor, was part of his research into the philosopher's controversial relationship with Nazism in his position as rector of the university in 1933.

Laubhüttenfest 1940, the book's German title, means the "festival of leafy huts" or the Jewish holiday of Sukkot, the autumn harvest celebration. Traditionally observed for eight days by dwelling in temporary shelters covered with greenery and fruits, it is reminiscent of the Israelites' forty years of homeless wandering. But why that title for his book? Professor Ott anticipated my first question. Because before Sukkot arrived on October 22, 1940, the harvest aspect of the Jewish festival drew attention from Hitler's government. With a fiendish nod to its symbolic meaning, he explained, Nazi reapers gathered 6,504 Jews, uprooting all they found in the western border regions of

Baden, the Palatinate, the Saar, and formerly French Lorraine. It was in memory of that grim occasion that Freiburg scheduled its reunions with Jewish former citizens to take place each October.

In 1940, when the holiday came, Professor Ott said, the Kaiserstuhl vineyards were ripe for harvest, and swastikas danced on red flags in the streets to celebrate Germany's recapture of Alsace. At dawn, the Gestapo burst into each Jewish home with a two-hour warning to pack valises and prepare to depart. Then, led through town to the railway station, the exiles were sealed into trains for a punishing journey to the camp of Gurs near the Pyrenees and the Spanish frontier in unoccupied France. In filth and terrible cold, by 1943 more than one thousand inmates had died of exposure, disease, and starvation. At that point, Fräulein Ellenbogen already numbered among four thousand others deported again, this time to death camps expressly designed to be more efficient.

Frau Loewy escaped that fate. On the day prior to the roundup, Professor Ott said, she paid her traditional holiday visit to the graves of her husband and daughter to pray and to leave small stones of remembrance. On the festival morning, in a dank and gray mist, the Gestapo showed up at her door, as at the others, with orders for her to get ready to leave. Before they returned to collect her, however, Frau Loewy, the pianist, then fifty-six, cheated the Nazis by slitting her wrists. She died that evening, not a Jew left in town to chant Kaddish for her, and was buried in Freiburg next to her husband. A year later, the Gestapo sent both of their pictures to the university to be included in racial research into the typical physical features of Jews.

. . .

So it was that with pad and pen and camera in hand, I immersed myself in work nonstop, while in the gloom of my hotel room I spent my lonely nights awake beneath the *Münster*'s unrelenting bells. Toward the middle of the week, I hosted a dinner for Mother's girlhood friends, eager to hear news of her. Then Michael Stock offered to introduce me to Berthold Glatt, the son of one of the two brothers who had taken over Sigmar's firm. I assumed that we would find him at the Rosastrasse showroom across the street from the Minerva, but Michael drove us out of town into a nearby countryside of modest homes with beaver-tail orange tile roofs set among the pines and with red geraniums blooming in every window even in October. We passed hillside vineyards and fields of *Spargel*, and then we came into an industrial zone stretching along the freight rail line that ran beside the mountains. There were Thyssen and Siemens, and then Eisen Glatt. I was astonished by the size of it, with a fleet of pea-green trucks and yards piled high with construction supplies and handsome, windowed warehouse buildings. Oh, what would Sigmar think if only he could see this!

The Eisen Glatt facility beside the freight rail line near the outskirts of Freiburg was a vast complex of offices and warehouses.

With us was Sissi Walther, an heir to the popular Freiburg brewery that produces Ganter beer. Then forty-seven, she said she had wrestled all her life with her father's support for Hitler, and from the first reunion of Freiburg's Jewish former citizens in 1985, she had been passionately engaged in working to reestablish German–Jewish friendship. A six-foot-tall Valkyrie with platinum blond hair cropped boyishly around her striking features, Sissi told me she was well acquainted with Berthold Glatt and wanted to facilitate our unique encounter.

"Herr Glatt?" a frosty receptionist in the lobby raised her voice in a show of incredulity after Michael explained the purpose of our visit. He had told her that a journalist from America, the granddaughter of the company's previous owner, was hoping Herr Glatt might spare a few minutes to speak with her in connection with her family research. "He's busy, you'll have to wait," the woman snapped.

Hours passed in the lobby, and I was drawn to investigate a stack of glossy brochures that commemorated the fiftieth anniversary of the company: "50 Years of Achievement and Partnership! ... that is Eisen Glatt," the cover said in German. Inside, a chronology traced the firm's development from its "founding" by Albin and Alfons Glatt in 1938. Beside the list of dates that trumpeted the sprouting of new branches in several other German cities, a small sepia-toned photograph showed two men dressed in suits and ties, posing before the wooden warehouse in its early days. But whether the two men were Albin and Alfons or Sigmar and Heinrich was indeterminable to me. When Sissi studied the chronology, she leaped to her feet and began to pace the narrow waiting room in her high black boots befitting Prussian royalty, waving the brochure like evidence high above her head.

"*Gründung des Unternehmens!*" she scoffed indignantly, reading the account of the supposed origins of the company. "But that was no founding! That was a takeover from a Jewish family!"

With that, an inner door suddenly slammed open and Berthold Glatt came storming out. A man seemingly in his middle fifties, nattily attired, he was red faced and fuming. "*Ich bin nicht interessiert!*" he bellowed when Sissi tried to tell him that my sole intention there was journalistic. "*Nicht interessiert!*" Not interested. Not today, not tomorrow, not even in another year. "Never!" he exploded. "What right do you have to bring her here?" he barked at Sissi and jerked his head in my direction.

"*Nicht interessiert!*" Sissi sputtered. Her face was drained and pale, and her lower lip was quivering. She thrust the Eisen Glatt brochure beneath his nose, and her finger stabbed the printed time line that purported to describe the founding of the company.

With that, Berthold Glatt seized Sissi Walther by both elbows and marched her through the lobby and shoved her out the door, while the receptionist came scurrying from behind her counter to assist her boss by grabbing me. Neither had the temerity to tackle Michael, who was tall and buff in a loose-limbed sort of way that seemed to advertise his latent strength, and who was, at any rate, already moving toward the exit.

That night I was agitated and excited to tell my parents what had happened, but when I called them from my hotel room, my mother's news eclipsed my own: Mom said she feared the cancer had moved into Dad's brain. And so I spent that night, too, sleepless and despondent, counting out the clanging bells that rang a mournful requiem. I hid my head beneath the pillows, but still the bells harassed me each half hour, demanding wakefulness to suffering. They echoed through the winding cobbled streets, across the valley and the foothills of the Schwarzwald, through the violet-tinted Vosges and the craggy Pyrenees, and over cold, wide waters to my parents' home.

The next day, I went with Walter to the Jewish cemetery on a hillside at the edge of nearby Ihringen, a former Nazi stronghold and the farming village where Sigmar had been born. One year earlier, visiting the little graveyard with my parents and my brother, we had found it locked, and Gary scaled its stucco walls in order to inspect the graves of Mom's great-grandparents. At that point all was well, but the following August unknown vandals also made their way inside and under cloak of night smashed and desecrated almost all two hundred tombstones. The massive monuments, their inscriptions all in Hebrew, had been hacked off from their bases and lay in rows, faceup on the grass like gray-clad soldiers mowed down on a battlefield. Blue and red paint swastikas, SS markings, and mocking Stars of David were suppurating wounds on the broken corpselike tablets. Several of the oldest slabs had been reduced to cracked and crumbled mounds of marble. Amid the ruins, it was difficult to identify our family graves.

Walter showed me a news article from the *Badische Zeitung* reporting there had been twenty-four attacks on Jewish cemeteries in Baden-Württemberg over the prior three years, with the one in Ihringen most destructive. But the German public rose in outrage: six thousand demonstrators flocked to the village to march in silent protest the Saturday after it occurred, and for several weeks that followed, visitors continued to arrive to deplore the desecration. On the day I went with Walter, the graveyard's high iron gate, which town officials normally kept locked, had been opened for viewing and bore a notice jointly signed by the mayor and the minister of the local church:

The Jewish cemetery has been defiled in the worst way by unknown culprits. We feel grief, indignation, and deep shame. Out of respect for the dead, we beg you, dear visitor, to enter the cemetery in reverence and to conduct your talks and discussions outside the cemetery.

Walter and I moved with other solemn visitors among the broken monuments bearing family names once so prevalent on both sides of the Rhine. Established in 1810, the graveyard's most recent tombstone was dated 1940, when the last of Baden's Jews were rounded up for

In 1990 vandals desecrated almost all two hundred grave sites in the small Jewish cemetery in Ihringen where Sigmar's ancestors lay buried, including the Günzburger whose tombstone is pictured above.

deportation. But the hatred that gave rise to centuries of persecution chased Jewish bones in Ihringen even into death, a curse they had escaped in the graveyard's hallowed ground all throughout the Holocaust. Scrawled in red and green across the cemetery's whitewashed wall were neo-Nazi threats, interspersed with swastikas:

HE—KOMM DU JUDE—WIR FAHREN NACH DACHAU. Hey, come you Jew, we're going to Dachau.
JUDE VERREKKE! Croak, you Jew!
JUDENSCHWEINE Jewish pigs

Many of those who walked about the cemetery, shaking heads in sadness and disgust, were holding children's hands and trying to turn the scene into a learning opportunity. Meanwhile, outside the gates, informal groups were clustering, exchanging reactions and debating how the government should respond. "They must immediately restore the cemetery as it was," a woman was arguing with her husband, who vehemently disagreed.

"My grandfather was in the Nazi Party in the beginning because they promised him a job," he said when I asked if they would share their views. "But after *Kristallnacht*, he quit the party. They took him to Buchenwald, and he was killed. Today I see this place, and I think it must be kept like this to be a warning to young people who can be attracted to those old and sick ideas."

That day I dreaded more than ever the prison of my hotel room. So when Michael and Karla invited me to spend the night at Poststrasse 6, where they planned a dinner party bringing together all my Freiburg friends, I gratefully accepted. Guests included Michael's chess mate Stefan, Walter and his wife Josefine, as well as Sissi. There was lively conversation over fresh *Spargel* and Riesling. Yet my thoughts kept sneaking to the past, with Alice and Sigmar presiding at their dinner table just floors below the place I sat, with the same gold October moon floating at the gabled rooftops, and the same Black Forest breeze rustling their curtains.

Hours later, when the house was still and dark, I lay awake beneath the massive beams of the pointed attic roof. Now my thoughts insisted on returning to the other women who had faced their nighttime fears in this same house. My grandmother, Aunt Trudi, and my mother preparing to wander out into a foreign world. Tremulous Frau Stock, trying to embrace the future. The grieving widow Loewy and helpless Fräulein Ellenbogen, both aroused at daybreak on a holiday exactly fifty years before.

Through an open window I heard the heavy wooden door open on the street and then bang shut, and there were footsteps on the staircase: I imagined the terror of SS men in jackboots storming to the attic to seize us all. It was just as Mom had told me of her close escape onto a rooftop in Marseille in the hour that she had planned to give herself to love, but fell into a dream that would claim its own reality. Sleep deprived, nerve ends frayed, I wavered in a timeless zone on the threshold of unconsciousness. Though freed of the domineering bells, on this night I was summoned from sleep by buzzing Vespas, traffic squealing at the corner, insinuating sirens, and the raucous blather of beer-emboldened students weaving down the sidewalk. Through waking nightmare's mist, I pictured drunken youths brandishing sledgehammers, scaling graveyard walls beneath the stars of Ihringen, bludgeoning the tombstones. Unremembered ancestors were crying out for peace, and then I saw my mother weeping—the frightened girl who had unhappily left Germany, yet found in France the tender man whose memory abided in her heart.

When morning came, I called my cousins in Mulhouse and asked if I might spend the weekend with them. It was a side trip I had not at all anticipated. But my airplane home was three days off, and like my grandparents in 1938, I decided that if I couldn't get to America immediately, the time had come to leave for France. Michael kindly volunteered to drive me there, and as we crawled to a stop at the checkpoint at the river—the long-disputed border that once divided the hope of life from almost certain death—I was shocked to see the guards just glance at us perfunctorily and wave us through.

Indeed, the watch on the Rhine spotted nothing worth investigating in the car that carried me on the path of my family from Poststrasse 6 in Freiburg to relatives in Mulhouse. Nothing unusual in our traveling together, German and Jew whose histories unfolded from the very same address. I myself was only starting to perceive the import of my journey—that the force and nearness of the past were luring me to France on a mission of salvation.

The lesson I'd learned in Germany was that the past was not a thing forever lost, but rather a place that was waiting to be found. Faces lined by years were waiting to be recognized. Yes, crossing the Rhine, I was following a route that my mother had mapped out and shared with me for decades, as if preparing me to meet the challenge of this moment. Now I would go to find Roland, as my mother had before me.

TWENTY-FIVE

THE AGENDA

—————————

THERE WERE THREE Arcieris listed in the Mulhouse telephone directory—one woman and two men—but to my disappointment, no one named Roland. Had I really let myself imagine that finding him would be so easy? The fact that my cousin Michel Cahen was still living in the same house where decades earlier *my* parents had visited *his* parents, Edy and Lisette, tempted me to hope that families in Alsace tended to stay rooted.

My cousins' house was located in the same residential section high above the city where I remembered Mother saying the Arcieris lived before the war. So as I drove with Michael Stock through the green and well-kept neighborhood, searching for the Cahens' address, the fantastic possibility began to blossom in my thinking that I might actually meet Roland that very afternoon. Living on the Rebberg, too, it seemed quite likely that my cousins knew him. Lisette, who had met him with my mother in the war, would certainly have introduced them—neighbors, after all.

But once among my cousins, I shrank from telling Michel and his wife, Huguette, and his sister Isabelle, just arrived from Paris for the weekend, the reason for my fervent interest in tracking down a Frenchman who was a stranger to me. Except for Isabelle, I didn't know my Mulhouse cousins very well and worried what they'd make of it. In recent years, moreover, Michel had startled all the family by embracing such strict new piety that within the very hour of our landing on his doorstep, he was rushing off to synagogue for closing Sabbath prayers with Isabelle and me in tow, there to be consigned to the women's section in the balcony. Thus it seemed unlikely he'd condone my seeking out my mother's former lover, a Catholic who was probably long married. With my father's days so numbered, how awful it would be if Michel wrongfully assumed that Mom herself had dispatched me on this quest, coolly looking forward to a future on her own. He was bound in any event to regard it as delusional for me to nourish hopes of bringing back a love long buried in Mom's past.

At dinner I aimed to strike a casual tone: I took a gulp and plunged ahead and asked about Roland. Michel was silent for a moment, then said, yes, he thought that Edy had represented Roland Arcieri's wife in a divorce. I tried to smother my delight—divorce!—and bit my lips to keep from betraying Schadenfreude. But my interest must have been transparent. That divorce was very long ago, Michel said, studying my face as he glanced up from his salad. He didn't have a clue, he added pointedly, whether either party had remarried.

"His former wife still lives in Mulhouse, *là, j'en suis sûr*," he said. "Her family has a prominent flower business. But I don't know about Roland." He paused as if debating how much to reveal, told his son to pass the bread, then added that he knew a woman lawyer, once a protégée of Edy's, whose maiden name had been Arcieri. Perhaps she was related to the man I hoped to find? (In an intersecting network of small-town relations, it turned out she was the daughter of Roland's first cousin, André; I would also learn that Mom's onetime classmate, Yvette, who introduced her to Roland in 1938, much later on became Isabelle's high school English teacher and a friend of the Cahen family.)

After dinner—Michel adding to my self-consciousness by settling in an armchair to read the newspaper in easy earshot of the telephone—I called the colleague he suspected might be related to Roland. But when I failed to get an answer, I was left with no alternative on my only night in town but to try all three Arcieris listed in the phone book. I dialed with no clear thought of what I'd say if anyone responded. Intentionally, though, I started with the men, feeling that before I called the woman I would have to brace myself to learn that Roland had ultimately remarried and subsequently died, leaving her his widow. But neither man replied, and when I called the woman, Emilienne Arcieri rewarded me by saying she was Roland's *sister*! Stammering for words, I said I hoped to reach him because my mother, known as Janine Günzburger before her marriage, had been

Roland's friend in Lyon in the 1940s. But if I hoped my mother's name would evoke a more cordial note of recognition, Roland's sister said she'd never met Janine and did not remember anything about her. Besides, she added brusquely, Roland no longer lived in town. Or in France, for that matter. Just when I thought she would hang up, however, she asked me to hold on for a moment. When she came back to the telephone, she surprised me by insisting that she'd prefer to speak in person, so I should come to see her.

The following morning I consequently found myself standing frozen with a drumming heart before the entrance of an apartment building where Isabelle deposited me on the avenue Robert Schuman in the lower city. No meeting of my life seemed as magically momentous as the one that I was facing. As I lingered in the empty lobby in the milky light of daytime behind frosted plate-glass windows, I felt fearful of resolving lifelong questions with answers that could lead to permanent unhappiness.

Slowly, debating my best approach with her, I made my way upstairs, rang the bell, and heard her footsteps echo on a hardwood floor. When the door swung open, I stared with disbelief into a face that imagination had imbued with all the perfect features I had admired since childhood in Mother's few remaining photographs of Roland. But Emilienne Arcieri was altogether different from her younger brother. In sorry fact, beneath the glare of the hallway's fluorescent light, she was alarming in her homeliness. The nose and mouth so harmonious on him lay heavy and masculine upon her wrinkled visage. Her thick brown brows drooped above her glasses and slanted toward her fleshy ears, which lent her the expression of a mournful basset hound. The rest was a study in challenging topography. Matching furrows were dug into her sallow cheeks, running southward from the midpeak of her alpine nose, and her jowls spread thick and soft. She stood erect in sturdy shoes with shoulders squared, armed against the autumn chill with a cardigan pulled across a belted shirtdress. Stretching to unexpected lengths below her elbows and her knees, her arms and legs were straight and bony, and she was taller than I had pictured. Her sole adornment was a simple golden crucifix that dangled from a chain about her neck.

We shook hands at the threshold, and inside Emilienne offered me a chair in a bright though sparsely furnished living room and then excused herself to prepare tea in the kitchen. When she returned, balancing a tray that provided us the buffering distraction of mutual activity, she perched upon a stool across a little table from me, giving the impression she might take flight at any moment. Conversation started cautiously. While I was awkward and ambiguous in defining why I'd come, presumably she also had a purpose—as yet unstated—for inviting me to meet her. Thus we poked around each other with guarded curiosity. I told her I had come to France after a few days' trip to Germany to see my cousins on the Rebberg, and she told me she had lived near them until she'd moved downtown.

Her life story was a poignant one, gradually revealed with prompting, but without self-pity. Society, like nature, had been stingy in dispensing gifts to her, and marriage had never been an option. She'd purchased her apartment nearly thirty years before, when the building seemed a marvel in its newness and crisp modernity. She had saved to buy it, working as a secretary in the office of a local potash-mining firm. After retiring in the 1960s, she'd devoted all her energies to serving God and caring for her mother, who refused to leave the home where she had reared her family. Only when her mother died at the age of ninety-nine and Emilienne was nearly seventy could she finally permit herself to move into her "new" downtown apartment—decades old by then, in need of paint and waiting for her, empty. Even as we sat there, it struck me that the cold and boxy space was suggestive of a person who had either trimmed her world to bare essentials or else, almost like a cloistered nun, Emilienne Arcieri had never roamed or tasted life enough to garner any keepsakes of memorable experience. At least, that is, mementos of her own.

"I don't get many visitors, but I'm very glad you're here," she said. At first I took her sentiment for standard hospitality. "Although I never knew your mother, I have something that belongs to her. I have always wanted to return it, but of course I had no idea of how to find her. This is why I asked you here."

Suddenly she stood and strode across the room to a contemporary shelving unit of glass and chrome, where an image of the Holy

Family, displayed within a modest frame, was one of several pictures in the room that seemed to have been salvaged from the pages of an illustrated Catholic calendar. On a higher shelf, from the middle of a row of books, she withdrew a little volume that she wordlessly placed into my hands. It was covered in red paper with a design of four-leaf clovers and bore a printed sticker glued onto the front:

Hanna Günzburger
Freiburg Br.
Poststraße 6
Tel. 2833

Inside the book, barely legible to me in that complicated German script called *Sütterlin*, Mom had also inked that same address, and beneath it, in more familiar penmanship, her address in Mulhouse. From cover to cover, the pages were filled with poems and messages dated from 1935 to 1938, most of them written by her friends in German as perplexing to decipher as her *Sütterlin* address. Still, I was astounded by the charming colored drawings that accompanied the entries. With

The autograph book that Janine left behind with Roland in 1942 is a creative jewel, filled with delightful pictures and poems from her girlhood friends, including this entry by Lore Brose.

exceptional artistry and whimsy, my mother's girlhood friends had drawn or painted elves with beards and pointed caps, children in folk-loric dress, animals and insects, flowers and gardens, illustrations of nursery rhymes, and early Disney cartoon characters. Silhouettes of dogs and cats and little girls and flowers were detailed cutouts from black paper that meticulously decorated several other pages.

My eyes welled up with grateful tears, and I couldn't trust myself to speak. I was holding in my hands the treasure I remembered Mother saying she had given to Roland in pledge before she left Lyon as tangible proof that someday she would return to him. It was not a thing she would abandon. For me, as once for Mom and for Roland, this cherished book of friendly messages provided lasting testimony of the truth of their relationship. How astounding that this devout and austere woman, seemingly starved of love herself, had kept it at her fingertips after all these years. In the archaeology of love, this discovery was priceless, a tantalizing shard that impelled me to keep digging.

"This is fabulous!" I cried, once I had composed myself. "How can I ever thank you? It was wonderful of you to keep this for so long. How did you come to have it?" I felt like jumping up and hugging her, but she turned her face and blushed, apparently unaccustomed to such outbursts of emotion.

"I found this among the things my brother left behind in his bed-room in our parents' house when he went to Canada in 1949," she said. "As I told you on the phone, I never knew your mother—Roland was much younger than I, and we had separate friends. When Roland lived in Lyon after France was occupied, I was here in Mulhouse with my parents and my sister. But I always thought this little book so special and creative that while, as you can see, I didn't take much with me when I moved here, I could never just get rid of it." She glanced around the bare apartment and then shrugged her shoulders as if to add that sometimes human action moves beyond the scope of logic. "When you called last night and spoke about your mother, it struck me that the family name you mentioned might match the label on the book, and I went to check. So I guess that I was *meant* to save it. I hope you'll take it to her. I imagine she'll be pleased to get it back after all these years."

That would prove Emilienne Arcieri's longest speech of our encounter, as well as our warmest interchange. Getting her to talk about
Roland was far more tricky, and there was nothing paranoid about my
sense that she was eyeing me suspiciously when I inquired into his life
and whereabouts. She asked me why I was so curious and whether I
had come because my mother sent me.

"*Non, elle n'avait aucune idée que j'essaierais de vous voir,*" I assured her.
My mother had no idea I would try to contact anyone in the Arcieri
family, I said. But in view of Mom's close friendship with Roland in
those dangerous war years before she fled the country, she had always
worried how he'd fared throughout the Occupation and whether he'd
gone on to live a life of happiness. As I chanced to be briefly visiting
my cousins in Mulhouse, it had simply occurred to me to try to ease
her old concerns. Emilienne said nothing, and, squirming in the heavy
silence, I began to prattle, telling her far more than I had planned. I
related how her brother had written to my mother following the war,
and how my grandfather had so unfairly intercepted all of Roland's
letters: Mom had come upon a telegram from him only by accident
long after it arrived, so that her failure to reply had never been intentional. "*Au contraire, ma mère en était vraiment désolée.*" Mom still despaired to think Roland could possibly believe she had refrained from
writing back to him on purpose. I ventured that I hoped she might be
able to relay that message to her brother.

When Emilienne ignored my little recitation and asked directly
about my father, I took it as a signal that I had crossed the bounds
of decorous behavior. When she asked me whether I was married, I
sprang to get my purse and showed her pictures of my children, as if
their open smiles and twinkling innocence at three and five years old
could purify my image or my motives. We spoke in French and, helplessly but shamelessly, I prodded her for details in a way that even I
could recognize would seem invasive to a European. Deliberately I
employed all the reporters' tactics that I had ever used to wheedle
information from cops and crooks and politicians—subjects rarely
disinclined to vaunt their knowledge and importance in response to
wide-eyed fascination or flattery. But Emilienne, not caring to impress me, proved tight-lipped.

She answered every question with skimpy facts, volunteering nothing, but what I learned was this: as my cousin had related, Roland returned to Mulhouse in the exhilarating period following the war, and in 1947, the same year that his father died, he married a local girl, Colette, whose family's thriving flower business exported cyclamens throughout the Continent. The couple promptly had a daughter, but barely two years later, they separated and divorced, and Roland set off for Canada. (That was when—I knew but did not say—he had tried to contact Mom.) Although he returned to France to visit in 1955 and often after that, he was fixed in his decision never to move home again. Starting life afresh in Montreal, he had risen in the ranks of a coppermining firm with properties in Panama, eventually becoming president. His second marriage, in 1960, this time to an English-speaking Canadian, was childless. His daughter from his first marriage lived in Paris, where she worked in pharmaceuticals and had just recently been widowed in her early forties. Roland himself, his sister said, was seventy.

I asked if she had pictures she would show me, half expecting a refusal. But she had already chosen several and placed them in an envelope hidden underneath a book on her coffee table, as if postponing the decision whether she would bring them out. Now she withdrew them one by one and tenderly examined each before she passed it over to me.

"He's as handsome now as he always was," she noted fondly. Then, in a tone of wry acceptance, she added a painful observation: "Lucky for him, he doesn't resemble me at all. Because I am so frightfully ugly, I have never had any real pleasure in my life." She leaned across the table where we sat facing one another and, becoming businesslike, began identifying when and where each photograph was taken. I knew it was no accident that the first one she showed me was a picture from her brother's second wedding, the beautiful new couple emerging from the ceremony through a great stone arch of some public doorway to face a storm of rice as white and dense as a February blizzard.

Tall and lean in an elegant black suit, white tie and shirt, with a white boutonniere in his lapel, Roland steps into the camera's frame with the grace of a male model posing in a photo shoot for a bridal magazine. His hair is thick and prematurely graying, which makes him look distinguished at thirty-nine years old, and his unlined face, solemn here, has only grown more striking, maturing into manliness, from the one that I remembered from the picture in my mother's wallet. Beside him, laughing, a pertly pretty, brown-haired bride squints against the hail of rice. She is carrying a white bouquet and a wears a lacy hat, long white gloves, and a dawn mink stole atop a blue silk dress floating over crinolines, short enough to show a pair of slender, shapely legs that end in matching blue silk high-heeled pumps.

I looked into the photograph and felt sore and hollowed out inside, as if the picture were a bomb that had left my dreams in tatters, while my excitement in having found the means to reach Roland withered in frustration. My thoughts raced backward to the year Roland remarried, and I realized it was right around the time that Dad had fallen for Ayn Rand and saw his egocentric muse embodied in Miss Chase. My parents' marriage had never been the same. If Roland had only tried again to reach Mom then! I mourned that window between 1949, when Roland arrived in Canada and Mom could not permit herself to see him, and 1960, when he'd wed this other woman. If not for Gary and for me, our mother might have found a happier life with him.

I studied the picture in my hand of the newly married couple and tried to reassure myself that it couldn't tell me everything, any more than my parents' wedding album could reliably predict the betrayals and the heartaches that would undermine their marriage. This photograph, however joyful, had captured just one moment more than thirty years before: it really told me nothing about this couple now. But Emilienne was passing me more pictures. Roland in liberated France, April 2, 1945, smiling broadly in suit and tie, as proud as if he'd chased the German Army back across the border by himself. He was sitting on a bench with his parents and two sisters, his arms spread wide, encircling his mother and Emilienne, then a moonfaced woman of thirty-two with a pouf of hair like a great profiterole balanced above her forehead. At the far end of the bench, Arcieri père, the textile manager, was the epitome of a Frenchman of his generation, in a three-piece suit, with a goatee and a beret and a pipe between his teeth.

Another gray-toned snapshot offered more than I anticipated seeing of the lanky form my mother still regretted: Roland in his early thirties was standing in a shallow, foamy surf in bathing trunks, his V-shaped torso lean and hairless as he smiled into the sun. Trailing up his groin toward his hip, a scar on his abdomen scrawled the story Mom had told me of nursing him back to health when his appendix ruptured.

The next picture showed Roland comfortably at home in Montreal, sitting cross-legged on a Persian rug in a sports shirt, slacks, and leather sandals, his graying mane of hair still streaked with black and swept straight back. A caramel-colored shaggy dog was cuddled adoringly beside him, and a bottle of champagne sat chilling in a silver cooler beside a red poinsettia on a marble table. The next shot was of Roland outdoors, cigarette in hand, sitting on a boulder. Another showed him stylish in khakis and a jacket, seated on a wall overlooking Lake Geneva. Roland at forty-three appeared a thoughtful man of business at a reception in Hannover. Slightly later, at a formal dinner dance in Tenerife in the Canary Islands, the dashing mining executive was magnificent in bow tie and tuxedo, laughing with companions. All pictures of a life he had lived without my mother, who had never ceased to yearn for him.

Disheartened, I forced gaiety into my voice, profusely thanked his sister, and stood to take my leave. Yet before I slipped into my jacket, I wrote out Mom's address and phone number for Emilienne to give Roland, though nothing in her attitude suggested willingness to do so. When I asked if she would be so kind as to provide his contact information, she took a little printed note card, crossed out her first name to replace it with her brother's, and above her own address wrote out his in Canada. But she added no phone number, an omission that I took to be intentional. I shook her hand, and as we headed for the door, I hesitated, then dared to ask her for a picture of Roland to bring back to my mother. Even as I told her Janine would be delighted to see a current picture of Roland, I actually felt unsure of how Mom would react. Being reminded of him now, under the present circumstances, might only grieve her more.

Emilienne kept silent for a moment, then moved back to the table, shuffled through her envelope of pictures, and to my surprise selected two, both fairly recent. In one, Roland stands at a lookout on a mountaintop with metropolitan Montreal sprawling far beneath him. In the other, he is seated at his dining table, his wife standing right behind him with her hands positioned firmly on his shoulders as if holding him in place.

Realizing the unlikelihood of my ever meeting her again, I said good-bye to Emilienne with something close to shame in having come into the home of this straightforward, clear-eyed woman with my secret aspirations. It was only through my disappointment, triggered by that second photograph, that I recognized the fantasies that had drawn me there, as well as the romantic folly of my optimism. Confronting what I was up to, I felt shady and embarrassed.

When I got back to New Jersey on October 24, I waited for a private moment to break the news to Mom about my meeting Emilienne. In my absence of a week my father had grown sicker, my mother more despondent, and I hoped the story of my exploit would help sustain her through this crisis by pointing to a future with unexpected opportunities. If not the one I wished for her, still a world of possibility. But Mom gaped at me, befuddled, and then pronounced herself aghast at the liberties I'd taken.

"I can't believe you just picked up the phone and called her, a perfect stranger!" she exclaimed. "How on earth did you explain your purpose? What *was* your purpose, anyway? What did you think you would accomplish?" She studied me with the same suspicion I'd seen from Emilienne. "Who did you say you were? How did you even know her name? I only hope to God you didn't say I sent you! And wait— how did you explain to Michel what you were doing? What on earth did *he* think of all of this?"

Still, she couldn't help but delight in the entries in her little autograph book, whose reappearance seemed nothing short of miraculous, and she hung on every word I reported of Roland. That he had actually remained on this side of the Atlantic, so near and yet so far, after coming to the United States to find her in 1949, hit her like a seismic shock. When I handed her the photographs, she was even more stunned to see the changes of the decades. She could scarcely fathom she was seeing her Roland, not yet twenty-three years old when she'd left him on the quai de la Joliette, now a man of seventy with silver hair. Thick, but silver all the same. She noted that his wife appeared to be a pretty woman, and then she gave the photos back to me. It was all too much for her. I felt terrible as well, not only for betraying Dad by searching for Roland, but also for adding to my mother's painful burden of emotions. She looked spent and almost as gray and gaunt as Dad.

Emilienne's picture of a silver-haired Roland—taken atop Mount Royal in Montreal—was Janine's first view of him after almost fifty years.

"I even got Roland's address," I murmured. Hoping to lift her spirits, I offered her the card with Emilienne's handwriting, but Mom just shook her head as tears sprang to her eyes.

"Not me," she said. "I'd never have the nerve to write to him. I don't know how you do these things. But even if I could, he's a married man. Why would I cause trouble for him now? I only know too well how terrible it feels to have your husband chased by some other woman. No, that's not for me. Definitely not."

. . .

"What's on the agenda? What shall we do next?" my father asked repeatedly on his last full day of life, as if he knew that something really big was happening. Despite our efforts to maintain a mood of normalcy and join him in denial, he may in fact have sensed the approaching hand of death, as he suddenly began to press me with that same unnerving question every hour: "What's on the agenda?" Like a busy top executive committed to appointments whose details were the duty of an underling to organize, he called the question out to me from the room where he was sitting with a dumbbell at his feet, ostensibly watching television, although his mind was fading. Or else, perhaps, there was only one inevitable appointment that he dreaded with such anxiousness he couldn't bring himself to name it. Whatever we had planned, he wanted reassurance we were doing it together.

"When you're finished with your toilette, tell me what's on the agenda, what shall *we* do next?" he called to me as I was getting dressed, his tone so companionably relaxed that it saddened me to realize I had never heard him speak that way before. Oddly out of character, something vague and vulnerable had permeated his personality. It was frightening to find our warrior laying down his armor with the enemy massing. If this supremely strong and vital man could die, I understood at last that none of us was safe.

The date, November 9, was the anniversary of *Kristallnacht*, a day already set aside by many Jews for mourning loss. Since coming back from Germany, I'd gone home to be with Zach and Ariel for Halloween, the quasi–holy day of childhood, before returning to my parents. I had somehow also felt impelled to spend a day reading in the library. Approaching death like cramming for a test, I was seeking expert guidance to explain it to my children—or so I told myself—as if there were an answer that would make it acceptable for anyone we love to disappear forever.

I passed the days that followed living with my parents in an intimate cocoon. At times, Dad lay in bed, curled upon his side with his head resting in Mom's lap, and she stroked his hair and rubbed his back, as if he were a schoolboy who had been bested in a fistfight and craved his mother's solace. It broke my heart to watch them come together in this way, with so much pure affection and so little time remaining. Few people came to visit, but Dad's secretary Zoanne would make her way upstairs and stand beside Dad's bed or chair to report to him or seek direction on the business she was still conducting. The moo-like buzzer for the office entrance blasted through the house, and the grumbling garage door rose and fell, and the UPS man entered with deliveries and exited with shipments, and Zoanne dragged on her cigarettes and blithely informed any customers who called and asked for Len that, sorry, he was out and would have to call them back.

In the evenings, when Gary came to see him after work, Dad had just one thing weighing on his mind. He didn't like the woman in my brother's life, and he roused himself from an unaccustomed fog of enveloping indifference only to harangue his son to give her up.

"That girl is not for you," Dad said, his only parting words of real advice for anyone. "Can't you get it through your head? There are lots of other girls out there. Remember my night nurse at the hospital? Donna—wasn't that her name, Janine? Now she was really something, and I could tell she liked you."

"Hell, after seeing *you*, she'd just find me a disappointment," Gary answered with a comic frown, half joking in his reference to Dad's endowments. Still, that Gary actually eloped with that same nurse within the year our father died—inflating Dad's suggestion and hurriedly entering a marriage that ended in divorce only three years later—was testimony to our father's enormous hold on him. Even with Dad gone, Gary was still clinging to that vestige of his guidance.

At nights, in that last week of his life, as might have been predicted, Dad's neuropathy was aggravated miserably by his new and deadly illness. Mom had given up their bed to him and was camping on the carpet, wanting to be close in case he needed something, while trying to protect herself from being whacked by flailing arms and legs. Restlessly, Dad tossed in bed, struggling to move his leaden limbs, and more than once he landed on the floor, bruised and moaning. Mom cried out in the darkness for me to come and help her lift him, and when we failed, we had to call the fire department.

Men in boots and yellow slickers came charging up the stairs—the white lamps of their truck's revolving lights bringing daytime to the sleeping street at three a.m.—the effort to restore my father safely to his marriage bed now finally become a medical emergency. With all good humor, exemplifying youth and vigor, the firemen lifted Dad and got him back between the sheets, but his helplessness in the face of their easy masculinity was mortifying to him. So on the morning we failed to recognize would be his last, Mom rented a hospital bed with railings. In order to make space for it, their queen-sized bed was dragged into the hallway and stood on its end, like a billboard advertising the temporary nature of the sickroom.

We spent that final afternoon sitting in my girlhood bedroom. Mom had turned it into a study, and there Dad generally watched television, clicking from sports to news to some familiar classic movie in which he could depend upon the hero's coming out on top. Now, however, suddenly and wordlessly, he twisted in his chair and fumbled on the skirted table at his elbow, clumsily attempting to reach the telephone. A large jar lamp wobbled precariously, and Mom shot up from the couch to steady it. She placed the phone onto her husband's lap, and intuiting the meaning of his effort, crossed the room in search of her address book. Then, with no time left to repair the hurts between them, resigned to all the sorrows of a marriage that might have ended differently, she dialed Carole Gordon's number.

"Hold on, Len would like to talk to you," she said into the phone, as efficiently impersonal as if she were his secretary. With such open-hearted tact that she gave no sign of knowing who was on the other end, she handed the receiver to my father and drew me from the room so that he could say good-bye to the woman he had promised to give up countless times before, never really meaning it. Mom closed the door behind us and only then gave in to the tears she never let him witness, so determined was she to allow him to believe he was truly getting better.

Indeed, all week, still following his lead as the doctor had advised, none of us indulged in any talk with Dad that seemed beyond the ordinary. To Mom, he had simply voiced regret that he was "a failure," meaning he had not attained the level of financial success he expected of himself.

"That's not what ever mattered to me," she answered him. "I only wish that you were faithful." Now she said that regardless of how much we craved the closure of a deep and meaningful conversation with him, forcing final talks would just be selfish. But how terribly I ached to tell him how much I'd always loved him. The oppressive weight of silence with so much left unsaid was almost unendurable, while the words I longed to say and longed to hear from him never entered into speech to be engraved in memory.

That afternoon I prevailed on Mom, who hadn't slept in days, to hire a nurse to spend the night. Before the nurse arrived, Mom decided to turn dinner into a sort of picnic. Since Dad no longer had the steadiness to make it down the stairs, she set up a card table in the study so that we could eat with him. She sent me to buy fish and vegetables—the meal she had been pushing on him ever since his first heart attack more than twenty years before—and for the first time in days I went out into the world. Like a hostage escaping from the scene where a madman held my parents captive, I wished that I could summon help to free them. I drove into Fort Lee as the lights began to glitter on the bridge into Manhattan and on all the storied towers across the Hudson River that my father so admired. I was stunned to find the world proceeding in its pace.

After dinner, as we helped him to his feet, his arms around us both, Dad went limp. Staggering together, Mom and I fought to keep him from sliding to the ground, and we called out to the nurse for help. We struggled to the bedroom with Dad's knees buckling, and we lifted him onto the rented bed. Hollow and cruelly wan, his handsome face was robbed of resolution, yet as we tried to raise the railings to ensure that he would not fall out again, something within him snapped. This loss of his autonomy proved one loss too many. The furious fire of life in him could not be tamed or caged. My father, a lion to the last, roared and thrashed against the railings and gasped for breath, his blue eyes staring wide in fear and rage.

I reached into the bed to calm him, but his arms were spinning crazily. His clawing fingers were ripping at the air, and some awful final panic took him, and he fought me off with all remaining strength, and wrestling in delirium, he slashed the skin below my thumbnail, drawing blood. Even now, the skin below the nail on my right thumb bears a small, white, ineradicable remembrance of my father, from that moment when we battled one another, fighting in our love, Dad asserting independence throughout his final hours.

His suffering that night was horrible. Weeping in frustration at our inability to soothe him, Mom tried to reach his doctor, a man whose interest in this patient had evaporated on the day that chemotherapy sparked a heart attack. Now, past midnight, when the answering service succeeded in relaying a message filled with sufficient anguish for the doctor to call us back, he told us to give Dad a stronger sedative. It might conceivably hasten death by slowing down his heart, he warned, but bringing peace would be a mercy. Mom hung up the phone and stared at me in silence, her face devoid of color. Then she said that the noble view of human life that had always been the cornerstone of Dad's philosophy was not well served by permitting him to suffer like a mute and wounded animal.

Numbly, I stood beside her at the kitchen counter where so often at this early morning hour in autumn she had fixed us a special snack reminiscent of her childhood: roasted chestnuts with sliced apples and white wine. In deference to Dad's limited dexterity, she always peeled his chestnuts for him, rummaging in the bowl to find him the biggest and the best. Now, with no less love but with tears coursing down her cheeks, she prepared to feed him one more time. Honoring the man with whom she'd shared her life, she took a pill and crushed it into applesauce and carried it upstairs. We sat with him until his limbs stopped thrashing and he drifted into sleep, but we failed to understand the ominous significance of the rattle in his chest. And so, past three a.m., I prevailed upon my mother to take a little rest herself. She told the nurse to call us the instant Dad awakened, and she came into the guest room with me, where, as we had done when I was just thirteen and Dad left home to try living with another woman, we lay beside each other in the dark.

Now the other woman with my father was a nurse, a woman who had never known his many charms. No, she had never heard his eloquence or the sensual music of his deep bass voice, had never been impressed by his lightning analysis of any complex problem, had never swirled across a dance floor with him, had never giggled as he trimmed her hair with a T-square to ensure he cut each strand precisely, had never watched him work all weekend to create a cozy home for her, had never heard him tell a joke in a faultless foreign accent, or seen the joy of life that sparkled in his eyes. No, never having known these things, she took advantage of the quiet of the night, sitting at his bedside in a chair where she was posted to keep watch, and fell asleep. And thus, at some unnoticed moment of a cruel, unguarded hour, my father fought with death alone.

Dawn was gray and seeping underneath the blinds when I woke up to the nurse pulling on my toes through the blanket. She put a finger to her lips and beckoned me to follow her. Wedged between my mother and the wall, I crept out from the bottom of the bed, so as not to waken Mom. I was glad that after so many sleepless nights on the floor, she was breathing deeply and restfully.

"He's gone," the nurse declared abruptly in the hallway where my mother's antique clock, unwound for many weeks, had also ceased its ticking.

I would have liked to build a barricade. I was afraid the nurse would summon some authority to steal him from us, and so I quickly ushered her out the door to keep the world at bay. I went back up and kissed Dad's vacant face, the fine sandpaper of one day's beard, and I clasped his cold and densely heavy hand between my own. Then, sinking into the yellow silk French provincial armchair that the nurse's dozing body had left warm, I grappled with the fact that even as he'd left me at a distance totally unbridgeable, my elusive father seemed more wholly available than he ever had before. I considered letting Mom sleep a few more hours, her duty to him over, to keep him to myself. But I sat with Dad a little while and then went to awaken her. I realized that I needed her to stand between her husband and still another woman who had, in her own way, always been in love with him.

TWENTY-SIX

MIDI MOINS DIX

ON A WINTRY EVENING almost three months after my father died, his longtime stockbroker came to see Janine and Gary in order to discuss the family's finances. A patrician German Jew with the sophisticated eye and necessary means to collect the edgy paintings of Lucien Freud, he made this house call to New Jersey as a favor, based upon regard for Janine's father that stretched back all the way to Freiburg. With loyalty to generations gone, he bent his head to analyze bank and brokerage statements spread across the dining table and concluded that the details of Dad's estate were particularly confusing.

Len had died with records of his assets locked in his computer, protected by a secret password. Local computer firms failed to breach the barrier, and when Gary sent the hard drive to a company in Texas that specialized in hacking, somehow it got lost. Given the predicament they were facing, when the phone rang in the kitchen a little after nine p.m. and Janine excused herself to answer it, both men counted on her cutting short any interruption and returning to them promptly. But neither of them, nor in fact Janine, had any expectation of another echo from the past that night.

"*Allô? Bonsoir, Janine? C'est vraiment vous?*" Is it really you? "This is Roland Arcieri. . . . I trust you still remember me, but I hope I'm not disturbing you. My sister in Mulhouse gave me your telephone number after your daughter visited her three months ago. But I confess I hesitated to call you until now."

The voice that came through the receiver was thickly accented in the Alsatian sort of French whose robust *r*'s slide into the throat, and the emphasis he placed on the first syllable of her name gave *ZHA-neen* its proper pronunciation, one that no American except for Len had ever tried to master. She heard Roland Arcieri speak her name and her knees began to tremble. The decades disappeared. Every weary muscle that had done its job to keep her moving forward, fulfilling all her duties to her parents and her children, her husband and his family, was jolted and revitalized. The world began to glimmer with endless possibilities she had summed up all her life in just one beloved name.

"*C'est Roland Arcieri!* . . . *J'espère que je ne vous dérange pas.*" I hope I'm not disturbing you. She realized he'd addressed her in French with the formal form of *you* (*vous*), and she fumbled for the phrases to alter that straight off, not content, after waiting almost half a century, to be a crusty *vous* to him, even on the telephone.

"Roland! I'm so happy to hear from you after such a long time. What a wonderful surprise! But couldn't we still say *tu* when we speak together? At least to me, that would seem more natural: *tu*, not *vous*." When she heard her words aloud in French, their waltzing trill, they surprised her by containing a grace note of flirtatiousness she no longer recognized as part of her personality.

"You know, we can even speak in English," he replied, disappointing her by skipping past her overture and seizing on our neutral *you*, with its disregard for degrees of familiarity. "I've been living in Canada since 1949, and if I say so myself, I've finally accomplished to speak the bloody language reasonably well."

Janine's girlish peal of laughter drew glances from the dining room, where Gary and the broker sat waiting impatiently. "Well, then, if you don't mind holding for a second, I'd like to take your call upstairs," she answered. Switching into English, she was eager for more privacy, and so she motioned to her son to hang up the receiver in the kitchen as soon as she grabbed the call in her bedroom.

"What the . . . ?" Gary began to question her, but she slashed the air to cut him off and, grinning, dashed past him up the stairs and shut her bedroom door. In the twenty-minute conversation that followed, Janine told Roland that she'd married on July 28, 1947, a marriage not without its difficulties, and that she'd lost her husband that November. She spoke about her children and Trudi and then about her parents, both now gone, and about her brother's dying prematurely in 1976, the victim of bad habits.

"I'm very sorry, for your husband and for Norbert. I was hoping sometime or another I might get to see him again," Roland said, a comment that buoyed her sudden hopes he meant to see her too. "You know, I always liked that fellow. But when it comes to habits, I'm no candidate for sainthood, either. I'm still quite loyally devoted to my scotch and cigarettes."

He told her that he'd married for the first time, though not by choice, exactly one month to the very day after she had married Len. He'd returned to Mulhouse in 1945 following his release from an uneventful stint with the Free French Army after liberation, and he'd bumped into Lisette. "She told me that you had a new life in America and that I should stay away from you or I'd only bring you misery," he said.

"Oh, my God!" Janine interjected. "She knew how desperate I was to hear from you. Did she really say that? You know, I think she never forgave me for the way I ditched her in a dump of a hotel room in Marseille to sneak off with you that night before we sailed for Casablanca. Even twenty years later, when she came here to visit me, she was still upset about it."

"What a shame, especially since you did me the discourtesy of falling asleep in our *own* very quaint hotel room, so in retrospect, you might just as well have brought her with you," he jabbed.

"After everything we went through, of course I was *kaputt*," Janine said, the dream-created memory of their escaping from the Nazis through a window to the hotel rooftop still entirely real to her. "But then you should have woken me! I've never stopped regretting how I fell asleep that night!"

"Ah!" he countered, his tone betraying more serious resignation. "That was just *one* of the irreparable mistakes we made in those days."

It was not until October, when he heard from his sister, that he finally understood how Janine's failure to answer his many letters might not have been intentional, but rather the result of her father's interference. Through all the years since they had parted, he assumed her silence meant she had resolved to move on and forget him, he said. She had obviously replaced him in America, much as Lisette intimated. Still, he remembered being terribly hurt that she had never even deigned to write to him and tell him so, instead of leaving him to wonder brokenhearted.

"You'll have to take responsibility—my cynicism about love in general is all your fault," he charged. There was a pause in which she heard him light a cigarette and take a drag, and that sparked her need for one as well, so she rummaged in her bedside drawer to find the pack she kept hidden for emergencies, despite the countless promises and resolutions she had made to quit. "Imagine my amazement," he continued, his speech precise and somewhat stilted, "when my sister wrote to tell me that you'd sent your daughter to track me down in Mulhouse. It was quite flattering, of course, but also quite surprising, after so much time. I assure you, I did not know what to make of it."

"But I didn't send her!" Janine interrupted, thoroughly embarrassed. "I had no idea that she was even going to Mulhouse. She was supposed to be in Freiburg at a meeting. I might have wanted to, but I would never have been that forward. It was entirely her doing! I only learned about it afterward."

"Well, that's not the way *I* heard it," Roland said, only partly teasing, "and my poor sister, *la pauvre*, is always very scrupulous in the way that she presents things. Here, I'll read you her letter. It's dated, I might add, October 22. I'm glad to say she wrote me far more promptly than you ever were inclined to do. So, I start:

'Bien cher Roland,

I must inform you right away of a visit that I received yesterday from a Madame Leslie Maitland, daughter of Janine Günzburger, whom you knew in the past. As she was making a trip to Europe, her mother charged her with seeking news of you, believing you were still living in Mulhouse. Leslie is a congenial person, speaking admirable French. She lives in Washington, and her mother near New York. Her mother had often spoken to her about you. Now I am supposed to tell you that if Janine never responded to your letters, it was because her father intercepted them, without destroying them. She only found them later, and then she was distraught at having failed to answer you. We spoke about you for a long while. . . .'

"But my sister, generally a person of irreproachable behavior, quietly decided not to pass along any information as to how or where I might try to contact you." Roland apparently stopped reading but still went rushing forward before Janine could dispute Emilienne's account of how I came to visit her. "Her letter—I tell you what, I'll send it to you—gave me not the slightest hint at all. As if I wouldn't notice that omission! 'Come now, dear,' I had to call her up and wheedle her, 'surely Janine's daughter left you her address or a phone number, considering she took the trouble to look you up and come to see you.' But then, I confess, once I wormed the information out of her, somehow I was afraid to call you. I thought your husband might not appreciate your former beau popping up out of the blue, and so it's taken me three months to gather up the courage."

"By that point," Janine said with a sigh, "Len was far too sick to object to much of anything anymore. But I hope your sister was not too shocked by my daughter's visit. Really, I had no idea she would try to get in touch with you. Now I'm not unhappy that she did—it's so wonderful to hear from you. . . . But tell me how you came to move to Canada. She told me you were living in Montreal?"

Before Roland could answer, they heard the sound of Gary lifting the receiver in the kitchen.

"Mom, what the hell is *wrong* with you?" he scolded her into the phone. "Just how long do you plan on keeping us waiting? We're about to call it quits here!" With that, he slammed down the receiver.

"Oh, excuse me," Roland said. "I can see I've interrupted something important. I should have asked you at the outset if my timing was convenient. Excuse me, it was so enjoyable to finally catch up with you that I've been selfish. Go now, before you get in trouble. I'll call again some other time."

"Wait! When?" Janine cried, terrified of losing the connection.

"I'll try tomorrow," he said, and again she noticed the French double *r* rolling down his palate, an accent in English much stronger than her own. "Tomorrow afternoon. Until then, I kiss you."

The following day, however, Trudi drove out to New Jersey from Manhattan for a rare visit, and when, as promised, Roland called again, Trudi insisted that Janine pass the phone to her so she could say hello to him. "Ooh, this is so exciting!" Trudi gushed into the telephone. "I really can't believe it's you after all these years." By the time she passed the receiver back to Janine, it was Roland's turn to say he had to go. He would do his best, he told Janine, to call again the next day. Yet that night, when she told me what had happened, Mother sounded every bit the schoolgirl in her anxious need for reassurance that Roland would actually contact her a third time. For my part, having kept a cautious silence on the subject of Roland since coming home from Mulhouse, I allowed myself to fantasize that, just maybe, I had set the stars in motion for them to find each other once again. Now, however, my mother was afraid to let herself imagine it.

"He probably won't call me back," she groaned. "It's just my luck." She enumerated for the hundredth time all the many things and people responsible for having kept them separated. First the war, of course. Then most to blame, her father, having hidden Roland's letters and his attempts to find her in New York. Then there was her cousin Herbert with his weekly lunchtime sermons on the dangers of leaving home and parents and going back to Europe by herself. She hadn't known before, but according to Roland, even her friend Lisette had meddled, warning him emphatically not to follow her! (Repressed and thus far unrecovered, Norbert's defamatory letter from Lyon in 1945 went unmentioned.) But Edy did his bit as well, years ago, she noted, with his dark insinuations that Roland had been corrupted. Then Emilienne had added to the pattern when she avoided passing on the information of where Roland could reach her now.

"On top of all of that," she added, "Gary was so outrageous when he picked up the telephone that I hated to admit he was my son. And the next time Roland called, Trudi nabbed the phone and took up all our time. What chance have I ever had with the man I've wanted all my life? . . . I guess I should be thankful—if it hadn't been for you, I wouldn't even know he was still alive. . . . But *honestly*, do you think he'll call me back? Do you *really* think he'll call again?"

The following night, she canceled plans for dinner with a friend in order to be home, just in case, and was rewarded with a phone call. This time, uninterrupted, they talked for hours, and she learned about his life, beginning with that last moment in Marseille when she'd watched him in a rowboat bobbing on the waves amid her sunshine-yellow, falsely gay mimosas, until his silhouette became a dot against the sky. On that brisk March day almost fifty years before, he said, adding his perspective, he rowed back to the dock and rushed to climb the hillside that rose above the city to the basilica of Notre-Dame de la Garde. From that summit above the Mediterranean, he followed the progress of her ship steaming toward North Africa for as long as he could make it out. Roger met him there by prearrangement, and as dusk approached and the *Lipari* disappeared into the clouds, they traveled back to Lyon. There, Roland had largely remained, living as unobtrusively as possible until the war was over.

Roger's fate, like that of Janine's cousins in Lyon, were topics both avoided, but the shadows of the dead hung between his words when Roland attempted to convey the country's joy at liberation. After five

Roland returns to his family in Mulhouse after liberation: (L to R)
Emil, Régine, Léonie, Roland, Emilienne

hard years of suffering, many of their generation, feeling cheated by the war, reveled in survival. In that euphoric, carefree interlude that followed peace, Roland maintained, he was not alone in his eagerness to party. Returning to Mulhouse, he started making money selling fabrics he obtained through his father's company. Then he enthusiastically engaged in spending every franc, earning more and playing even harder after his father's untimely death in 1947. Sometime before that, though,

Norbert came to town for a day from his base in Germany in an American Army uniform, driving an impressive car—a Packard with a knob on the steering wheel—with a German shepherd dog on the seat beside him. They went to have a drink together.

"I begged him to tell you that I was waiting for you—I needed you and loved you. I didn't understand your silence," Roland recalled. "He promised me he'd tell you, and after that I was certain that you'd write, but I didn't hear a word from you, in spite of all the beautiful pledges we had made to one another. So I guess eventually I just got angry. *Tant pis. C'est ça.* I decided to amuse myself with any girl who wanted me. I vowed I would never fall in love again. Thanks to you, I became, *comme on dit, l'homme le moins romantique du monde*"—as they say, the least romantic man in the world—"And that, *ma chère*, has never changed."

Janine did not know how to answer him. Norbert's calculated silence, his failure to keep his promise and pass on Roland's message, stunned her with the recognition, yet again, that the people who claimed to love her most had robbed her of the freedom to shape her life herself.

"You wouldn't have liked me then, the guy I became with nothing to believe in. I'm almost glad you couldn't see me," Roland was continuing, confessing that in a casual sexual encounter, he had found himself responsible for an accidental pregnancy. Colette, the girl involved, then just twenty-one years old, had been similarly enjoying the pleasures of the postwar period. But when her parents, prosperous flower dealers, learned of her condition, they forcibly took charge. "That was the beginning of a whole hullabaloo," Roland said, using an expression that Janine found startling, coming from her Frenchman. An image of Colette—a petite and bosomy blonde with curls—swam into her mind as a former schoolmate from the happy year she had spent in the all-girls lycée in Mulhouse before the war.

Colette boasted a higher economic status, he observed. Her mother, a Swiss Calvinist, was the aunt of the woolen textile magnates Hans and Fritz Schlumpf, who would go on, albeit scandal tainted, to found France's National Automobile Museum in a former mill in Mulhouse. Her parents were therefore anything but eager for a son-in-law who, at the age of twenty-seven, had yet to define his financial prospects. Colette's pregnancy, however, left no other choice. They hastily arranged

a wedding in the council chamber of the Mulhouse City Hall. He was
not in love with her, yet that no longer seemed to matter to him, and it
was easier to comply than fight. They wed on August 28, 1947 (exactly
one month after Janine's nuptials), and their daughter was born seven
months later, with the marriage doomed before it started.

"How could you let that happen?" Janine blurted out. "You didn't
take precautions?"

"What can I say? I was young and careless? In the end, I was punished for it."

He moved into his in-laws' home, while Colette's parents saw to
the remodeling of a fine apartment that was their wedding present.
However, given his own increasing resentment and rebellion, he said,
it soon proved a catastrophic arrangement because it placed him beneath the scrutiny of the family's longtime housekeeper, Fifine.

"With Colette's mother always busy in the flower business, Fifine
took care of Colette from the time she was a baby and still watched
over her as if she were a perfect pearl. When my predinner absences
attracted Fifine's attention, she had me tailed by a detective, who
tracked me with admirable efficiency to a popular *maison de passe*."

"What's that?" Janine asked.

"A place at the edge of town, a modest sort of bar with some private rooms, where women who needed a little extra money discreetly
came to sell their favors," Roland replied. "But fortunately or unfortunately, the establishment happened to be a place where Colette's
father was among the clientele. And so one night I met the old guy
there just as I was leaving and he was coming in."

By the time Roland returned home, after stopping to meet some
friends en route, both of Colette's parents *and* Fifine were assembled
in the living room, ready to condemn him.

"'If you'd only had the judgment to come along with me when I
make my little visits there *after* dinner, instead of raising eyebrows by
coming home to dinner late, you would have saved us all a lot of trouble,'" Roland quoted his former father-in-law secretly admonishing,
even as the florist called his lawyer, Maître Edmond Cahen, to handle
the divorce he imposed upon his daughter. "It was testimony," Roland
archly told Janine, "to your illustrious cousin's skill as an attorney,

as well as to the status of my in-laws and the undisputable guilt of the wayward husband in this case, that divorce proceedings generally known to take a year, at least, were concluded in just two months. For my daughter's sake, I would have kept the family together. But Colette's parents insisted on divorce, and it was all quite friendly. After court, I even went out to lunch with Colette and Edy. And I think that was the last time I ever saw your cousin."

"Don't worry," Janine said. "You left him with an indelible impression. When I was visiting Mulhouse in the 1960s and asked Edy if he knew what had happened to you, he warned me to stay clear of you. 'Forget him!' he told me. 'He's finished. Roland Arcieri was ruined by women.'"

"I was," he said.

In the pointed silence that Roland allowed to trail behind the accusation hiding in that simple statement, she heard the metallic click of his lighter as he lit another cigarette. "After my divorce, I became the laughingstock of Mulhouse," he went on. "You're familiar with the game of gossip there. All the nasty tongues were wagging. And I'll have you know, not a single blabbermouth who found my fall from grace so humorous was forced to march through town with the *Klapperstein* around his neck. So much for local custom. Even all my friends were laughing at me. First, I'm forced into a marriage I didn't want. Then, for just a youthful indiscretion—nothing the other chaps weren't doing, making up for time we'd all lost to the war—I'm tossed back on the street, having served my usefulness!"

"How awful for you!" Janine voiced sympathy, though she felt anything but pleased with his account. She couldn't help but wonder what *their* marriage might have been like. Her torment would have been beyond endurance had she found Roland untrue to her. It was hard enough with Len. "I guess Lisette was right," she added. "When she came here to visit me, she said it was a lucky thing that I never married you because I loved you far too much for my own good."

"Looking back, maybe she *was* right," he said, a candid answer that was not the one she longed to hear. "After all, what did I have to offer you?"

"But you know that never mattered to me!" she insisted ardently, as if that practical reality were still ripe for their debating. "I always swore I would have gladly lived my life in an attic with you, scrubbing floors, just for us to be together."

"Ah, well, I did come looking for you," he replied. "But as you may remember, when I got a friend—a chap I met aboard the ship to Canada—to write to your employer to get word to you that I had landed in Montreal and was planning to come for you, you no longer cared enough to send me any answer."

"But I was pregnant! I didn't see how I could run off carrying my husband's unborn child! I didn't trust myself to see you. . . . I was afraid what I might do. . . ."

"*Bien sûr*, of course, you had no alternative," he said. "Yes, by then it was too late. I guess I didn't understand that at the time. But all the same, after that, I no longer expected very much from my amorous relationships."

Both of them fell silent. "Tell me how you chose to move to Canada," she ventured.

"After the divorce, I wanted to get as far away as possible," he said.

When a contact in the textile business put him in touch with a counterpart in Canada who offered him a job selling fabrics around Montreal, he grabbed the chance to start out fresh in another country where being French might prove an asset. That it was closer to New York and the possibility of finding her was another impetus, but he wouldn't tell her that until a later conversation. Now he told her that the early years were lonely ones and difficult, not least because he arrived not knowing any English, a greater handicap than he'd anticipated. Moreover, he disliked and quit his job and then struggled to scrape by, driving cabs at night while scouting a more promising career. As it happened, he met a man who offered him a foothold in a copper-mining firm, and he thrived in that, climbing up the corporate ladder and ultimately becoming president. He had retired a few years earlier and had a lovely home that overlooked the city in the fashionable English-speaking Westmount district. As to his second marriage, to a woman eight years younger, he described it as a peaceful partnership that had never been a great romance, for once again, he had passively succumbed to wedlock to satisfy demands imposed by other people.

"I did not expect to fall in love again in my life," he said. "The girl I married was a nice and caring person, and we had already been together for six years. Getting married didn't matter much to me—it was basically a piece of paper, a contract—but it meant a lot to her and to her mother, so I went along with them."

The fact that his wife spoke not a word of French, he noted, helped perfect his English. Although he returned to France every other year to visit his family, he had not been able to develop the relationship he'd wanted with his daughter. He sent her presents every year for Christmas and her birthday but almost never received an answer. Then, too, he said, his second wife would not allow him to invite his daughter to visit them in Canada. He never had another child. His days were quiet, now mostly spent in reading—history and politics remained his favorite subjects—yet the state of world affairs made him pessimistic. "In the war I started learning to expect the worst, and I was right," he gibed.

Hours had passed in relating the details of the years, and when Roland realized how late it was, he told Janine that if she liked, he'd gladly call again the following Tuesday evening. There was nothing wrong with two old friends talking on the telephone, he said, but it would be much easier to indulge in conversation on the nights his wife was out, and on Tuesdays she always met her friends for bridge. No need to make her worried or suspicious. (The irony, that Tuesday had been the day Len dedicated to his weekly trysts with Carole Gordon, did not escape Janine's reflection.)

Thus began a pattern of disembodied conversations that reignited Janine's zest for life. Each week when Roland called, she was transported to a period that, despite the war, she thought of as her happiest—that time in Lyon she'd spent with him. They laughed, they flirted, they recalled the people they had known and the places they had been and the hardships they'd endured, and they gradually dispensed and earned forgiveness for their bitter disappointment in having failed to find each other in time to share the future. There was healing in exploring dormant feelings, if only through the phone line that once a week connected them. Janine wished the weeks away in waiting for those Tuesday evenings.

Not seeing one another, both knew they still existed in the other's eye of memory as the innocent and blushing lovers they had been, a flight of fancy that lent them youth again. At seventy and sixty-seven, they walked in recollection hand in hand down Lyon's rue de la Ré-publique, stealing kisses in darkened doorways while world war raged. There was no one else for either who could share the intensity of their memories of years when they were young and beautiful, strong and hopeful, and wholeheartedly believed that nothing could divide them. There was seductive magic to such talk that transported them through decades to a time preceding the mistakes that they regretted and gradually allowed them to fantasize about the future. Still, his marriage and her period of mourning confined them to the telephone, and many months went by before they even talked of meeting.

Meanwhile, though Mom was lonely and grieved that Dad had suffered and died so relatively young, she felt that she had actually lost her husband many years before—through repeated infidelity, his obsession with Ayn Rand, and a pattern of illness that fostered self-absorption. With the mercy of selective recall, she nonetheless blotted out the negative and extolled her husband's noble qualities and often even claimed the flaws within her marriage had, in fairness, been *her* fault. She devoted too much time to her parents and her children, she told me in rueful warning not to follow her example. She should have put her husband first, Mom said. She should have treated Len with the same adoring love she had lavished on Roland. She saw that now.

"Perhaps if I had treated Dad the way I'd treat Roland, he might not have had the need to run around," she theorized. "Lord knows why, but Daddy was actually very insecure. He needed a woman to look up to him. But after Betsy Chase, I simply couldn't offer him the complete respect he always wanted from me. And after Carole Gordon, I was through with him romantically."

Early the following October, almost a year after my father's death, she stunned me by announcing she had decided to fly to Montreal. She had already bought herself a round-trip ticket and would stay for one night only. Perhaps she was afraid that I would try to talk her out of it. In truth, I was both elated and terrified she would come home disappointed, either because the man she met might not match her expectations, or else because the feelings Roland aroused might not be reciprocated. The fact that he was married could not be ignored. It felt so dangerous; she seemed so vulnerable; it was the single most affirmative, self-directed, and aggressive action I had ever witnessed from her in my life. I encouraged her to buy something fabulous to wear.

"No," she said emphatically. "He'll have to see me as I am."

But it was she who saw him first. She spotted him in the airport outside the gate where he had come to meet her flight. He was tall, trim, and well dressed in a navy blue suit, white shirt, red striped tie, Bally loafers, and metal-rimmed aviator glasses. He stood waiting with the posture of General de Gaulle and wore a crown of thick snow-white hair combed straight back from a flawless horizontal hairline. She stared, aghast, and cursed herself and began to edge away. He was far too handsome and commanding—the sight of him unnerved her. She would slip into the crowd before he noticed her and fly straight back to the routine to which she'd grown resigned. She couldn't let him see her. At least she'd have him on the telephone. But turning back proved not to be an option.

"*Midi moins dix!* Janine! Over here," he waved as he came rushing toward her. She extended her hand, but before she had a chance to move, he had grasped her by both arms.

"You can, after all, give me a kiss," he said, and he bent to kiss her on each cheek. Then, squinting, he looked her up and down.

"What's with the blond hair?" he demanded with a scowl. "I was expecting a brunette."

"Well, then, what's with the white?" she bristled involuntarily. "I could say the same to you."

"*Mine* is natural," he countered. "But I didn't picture your becoming such a modern and flashy American."

He led her to his car, and they checked into her hotel, then he took her on an abbreviated driving tour around the city she had visited just once before, with Len on her honeymoon. They parked and walked, and he surprised her by daring on a public street to link her arm through his. When a cold rain began to fall, he took her to a restaurant for lunch, but like an awestruck teenage girl on her first date, she had no appetite and declined to order anything but coffee. Despite their months of talking on the telephone, she was completely unprepared for the shock of his reality. The dream of decades sat across the table, and once again she saw him as epitomizing everything she had always wanted in a man. The mutual history they explored, validating memories that no one else could share, brought a thrill that was unparalleled, for both had made their lives as immigrants in countries where their families had neither roots nor pasts. He was a man, Roland declared, without a nationality.

As they spoke, he solicited her views and feelings with the sort of interest that Len, so certain of his own opinions, had long since ceased to show her, and she found that she was tongue-tied. Still, Roland's courtly Old World manners made her feel like royalty. He lit her cigarettes, he opened car doors for her, he helped her with her coat, and with a wicked grin, he dubbed her *la Baronne*, Baroness. After lunch, they strolled throughout the vast commercial networks of Montreal's Underground City, which tunneled through a nine-mile course beneath the urban center. Janine's rain-soaked suede high-heeled boots, rarely worn at home, pinched and rubbed her feet such that every step was painful and created bleeding blisters; she said nothing for fear that he would think her feeble or complaining. Self-conscious, wanting more than anything to please him, she harshly judged herself.

"I regret to say I cannot leave my wife," Roland asserted out of nowhere.

"Who asked you to?" she said, indignant that he could think she would so easily assume the guilt of destroying another woman's marriage. What *did* she want? She felt challenged, all the same, to win him back—a strong, defiant part of her felt entitled to him. He had been hers, and lamenting years they might have spent together, she was determined not to lose him now.

"It's just that while I don't pretend to be a saint, I *am* a man who keeps my word," he persisted. "When I agreed to marry a second time, I told my wife I had reached a point in life when I could not tolerate contention. In exchange, I promised that I would never leave her. Those were the terms of my unsentimental contract."

When evening fell, he briefly went back home to walk his dog and then returned to the hotel to take Janine out to dinner. They talked into the early hours, nursing scotches at a bar, and after making plans to meet her in the morning, he embraced her noncommittally at the door of her hotel room. "When you build a thing of value," he suggested, "like an old cathedral, you must go stone by stone and slowly build a firm foundation."

The following evening, Gary met her at the baggage carousel at La Guardia Airport in New York, and she wept beside him in the car the whole way home. Twisting in her seat to avert her face, she told him she felt mortified. She attacked herself for behaving with Roland like a silly lovesick girl, lacking the confidence to speak her mind, when she should have let him get to know the woman she'd become. Twice before, she'd lost him in the past, in Mulhouse and in Lyon, neither loss her fault, but this time was different and maybe even worse, with just herself to blame.

"Oh God, I wish I'd find a cure for the way I feel about him," she despaired. "It's been a lifelong illness. And now I've wrecked my only chance with him."

"Mom, please, I'm sure you'll hear from him again," Gary stroked her shaking shoulder as she slumped beside him, giving in to tears of sorrow and pent-up rage. She was angry with Roland for presuming that she wanted him and furious with herself for having made her ardor so apparent that he'd attempted to discourage her from expecting more than he was free to give.

Gary tried another tack. "I'm sure he saw you as the woman he always loved before." But nothing reassured her: she sensed that this most decisive of reunions, the meeting she had painted in her dreams, had not gone well. She knew with piercing clarity that she would never dare to go to him again, a feeling that remained even though he called her the day after she got home.

"You're still my Hannele from Mulhouse," Roland said affectionately, thanking her for visiting. "Granted, at first, it was hard to see you as a blonde—I remembered you *châtaine*, like the chestnut trees in the park behind your old apartment on the avenue Salengro. But for the rest, you haven't changed at all."

· · ·

A few months later, a leaky pipe required Janine to call a plumber to the house. It was the sort of fix-it job that Len would have handled in his prime with meticulous precision, but the plumber, with indifference born of strictly practical priorities, smashed a ragged hole into her yellow-flowered bedroom wall, Mother gloomily observing him. Behind it, though, they were astonished to discover a porcelain figurine of a little German girl, standing in between the wooden studs, securely fixed to a lump of hardened concrete. Her hair was golden brown, her eyes were blue, her cheeks were pink; she was wearing a dirndl and clutching a doll between her arms. In secrecy and darkness, she had been trapped throughout the decades within the deepest framing of our house—a place where no one ever lived before us. Entirely inexplicable, a mystery, how she came to be there, utterly unknown! I couldn't help but see her as a token of my mother's girlish spirit, always present, yet in hiding, waiting to be found.

In the time that followed, as Mother and Roland resumed their relationship, if only on the telephone, I was delighted to observe something of that youthful spirit infuse her personality. It seemed as if Roland had also broken through a wall that long confined the Hannele he remembered—the girl who animated all the stories of love and war that had sent me off to look for him.

The porcelain figurine embedded in a lump of cement and hidden for more than three decades behind the wall in Janine's New Jersey bedroom

TWENTY-SEVEN

A LA FIN

"Good girl, I can tell you've been eating your broccoli," Dr. Zuckerman remarked to Janine half facetiously as he palpated her breasts prior to a routine mammogram in November 1994. "I don't feel anything unusual." But a half hour later, after her films had been examined, he snapped at her accusingly, "You've got cancer!" A tumor in her left breast would require surgery, and depending on whether the lymph nodes were involved, either radiation or chemotherapy. By the next afternoon, a second specialist confirmed the diagnosis, and Janine was consulting a surgeon. Forced so unexpectedly to contemplate the possibility of death and the imminent prospect of disfiguring surgery and treatment, her thoughts turned to Roland.

Three full years had passed since their rendezvous in Montreal. Since that first and only meeting, his calls to her had steadily increased both in frequency and tenderness. Soon, several times a week and then every day, defying the frigid Canadian winter weather or rallying against the torpor of its humid summer heat, Roland would leave his house in Westmount near six p.m. and drive downtown to a public telephone. He escaped from wife and home with the excuse he needed cigarettes or a fresh baguette or wine for dinner, and sometimes he took his dog along, claiming it needed exercise. For her part, Janine made a point of getting home and waiting at the telephone by five-thirty every afternoon. The ritual of an appointed hour together was one that neither would exchange for the instant accessibility of a mobile phone, even when their use expanded. As it was, however, if Janine missed a call, she couldn't call him back, so absolutely nothing was allowed to interfere with the schedule of their conversations. If we went out when I was visiting, she would check her wristwatch with military vigilance throughout the afternoon to be certain we'd get home in time. And on those very rare occasions when Roland called at an unanticipated early hour, and she wasn't there to answer, she would listen to his message several times over, as if drinking in the daily dose of him that she required. Not until the next day, when she knew that he would call again, was she able to forgive herself. Tuesday nights, when they could talk for hours, were inviolable. And with every call I witnessed, long or short, I'd see her face flush pink with pleasure and the music of her laughter overtake the customary solemn timbre of her voice.

In deference to Roland's marriage, Janine sidestepped all his invitations to return to Montreal. It nonetheless remained her fervent dream that they would meet again someday. Now, in the face of a terrifying medical diagnosis, it became maddening and intolerable to realize that life could end without her ever knowing the consummation of their love. Envisioning the end of life or, at best, the end of her capacity to feel sufficiently alluring to offer him her nakedness—with the expected ravages of surgery and chemotherapy compounding the indignities of age after so many squandered decades—Janine decided to allow herself an unaccustomed act of selfishness. Furious at fate, she refused to die at seventy-one without her dream fulfilled. And although she knew she'd bear the weight of guilt and maybe even punishment for this wrongdoing toward Roland's wife, she felt that she was owed this singular experience of love. After her surgery, scheduled two weeks hence, the romantic encounter she hoped to engineer could never be repeated.

As Janine pondered how to go about it, she recalled the ruse that she'd devised in 1947 to encourage Len's proposal by pretending that Aunt Marie's steamship ticket back to France was really hers. This time, with Roland, she would need to figure out a way to encourage him to visit her. She wanted him entirely to herself, not merely to steal a few hurried hours in the impersonal confines of a hotel room and then be left to spend the night alone. She resolved to keep her diagnosis and impending surgery a secret, wanting neither sympathy nor to cast a pall on a uniquely magical occasion whose memory would be all she had. And so, searching for a plausible explanation to propose a sudden get-together, she hit on the idea of telling him that she wanted to make use of expiring frequent-flier miles. In fairness, she would say then, it was *his* turn to visit her this time. She would suggest that he arrive on the Wednesday afternoon and leave that Friday before her Monday operation, allowing them two days and nights together. It seemed to her the decent thing to make sure he got back home in time to spend the weekend with his wife. Janine felt guilty enough without trying to keep him with her longer.

Roland arrived as handsome and impeccably attired in suit and tie as he had been in Canada. She met him at La Guardia and drove him home, and although she had always imagined sitting closely on the couch in the gentle glow of lamplight in her living room, instead they settled somewhat awkwardly at the kitchen table. She was conscious of the disparity that in Canada she had seen him extracted from his personal environment, yet now her world was spread before him in all its intimate reality. In old allegiance to her husband, she had hidden just one thing—a framed picture taken by *The New York Times* photographer in Freiburg that showed Gary pushing Len in a wheelchair down the Poststrasse with her walking at their side. Len would not have wanted his longtime rival to see him as disabled, so she put that picture facedown in a drawer. But for the first time in her life Janine had her own photographic aspirations, leading her to purchase a disposable camera to document Roland's visit. She did not expect another opportunity, so at least she would have pictures of his visit to sustain her ever afterward.

She prepared a snack and they talked all afternoon, chiefly of the past and the people they had known. But Roland also told her he had missed her terribly: he was surprised and overjoyed when she finally invited him. He fully understood her unwillingness to return to Montreal for a few clandestine hours together, but it seemed presumptuous for him as a married man to expect her to invite him to her home, so he never dared suggest it. When night fell, they went out to dinner, and afterward they gravitated once again to their separate swivel chairs at the brightly lit kitchen table, where she poured nightcaps, scotch for both of them. She could hardly have settled on a more

Roland's visit to Janine's home prompts her first attempt at photography.

domestic, less romantic spot in which to entertain him. Still, the hours
wore on. Through the glass doors to the terrace, they saw the lights
of the neighborhood extinguish all around them, the illumination of
Manhattan rosy through the trees and across the Hudson. Yet she
hated to bring things to a close, largely because she didn't know how
to handle which bedroom to offer him. Past two thirty in the morning,
her inhibitions weakened by emotion, fatigue, and drink, she sketched
out three alternatives.

"You can sleep in the downstairs guest room," she said, pointing
to the room next to the garage, Dad's former gym, which she had re-
furnished with twin beds and dressers for visits from Zach and Ariel.
"Otherwise," she added shyly, "upstairs of course there is my room
and another guest room across the hall." He was quiet for a moment
and then chose the upstairs guest room, so near to hers and yet so
far. Roland mentioned that he always read in bed at night but had
neglected to bring a book along, and from a corner bookshelf she unaccountably picked out a history of the Jesuits. It was written by a
German Jewish refugee she'd met in Cuba in the war and who con-
tacted me after my article about our European trip appeared in *The
Times* in order to reach her and resume their friendship. Recalling
that Roland had studied as a youth in a Jesuit lycée, Janine handed

him that volume, dense and serious, and after modestly kissing him good night, retreated to her bedroom.

But no sooner was she beneath the blanket, attempting to concentrate on a book herself, than she realized she was wasting her precious opportunity. With just two nights together to make up for all the losses of the past and of the future, she couldn't bear to spend another minute separated from the man she loved. She climbed out of bed, rummaged in her armoire to find a sheer black nightgown—a gift from Trudi years before, though never worn—and hurriedly changed into it. Then, emboldened by the evening's scotches and Monday's scheduled surgery, she crossed the hallway with its antique French clock ticking in the silence and lightly rapped upon his door. She opened it to find him lying on his side, wearing pajamas, intent upon the Jesuits. On the wall facing him, in frames, were her great-grandparents and her grandparents and her parents and Norbert and Trudi and Len and Gary and me and numerous other members of the family. It was what she called in German her *Ahnengalerie*, her gallery of ancestors. Roland was lying on the outside right-hand edge of the queen-sized bed next to the night table.

"As long as you've left so much room against the wall, I might as well sleep there," Janine said, as if moving toward a vacant subway seat. "But don't worry. I'm not expecting anything but your company."

Roland lowered the book and gazed in unspoken disbelief at her youthful breasts, her narrow waist, and the promise of her hips and thighs visible through the black transparent veil that flowed around her and reached her ankles. Her feet were bare and her toenails were painted a happy cherry red.

"Come on, move it, buster, I'm climbing in here," she said lightly, sounding far more confident than she really felt, drawing back the covers and settling beside him. "Okay, now you can continue reading," she added. "I guarantee I'll be very quiet here against the wall." And so she was.

Roland tried to read but soon confessed he could not focus on the pages. "Maybe if you'd given me *Playboy* instead of the Jesuits I might have expected this." He laughed.

"That's okay," she answered. "It's so late anyway—why don't you just put the book away, and turn out the light, and we can go to sleep. You know, I didn't wait so many years not to enjoy the pleasure of resting my head on your chest as I drift off."

Later on, each would claim it was the other who acted first. But of course I must believe my mother. She reported that he placed an arm across her waist and slid the other behind her neck and slowly started kissing her. Soon there was nothing left between them—not time, or distance, or meddling family, or political upheaval, or duty, or even the fabric of their nightclothes. Aloud, with words and wordless sounds, he marveled at the soft and scented beauty of each part of her. He was generous and worshipful, and she felt tenderly loved as she never had before.

How easy to imagine: it was past the midnight hour of March 13, 1942, and they could hear the halyards clanking, foghorns groaning, hungry cats complaining, and drunken sailors and their women singing on the twisted streets beyond the windows of their hotel room in Marseille. Still they saw each other—young and perfect and trusting but untested—in the moonlight that danced indifferent to the war across the waters of the Mediterranean, filtering through the shutters to paint their bodies silver.

Now they would again too soon be separated, but they had this single moment and, with the greater understanding of life's vagaries that comes with hard experience, this time they would not squander it. They reveled in each other and kissed each other's tears away, and then she suddenly leaped up from the bed, pulled him by the hand, and ran completely free and laughing past the swinging golden pendulum of the French clock in the hallway, and drew him to her own bedroom. Hand in hand this time, they escaped the family and crossed the border. There, in her marriage bed with an antique cupid, that most clever archer, perched atop the headboard, at long last Janine held Roland against her pounding heart, and with a vast and soul-deep sigh of coming home, they joined together.

"Whatever happens now, I will have had the two happiest days of all my life," she called me to confide after he'd returned to Montreal. "And they were thanks to you."

The following Monday morning I flew to New York and sat in the waiting room of the hospital, my eyes anxiously riveted on the doorway, watching for Mom's surgeon.

"I was able to preserve her breast," Dr. Peter Pressman said. "The tumor was very small, and I did a lumpectomy." A sampling of the lymph nodes in a second operation the following week thankfully showed the cancer had not spread. There would be weeks of daily radiation, the only side effect fatigue but nothing worse. The only sign of surgery would prove to be a delicate line of stitches on her left breast. It seemed to mark the spot where a broken heart had been repaired.

That spring, Gary, Dan, and I met Roland and Mom for lunch in Manhattan at the Symphony Café near Carnegie Hall. He was visiting her again, and to say we were eager to get to know him would be an incalculable understatement. Alone at the bar when I came in, they failed to notice me. Their heads, silver and blond, were bent and touching, and Roland was kissing the palm of Janine's hand. She looked girlish, her blue eyes full of joy in a way that I had never seen them. I stood there undetected, watching, and it seemed that I was peeking surreptitiously at my daughter on her first date. Roland threw back his head, robustly laughing in response to something that she told him, and he was everything I had imagined: elegant and handsome and obviously in love with Mom. I felt full of gratitude to view this spectacle of myth become reality.

When Gary arrived, he surprised Roland—particularly dignified and formal in demeanor—by clasping him in a jovial embrace. "So you're the man who was almost my father!" he exclaimed to Mom's chagrin. "I've been hearing about you all my life. It's amazing to get to meet you!"

For my husband, however, it would turn out to be more difficult to regard Mom's involvement with a married man as positive, no matter how charming and intelligent he found Roland to be.

"Aside from the issue of *his* marriage," Dan objected, not unreasonably, "this will keep her from exploring other relationships with men who are available. I'd hoped someday she might remarry."

"There could be no other man for her," I countered, and Gary agreed with me.

"Honestly, there never has been," my brother added. "He's the only man she's ever fully loved. No one else would interest her. To whatever degree that she can be with him, he's the only one she's ever wanted."

After lunch that day, I accompanied Mom and Roland as they walked along Fifth Avenue arm in arm, very slowly, a royal couple in procession, glowing. Their feet barely moved along the pavement, and as I found myself outpacing them, I stopped to turn and wait, replete with something that resembled the contentment of creation. I would not have been surprised to see New Yorkers, however jaded, line the street to cheer in honor of a love reborn, now transcending every obstacle.

During Roland's next trip to New Jersey six weeks later, the happy couple invited me to spend some time with them. Dan was back in Maryland with our children, and I was at my mother's house, staying in the upstairs guest room. Over dinner at a local restaurant—the scene of many memorable meals I'd shared with both my parents—Roland indulged me by recounting the story of his life and origins, beginning with his grandfather, the shoemaker from Genoa. It was fascinating to come to know the man who had always been a mystery, a picture in my mother's wallet.

"I feel robbed," Mom told me later, when we got home. "It's sometimes hard to keep in mind how lucky I am to have him back, when I consider how very much time I missed."

Before they retired to bed that night, Mom suggested that given my own curiosity for all things past, she'd be pleased to offer for my late-night entertainment her so-called Old Maid Box. She'd recently come upon it while cleaning out a closet, she explained, but hadn't troubled to peruse its contents. Indeed, she seemed completely satisfied to be living in the present now. I found the box on a shelf in the closet and sat with it on the bed, facing the display of Mom's *Ahnengalerie*, including many pictures of my father. There was a *New York Daily News* article that recounted his novel 1955 court fight against the use of radar in speeding cases, which he'd proudly printed on aluminum and mounted on a wooden plaque; a snapshot that showed him seated with one hand on his hip and a tiny white kitten I had adopted creeping down his arm; a stiffly stylized portrait of the four of us at Gary's bar mitzvah; and even a large, matted chiaroscuro photograph of Dad as a dimpled child, in velvet shorts and kneesocks, like little Lord Fauntleroy with bangs across his forehead.

Mom's memory box was full of kitschy greeting cards from the 1950s and '60s and many yellowed letters written by my father—full of boyish swagger, ambition, and young love, written in their courtship and early marriage. It was difficult in that moment, knowing Roland was in my father's bed and that I was at least partially responsible, not to feel remorse toward him. Dad would not have expected his widow to remain forever chaste, yet the fact that Roland was in his place, as he had always been in Mother's heart, made me question whether I'd betrayed him—not just in bringing Roland back, but always, through my fascination with the story of my mother's first romance.

It was then, digging deeper in the box, that I first found the letter on thin blue airmail paper that Norbert sent Janine in 1945, after spending a dissipated night in Lyon with Roland. I was shocked to find it full of threats and coldly worded warnings. "*In the event you return to Europe and marry Roland,*" her brother had written, "*YOU WILL SAIL OUT OF MY LIFE FOREVER.*" How baffling that Mom had never mentioned it, a letter that would have helped explain the pressure that prevented her from returning to the man she loved! Had she truly managed to erase this letter from memory? Or had she just concealed it from me in order to preserve my feelings for my uncle?

Norbert's letter was burning in my hand, and I only wished that I could wake Mom up immediately to ask about it. I felt disturbed by Norbert's criticism of Roland, while unable to assess its truthfulness. And yet, I wasn't sure: come the morning, should I tell them what I'd found, or should I rather keep this ugly letter to myself? How would it affect them now, almost fifty years after it was written and with Norbert gone, to confront this buried evidence, which helped elucidate so much? I felt confused and hot and tired and engulfed by more of the past than I could handle, so I opened the window to get fresh air. The burden of too much knowledge was suffocating.

"YOU HAVE VIOLATED A PROTECTED AREA! THE PO-LICE HAVE BEEN CALLED! LEAVE IMMEDIATELY!" Instantly, a man's voice reverberated throughout the house, intensely loud and menacing. I jumped in terror, and he bellowed deeply once again: "YOU HAVE VIOLATED A PROTECTED AREA! THE POLICE HAVE BEEN CALLED! LEAVE IMMEDIATELY!"

Oddly, despite my midnight probing, I felt the voice was not addressing me. Rather, it almost seemed that by delving in the box I had summoned up my father's ghost, like Agamemnon's, with Norbert's there to serve as ally, to condemn and to expel the usurper lying even now beside my mother in my parents' bed. Mom's door burst open, and she came running out in her nightgown, frightened, as the booming voice repeated, "LEAVE IMMEDIATELY!"

"Are you okay?" she gasped, blinking in the light.

"Yes," I stammered, Elektra after all. "Who is that? What the hell is going on?"

But Mother didn't answer me. She was already flying down the staircase to silence the commanding voice of her new security alarm, which had failed to guard against spirits of the past entering the house unbidden.

· · ·

In May 1999—a decade after traveling to Germany and France with my parents and Gary—I went back again, this time with Mother and Roland. I had become an aficionada of this sort of pilgrimage, it seemed, a reporter whose favorite beat meant inching in rediscovered pathways through the geography of the years. I needed to see the stories fleshed out in front of me: the house, the river, the railway station, the theater, the café table, and the pier. I wanted to enter every scene myself and smell the air and feel the ground beneath my feet and count the steps at every door and evaluate the neighbors' smiles.

Roland had long since informed his wife that he was doing consulting work for a company in the United States, which enabled him to travel freely and get away discreetly for regular extended visits. And while he and Mom were neither emotionally nor morally content with the compromises they were making, both recognized that their options were very limited. Roland hated being responsible for Janine's living by herself, yet she insisted she preferred to have whatever time she could with him, rather than make her life with anyone else on earth. Given that assurance, he refused to consider losing her again. It was not their fault that destiny had driven them apart, he said, and they owed it to themselves to seize this unpredicted happiness. Still, both agreed it would not be fair for Roland to abandon his blameless wife after more than thirty years of marriage. Janine insisted she would not want that on her conscience. So every six weeks since 1994, he had come to spend two weeks with her, and from time to time they traveled in the United States or France.

"*Two days only have passed since my return and it already feels like months,*" he wrote her after one such visit. "*I miss you terribly. You see, you always talk about getting cured of our romance, and I did my best to help! But now you have me definitely and hopelessly 'contaminated' to the extent that I am sick at heart. Strangely, I do not want to be cured! I love you completely.*"

To me, Roland explained, "No matter how long I stay, when I have to leave, it's definitely very painful for us both. All the same, we have to try to be grateful for what we have."

For the rest, they spoke by telephone every day, twice a day—as evening fell and then again past one a.m. for a whispered good night kiss. And so Roland, the man whose name had always been familiar to everyone who knew Janine, became real and dear to all her friends and family.

The year before our trip, in 1998, Roland had come to Washington for Zach's bar mitzvah. I invited him and Mom to stay with us for a few days in advance, and I dodged the children's questions about their relationship until the point when the phone rang with only Zach at home, and he found himself uncomfortably talking to a woman who gave her name as Mrs. Arcieri. What she may have thought about her husband's absences—how much she guessed or tolerated—we would never know. She asked Zach to take a message for Roland, and my soulful son, on the brink of ritual manhood, confronted me as soon as I got home. Urgently, he drew me to his bedroom, peered into the hallway to make sure no one was approaching, and quietly closed his door.

"You won't believe this," he whispered. "I think Roland is married!" He imparted this intelligence with all the grave intensity of a spy reporting back on the opposing camp's position. "A woman who said she was his wife called here while you were out. Whoa, I didn't know what to say! Don't you think we should tell Nana?"

We sat down on his bed, and I outlined his grandmother's cruel dilemma. She could give up Roland entirely, or make do to reclaim in little interludes, now that she was in her seventies, the love stolen from her in her youth. In respect to Roland's wife, yes, the situation was deplorable. But a divorce at this point in life might be even worse for her, and Roland was trying to shield her feelings by keeping his relationship with Nana secret. It was a complex ethical conundrum to present to a thirteen-year-old boy, and so it was and would remain for all of us, especially for Janine, with her own experience of infidelity.

From my place on the bimah at Zach's bar mitzvah that Saturday, I wept silently for Dad when the moment came to recite the Kaddish, remembering how he'd always said it was his goal, despite his lack of religious faith, to live to celebrate this milestone in his grandson's life. But I had only to look down at the congregation and see Mom seated with Roland, her hand entwined with his, to know that while I missed Dad terribly, there was reason here for thankfulness. And so I hoped there was a God who would understand and tolerate that living in a ruthless world could sometimes lead us to unholy bargains.

Our trip to Europe in 1999 began for Mom, Roland, and me in Freiburg, as had our family adventure in 1989. But if the previous journey was a sort of pilgrimage for Mom and an opportunity for us to understand our roots, this one enabled her to share her German past with Roland, who had never traveled there before. For the sake of history, I had arranged for us to stay on the Poststrasse in the Hotel Minerva, long boarded up and empty but recently refurbished and reopened next door to Mother's childhood home. At Michael Stock's suggestion, we even parked our rental car in the driveway of Poststrasse 6, and from her corner window Mom could see the site of Sigmar's former business, still an Eisen Glatt showroom, on the Rosastrasse. Once again, we went to services on Friday night in the modern Freiburg synagogue. This time Roland was seated with the other men across the aisle from us. Seemingly at ease among the Jewish worshippers, many of them

In front of the 1987 Freiburg Synagogue, the waters of a Bächle *(dark line at bottom right) run across the sidewalk and up to the center of a large steel Star of David.*

recent Russian immigrants, he wore a yarmulke floating on his head of thick white hair. My sixteenth wedding anniversary fell that week, and when Dan arranged to have a bright bouquet sent to my hotel room, I presented the flowers to Rosemarie Stock before we said good-bye to her. Posing for a picture in the very room where Mom was born, she and Mother stood together, side by side. And in a gracious nod to the background that connected us, Michael surreptitiously covered our hotel bill, subsequently insisting over our objections that no one from our family should ever have to pay to sleep on the Poststrasse.

In Ihringen, we found the chestnut trees inside the desecrated Jewish graveyard blooming pink and white, with crimson poppies winking through the nearby vineyards. The cemetery's walls were clean again, the vileness painted over, and patches of cement, smooth and slightly raised, filled jagged cracks on all the broken tombstones like keloid scars. Notwithstanding the offer of a large reward for information leading to the vandals, Walter Preker told us, no arrests were made, and in 2007 the little graveyard would be attacked again.

Mulhouse proved far more painful. My cousin Michel Cahen, Lisette and Edy's eldest son, had only recently at the age of sixty died of a brain tumor. Roland's sister Emilienne was also gone, the victim of a violent mugging in 1993 at an ATM not far from her apartment. As it was, we had dinner with Michel's family, and his widow, Huguette, surprised us with two other guests: Martine, the daughter of Roland's first cousin André, and her little son, who hid behind his mother as he studied his previously unknown relative from Canada.

"It's funny," Mom observed to Roland, meeting these new members of the extended Arcieri family. "Here we come to see *my* cousins, and we meet *yours*! Whoever would have guessed our families would finally sit together at a dinner table in Mulhouse?"

Roland's cousin, married to a Jewish man, was a lawyer and had been Edy's former protégée. It was in fact Martine, Huguette explained, whom Michel had suggested I contact on that night in 1990 when, going through the city phone book, I randomly reached Emilienne.

"I recognize you by your old photographs—*un très beau, brun ténébreux*," a very handsome, dark, mysterious guy, Martine told her newfound cousin. "My father has always admired you. He says you were always the exception to every rule. I must tell you, even now, you're known throughout our family as *l'aventurier*," the adventurer.

The next day I strolled with Mom and Roland on the rue du Sauvage, where as bashful teenagers they had so often hunted for each other in the evenings. We passed the birthplace of Captain Alfred Dreyfus, stopped into the pine-scented council chamber where Roland had married his first wife, and laughed beneath the *Klapperstein* with its bulging eyes and obscene protruding tongue. In respectful silence, we stood in the Catholic cemetery before the tombstone of one of Roland's martyred friends, "*mort pour la France*" at only twenty-two in 1944, on his first day in action fighting for the Resistance. And finally, leaving town, we pulled off the road for a nostalgic glance at the green and swollen springtime river where Janine and Roland had first expressed their love in 1939 among the reeds and willows. Roland was at the wheel as we headed southwest toward Gray, the sky releasing a heavy downpour, and Mom pronounced Mulhouse as having been far more gemütlich or cozy in the year when she first met him there.

Roland: "Now I love you twice as much."

"Oh, my poor baby," Roland crooned to her. "Don't you know that everything in Europe was more gemütlich before the war?" With that, he reached to take and kiss her hand, adorned by a new silver ring with a blue stone twice as large as the one that he had given her before their separation in 1942. "Twice as large," he'd told her when he placed it on her finger before our trip, "because now I love you twice as much."

We drove on through rolling hills on roads bordered by mustard and wildflowers, through quiet, forgotten villages, and past wheat fields where the wind blew undulating ripples like waves across a golden ocean. In the backseat I listened as they reminisced. They told me again how they had found each other in Lyon after France was occupied, and then they talked about the grievous day they were torn from one another in Marseille. It was seven years later when he tried to see her in New York, Roland reminded me, and by then she was no longer free. He turned around to face me, and in a tone he may have thought would camouflage such resentment as he harbored, he told me this: "Basically, my dear, *you* were the culprit. The woman I adored, the most extraordinary woman I ever met, couldn't be pursued because you were around. It's the sad story of life—either one arrives too early or too late. Everything that happens in life, in love, or in war is a question of timing."

True enough, I thought, as I contemplated how the timing of my father's fatal illness, coinciding with my second trip to Freiburg, had spurred me to begin a search for Roland Arcieri that I could have undertaken years before. Now, however, instead of traveling with my parents, I was with my mother and her long-lost love. If casual observers assumed I was their daughter, for my part, I sometimes felt an interloper, intruding on their romance, and at other points a "scribe"—my father's nickname for me. Everywhere we went, I was documenting stories that they shared, as in town after town we toured locations that were memorable to each of them. She showed him Gray, and he took us to Villefranche, where they bemoaned the war that had sent their families running from Mulhouse to seek refuge in different places. Now, so happy were they both just to be together, in the same place at the same time, that at every stop I had to push them to seek out specific sites and look up former friends.

In Lyon, eager to meet Roland, Lisette's youngest daughter Isabelle joined us from Paris. She had been named in memory of her grandmother Marie's beloved attendant, Isabelle Picard, and we stood rapt in silent prayer before the wooden door with its fruits and cherubs at the building where Cousin Mimi, her three children, and Bella were arrested. Mournful memories shrouded that afternoon as we toured the gare de Perrache and the Hôtel Terminus where Roland had worked as a translator, the Gestapo breathing down his neck.

He stumbled and we grabbed him to break his fall at the very spot where he had witnessed Roger's arrest—the last time he ever saw his friend before Roger was transported to Drancy and then to death at Auschwitz.

"Today, I could have warned him, but communication then was awful," Roland despaired, still haunted after more than half a century by his inability to save his friend.

Past Lyon, the leafy plane and chestnut trees along the roadside gave way to slim columns of deep green cypress before we descended on Marseille, with its chalky limestone cliffs and orange rooftops, and with the Mediterranean a sober blue in front of us. It was Janine's first return there since she'd fled, and she fell grim and silent. Gamely, Roland worked to stir a lighter mood. "Ya, ya, my darling"—he laughed and reached to squeeze her knee—"whatever you do here in Marseille, just don't sail away from me again."

We drove to the quai de la Joliette, the point from which her ship had steamed off toward Algiers en route to Casablanca, and squealing gulls dipped overhead as we walked out on the pier. Now Janine had come full circle and her eyes were wet with tears as she recalled the girl who had been pried from Roland's arms and led along the gangway to find a distant world of strangers. Her parents too had not been old when they lost everything and on unfamiliar ground became reliant on their children.

Once again, she stood staring out to unknown shores with Europe at her back and her beloved Roland beside her. But for the greater tides of history, a different daughter might have stood with them. Still, by whatever hand of God or fate or simple circumstance the three of us had come into that moment, I rejoiced in having played a vital role in how their story ended. Somehow, it even seemed to validate my father, who had taught me to believe that anything was possible.

Near the close of day we found ourselves at the park behind the Palais du Pharo, perched above the sea on a lofty promontory. A great red sun was sinking toward the water, and the pale stone walls of the ancient forts guarding the harbor's mouth blushed pink. Dogs ran free—a German shepherd and a dalmatian romped in the grass as their masters watched from benches—and far below, a few intrepid sails still bobbed along the waves. We sat there for a while before Mom and Roland told me they were tired and would walk back for a rest at our hotel. I watched them go off hand in hand, the sorrow of their next parting already sneaking up on them. Our journey was almost ended, and two days later Roland would have to leave Janine in New Jersey and return to Montreal. For two tall people, their steps were short and slow, as if by reining in their pace they might hold back the waning hours.

On a bench not far from mine, a young couple sat together kissing. They each wore jeans, T-shirts, and sandals, and the boy cradled the girl within his arms as she cuddled on his lap. He gazed into her eyes and lovingly stroked her hair, blond with dark brown roots. Soon, the evening growing cooler, they too got up to leave. The boy draped a lanky arm across her shoulders and she wound hers about his waist and tucked her fingers in his belt. Both couples were retreating toward the castle and the road beyond—the older pair in front, the younger following—and it was tempting to regard them as the same, just in different stages. Would that boy and girl, I wondered, still be walking in close embrace after half a century? Or did it take a world of turmoil, of loss and then recapture, to treasure properly the people we mean to hold most dear?

Above the city, as stars began to climb, the bells of Notre-Dame de la Garde rang the seven o'clock hour for all her sailors left at sea and for all of us on land to mark the passing of the day. The bells tolled along the coast of France, the shadowed waters ran toward Africa, and America lay waiting.

Long before I ever imagined trying to locate Roland Arcieri, I was entranced by my mother's account of her life. Sleeping in my heart for decades was the desire to share her dramatic stories of love and war and escape, yet as a journalist I needed a great deal more information to ground her account in historical facts. The events she described occurred a long time ago, and while I trusted my source, I would rely on her recollections of violent political upheaval and persecution in Europe under the Nazis only as points of departure. To establish the context of all she had told me demanded extensive reporting and research. In terms of her personal memories also, I needed to be able to state with confidence, for myself as well my readers: this story is true; this is what happened.

Confronting Hitler's dread transformation of Europe is no simple matter, and nowhere more complex, perhaps, than in France. Research sent me on five trips there, as well as to Germany, one to Canada, and another to Cuba. Besides Janine and Roland, who participated in innumerable hours of interviews, I am beholden to those who shared their experiences or studied the period. Over the years I spent delving into a time that must not be forgotten, my own scope enlarged to include those whose lives intersected my mother's—too many of whom, like our cousins in Lyon, did not survive to tell their own tales to a new generation.

Indeed, compared to the hellish suffering inflicted on millions under the Nazis, the star-crossed love of two young people was something I wanted to keep in perspective. Or as Rick unforgettably insisted to Ilsa in the 1942 film *Casablanca*, in their own parting scene: "It doesn't take much to see that the problems of three little people don't amount to a hill of beans in this crazy world." Losing Roland felt like a death to Janine, but her escape onto a ship sailing from France at the eleventh hour placed her among the most fortunate few at that place and time.

The fact that our family is here today is proof enough to require me to say so.

As a reporter I faced two professional issues. First, I opted after much debate to change the names of a limited number of individuals—among them the man I've called Roland Arcieri—to protect their privacy and that of their family members. On the other hand, there were two who requested anonymity and were unhappy to learn that I could not comply because their names were already a matter of public record. A second journalistic concern involved recounting conversations that took place in the distant past. In such instances, I have done my best to relate the dialogue as accurately as possible, based on interviews with those who were present to hear or speak the words once exchanged.

My mother has obviously been my most crucial source, and her recall, standing up to rigorous research, proved remarkable. Her capacity to give of herself has made her a truly exceptional mother, and I have been blessed by her friendship. I am profoundly aware of her courage and generosity in permitting me to explore her personal relationships so honestly, in all their manifold human reality. Indeed, though I have trespassed on the delicate terrain of my parents' marriage, I hope the resulting portrait reflects my undying love for both my mother and father.

I am indebted, as well, to the true Roland for his assistance with this project, not a facile decision for him either. I was especially appreciative that he joined Mother and me on a research trip from Freiburg to Marseille, during which we toured each locale of their youthful years. Roland furnished pictures and details about his life and his feelings, and while not a man to seek center stage, he responded with candor and humor to all of my questions, however intrusive.

I thank Ronald Goldfarb for his immediate enthusiasm in encouraging me to write their story and for taking it to Judith Gurewich, the wise and extraordinary publisher of Other Press. Judith's clear vision, dynamism, and dedication took this work to completion. As an editor, she fully endorsed of my aim to contextualize the love story of Janine and Roland within their turbulent times, which made Other Press an ideal home. I deeply appreciate the personal care Judith lavished on every detail. Senior editor Corinna Barsan and production editor Yvonne E. Cárdenas brought scrupulous nurturing to the manuscript and the creation of this volume, and it was a superbly rewarding collaborative experience to work with them both. Also at Other Press, I sincerely thank Paul Kozlowski, Sarah Reidy, Carol Lazare, Sulay Hernandez, and Marjorie DeWitt for all that they have brought to this book. I thank attorney Ellis B. Levine for his thoughtful comments, and the excellent mapmaker Valerie M. Sebestyen for her patience and artistry.

My brother, Gary, certainly lived the story with me from the start. He not only offered his perceptive insights and judicious guidance, but also rode to the rescue each time I called. To our grandparents, Sigmar and Alice, I am boundlessly grateful. The little, scuffed brown leather valise or *Köfferle* in which they clung to a trove of official documents, identity cards, visas, letters, telegrams, and photographs made it possible to follow their fates under Hitler's regime and to trace our family roots through the centuries. With the owners gone, it was hard to fathom the resilient endurance of the vibrant, pulsing artifacts of lost days that imparted a world of information to me.

The discerning counsel of my cousin Richard Herzog was an incalculable gift, and with his wife, Barbara, he provided painstaking dissection of every issue on which I sought his opinion. Other cherished relations here and in France proved notably helpful, as well. Among them, I thank Hanna "Hannchen" Hamburger; Isabelle, Janine, and Huguette Cahen; François Blum; Lynne Marvin; Lynn Ullman; Suzanne Steinberg; and Carol Weil. My Parisian cousins on my father's side, Danielle Fakhr and Hélène Putermilch, prepared me to tackle this book years ago when they taught me to speak French and introduced me to their beautiful country.

Of course reporting in France was no hardship assignment. The story took me to Mulhouse, Paris, Gray, Langres, Lyon, and Marseille, and in each city I found gracious and ready assistance. In Mulhouse, where I owe so much to Roland's sister, Emilienne, I am also obliged to Benoit Bruant and Geneviève Maurer. In Marseille I thank Guy Durand of the Direction du Patrimoine Culturel. In Lyon, I am thankful to Marc-Henri Arfeux, who welcomed me—a stranger who showed up unannounced at his remarkable door—with genuine interest and warmth. A writer himself, he greatly furthered my knowledge regarding my cousins who had lived in his building and, in an instant, arranged for me to meet with his mother, Monique Arfeux, and his upstairs neighbor, Pierre Balland, who had both personally known the Goldschmidts and related still-haunting memories of them.

Also in Lyon, I thank the Centre d'Histoire de la Résistance et de la Déportation and Roselyne Pellecchia. Through the Centre de documentation juive contemporaine of the Mémorial de la Shoah in Paris, she located the chilling documents that detailed what happened to Mimi Goldschmidt and her three children, as well as to Roger Dreyfus and Bella Picard, among twelve hundred Jews deported on Convoy 62 from Drancy to Auschwitz.

Yannick Klein, former Directeur Général des Services Municipaux of the city of Gray, performed an immense service in connecting me with André Fick—my mother's friend and one of Mayor Fimbel's key aides during the occupation of Gray. André Fick's eyewitness account of that period, *Gray à l'Heure Allemande: 1940–44*, provided vital historical detail for my chapters describing the fears and compromises imposed by that time, as well as its moments of quiet heroism. In Gray, as well, I thank Rémi Hamelin for the background and tour he provided.

In Germany, Walter Preker extended constant assistance and lasting friendship. His expertise is well demonstrated by the fact that when we first met in 1989, he was the mayor of Freiburg's press secretary, a post he continues to hold to this day, even as city hall has changed hands. On each of my trips there, Walter facilitated my reporting in Freiburg and Ihringen, and when I returned home, he followed up my every request for added information or pictures. A real favor—he even politely corrected my German! It was on my first visit that Walter set up an interview with Mayor Dr. Rolf Böhme, whose initiative to invite Jewish former citizens to return to their homeland actually served to launch my endeavors.

Through Walter, I met with Professor Hugo Ott, the renowned Heidegger scholar, who shared his research into the 1940 deportation of all Freiburg's Jews and the suicide that day of Therese Loewy. I am equally indebted to Dr. Hans Schadek, the former chief archivist of Freiburg and an authority on its Jewish history, and to his successor, Dr. Ulrich Ecker, who both devoted much time to discussing the painful history of Jews in the region under the Nazis and back through the centuries. From the archives, they and Dr. Hans-Peter Widmann unearthed important pictures and documents for me.

Among others in Freiburg who aided my research, I note with appreciation Sissi Walther and Michael and Rosemarie Stock. In addition to his other kindnesses, in 2005 Michael permitted the artist Gunter

Demnig to imbed so-called *Stolpersteine*—"stumbling stones," or blocks engraved with my grandparents' names—in the sidewalk in front of Poststrasse 6, as part of a project that has already memorialized more than 30,000 victims of Nazism throughout Europe. The *Stolpersteine* on the Poststrasse literally paved the way for a first family reunion, because an unknown French cousin, François Blum, happened to notice them on a trip to the city and began a quest to find Sigmar's descendants. In the dispersal of the Nazi years, branches of the family had become disconnected, but François figured out that our great-grandfathers were brothers, and I was thrilled to be found.

When it came to researching my mother's escape from France, the archives of the American Jewish Joint Distribution Committee in New York proved invaluable. One has only to read the wartime documents in the relief agency's files to feel the desperate urgency of its efforts to save lives. I came away inspired by profound respect and gratitude for its mission and staff.

My account of the voyage of the *San Thomé* owes a great deal to Dr. Margalit Bejarano, former academic director of the Oral History Division of the Avraham Harman Institute of Contemporary Jewry at the Hebrew University of Jerusalem. She generously allowed me to use the transcripts of two oral histories she conducted in 1987 with passengers Lotte Burg and Emma Kahn, who had escaped to Cuba on the same voyage as the Günzburger family.

Dr. Michael Berenbaum, former director of the United States Holocaust Research Institute at the U.S. Holocaust Memorial Museum, arranged with Sarah Ogilvie and Scott Miller of the museum to put me in contact with numerous former refugees who had been interned at Tiscornia. I was surprised to learn that the long-term detention of Jewish refugees there had never before been closely examined and, moreover, that no one could tell me where the one-time camp might have been situated. Not former refugees who had spent six hard months there, nor American or Cuban officials, nor scholars, nor anyone I consulted in several agencies that regularly deal with worldwide Jewish issues. The camp's location appeared on no map, and guidebooks and histories shed no light on the matter. That I finally managed to stand outside its gates I owe to a marvelous Cuban woman whom I cannot name for fear of causing trouble for her. She led my mother and me to the barred compound—transformed into the Instituto Superior de Medicina Militar—where heavily armed military guards ordered us not to approach or take any pictures.

Maritza Corrales, an expert on Cuban Jewry, proved a remarkable guide in Havana. She took us to the places that Mother remembered and brought us to meet another alumna of St. George's School who, after sharing recollections and yearbooks with us, succumbed to tears as she and Mom ventured to sing the old St. George's anthem together.

In regard to Moisés Simons, musicology professor Robin D. Moore, now of the University of Texas at Austin, steered me to fascinating research that traced the Cuban-born composer's mysterious lineage to Jewish immigrants from the Basque region of Spain. According to Dr. Moore, the musician—while living in Paris before World War II—quite likely changed his name from Simón to Simons to disguise the fact that his background was Jewish.

In Washington, Norman Chase of the periodicals collection at the Library of Congress helped obtain French and English newspapers from the late 1930s and early 1940s that sketched a first view of history. I was grateful, as well, to my esteemed *New York Times* colleague, William Safire, who entrusted me with large stacks of personal copies of *The Times* he had lovingly saved through the war and ever thereafter. Though their brittle pages risked damage from handling, he unstintingly urged me to use them, as was his way. For broader and deeper analyses of the period, I commend with gratitude and respect the dedicated scholars and historians whose works provided a firm and essential foundation for all that I wrote. I list many of their superb studies in the bibliography at the end of this volume.

I have been truly lucky over the years to be bolstered by dear friends who remained interested and kept faith for so long. Susan Goldart has been my treasured ally from the very first day—a trusted confidante, caring advisor, and nuanced reader. I have prized the heartfelt camaraderie of Naomi Harris Rosenblatt, who, as a writer, shared my adventure and lent her perspective, both as a biblical scholar and, like Susan, a psychotherapist with valuable insight on family dynamics. Barbara Wolfson and Harvard English professor Elisa New each read early drafts of the manuscript and provided astute observations. Anne-Marie Daris was a valued consultant on all things French: she checked my language, brought me Lamartine verses, and invited me to the mountains of France, where Roland had served with the Chantiers de la Jeunesse. Jean B. Weiner, our lifelong family friend, openly shared her memories with me. Kendra and Mark Sagoff, Miriam and William Galston, Margery Doppelt, Larry Rothman, and Rangeley Wallace comprised a responsive council of intelligent voices on intricate questions.

I am thankful to Rabbi M. Bruce Lustig, our clergy, and all our wonderful friends at the Washington Hebrew Congregation, too many to name, who formed a circle of care that felt like a family and enabled two transplanted New Yorkers to feel at home in the nation's capital.

Our incisive daughter, Ariel, read the whole book aloud and gave me important feedback. I was grateful to have her zesty prodding at moments when my energy faltered. She and her brother, Zachary, grew up with this book as a selfish sibling, and I am sure they are thrilled to see it kicked out of the nest. To my son, I extend a special measure of thanks for, second only to me, Zach lived with this book on his desktop. I am profoundly indebted to him for the countless late hours he spent reading and editing, reacting with eager delight to the task of weighing a problem of phrasing, regardless of every other demand on his time. Like Ariel, he brought to the manuscript a sharp eye, keen ear, and sensitive grasp of the story.

Finally, this book could not have been written without the vast and forbearing support of my husband, Dan Werner. He has endured its many fitful demands for time, attention, and travel. His only complaint throughout came on a visit to Gray, when he grumbled that the next time his mother-in-law felt compelled to escape, he hoped she might pick a more lively refuge. A journalistic advisor, technological savior, moral compass, and devoted partner, he has been unfailingly helpful and thoughtful in ways that would take a book to describe.

FAMILY TREE

GÜNZBURGER

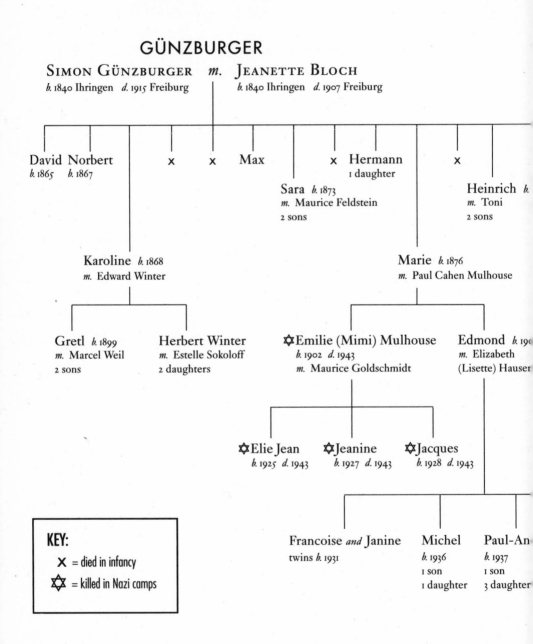

SIMON GÜNZBURGER   *m.*   JEANETTE BLOCH
b. 1840 Ihringen   *d.* 1915 Freiburg   *b.* 1840 Ihringen   *d.* 1907 Freiburg

David   Norbert   **x**   **x**   Max   **x**   Hermann   **x**
b. 1865   *b.* 1867   1 daughter

Sara *b.* 1873   Heinrich *b.*
m. Maurice Feldstein   *m.* Toni
2 sons   2 sons

Karoline *b.* 1868   Marie *b.* 1876
m. Edward Winter   *m.* Paul Cahen Mulhouse

Gretl *b.* 1899   Herbert Winter   ✡Emilie (Mimi) Mulhouse   Edmond *b.* 190
m. Marcel Weil   *m.* Estelle Sokoloff   *b.* 1902 *d.* 1943   *m.* Elizabeth
2 sons   2 daughters   *m.* Maurice Goldschmidt   (Lisette) Hauser

✡Elie Jean   ✡Jeanine   ✡Jacques
b. 1925 *d.* 1943   *b.* 1927 *d.* 1943   *b.* 1928 *d.* 1943

Francoise *and* Janine   Michel   Paul-An
twins *b.* 1931   *b.* 1936   *b.* 1937
                        1 son   1 son
                        1 daughter   3 daughter

KEY:
x = died in infancy
✡ = killed in Nazi camps

HEINSHEIMER

Maier Heinsheimer   *m.*   Johanna Kahn
b. 1855 *d.* 1913 Eppingen   *b.* 1862 Kuppenheim *d.* 1941 Zurich

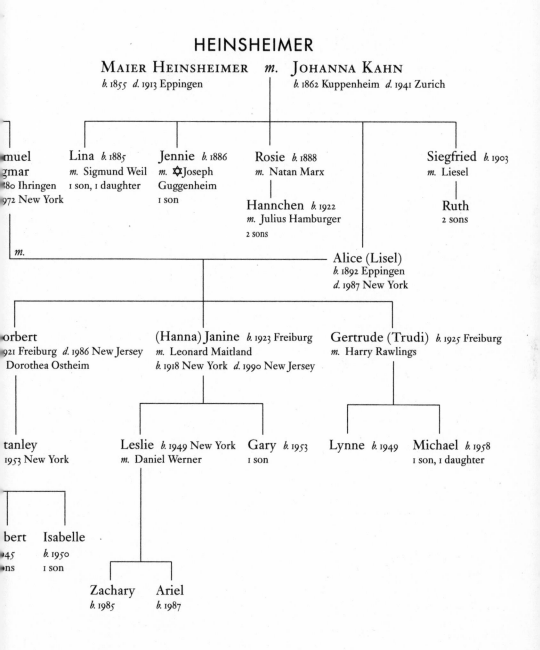

muel
gmar
80 Ihringen
972 New York

Lina *b.* 1885
m. Sigmund Weil
1 son, 1 daughter

Jennie *b.* 1886
m. ✡Joseph
Guggenheim
1 son

Rosie *b.* 1888
m. Natan Marx

Hannchen *b.* 1922
m. Julius Hamburger
2 sons

Siegfried *b.* 1903
m. Liesel

Ruth
2 sons

m.

Alice (Lisel)
b. 1892 Eppingen
d. 1987 New York

orbert
921 Freiburg *d.* 1986 New Jersey
Dorothea Ostheim

(Hanna) Janine *b.* 1923 Freiburg
m. Leonard Maitland
b. 1918 New York *d.* 1990 New Jersey

Gertrude (Trudi) *b.* 1925 Freiburg
m. Harry Rawlings

tanley
1953 New York

Leslie *b.* 1949 New York
m. Daniel Werner

Gary *b.* 1953
1 son

Lynne *b.* 1949

Michael *b.* 1958
1 son, 1 daughter

bert
45
ns

Isabelle
b. 1950
1 son

Zachary
b. 1985

Ariel
b. 1987

American Jewish Joint Distribution Committee Archives: Files 366, 388, 594, 596, 616. 711 Third Avenue, New York, NY 10017.

Amoretti, Henri. *Lyon Capitale, 1940–1944.* Paris: Editions France-Empire, 1964.

Anderson, Mark M., ed. *Hitler's Exiles: Personal Stories of the Flight from Nazi Germany to America.* New York: New Press, 1998.

Arad, Yitzhak, Israel Gutman, and Abraham Margaliot, eds. *Documents of the Holocaust.* Trans. Lea Ben Dor. Lincoln: University of Nebraska Press, 1999.

Arendt, Hannah, and Karl Jaspers. *Correspondence 1926–1969.* Ed. Lotte Kohler and Hans Saner; trans. Robert and Rita Kimber. New York: Harcourt, 1992.

Asheri, Michael. *Living Jewish: The Lore and Law of the Practicing Jew.* New York: Dodd, Mead, 1983.

Bauer, Yehuda. *American Jewry and the Holocaust: The American Jewish Joint Distribution Committee, 1939–1945.* Detroit: Wayne State University Press, 1982.

Bejarano, Margalit. Interviews with Lotte Burg and Emma Kahn, passengers aboard the *San Thomé.* Archives of the Avraham Harman Institute of Contemporary Jewry, Hebrew University of Jerusalem, 1987.

———. "The Jewish Community of Cuba Between Continuity and Extinction." *Jewish Political Studies Review* 3, no. 1–2 (Spring 1991).

———. *La Comunidad Hebrea de Cuba: la memoria y la historia.* Jerusalem: The Harman Institute of Contemporary Jewry, 1996.

Berenbaum, Michael. *The World Must Know: The History of the Holocaust as Told in the United States Holocaust Memorial Museum.* Boston: Little, Brown, 1993.

Bobenrieth, Charles. *39/45 A Lyon.* Lyon: Centre d'Histoire de la Résistance et de la Déportation, 2001.

Branden, Nathaniel. *My Years with Ayn Rand.* San Francisco: Jossey-Bass, 1999.

Brissinger, André. *Joseph Fimbel, Marianiste 1897–1978.* Bar-le-Duc: l'Imprimerie Saint-Paul, 1980.

Burns, Michael. *Dreyfus: A Family Affair, 1789–1945*. New York: Harper, 1991.

Burrin, Phillippe. *France Under the Germans: Collaboration and Compromise*. Trans. Janet Lloyd. New York: New Press, 1996.

Carroll, James. *Constantine's Sword: The Church and the Jews*. Boston: Houghton Mifflin, 2001.

Chauvy, Gérard. *Lyon 40–44*. Paris: Plon, 1985.

Claerr-Roussel, Christiane. *Gray, Haute-Saône*. Paris: Editions Erti, 1998.

Davidson, Edward, and Dale Manning. *Chronology of World War Two*. London: Cassell, 1999.

Dawidowicz, Lucy S. *The War Against the Jews, 1933–1945*. New York: Holt, Rinehart, 1975.

Elon, Amos. *The Pity of It All: A History of Jews in Germany, 1743–1933*. New York: Henry Holt, 2002.

Epstein, Helen. *Children of the Holocaust: Conversations with Sons and Daughters of Survivors*. New York: Penguin Books, 1988.

Fick, André. *Gray à l'Heure Allemande 1940–1944*. Langres: Editions Dominique Guéniot, 1998.

Gaster, Theodor H. *Festivals of the Jewish Year: A Modern Interpretation and Guide*. 4th ed. New York: Sloane, 1968.

Gatin, Jean Henri, and Louis François Nicolas Besson. *Histoire de la Ville de Gray et de ses Monuments*. Paris: Imprimerie Firmin-Didot, 1892.

Gay, Ruth. *The Jews of Germany: A Historical Portrait*. New Haven: Yale University Press, 1992.

Gilbert, Martin. *The Holocaust: A History of the Jews of Europe During the Second World War*. New York: Henry Holt, 1985.

Gildea, Robert. *Marianne in Chains: Daily Life in the Heart of France During the German Occupation*. New York: Picador, 2004.

Goldhagen, Daniel Jonah. *Hitler's Willing Executioners*. New York: Knopf, 1996.

Grass, Günter. *The Tin Drum*. Trans. Ralph Mannheim. New York: Pantheon, 1961.

Hertz, Joseph H. *Authorized Daily Prayer Book with Commentary, Introductions and Notes*. New York: Bloch Publishing Company, 1961.

Hertzberg, Arthur. *The French Enlightenment and the Jews: The Origins of Modern Anti-Semitism*. New York: Columbia University Press, 1968.

Hijuelos, Oscar. *A Simple Habana Melody*. New York: Harper, 2002.

Hilberg, Raul. *The Destruction of the European Jews*. New York: Harper, 1961.

International Herald Tribune, 1939–1941. Library of Congress.

Jackson, Julian. *France: The Dark Years 1940–1944*. New York: Oxford University Press, 2001.

Jarman, T. L. *The Rise and Fall of Nazi Germany.* New York: New York University Press, 1956.

Kalchthaler, Peter et al. *Freiburger Biographien.* Freiburg: Die Stadt, 2002.

Kaspi, André. *Les Juifs pendant l'Occupation.* Paris: Editions du Seuil, 1991.

Klarsfeld, Serge, ed. *French Children of the Holocaust: A Memorial.* Trans. Glorianne Depondt and Howard M. Epstein. New York: New York University Press, 1996.

Klemperer, Victor. *I Will Bear Witness: A Diary of the Nazi Years 1933–1941.* New York: Random House, 1998.

Laqueur, Walter. *Generation Exodus: The Fate of Young Jewish Refugees from Nazi Germany.* Hanover, NH: Brandeis University Press, 2001.

Levine, Robert M. *Tropical Diaspora.* Gainesville: University Press of Florida, 1993.

Lipstadt, Deborah E. *Beyond Belief: The American Press and the Coming of the Holocaust.* New York: Free Press, 1986.

Marrus, Michael R., and Robert O. Paxton. *Vichy France and the Jews.* New York: Basic Books, 1981.

May, Ernest R. *Strange Victory: Hitler's Conquest of France.* New York: Hill and Wang, 2000.

Mayer, Arno J. *Why Did the Heavens Not Darken? The "Final Solution" in History.* New York: Pantheon, 1988.

Mendes-Flohr, Paul. *German Jews: A Dual Identity.* New Haven: Yale University Press, 1999.

Miller, Arthur. *Death of a Salesman.* Ed. Gerald Weales. New York: Penguin Books, 1996.

Moore, Robin. *Nationalizing Blackness: Afrocubanismo and Artistic Revolution in Havana, 1920–1940.* Pittsburgh: University of Pittsburgh Press, 1998.

Orlow, Dietrich. *The History of Modern Germany: 1871 to Present.* Englewood Cliffs, NJ: Prentice Hall, 1995.

Ott, Hugo. *Laubhüttenfest 1940: Warum Therese Loewy einsam sterben mußte.* Freiburg: Herder, 1994.

Ousby, Ian. *Occupation: The Ordeal of France, 1940–1944.* New York: St. Martin's Press, 1998.

Paris Soir, 1939–1941. Library of Congress.

Rand, Ayn. *Atlas Shrugged.* New York: Random House, 1957.

———. *For the New Intellectual: The Philosophy of Ayn Rand.* New York: Random House, 1961.

———. *The Fountainhead.* New York: Bobbs-Merrill, 1943.

Rayski, Adam. *The Choice of the Jews Under Vichy: Between Submission and Resistance.* Notre Dame: University of Notre Dame Press, 2005.

Rockmore, Tom. *On Heidegger's Nazism and Philosophy.* Berkeley: University of California Press, 1992.

Röhl, John C. G. *The Kaiser and His Court: Wilhelm II and the Government of Germany.* Trans. Terence F. Cole. New York: Cambridge University Press, 1994.

Rosshandler, Felicia. *Passing Through Havana: A Novel of a Wartime Girlhood in the Caribbean.* New York: St. Martin's/Marek, 1984.

Ryan, Donna F. *The Holocaust and the Jews of Marseille: The Enforcement of Anti-Semitic Policies in Vichy France.* Urbana: University of Illinois Press, 1996.

Safranski, Rüdiger. *Martin Heidegger: Between Good and Evil.* Trans. Ewald Osers. Cambridge, MA: Harvard University Press, 1998.

Schadek, Hans. *Freiburg.* Stuttgart: J. F. Steinkopf Verlag, 1997.

Schlant, Ernestine. *The Language of Silence: West German Literature and the Holocaust.* New York: Routledge, 1999.

Schwineköper, Berent, and Franz Laubenberger. "Geschichte und Schicksal der Freiburger Juden." *Freiburger Stadthefte* 6 (1963): 1–15.

Shirer, William L. *The Rise and Fall of the Third Reich: A History of Nazi Germany.* New York: Simon & Schuster, 1960.

Silvain, Gérard. *La Question Juive en Europe, 1933–1945.* Paris: Editions Jean-Claude Lattès, 1985.

Staatsarchiv, Freiburg im Breisgau.

Thalmann, Rita, and Emmanuel Feinermann. *Crystal Night, 9–10 November 1938.* Trans. Gilles Cremonesi. New York: Coward, McCann, 1974.

Thrush, Elizabeth. "Alsace by the Yard" *France Magazine,* Fall 1999.

Van der Kiste, John. *Kaiser Wilhelm II: Germany's Last Emperor.* Stroud, UK: Sutton Publishing, 1999.

Weiss, Aharon, ed. *Yad Vashem Studies* 22. Jerusalem: Yad Vashem, 1992.

Wyman, David S. *The Abandonment of the Jews: America and the Holocaust 1941–1945.* New York: Pantheon, 1984.

Zeitoun, Sabine, and Dominique Foucher. *Lyon 1940–1944: La Guerre, L'Occupation, La Libération.* Rennes: Editions Ouest-France, 1994.

———. *Résistance & Déportation: Catalogue générale de l'exposition permanente.* Lyon: Editions Ville de Lyon/CHRD, 1997.

Zola, Emile. *The Dreyfus Affair.* Ed. Alain Pagès; trans. Eleanor Levieux. New Haven: Yale University Press, 1996.

Zweig, Stefan. *The Burning Secret and Other Stories.* Trans. Jill Sutcliffe. New York: Dutton, 1989.

PHOTO CREDITS

Page 186: Gebrüder Strauss Phot., Mannheim, Germany, circa 1920

Page 219: From *Le Sémaphore* newspaper, Marseille, France, March 1943

Page 221: Cliché Labbé, France

Page 227: Postcard by Mireille, Marseille, France, circa 1942

Page 270: Museo Nacional de la Música, Havana, Cuba

Page 292: Centre de documentation juive contemporaine, Mémorial de la Shoah, Paris, France

Page 322: John U. Vogel

Page 341: Hannah Weil Schreiber, New York

Page 381: *The Record,* Bergen County, New Jersey, June 28, 1965

Page 471: Walter Preker, Freiburg i. Br.